Manners and Mischief

Manners and Mischief

Gender, Power, and Etiquette in Japan

EDITED BY
Jan Bardsley and Laura Miller

UNIVERSITY OF CALIFORNIA PRESS
Berkeley · Los Angeles · London

University of California Press, one of the most distinguished university presses in the United States, enriches lives around the world by advancing scholarship in the humanities, social sciences, and natural sciences. Its activities are supported by the UC Press Foundation and by philanthropic contributions from individuals and institutions. For more information, visit www.ucpress.edu.

University of California Press
Berkeley and Los Angeles, California

University of California Press, Ltd.
London, England

Sanrio Co. Ltd. is home to Hello Kitty, Dear Daniel, and more than 400 character properties. The worldwide lifestyle brand was founded in 1960 based on the "small gift, big smile" philosophy—that a small gift can bring happiness to people of all ages. Today, over 50,000 Sanrio-branded items are sold in over 70 countries around the world. In the Western Hemisphere, Sanrio character-branded products are sold in upwards of 12,000 locations including department, specialty, and national chain stores and Sanrio Boutique Stores. For more information, please visit www.sanrio.com.

Library of Congress Cataloging-in-Publication Data

Manners and mischief : gender, power, and etiquette in Japan / edited by Jan Bardsley and Laura Miller.
p. cm.
Includes bibliographical references and index.
ISBN 978-0-520-26783-1 (hardcover : alk. paper)
ISBN 978-0-520-26784-8 (pbk. : alk. paper)
1. Etiquette—Japan. 2. Sex role—Japan.
3. Power (Social sciences)—Japan. 4. Japan—Social life and customs. I. Bardsley, Jan. II. Miller, Laura, 1953–
BJ2007.J34M36 2011
395.0952—dc22 2010041905

Manufactured in the United States of America

20 19 18 17 16 15 14 13 12 11
10 9 8 7 6 5 4 3 2 1

This book is printed on Cascades Enviro 100, a 100% post–consumer waste, recycled, de-inked fiber.
FSC recycled certified and processed chlorine free.
It is acid free, Ecologo certified, and manufactured by BioGas energy.

For Lucy, Raquel, Snickers, and Truffles

Feeling self-conscious is your first step on the way to improvement.

—Agasa/Agatha
Author, *Ugly Chick Inspection* (Tokyo, 2004)

Contents

List of Illustrations

Acknowledgments

Was it manners or mischief that got us started on this project? Probably a little of both. Ideas for the book began percolating in the fall of 2005. We'd had afternoon high tea at the Drake Hotel with our good friend Laura Hein and her two lovely daughters, Cora and Vinca. Although it was early November, the weather in Chicago was crisp and clear, and we enjoyed the time we spent walking around downtown. Back in our room on the concierge level of the Palmer House, we were snug in big, white fluffy robes, making margaritas in the water glasses, and watching the *mazā-kon* TV drama that Laura had brought, *Mazā & Rabuā: Mazā-kon de nani ga warui?!* (2004) (Mother and lover: What's so bad about a mother complex?!). Our first edited volume, *Bad Girls of Japan* (Palgrave, 2005), was about to debut. Friends were already kidding us about whether or not there would be a sequel, *Worse Girls of Japan* or *Really Bad Girls of Japan*. Or, what if we did a complete turnabout, reformed, and produced *Good Girls of Japan*? Thinking about what a volume on good girls would look like brought us to etiquette manuals and manners guides, a topic both of us had already been working on for some time. Talking about various Japanese guides, recalling movies and TV shows, and remembering our own faux pas in Japan quickly made us realize that this book on manners was going to involve lots of mischief as well.

We thank Reed Malcolm at the University of California Press for being such a fantastic, supportive editor. Although it took us longer than expected to get this volume gloved, hatted, and ready to debut, we're happy to say that she's ready to go out into the world now, thanks to his encouragement.

We are grateful to our colleagues for contributing these fine chapters. Their friendship and writerly manners, and even the bits of mischief they added to make this project more fun, are all much appreciated. For sticking with us and for doing even that last round of revisions with good humor, we thank Hideko Abe, Gavin James Campbell, Linda H. Chance, Kelly M. Foreman, Sally A. Hastings, Hiroko Hirakawa, Maki Isaka, Amanda C. Seaman, and Janet Shibamoto-Smith. We appreciate the support for this project offered by Rebecca Copeland, Liza Dalby, and William Tsutsui.

We would like to thank the following for kindly giving permission to use images: Kumagai Hiroshi, a senior editor at H & I Kenkyūjo; Mimura Keisuke, a senior editor at Shufu to Seikatsu-sha; Hibino Reiko, an editorial administrator at JTB Publishing; Kurata Akihiro, a senior editor at Shōbunsha Publishing; and Daiwa Shobō. We made every effort to contact copyright holders for their permission to reprint images in the final chapter. The editors would be grateful to hear from any copyright holder who is not herein acknowledged and promise to rectify any errors or omissions in proper credit in future editions of the book. We also thank Margaret Price for help with organizing the image permission letters. We thank the editors of the *U.S.–Japan Women's Journal*, and Josai University for granting kind permission to reprint a revised version of Sally A. Hastings's article, "A Dinner Party Is Not a Revolution: Space, Gender and Hierarchy in Meiji Japan," originally published in the *U.S.–Japan Women's Journal English Supplement* 18 (2000): 107–132.

We appreciate the support for *Manners and Mischief* provided by the University Research Council at the University of North Carolina at Chapel Hill.

We owe a lot to our feline children, who magically de-stress our lives. In Chapel Hill, Snickers and Truffles snuggle up with Jan; in Evanston, Lucy and Raquel provided much comforting diversion for Laura. It is to their feline elegance and confidence, their cunning, and their companionship that this volume is dedicated with love and admiration.

Jan Bardsley and Laura Miller
April 2010

Manners and Mischief

Introduction

JAN BARDSLEY AND LAURA MILLER

One fine day a robust Japanese man with a boyish mop of hair, a colorful aloha shirt, and a grin of anticipation sits down at an ordinary lunch counter in Tokyo. He has come for a lesson in eating ramen noodles by a master who has studied the art for forty years. The elderly expert, elegant in his kimono, sits subdued next to him. He instructs the novice in each step of proper noodle consumption, from appreciating the aesthetic whole to attending to the meal's superb particulars. He expresses affection to the pork slices with a fond, "See you soon!" Every move made by the master appears steeped in significance; every taste is a symbolic act of reverence for the thin ropes of dough. Yet when the young fellow asks the master why he ceremoniously taps the pork slice three times against the bowl, he replies, "Just to drain it."

Fans of Itami Jūzō's movies will recognize this scene as one of the early vignettes in his film *Tampopo* (1986), a satire about the pleasure that Japanese take in food, sex, and rituals.[1] As the vignette is all about manners and mischief, it provides the perfect opening to introduce the goals and scope of this book. Whether made instantly or eaten at one of the trendiest noodle shops in town, ramen is considered one of the most commonplace meals in Japan. Itami makes this scene comical by imagining a professor of pasta who approaches noodles with all the grace and seriousness of purpose associated with the Zen priest or the tea ceremony master, iconic practitioners of Japanese high taste and esoteric thought. The student has no way of knowing what the significance of any movement might be but begins to think that all have some deeper meaning. He relies entirely on the ramen master, a situation that leaves him open to being duped. Luckily for him, the master tells him when the movement—tapping the pork slice against the bowl—is merely functional. The scene is a story-within-a-story, for the viewer knows that it is being read by two long-haul truckers to pass the time as they drive on a rainy night. One trucker cannot help but comment on the absurdity of eating ramen this way, but the other asks him to continue reading. As Itami returns the viewer to the ramen lesson, the camera zooms in for a close-up of the master. We observe in the expression on his face that this seasoned master savors every pleasure that can be extracted from the humble bowl of noodles. Then again, we may ask, Is the master smiling because he is up to no good, having hoodwinked the student into buying his ritual and his bowl of ramen to boot? One thing is for sure: by the end of the scene, the truckers are hungry for a bowl of ramen and so are many viewers.

Manners and Mischief: Gender, Power, and Etiquette in Japan trains critical attention on similarly evocative moments in the history of Japanese manners. Etiquette books as the means to vicarious pleasure, refined ritual as a leap of faith, and manners as a site for constructing and contesting gender, class, race, and national identity all figure here. Although this volume focuses on conduct in Japan, it does not aim to teach readers how to perform Japanese etiquette, nor does it survey the complex history of Japanese manners. Rather, by offering close readings of selected texts past and present, examining cultural practices in their historical or ethnographic context, and interpreting graphic images of proper and offensive behavior, we will show how conduct instruction has given meaning to both everyday life and extraordinary occasions alike.

Manners and Mischief examines the ways in which notions of good conduct reinforce the power of particular interests, whether institutional, as evident in government and corporate manuals, or informally in the household. Our prime concern is to investigate how such notions naturalize concepts of femininity and masculinity in Japan. We look at the ways in which this naturalization works to create gender distinction both as a kind of common sense and as an idealized view of the way the world *should* work. As Maki Isaka's chapter on the Kabuki female role players known as *onnagata* shows, such gender work does not depend on biological sex. Research on conduct literature also attracts our attention because so much of it tries to entertain. Many guides ask readers to imagine themselves in lavish settings such as galas and first-class hotels, others solicit laughter at caricatures of bumbling behavior, and many, especially contemporary ones, cheer readers on the road to self-improvement with endless optimism. Japanese parodies such as *Tampopo* poke fun at the very idea of elaborate prescriptions for conduct. Pursuing the normalizing and entertaining aspects of conduct literature pushes us to search for moments of potential resistance as well. We look at why people refuse propriety, rewrite the rules, or, as in the case of advice columns in lesbian and gay magazines discussed in Hideko Abe's chapter, employ the conventional language of conduct to claim normality for groups often ostracized.

As the chapters in this volume illustrate, participants in a variety of cultural scenes draw on different etiquette repertories for "doing gender." The introduction sets the stage for our inquiries into Japanese conduct by laying the groundwork common to all the chapters in *Manners and Mischief*. Here, we describe the centuries-old popularity of manners guides in Japan, their link to notions of ethical behavior, and the proliferation of advice today. Turning to the language of conduct, we highlight the Japanese terms that appear most frequently in this literature and explain the influential concept of *kata* as well as both romantic and satirical approaches to it. We also look at some of the more irreverent takes on conduct in Japanese popular culture before concluding with a guide that illustrates the topic and arguments of each chapter.

As a window into the changing dynamics of manners and etiquette, *Manners and Mischief* presents cases of impeccable manners, comic faux pas, and resisting rudeness that highlight the politics of mores and morality informing everyday performance. Efforts to present manners as common sense and as naturally embodied behavior disguise the interest of the creators of conduct ideologies, and those who want to promote or sustain such ideologies recede from the picture. Thus, a study of conduct literature offers an analysis of some grounded aspects of this naturalization process, contributing to our understanding of gender in Japan and adding to a rich literature that has already established many of the political, historical, and cultural bases for gendered constructions.

THE LITERATURE AND LANGUAGE OF JAPANESE CONDUCT

Bookstores in Japan at the turn of the twenty-first century carry all kinds of colorful books on conduct that intermingle messages about proper behavior, etiquette, and polishing one's appearance. As Janet Shibamoto-Smith writes in her chapter on newspaper advice columns, messages on proper behavior abound not only informally in magazines, in newspapers, and on Internet sites, but also in official sources such as the "Survey on National Characteristics of the Japanese People," a study sponsored every five years by the Institute of Statistical Mathematics. Shibamoto-Smith observes that all combine to "tell various targeted groups of readers (women, men, young, old, career-oriented, or domestically inclined) how to be the 'best'—or at least, how not to be the 'worst'—at being whatever sort of Japanese person they are." Indeed, we can say that the proliferation and acceptance of conduct literature have long been one of the means by which Japan has taken shape as an imagined community and been institutionalized as a nation-state.

As the sociologist Eiko Ikegami has shown, Japanese taste for reading conduct literature surged in the Tokugawa period (1600–1868) with the advent of commercial print culture. In her book *Bonds of Civility: Aesthetic Networks and the Political Origins of Japanese Culture* (2005), a study of the role of aesthetics in shaping public life in pre-modern Japan and the most influential work to date on Japanese manners, Ikegami explains that conduct books were among the earliest best-sellers.[2] Illustrated and easy to read, "how-to" books had particular appeal for urbanized commoners, but even readers outside cities desired such guidance. Although every community already had its own codes in everything from dress to seating arrangements, these books nurtured "popular recognition of more culturally prestigious" rules of sociability emerging in cities. Putting their advice into practice enabled one to act beyond one's local network and in ways that might lead to upward social mobility. The commercial vitality of such books, and their wide distribution, led to the establishment of conventions that expressed politeness and sensitivity to differences in individual status. Although Ikegami contends that such conventions functioned as a means of social control, she also sees them as creating a "distinctive aesthetic consciousness."[3] Shifting to the present, we see that accessible language and graphics continue to appeal to Japanese readers, and that contemporary guides often become best-sellers. As Amanda Seaman's chapter shows, magazines specifically designed for pregnant women are selling well in Japan despite concern over the nation's low birth rate. Moreover, Bandō Mariko, an elite career woman, authored *The Dignity of the Woman* (2006), a book that sold more than a million volumes.[4] However, as Hiroko Hirakawa's chapter explains, reader dissatisfaction with the book demonstrates that the mere purchase of guides does not mean that readers follow them or even always agree with them. This prompts us to imagine that many a Tokugawa reader may also have disagreed with the handbooks of that age.

Japanese conduct literature embraces a lengthy lexicon for denoting proper deportment. Like the common English terms "manners" and "etiquette," Japanese terms tend to overlap in usage and can blur the boundaries of one's moral character (manners) and one's ability to execute protocol (etiquette). Japanese expressions for conduct, too, have a long history, one altered by the inclusion of Chinese and European terms. Following the language of Japanese etiquette can take one from the trendiest ideas of cool back to ancient times. Contemporary advice in Japan, especially that which targets women and girls and focuses simultaneously on proper speech and movement, will use the terms *manā* (manners) or *echiketto* (etiquette). Although the terms *manā* and *echiketto* were used as early as the Meiji era, they became increasingly popular from the 1980s. One reason is that the forms of etiquette associated with them allow broader applications than do older native terms, which could evoke old-fashioned decorum in a reader's mind. *Sahō*, commonly translated as manners or etiquette, is one such word. Looking up *sahō* in a comprehensive dictionary will take you to a host of references to classical Japanese literature from court-lady tales to stories of samurai and various meanings from formalities to the proper ways to compose prose and poetry. The entry will also explain that by the 1840s *sahō* connoted the "sense of codes passed down from ancient times," thus implying a way of behaving in the world that bore the weight of tradition and an indefinable past.[5] Even though *manā*, *echiketto*, and *sahō* have these different connotations, all work well as search terms in the digital age, and one will find Japanese advice guides that mingle them, as one can see in the contemporary manuals discussed in the chapters by Bardsley and Hirakawa.

Tracing the use of the term *shitsuke* offers another fruitful path to exploring the history of Japanese conduct. Translated as "social discipline," the word *shitsuke* predates the use of the Chinese writing system in Japan and refers to the physicality of etiquette. The character the Japanese fashioned for this term combines the Chinese characters for *shin* (body or person) and *bi* (beauty).[6] As Ikegami explains, the character for *shitsuke* "implies physical grace allied with habitual discipline of the body."[7] Tracing the use of *shitsuke* as a teaching tool takes us to the medieval origins of the most influential school of Japanese manners, the Ogasawara School. Initiated in the Muromachi period as a kind of secret teaching that drew from Zen monastic etiquette and the neo-Confucian ideals of Chinese literati, the Ogasawara codes envisioned a way of living in the world that was at once beautiful and ethical.[8] Associated with swordsmanship, samurai, and courtiers, the Ogasawara School became popularized in the Tokugawa period through the commercially published manners books described above.[9] In the rapidly changing times of the Meiji era, many still looked back to Ogasawara precepts. As the historian Jordan Sand points out, for instance, Meiji-era progressives and conservatives alike "treated the dictates of the Ogasawara School as the essential canon of manners" and believed it was particularly appropriate for girls to learn.[10] This belief opened a path for textbooks for schoolgirls that were drawn from Ogasawara School teachings.

Pushing Meiji girls to be on their best Ogasawara behavior no doubt shaped notions of modern ladyhood, but it laid the ground for class divisions as well.

Take, for example, the moment when the lead character of Higuchi Ichiyō's 1895 short story "Nigorie" (Troubled waters) invents her own school of etiquette. The alcoholic beauty of a second-rate Tokyo teahouse known as the Kikunoi, Oriki is unabashed in pulling potential customers right off the street. One challenges her serving abilities, demanding, "Pouring sake without even lifting the cup from the tray! What is that, the Ogasawara school of etiquette?" She retorts, "No, no, no, of course not. It's the Oriki school. That's what we follow here. There's an even more esoteric school where we pour sake on the floor and let the mats soak it up. We serve it to guests in the lid of a big bowl. And if we don't like someone, we don't serve him at all."[11] Despite the cheekiness of Oriki's retort, she later mourns the fact that she will never become a respectable married woman. In fact, as a woman forced into sex work, she can only be the parodic inversion of Ogasawara codes, a theme that heightens the tragedy of this doomed character.

As prolific publishers of Meiji-era guidebooks, the Ogasawara are responsible, too, for developing modern styles of standing and bowing in Japan. The historian Selçuk Esenbel describes Ogasawara's creation of the three-tiered bow as an adaptation to Western-influenced architecture and a new standing culture. She describes how an Ogasawara etiquette book for ladies eased Japanese concerns about navigating a new physical environment, picturing a gentlewoman in a kimono gracefully bowing while poised beside a chair.[12] Modified over centuries to keep up with changing times, the Ogasawara School's teachings have demonstrated remarkable staying power. Even today in Japan, a shorthand way of putting people at ease is to say, "Let's dispense with the Ogasawara School."

Bowing, a convention strongly associated with Japan in the global imagination, indicates degrees of formality. The action is often misread by foreigners, who view it as the quintessential performance of subservience to hierarchy. The U.S. public has reacted negatively to its presidents bowing in Japan. In 1989 President George H. W. Bush bowed his head in respect at the state funeral of the Shōwa emperor, Hirohito, angering numerous veterans at home. More recently, President Obama's bow to the Japanese emperor on his 2009 visit to Japan was widely criticized by the U.S. Right as showing submission rather than respect. Yet, bowing can also be a source of comedy. Hollywood films depict foreigners trying to bow as foolish and clumsy. Humorists in Japan spoof the custom by taking bowing to the extreme. Laura Miller's chapter gives a prime example of this, offering a comic showing ladies formally bowing to each other as one surrenders the toilet to another.

Most of the guides and practices discussed in *Manners and Mischief*, whether meant for Tokugawa actors or twenty-first-century commuters, emphasize decorum as the means to displaying a beautiful appearance. This recalls the term *midashinami* or "personal grooming." One can find reference to *misdashinami* in early Tokugawa comic plays known as *kyōgen*, in late Tokugawa sentimental love stories (*ninjōbon*), and in early twentieth-century novels.[13] Contemporary beauty and style guides are replete with tips on how to spiff up one's *midashinami* by developing a polished look from head to toe. Although these guides stress the personal pleasure gained from spending time on one's appearance, *midashinami* has also long carried the sense of perfecting one's self-presentation in order "not to offend others," a concern still evident in contemporary guides. Such stress on visual appearances leads to self-surveillance in which the virtuous person monitors her or his body, movement, odor, and dress in ways to avoid giving offense. This ideal of presentation also creates a divide between private space, where one grooms modestly, and public space, where one presents a finished, polished appearance. What we may call commands to control *midashinami* have been directed with notable vehemence at young women from the advent of mass transportation to the present. Still, as Laura Miller's image chapter points out, girls resist the call to present their best self to anonymous fellow passengers by openly applying makeup and performing other grooming behaviors on trains, instead claiming the public space as their own private domain.

TRAINING THROUGH *KATA*

A key element in much Japanese conduct writing is the intertwined notion of body and mind, a unity of the corporeal and spiritual found in the concept of *kata* and related to the philosophy of the Ogasawara School. *Kata* are standardized postures and movements that accompany spiritual or aesthetic activities, such as martial arts, the tea ceremony, the composition of classical poetry, and the execution of calligraphy (and perhaps the way of eating noodles). Students of these arts learn *kata* by continually observing and patterning their own movements after a master–teacher. This practice aims to cultivate a student's body and mind to the point where he or she can stand or move fluidly without conscious effort. As the anthropologist Christine Yano explains, *kata*-training seeks "to fuse the individual to the form so that the individual becomes the form and the form becomes the individual."[14] Maki Isaka's chapter on the training of Kabuki actors and Kelly M. Foreman's chapter on geisha show how important *kata* are to the subjects' cultivation as artists. But *kata* are not restricted to the world of the arts. They are also important in Japanese social contexts. Bowing, smoothly exchanging business cards, and gracefully serving tea to visiting clients may all be considered types of interactional *kata*. *Kata* are a powerful means for encoding gender as well. The anthropologist Takie Lebra introduced us to the gendered aspect of this melding of body and language with her inclusive concept of "femininity training," which we might conceive of as *kata* for correct ladylike speech and postural propriety.[15] Such training is formalized in guides designed to prepare young people for job interviews with Japanese companies. These guides include images that show the gendered *kata* of this interview ritual, clarifying how women and men should sit, and naturalizing these postures as correct behavior that all who want to enter the corporation should know.[16] The concern explored in *Manners and Mischief* is how *kata* of all kinds codify gender, in effect naturalizing behaviors and making infringements of them improper. By the same token, we may ask, does gaining authority allow one to make changes in *kata*? How have *kata* been understood in relations between Japan and the West and as aspects of culture that create the image of Japanese tradition?

The mystical aura surrounding *kata* has long fascinated Westerners and given rise to wicked parodies in Japan. Western fiction recounts many scenes of *kata* performed in the West, but it is their display in movies that is most dramatic. Tom Selleck learning to swing his bat Japanese-style in *Mr. Baseball* (1992),[17] Sean Connery instructing Wesley Snipes in the (inscrutable) formalities practiced by Japanese businessmen in *Rising Sun* (1993),[18] and Tom Cruise slicing the air with his samurai swords in *The Last Samurai* (2003)[19] all exemplify Hollywood's take on training in Japanese *kata*. In the process, the Western characters mature as men, becoming calmer and wiser. Selleck improves his batting record, Connery's command of Japanese and Western ways of knowing ensures he solves the murder, and Cruise's character finally overcomes his alcoholism and self-hate through getting down with *kata*. In contrast, moments in contemporary Japanese media offer hilarious spoofs of *kata*. The YouTube sensation "The Japanese Tradition" (*Nihon no kata*, literally, Japanese *kata*), featuring a comedy duo known as the Rahmens (Rāmenzu; the two performers are Katagiri Jin, and Kobayashi Kentarō), is a series of short videos that, at first glance, seem to be reverent introductions to such common Japanese customs as bowing, making tea, using chopsticks, and so forth.[20] Gagaku music at the beginning of each video sets a mystical tone of high seriousness. Public television–style graphs, the well-modulated voice and careful enunciation of the narrator, and step-by-step examples of each movement add even more gravity. But one quickly sees the satire. "Japanese Traditions: Chopsticks" explains the difference between a chopstick and a fork, declaring that Japanese, of course, *always* use chopsticks. One graphic delineates the precise hand placement to use when holding and then separating a pair of ordinary throwaway chopsticks. The instructions get more and more absurd until we end up with chopstick-related accidents and chopstick sculptures.

Although it is tempting to see *kata* as uniquely Japanese in the vein of Hollywood films, the idea of *kata*-training recalls the frequently used sociological term "habitus," a word that refers to all the habits of thinking, moving, and interacting with the world that are so thoroughly ingrained in childhood that they become "second nature." Habitus becomes our common sense, so innate that we can easily fail to see how much this training has marked us as part of a certain social class, region, nation, and gender. *Kata*-training, then, is the deliberate and conscious adoption of a new habitus. Much teaching outside of Japan employs this kind of education, aiming, too, to guide the student to "learning through the body," such that movements can be performed efficiently, gracefully, and without a second thought. We can draw similarities with the discipline of students of figure skating, ballet, sports, and cooking. One hopes to master physical movements that ultimately enable top performance, which in turn opens up possibilities for the "master" to innovate. This could as easily be a Kabuki actor's virtuoso performance or a skater's decision to add a triple Lutz to the program. Learning a new language as an adult may also be likened to *kata*-training. One observes, imitates, memorizes, and hopes to reach the point where speaking the new language becomes second nature, one's own, and open to creative manipulation.

MAKING FUN OF GOOD CONDUCT

Perfectly executed etiquette can be a marvel of grace but is difficult to achieve. Even making the attempt opens the way for no end of missteps. Sake sloshes out of dainty cups, words come out all wrong, and the unruly body's own natural processes may emit ill-timed noises. Japanese comedy has long depicted missteps in conduct to delight audiences. Gender has also played a role here, accounting for many scenes of ordinary men and women inadvertently making fools of themselves despite their diligent efforts. Although many Japanese feel increasingly shaky about their command of honorific speech, those who make particular types of errors find themselves characterized as linguistic buffoons. Women who say such things as *o-biiru* (honorable beer), *o-jagaimo* (esteemed potato), or *watashi no o-denwa bangō* (my honorable telephone number) are often ridiculed.[21]

Likewise, the would-be gentleman who misses the mark has entertained readers and audiences from the Tokugawa period to the present. The stories in "witty books" (*sharebon*) of the late 1700s offer a case in point. Set in the licensed quarters of the Yoshiwara, these stories sketch a comedy of manners, making fun of playboys who yearn to be sophisticated in every way. Unfortunately, the men end up being ridiculed by courtesans for their clumsiness in everything from tipping to making love.[22] One of the most biting scenes in *Tampopo* takes viewers to an elegant business lunch among Japanese executives at a French restaurant. The diners are dwarfed by the grandeur of the room, the giant table, and the enormous bouquet on it. The most senior men do not wish to let on that they clearly cannot read the French menu. All are put to shame when the lowest man on the corporate totem pole, the lowly "briefcase carrier" (*kaban mochi*) orders last and most expertly, revealing his extensive knowledge of French wine and cuisine. A gentler humor surfaces in the 2005 film *Train Man* in which strangers who log on to the same Internet forum band together to guide a nerdy young man through a makeover. With their help, he improves his appearance (getting a new haircut, contacts, and clothing) and learns how to conduct himself on a date.[23] His fellow Internet geeks provide him with a Preparation Flow Chart for his first date ever, in which they tell him to Febreze his clothes and underwear, trim nose hairs, and take along a supply of "etiquette items," such as tissues, a handkerchief, breath mints, and facial blotting paper. Even thus prepared, Train Man's attempt to eat lobster at an elegant restaurant sends the crustacean delicacy flying across the table. In each case, consumers of this comedy get a lesson on masculine deportment, though they are comfortably positioned to laugh at the male characters. Although the humor underscores the arbitrary, even nonsensical, elements of protocol, the target of the satire is the pretender himself.

GUIDE TO THE CHAPTERS

The eleven chapters in *Manners and Mischief* are written by scholars from a variety of academic homes—anthropology, ethnomusicology, Japanese literature, theater, and cultural studies—who explore Japan's practices and guides to good manners from a range of standpoints. By examining a spectrum of cases, contributors illustrate how members of society engage with their culture and its ideology in practical ways that also express adherence or resistance to convention. Each chapter investigates models of ideal behavior but calls attention to infringements of these models. Authors show how even the strictest rules create plenty of room for mischievous subversion. Specifically, the chapters dissect how fundamental ideas about society and morality are refracted through the idiom of manners and then presented as something that may be learned, performed, and packaged for individual consumption.

You do not have to read many guides to see that those who pronounce on manners and morals come across as the most self-assured of all authors, authoritatively promising the keys to a happier, more beautiful life. They presume to know how the world works and how individuals should live. As scholars of conduct literature, we take a uniformly different tack, unpacking its optimistic and didactic quality to ask what kinds of assumptions about society and the individual prop up the advice.

We seek to point out the tensions concerning class, gender, or race, for example, that may be papered over by conduct literature's homilies on becoming a "better you." As the chapters here prove, advice literature grapples with social and cultural changes in the construction of roles and identities. Prescriptions for good conduct inevitably adjust with the times, responding to evolving social mores, shifting populations, and altered physical environments, as evident in the growth of cities. New forms of transportation and communication from nineteenth-century trains to twenty-first-century e-mail have spawned guides to their proper use.[24] For example, women are told how to become an "e-mail beauty" (*mēru bijin*) by not using emoticons in business e-mail, and are given advice about cleaning up their computer by organizing documents into neat folders rather than leaving the desktop cluttered with icons.[25] By responding to change and proposing innovative codes, conduct literature and practice also help generate a new common sense. These recipes for behavior are not fixed or unchanging but rather are windows into social and cultural transformations in Japan. As the chapters show, these guides and practices are also enjoyable to contemplate, giving readers pause to reexamine their own everyday lives and question why they hold the beliefs that they do.

It is fitting to begin *Manners and Mischief* with a chapter on the most celebrated work of all Japanese literature, the *Tale of Genji*, a work prized for its depiction of aristocratic sensibilities and decorum. The year 2008, declared (by committee) to be the classic's one thousandth anniversary, saw numerous festivities in Japan and abroad that honored the author Lady Murasaki and the *Tale of Genji*, and recognized the centuries of appreciation and other kinds of art and products that her work had inspired. Allusions to *Genji* have long been employed to add panache to one's style and poetry. During the Edo period, courtesans in the Yoshiwara pleasure quarters used to keep a copy of the *Tale* on their writing desks to show their refinement, and invented their own vocabulary by taking words from its chapter titles.[26] Today one can find exquisite Japanese candies, flower arrangements, and even plastic letter files that evoke famous scenes from the *Tale of Genji*.[27]

As Linda H. Chance's chapter, "*Genji* Guides, or Minding Murasaki," contends, however, approaches to the classic have varied widely over its long history, and appreciation for its surface beauty has neutralized the challenging aspects of Murasaki's work. Lofty aims to foster a climate that nurtures the "right person reading the right material in the right way" defeat the potential complexity and diversity of readerly engagement. *Genji* guides that focus on its "bits and pieces," whether medieval compendiums of its poetry or postwar study manuals for college-prep students, miss the way that Murasaki troubles concepts of "gender, genre, and morality." Chance investigates premodern and modern guides, and even twenty-first-century experiments with a cell-phone literature contest, magazine parody, and literary tourism, to ask what happens to the *Tale of Genji* when readers "mind Murasaki." Playing with the double meanings of "mind," that is, "supervise" and "heed," Chance argues that such guides attempt to discipline readers' approaches to the *Tale of Genji*. They dissuade the readers from minding the text's most unruly themes and the author's subversive moments. As Chance puts it, the guides have created an "etiquette of reading" the *Tale of Genji* that crafts a "split between surface and depth, form and content, forcing readers to feel that there is a realm of the text that is proper to be conversant with, and one that is better left hidden." Although Edo moralists, for example, warned that women should avoid the *Tale of Genji* for its lewdness, the work regularly found its way into bridal trousseaux and, as we have seen, onto the courtesan's writing desk. Chance also shows how Murasaki, too, mischievously brooked the conventions of gender and genre of her day by having Prince Genji praise tales (written in the vernacular by women like her) as more truthful than histories (written by men in academic language and Chinese characters). Fortunately, today's readers have access to both the guides to reading the *Tale of Genji* and *Genji*-inspired products and events and they can pick up the book translated into the modern Japanese language or into other languages. If feeling subversive, one has only to lock the door and read the book.

Guides to gender-specific conduct, whether containing advice directed to women climbing the corporate ladder or to men preparing to become fathers, assumes a symmetry between gender and biological sex. In Japan, however, despite (or perhaps because of) its strong adherence to gender distinctions, one finds instances where gender and sex do not match. The all-women's Takarazuka Theater entertains its fans, most of whom are women, with displays of beautiful male characters who have tall, slim bodies, big eyes, and deep voices, and who can play across not only race and ethnicity (think Rhett Butler and Chinese princes) but also sex. Similarly, the all-male Kabuki stage is home to *onnagata*, who are actors, usually male, that perform female roles to the delight of audiences composed of both women and men. In contemporary Japan, popular books by transgendered individuals, and their appearances in the media as celebrities, have further complicated notions of gender and sex. The makeup artist and media celebrity IKKO, a male-to-female (MtF) transgendered person, has recently authored beauty guides for women that feature her as the model.[28] In 2006 Nōmachi Mineko, another MtF transgendered individual, published a book that comically but poignantly described her efforts to pass as an Office Lady (OL).[29] Her observations of the changes she had to make in her appearance, speech, and attitude, and in a host of behaviors, in order to pass as a woman highlight the politics of gender in the office. That Nōmachi feared being found out by her coworkers speaks to the fact that, for all its colorful presentation onstage and in the media, the phenomena of being transgendered, cross-dressing, and exhibiting other variations on gender norms are not mainstream. They still disrupt "common sense."

Questions about decorum and gender play are explored in a different light in chapter 2, "Box-Lunch Etiquette: Conduct Guides and Kabuki *Onnagata*," contributed by Maki Isaka. Analyzing guides written in the Edo period for actors aspiring to be *onnagata* and critiques of actors written for Kabuki fans, Isaka traces the formation of codes of ideal femininity. She also speculates on the influence that such commentary and the vivid performances of *onnagata* may have had on women. Although the Japanese government now subsidizes Kabuki as a cultural treasure, in the Edo period Kabuki suffered government bans, its theater was regarded as an evil space, and actors, despite their glittering celebrity, occupied the lowest rungs of a class-conscious society. The same neo-Confucian curmudgeons who warned women away from the *Tale of Genji* cautioned them not to emulate *onnagata* fashion. Both proscriptions show, of course, that women were indeed enjoying such mischievous pleasure. But as Isaka explains, the femininity performed by *onnagata*, who intended to present themselves convincingly as women on stage and off, helped shape stereotypes of as well as constraints on women's behavior. Guides for actors based their advice on observations of women and what the authors took to be representative of femaleness. Disseminated in booklets for Kabuki lovers and performed on stage by talented *onnagata*, such notions of ideal femininity came to seem both natural and appropriate. Thus the transmuted ideal became the real.

The case of the *onnagata* also exemplifies an important feature of advice literature, that is, the possibility of its perfect embodiment. Contemporary beauty and manners guides in Japan and elsewhere, and even compliments to world figures and movie stars for their "effortless elegance," all embrace this ideal. In contrast, failed performances are the stuff of comedy. For example, when people perform some aspect of etiquette with obvious effort, too much enthusiasm, or simply ineptly, the result is humorous. The gap between the ordinary person's ability and the sophistication attempted makes us laugh (or cringe in memory of our own faux pas). As the embodiment of ideal femininity, however, the *onnagata* demonstrates elegance achieved so perfectly that audiences cannot detect the faintest hint that the actor is a man, whether they spy him onstage or off. Analyzing this performance within its historical context, Isaka points to Edo society's belief that surface appearance was not superficial. Following Ikegami's concept of appearance as one's Edo-era "identity kit," Isaka states that in this milieu, where one's social position was visibly marked in many ways, "how you appear *is* who you are." Moreover, *onnagata* followed a Buddhist-inspired philosophy of learning through the body, known as *shugyō* (cultivation), practicing the *kata*-training described above. *Shugyō*, too, posited no division between mind and body or between the *onnagata* and the ideal woman he was to embody, whether on the street or on the stage. Perfection was to be perfectly whole.

A search for manners guides for women in Japan today will turn up several authored by geisha. As the chapters by Kelly M. Foreman and Sally A. Hastings show, the geisha's place in polite society has undergone enormous changes, demonstrating how morals, manners, and changing ideas about female sexuality have become intertwined. Contemporary women regard geisha as practitioners of traditional arts and feminine refinement. But the idea that a geisha could serve as a role model of grace for a respectable lady would have shocked the ladies of Meiji, who took pains to distinguish themselves from the bawdy, outspoken geisha. In fact, part of the Meiji lady's need to adhere to Ogasawara School guides was to differentiate herself from the hapless Oriki types of the pleasure quarters. Much like the *onnagata*, geisha are now regarded as representatives of Japanese traditions anchored in the vitality of the Edo commoners' culture. Whereas famous Kabuki actors enjoy elite status in Japan, geisha, for all their polish, can still be considered somewhat suspect. As Liza Dalby, an expert on geisha, writes, "Would one boast of one's connection with geisha or proudly present an evening of their entertainment to the visiting Queen of England? Most certainly. Would one want one's daughter to become a geisha? Probably not."[30] In chapter 3, "The Perfect Woman: Geisha, Etiquette, and the

World of Japanese Traditional Arts," Foreman takes on these contradictions, explaining how the geisha's involvement in arts practice in the twenty-first century becomes her identity and her profession.

Like the *onnagata* and other practitioners of traditional arts in Japan, geisha learn through observing others. Spending most of their days in lessons in the arts of dance, music, flower arranging, and tea ceremony, geisha must thrive in a culture that Foreman describes as "saturated in etiquette, utterly defined by rules." Guides to manners written by geisha give readers a glimpse of this refined life, describing how a woman may stand, move, speak, and pour sake with the utmost grace. Yet, geisha themselves do not use manuals to hone their own artistic acuity. Rather, they master what they call "common sense" by following the tutelage of arts masters (*iemoto*), with whom they study dance and music. Geisha know how to show respect to their customers and others, but it is to their arts masters that they show heartfelt deference and loyalty. Geisha see the culmination of this training in the spectacular public dances that they perform and to which they devote much time and money.

Misconceptions in Japan and abroad continue to link contemporary geisha with prewar geisha and their association with the pleasure quarters. In contemporary Japan, however, no one is forced to become a geisha nor does a geisha perform sex work. Nevertheless, as Foreman explains, the geisha still confounds expectations for women. It is the geisha's choice to remain single and singularly devoted to the arts rather than assuming the role of a "normal" wife and mother that marginalizes her today. We can imagine that readers of the guides that geisha publish today may wish to peek into the lives of geisha and, like the Edo women who took fashion tips from the *onnagata*, bring a bit of the extraordinary and the risqué into their own lives. The geisha, like the *onnagata*, demonstrates the allure of refinement made all the more exquisite by serving no purpose other than to produce beauty.

Much as the traditional arts have influenced Japanese conduct, so have the manners and mores originating in the Euro-American West. Indeed, it would be impossible to discuss advice literature in modern Japan without referring to the effect of Western practices. At the same time, as the next chapters make clear, this influence did not—and to this day does not–occur without much negotiation, resistance, and even humorous self-reflection. Much of the story of the Japanese–Western encounter, when viewed through the lens of conduct, is a tale of dueling etiquettes, where adaptation to one another's ways is most often motivated or forced by changing diplomatic and economic relations. Americans, for example, showed a keen interest in learning Japanese conduct in the 1980s during the Trade War, while Japanese had an obvious interest in learning U.S. customs during the Allied occupation. Japanese and Western observations about the other's conduct have led to essentialistic views of the other, resulting in generalizations about national character, virtues, and pathologies, all by looking at the way Japanese bow or Victorian men tip their hat to women. Such essentialism occurs even when both parties assume they are working toward such mutually beneficial and inclusive goals as international understanding, democracy, or the expansion of women's rights. The 1986 U.S. movie *Gung Ho* serves as an example of this, imagining a Japanese firm rescuing a U.S. auto factory. The film plays up the ordeal of each side learning the other's etiquette, values, and corporate cultures. Ultimately, the two sides broaden one another's horizons—and increase profits.[31]

Manners and Mischief engages with the Japanese–Western encounter in two parts. Chapter 4, "Mortification, Mockery, and Dissembling: Western Adventures in Japanese Etiquette," by Gavin James Campbell, provides a compelling overview of Western commentary. Chapter 5, "A Dinner Party Is Not a Revolution: Space, Gender, and Hierarchy in Meiji Japan," by Sally A. Hastings, narrows the scope to focus on the nineteenth-century dinner party, analyzing the specifically gendered nature of the politics involved in this arena and drawing our attention to the way women's access to public space has been at the center of much Japanese–Western discussion of proper manners.

A common theme in Western writing on Japan, as Campbell observes, is the nation's "reputation for ferociously unforgiving standards of etiquette." He argues, however, that the history of Western guides to Japan reveals more about the psychological needs of the foreign traveler than about Japan itself. Some travelers, such as the Italian Jesuit missionary Alessandro Valignano, believed that learning proper Japanese customs and manners was essential. In 1581 he wrote a book on how Jesuits should conduct themselves while in Japan, outlining the types of local etiquette that missionaries ought to adopt, including how to greet nobles and how to serve sake.[32] Other sojourners, as Campbell points out, have wondered if such attention was worth the effort, observing that many later Western guides tended to harbor suspicions about how Japanese deploy etiquette. Potential deceit has been one issue, coldness another, and some Westerners have even wondered whether the Japanese are no more than performers of ritualized formalities, entirely lacking the ability to express genuine feelings. As Campbell explains, such doubts about Japanese conduct have produced a self-congratulatory sentiment among Western guide writers, leading them to conclude that their own conduct is the more liberated and humane. Although Victorian writers were completely convinced of their own superiority, more recent guidebooks urge readers to adapt to Japanese ways, promising that doing so will take them past the superficialities of the tourist experience and allow them to integrate into the "real Japan." When no mystical moment of engagement occurs, however, travel writers blame the Japanese, faulting them as frigid and bereft of emotional depth and honesty.

Campbell detects a common disappointment in Western writing on Japanese conduct. According to Western guide writers, "The central 'problem' with Japanese etiquette, and therefore with Japan, is that it refuses to cooperate in the psychological needs of the modern traveling public." Rather than reflect on their own excessive expectations, travelers channel their frustration into criticizing "the Japanese and their entire culture—from feudal times to the present—for denying them 'authentic' encounters that stretch the boundaries of self-awareness," even though the Westerner has followed every tip on courtesy in the guidebook. Notably, these Western guides to Japan do not suggest bringing Japanese ways into North American or European lifestyles but rather presume that one practices them only in Japan or when with Japanese. One is not advised, for example, to start bowing when greeting other Americans. Yet, as we see below, Western etiquette has been and continues to be recommended to Japanese by Japanese to elevate the pleasure and sophistication of their daily lives or even, as Hastings's chapter proves, to bolster the nation's image in the global imagination.

Analyzing the nineteenth-century dinner party as "a contested site," in her chapter Hastings finds that Japanese and Westerners brought quite different beliefs about social events to the table, and what's more, even their tables were different. The elite of Meiji Japan preferred small, individual, footed tray-type tables, while Westerners seated people in groups around a single shared large one. But more importantly, they had different views about seating women at the table. Japanese were surprised at Westerners' inclusion of wives and daughters, while Westerners were alternately bemused and shocked by the presence of lively geisha and dismayed by the reserve of Japanese wives and daughters, whom they saw as "slaves to etiquette." Complicating this encounter for the Japanese was the fact that unequal treaties were in place that vastly favored Western interests, forcing Japan into a semi-colonial status. Performing well at Western-style dinner parties, dances, and other social events became a way for Japanese to prove that they understood what the Euro-American elite deemed to be the protocols of civilization. This in turn would prove that they deserved equal status in the realms of diplomacy and trade. As Hastings makes clear, the Japanese were well aware of the hypocrisy of Western pronouncements on civilized behavior, and saw contradictions, for example, in Western homilies on women's virtue, considering the flourishing red-light districts in the United States and Europe. Westernized social rituals became further politicized in the late 1880s, when the Japanese public began to protest against their leaders engaging in events such as a fancy masquerade party with Western guests at a government-built guest house known as the Rokumeikan. To the public eye, such performances of Western conduct did not appear to be effective strategies for increasing Japan's status in the global arena, but merely reflected Japanese subservience to foreign powers. In retrospect, both Japanese and Westerners have applauded this moment as showing resistance to the imposition of values from abroad and as being a healthy reassertion of Japanese ways.

Hastings observes that Japanese men understood that the witty conversation expected at dinner parties required women to excel in skills that, in Japan, were the specialty of geisha, and they were uneasy about placing their wives and daughters in that ambiguous position. Japanese men were likewise aware that in the West the dinner party, along with the parlor, served as the site of courtship. Japanese parents had no intention of ceding the choice of marriage partners to the younger generation. Moreover, the dining room as arena for courtship placed geisha in competition with wives and daughters. Mothers feared that their daughters, taught to be quiet to show their refinement, could not capture men's interest when pitted against geisha. Dinner parties fell out of favor, Hastings explains, because men did not want to give up the patriarchal privilege that allowed them both geisha entertainment and their married status. Consequently, Japanese men's decision to give up the dinner party had more to do with retaining their own status vis-à-vis women than resisting Western influence. For wives, however, fighting for a place at the dinner party was tantamount to demanding greater equality and respect in their marriage.

Fast-forwarding from nineteenth-century masculinity to twenty-first-century men's guides, we ask what kinds of advice are aimed at men in Japan today. Chapter 6, "The *Oyaji* Gets a Makeover: Guides for Japanese Salarymen in the New Millennium," by Jan Bardsley, examines three recent guides to men's deportment. All include wit and include *manga* to make their points about what is offensive and what is proper behavior. As Bardsley discusses, the guides underscore the poor reputation the old-fashioned salaryman now has in Japan. Once, he was the corporate warrior who led Japan to high-speed growth in the 1960s and steered a course toward the heady days of the "bubble economy" of the 1980s. Today, the salaryman seems most closely associated in popular culture with the recession of the 1990s, the economic downturn of 2008, and the disappearance of the lifetime employment system that had been his salvation. *Oyaji*, a sometimes affectionate term for older men, has increasingly been used in derogatory ways to satirize older salarymen who self-importantly cling to their status as white-collar company men despite the failure of the system they built and represent. As Bardsley discusses, men's guides persuade readers to rid themselves of the arrogant mannerisms and provincialism, and even the fashion associated with *oyaji*. One can still be a white-collar executive, but not in the same old Japanese way, the guides imply. Comics and anecdotes in the manuals reveal what Bardsley describes as a "spectrum of racial cool," which positions young, sophisticated Japanese men near the ideal of the (Anglo) cosmopolitan man, and envisions the *oyaji* as his frumpy opposite. *Manga* images reinforce this image: cartoons of the *oyaji* exaggerate his East Asian features, while drawings of the successful man show a vaguely Anglo figure. Bardsley also observes that these guides portray OLs as mocking the salarymen while fantasizing about a man so beautiful that he is as unreal as the *bishōnen* (beautiful boy) commonly found in *manga*. She argues that the OLs' mockery refers to assumptions about young Japanese women's ease with Western ways. In contrast to the *oyaji*, the OL is imagined to be familiar with European foods and fashion and at home speaking English. Such traits give the OL a cultural capital that aligns her with the power of the idealized figure of the Western man, justifying her smirking at salarymen. Yet Bardsley also detects signs of *oyaji* resistance. One guide writer asserts that, for all his love of Western dinner rituals, as a Japanese man he insists on his right to slurp his noodles *oyaji*-style. Another kind of resistance takes the form of some younger men, dubbed the "grass-eaters" (*sōshokukei danshi*), who, in contrast to the "carnivorous," aggressive career women, wish to develop a private life with ample leisure time to enjoy aesthetic pursuits rather than to become exemplary executives.

Turning from salarymen to women working in the corporate world, we examine the advice given Japanese women who want to be successful in both their careers and their personal lives. In major Japanese bookstores, what books stand out among the numerous lifestyle and beauty guides for women? In chapter 7, "The Dignified Woman Who Loves to Be 'Lovable,'" Hiroko Hirakawa examines this question by analyzing the phenomenally popular guide *The Dignity of the Woman* (2006), written by Bandō Mariko, a woman who has won acclaim as a diplomat, a university president, and the head of a major brewery. In other words, she is a "superwoman" who seems to have it all, and this success has drawn women to her book. Hirakawa locates Bandō's book in a "dignity-book boom," a spate of guides, serious and satirical, that drew inspiration from another best-seller's title *Dignity of the Nation* (2004), by the mathematician Fujiwara Masahiko. The book called on Japanese to stave off rampant Americanization by remembering their nation's unique tradition of "form and feeling," a sensibility so powerful that, Fujiwara argued, it could light the way to saving the world. As it turned out, *The Dignity of the Woman* sold the best of all the "dignity" books, and yet, surprisingly, it has received consistently poor reviews from readers.

Examining the reader reviews posted on Amazon.co.jp, Hirakawa traces readers' disappointment with Bandō's advice to the point "when they find that the book's advice is mainly about becoming adept at pleasing men in power." One reviewer branded Bandō as an "*oyaji* manipulator" (*oyaji korogashi*) and not a strong advocate for women's rights in the workplace. Essentially, Bandō advises that young women can get ahead by becoming "lovable" and by avoiding becoming like *oyaji*, the male model described above. They should be feminine, prettily dressed, and always polite, especially taking care to use respectful language when speaking to men. Women should not be strident in claiming their rights but should instead show gratitude to their coworkers when, for example, they are granted maternity leave. On top of that, Bandō believes that career women must be consummate homemakers. In short, they must be overachievers who can combine career acumen with domestic talent. She does advocate hiring maids to help with the housework, but even this remark shows how out of touch Bandō is, since most working women cannot afford domestic help. The comic illustrations of this dignified woman punctuating the volume depict an Anglicized figure similar in style to the senior executive described in Bardsley's chapter above. Neither the Anglicized man in the men's guides nor the Anglicized woman in Bandō's book is meant to be funny. Both are intended as model figures. In her conclusion Hirakawa presents the example of a much different working woman, a character in a

TV show called *The Dignity of the Temp*, a temporary hire at a company who wins everyone's respect even though she is assertive and refuses to do any work not specified in her job description. Hirakawa contends that *The Dignity of the Woman*'s best-selling status and its poor reviews construct a remarkable gap and that "this fissure should be understood in the context of the collective insecurity over the fate of post-bubble Japan that the dignity book boom has successfully exploited."

Women may turn to different kinds of guides when pregnant. Advice for pregnant mothers in contemporary Japan, and its connections to consumerism, the social importance of mothers, and the idealization of the female body are scrutinized in chapter 8, Amanda C. Seaman's "Making and Marketing Mothers: Guides to Pregnancy in Modern Japan." Arguing that such guides have long "served as a medium for the representation and (just as significantly) the regulation of the female body," Seaman explores guides for pregnant women by taking us from Tokugawa-era Confucian-inspired texts through modern manuals that emphasize scientific knowledge and hygiene, and then concentrates on an analysis of the new pregnancy magazines: *Pre-Mo, Nin-sugu,* and *Pregnant Living*. Seaman's investigation illuminates how views of the reproductive body have changed over hundreds of years; but in tracing these changes, she shows how society has consistently employed pregnancy manuals "to create, discipline, and define women, their bodies, and their choices." She observes that today's magazines approach pregnant women as comprising a kind of niche market that can be further segmented according to age and income, and to which a variety of products geared toward making pregnancy more pleasant and less stressful can be marketed.

In the world of magazines, pregnancy is a "lifestyle moment" that will be healthier and more pleasurable if advice is heeded, services used, and many specialty products consumed. Moreover, these magazines employ standard marketing techniques for cultivating a long-term readership that seeks to engage readers who will eventually turn to the companies' magazines for mothers and related products for advice in rearing, educating, and clothing children. Although much advice in pregnancy manuals from Tokugawa times to the present focuses on birthing a healthy child, Seaman observes that today's advice to women living in this era of abundance incorporates cautionary language about weight gain and emphasizes maintaining a careful eating and exercise regime. She finds that such concern underscores women's ambivalence about their expanding bodies at a time when the slim woman is regarded as the most competent, successful, and desirable. Seaman contends that the magazines attempt to assuage pregnant women's fears and fulfill the magazines' mission to sell products by promoting materialism as the answer. Consumption of such items as a "cute Italian maternity outfit" compensates for the slimmer body one is losing. Seaman concludes her chapter by speculating that this "reconfiguration of pregnancy, and its integration within the body and lifestyle discourse of young womanhood, is part of a broader transformation in the significance and nature of motherhood itself as Japan faces the looming dilemma of declining fertility."

Advice columns that respond to readers' letters, common in Japanese newspapers and magazines, give visibility to individuals' concerns and recommend certain courses of action as solutions. They also provide voyeuristic entertainment as readers glimpse the scrapes, awkward moments, and unhappiness of others. Such columns reveal a sense of the insufficiency of long-standing customs or commonsense ethics and illustrate that new situations may be prompting fresh questions. In chapter 9, "When Manners Are Not Enough: The Newspaper Advice Column and the 'Etiquette' of Cultural Ideology in Contemporary Japan," Janet Shibamoto-Smith examines sixty letters to an *Asahi* newspaper advice column published between 2005 and 2006. Most of the letter writers ranged from fourteen to sixty-five years of age and requested advice about relationships or self-dissatisfaction. Shibamoto-Smith contends that such columns give shape to "the often unspoken yet ever-present rules laid down by dominant ideological constructions of the good person, the good family member, the good lover or friend," and the advice is often "to undertake a project perhaps best described as 'ideological etiquette.' "

Analyzing these columns, Shibamoto-Smith discerns changes in attitudes toward gender, family relationships, and "ideologies of what makes a good person." Unlike the pregnancy advisors described by Seaman, who often are—or rely on—medical experts, *Asahi* advisors include people from many walks of life whose ages range from mid-thirties to seventies. Readers hear from such advisors as a fashion critic, a mountain climber, a romance novelist, a comedy team, and a former model. Shibamoto-Smith discovers that, whereas in the past, readers, especially women, might be encouraged to endure their situation, now "action is where it's at," and this is true of advice to both men and women. Everyone is urged to find a resolution either by openly discussing a problem with others or by finding a passion. In other words, most advice follows a "liking strategy," with readers advised to find a project or activity that excited them, to follow that to their heart's content, and then to expect that good things would come to them by the positive energy they generated. Shibamoto-Smith observes a marked difference in the columns of the 1980s and 1990s with regard to gender roles. Whereas the advice in preceding decades tended to guide readers into appropriate gender roles, today's advice embraces tolerance and valorizes the notion of readers finding their own paths. At the same time, Shibamoto-Smith speculates, it is this tolerance for different life choices that prompts readers to ask if their own goals and their problems are "normal" in this new and ever-changing environment.

Intimate relationships have long been a part of life ripe for advice of all kinds. In fact, there is almost no end to guides in Japan and elsewhere that claim to hold the key to developing the self-confident personality that will win love and result in marriage. In the twenty-first century, romance novels and movies, the stories of celebrities' lives, and advertisements for everything from weddings to honeymoons to first homes, construct the culture of heterosexual love. But where can lesbian, bisexual, and gay individuals turn for advice and models of satisfying relationships? In chapter 10, "A Community of Manners: Advice Columns in Lesbian and Gay Magazines in Japan," Hideko Abe explains how magazine editors have attempted to fill this need. Examining the advice columns in four post-1990s magazines—*Anise* and *Carmilla* for lesbians and bisexuals, and *Bádi* and *G-men* for gay men—Abe demonstrates how these publications frame an imagined community "where sexual minorities live, interact, exchange, and negotiate their everyday lives." These columns offer almost nothing in the way of conventional etiquette advice. Rather, they reflect the editors' "foundational, self-conscious commitment to openness and affirmation," welcoming those who often feel ostracized. Abe reads the columns to discern the behavioral ethics they establish, the messages they send about queer identity, and the ways that discussion of good conduct injects meaning into daily life. She notes that the advisors writing these columns are not experts with training in psychology but rather members of the community they serve. They support readers' desires and self-revelations, while urging them to be honest and to avoid hurting others. Abe observes, however, that advice columns in lesbian magazines are much longer than those in magazines directed to gay men, an indication that it may be more difficult for lesbians to meet and talk openly. This may explain, in turn, why lesbian readers ask questions about lesbianism in general, specifically inquiring about such topics as types of lesbians, marriages of convenience, and ambivalence about their sexual identity. They also ask for relationship advice. Interestingly, lesbian readers and advisors flexibly use a variety of voices "stereotypically categorized as feminine, masculine, and neutral," giving the impression of an egalitarian community of readers. This differs from the conservatively gender-coded, hierarchical linguistic preferences found in magazines for gay men. What ties the four magazines together are their creation of queer community and the presentation of that community as equally human and complex as the straight world.

Manners and Mischief closes by reflecting on one of the simplest yet most effective means for teaching good conduct: the graphic image. In chapter 11, "Behavior That Offends: Comics and Other Images of Incivility," Laura Miller emphasizes the power of the image to shape our ideas of propriety. Public-service posters, funny comics, and clever illustrations in manuals and magazines have a way of capturing our attention and getting their messages across immediately. When we laugh at the joke, that means we understand the difference between good conduct and the ridiculously bad. Eye-catching images can slip into the public imagination in ways that make us forget that there ever was an author, a publishing house, or a government agency behind them. As Miller argues, images "work to discipline our focus and expose in a concrete way the ideology of manners." Her chapter invites scrutiny of several images, most taken from contemporary Japanese guides and magazines, and peels back the humor to reveal how each graphic frames culture and subculture, location, actors, and the desired interaction. Such images not only suggest ways that we may criticize others' habits but also prompt us to imagine new experiences and identities in a cultural landscape. What Miller writes about the image may also hold true for many of the etiquette books discussed in *Manners and Mischief*, bringing the discussion full circle: "There is a degree of instant gratification involved. In place of years of good breeding, one can acquire knowledge of good conduct, and become a good person, by learning them quickly."

Following East Asian practice, all Japanese names give the family name first and given name second, except in cases where the person works primarily in English. Following most of the Japanese texts we discuss here, we use the terms "West" and "Western" largely in reference to the United States and the countries of western Europe. This usage captures the weight of this particular "West" in the Japanese imagination, notwithstanding how imprecise and politically charged the term is.

Manners continue to evolve in Japan, although some Japanese may misread new conventions as an affront to national pride. Contemporary journalists writing about Japan's generation gap often point to a seeming disparity between the expectations of the old and those of the young concerning manners, claiming that young people don't seem very interested in learning etiquette from their parents or elders. Yet even the most outré of Japanese youth subcultures show the same desire for behavior guidelines that one finds in any society; they simply require that the guidelines be suitable in their own social settings. Thus, it is not surprising to find that the Nihon Meido Kyōkai (The Japan Maid Association), formed in 2007, provides certification for those who want to work as waitresses in the Maid Café industry, requiring that aspirants pass courses on manners and the history of the service industry as part of the licensing examination. Those who conduct work on Japan would do well to pay attention to shifting mores and manners while taking note of the mischief that arises in the wake of these changes.

NOTES

1. Itami Jūzō, director, *Tampopo* (Dandelion) (Tokyo: Itami Productions, 1986).

2. Eiko Ikegami, *Bonds of Civility: Aesthetic Networks and the Political Origins of Japanese Culture* (Cambridge: Cambridge University Press, 2005).

3. Ikegami, *Bonds of Civility*, 345.

4. Bandō Mariko, *Josei no hinkaku* (The dignity of woman) (Tokyo: PHP Shinsho, 2006).

5. Shōgakukan, *Nihon kokugo daijiten* (Comprehensive dictionary of Japan's national language) (Tokyo: Shōgakukan, 1974, 2001), 164.

6. Characters invented in Japan through the creative recombination of existing Chinese characters are known in Japanese as *kokuji* or "national characters."

7. Ikegami, *Bonds of Civility*, 344.

8. Kōzō Yamamura and John Whitney Hall, eds., *The Cambridge History of Japan: Medieval*, Vol. 3 (Cambridge: Cambridge University Press, 1990), 602.

9. Ikegami, *Bonds of Civility*, 333.

10. Jordan Sand, *House and Home in Modern Japan: Architecture, Domestic Space, and Bourgeois Culture, 1880–1930* (Cambridge, Mass.: Harvard University Press, 2003), 50.

11. Robert Lyons Danly, *In the Shade of Spring Leaves: The Life and Writings of Higuchi Ichiyō, A Woman of Letters in Meiji Japan* (New Haven, Conn.: Yale University Press, 1981), 221.

12. Selçuk Esenbel, "The Meiji élite and Western culture," in *Leaders and Leadership in Japan*, ed. Ian Neary (Richmond, Surrey, U.K.: Japan Library, 1996), 111.

CHAPTER I

Genji Guides, or Minding Murasaki

LINDA H. CHANCE

What is the proper way to read the *Tale of Genji* (*Genji monogatari*), the greatest classic of Japanese literature, and who are its proper readers? We, modern seekers after the "truth" of literature, might chafe at being told how to correctly read a poem, or be wary of conduct manuals used to create disciplined social groups, but when confronted with the almost eight hundred poems larded into the famously allusive prose of *Genji monogatari*, some kind of guide begins to seem welcome. The fifty-four-chapter bulk of the text has no doubt left many a student wondering whether it might not be preferable to be told that the *Genji* is, unfortunately, not the thing for a youth to read. This monumental work is an argument for instructional aids, if ever there was one. Long before centuries of language change intervened between the modern audience and Murasaki Shikibu's (c. 978–c. 1016) prose, the fact that most characters were identified by official titles rather than personal names, and that these titles changed from chapter to chapter with a character's promotion or change of social role, led to the production of genealogies for tracking them, not to mention nicknames for conveniently making reference to the main heroes and heroines among the more than five hundred individuals who put in an appearance. Dilettante and professional readers alike were in need of these "handles," without which few could grasp the salient plot points.

SAMPLING THE *GENJI*

It would seem that guides to a major work of literature, particularly one that presents special problems due to its historical distance, are something to celebrate. This is especially true in the case of the *Tale of Genji*. First of all, the reader must come to terms with an elite, hierarchical world in which lords and ladies pass the time with arts and seductions. One also has to figure out which character is acting, speaking, or being spoken to or about at any given time in *Genji monogatari* (true pronouns are mostly absent; grammatical inflections signal the relative social position of parties to a conversation).

The eighth chapter, "Under the Cherry Blossoms" (*Hana no en*) provides a useful example of the charming and yet slightly alarming way the narrative moves through highly charged territory, giving us a good idea of why generations have turned to guides for clues to navigating this classic. For the sake of convenience, I will refer to the main man as Genji (a pronunciation of the family name "Minamoto," given to princes who are removed from the royal succession) but not rely on other sobriquets. Although the chapter is a mere half-dozen pages in English translation, it is dense with references to courtly romances and pastimes.

The chapter begins with the court gathered to fête the cherry tree before the royal palace. The introduction of each participant brings allusions to the complicated emotions among them, from the resentment of the sovereign's first wife toward the honor shown the current empress, to the nervousness of Genji's best friend and rival as he is called on to produce Chinese poems or dance just after the incomparable hero, to the tears of the father-in-law who thrills to Genji's dancing, even though he wishes the young man were more attentive to his daughter. The empress watches her stepson Genji with mixed feelings, since she and he have been involved in an affair. Her precarious situation is revealed in a poem that the narrator admits it is strange for her to be able to report. Having had a lot to drink, Genji tries to get in to see the empress, but the door through which he might gain access is locked. He continues until he finds an unlocked door. There begins one of Genji's many affairs, a perilous liaison with a high-ranking woman whose parents intend for her to marry well, to Genji's half-brother, the heir apparent. Genji suspects but hopes this is not the woman he has found under the misty moon (until he realizes it could be a convenient out for her to marry his brother). As he frets over the identity of the lady, from whom he had received only an appealing display of fright, a poem and a fan, Genji runs a mental comparison with the empress (a repeated topos, as he never forgets a relationship), plays music, calls both on the girl he is raising to be his model wife and on his first, less friendly, wife, and is finally invited to an archery contest by the father of the mystery lady. The chapter ends with Genji clutching the hand of the one he guessed to be his conquest, filled with joy and misgivings when she offers him a verse in response.

Joy and misgivings over Genji fill the many women in his orbit: the girl he brings up, young Murasaki, must adopt the daughter of a mistress while having no children of her own; and his first wife, Aoi, is struck dead by the spirit of a rival just after having a son. The parade of ladies, their letters, their attendants, and even their locations behind screens and under layers of robes keeps the reader's head whirling. If the producers of manuals to such a text are themselves good readers, scholars with access to contextual knowledge (knowing how archery contests proceeded, for example), and educators who have the public's best interests and edification at heart, and if their efforts encourage larger audiences to read the work, as surely they must, what can be the objection? But the rhetoric of "best interests" often hides a threat of coercion. When the interpreter tells the reader what to look at and therefore what to ignore in order to read correctly, text and reader are at that interpreter's mercy. Some guides to the *Genji* seem more like guards keeping us *from* the *Genji*, from Murasaki Shikibu, or even from ourselves. They promise to narrow and straighten us (as the English banner at the top of one cover proclaims, JAPANESE TRADITIONAL CULTURE OFFICIAL APPROVAL [*sic*][1]), in essence to prevent an uninhibited embrace of the material. Even as they bring the text to our notice and herald it as a classic, they aim to organize and institutionalize our reactions. Indispensable though they may be—and, no, I could never have read the book myself without them—they invite suspicion.

In saying this, nonetheless, we face a paradox and a question about the nature and purpose of reading itself. Handbooks to the *Genji* have historically tended to try to simplify the process of the encounter with the text, and to focus our attention on the shared values of the community of readers that such guides presuppose and work to reinforce. They imply a correct reading that is arguably less diffuse and more shallow than we could acquire by approaching the text without their mediation. Were we to read the text directly, a freer, deeper experience might emerge, one that would not necessarily produce a directed and shareable response. Such an unencumbered reading seems ideal. And yet it is equally dogmatic to insist that the proper way to read the *Tale of Genji* is in an immediate, undisciplined, and singular encounter.[2] Whether we say that the right reading is the unfettered or the guided, we are still calling for control over how the text is consumed, and implicitly calling for seriousness. Yet it is impossible to fully admire the variety of readings the text courts—its profound creativity—while rejecting the handy chart, the digest, the comic book, or even the attractions of the Super Dollfie designer doll modeled on the male lead, the Shining Genji.[3] Each of these has its place and may be the natural and preferable response to a tale that so often remarks on the devastating good looks of its hero. Scenes of voyeurism beckon us to look at handsome men or unavailable women and sigh. Love relationships do emerge as the highest goal for women (with committing suicide or becoming a nun the frequent, but lamented, alternatives). The world of the tale (*monogatari*) is one of women gathering in groups; we hear the things (*mono*) they tell one another (*katari*). Genji is always ready to substitute likely candidates for the women he has loved and lost, beginning with his mother, and reading requires we keep track of them. Guides have their utility, and can expand our horizons by sharpening our focus. What I hope to show, however, is that some have used their mastery over the text as a way of suppressing a range of discoveries, especially those that open up a critique of gender. The fact that the author is a woman, and that the intended audience was evidently female, has raised the stakes for those who felt charged with making the best parts of the text legible. Women, as much as the text, are the object of advice for good conduct when it comes to this tale.

Why we must read, who "we" are, and why we ought to read particular things are topics for a philosophy or an ideology of reading. Educators must be aware of their own answers, which, in turn, form the structuring principles of a canon. But such moral imperatives are not entirely divorced from the question of *how* we should read, in the literal sense of what physical posture to assume, or where it is appropriate to be seen reading, for example (until recently, it was not common to see women reading on trains in Japan). This etiquette of reading—how to turn the pages or wind the scroll, which material details to remark upon, which characters may be part of polite conversation—participates with the larger project of training one's sights on the classics and avoiding trash. The aim in both cases is to produce the educated, refined person who upholds propriety. Such a person reads the right things, in the right fashion, and draws the right conclusions. The etiquette of reading *Genji monogatari* does not focus on form to the exclusion of content. In fact,

I will argue that it raises attention to certain matters of form as a means of patrolling the content and, perhaps more significantly, responses to it. The etiquette imposed on readers, furthermore, can be seen as keeping the author, or at least her ideas, in check as well.

DANGERS OF THE *GENJI*

The question of proper readings and readers for the *Genji* has, moreover, always exceeded mere issues of organizing information or classifying possible responses. In its own pages the tale raises such issues as gender, genre, and morality; continuing debate on each of these has shaped its reception down to the present. Whether eager readers, avid canonizers, or detractors, pundits in every epoch have taken little for granted. (And how could there be a muted response to a story such as this? It begins with death by bullying, progresses through the amorous adventures of the royally born Genji—seeking a substitute for the stepmother with whom he trysts only long enough to make her pregnant—his rivals, and progeny. It finally ends with a woman who tries by all means to resist the bonds of romantic submission to two men, the grandson and the putative son of Genji, who represent society's highest aspirations for male behavior.) How the *Tale of Genji* is read reflects the concerns of the historical period in which it is read. The tale functions as a touchstone for views of the past, of literature, and of properly male or female spheres. In what follows, I will briefly trace representative premodern views of how to handle this most capacious of texts, beginning with visions that take the *Genji* itself as the guide, before returning to some of the ways it has been parsed for modern audiences, both within and outside Japan. While this will hardly be an account of all the customs that hem in the reading of the tale today or in times past, it suggests some of the reasons that an etiquette of reading (one with much ideological force) often trained on the superficies of the book has developed around *Genji monogatari*. Although early moral reactions can be stern in their critique of the tale, the fortunes I sketch are not always on an upward trend to a modern, increasingly enlightened acceptance of the *Genji*. Rather, periods of intense interest in the tale at a national level have sometimes apparently done the least to promote a balanced appreciation of it. The year 2008, recognized (by committee) as the one thousandth year of the tale's existence, has seen the work receive its fullest local, global, and virtual exploitation. Nationwide, "culture centers" offer reading groups, exhibitions proliferate, and even the

Kyoto branch of the Bank of Japan draws on the *Genji*'s cachet to lure customers on a tour of their local financial institution.[4] The tale is at the center of a marketing effort that is probably unprecedented, and yet there is a certain hesitation to embrace the whole saga, an always resurfacing ambivalence about this work that is so closely identified with, but still so dangerous to, traditional Japanese culture. How this can be so should be obvious to anyone who has read it, although readership never seems to grow quite in proportion to the energy that goes into exhorting people to read the book, at least in our time.

THE *GENJI* AS GUIDE IN PREMODERN TIMES

Evidence suggests that the tale attracted readers much more easily in its own day, at least among the tiny percentage of the population that comprised the literate elite. In her journal, Murasaki Shikibu at one point laments that her patron has taken an inferior version from her room to give to his second daughter, implying that fans were anxious to peruse the latest installments.[5] She also reports that the sovereign Ichijō (r. 986–1011), to whom the central woman in her salon, Shōshi (also known as Akiko, 988–1074), was married, remarked upon hearing some of the tale read that the author must have read the history *Nihongi* (properly, *Nihon shoki*, *Chronicles of Japan*, 720). This remark inspired the lady-in-waiting Saemon no naishi to tease the writer with the nickname "Our Lady of the Chronicles."[6] Ichijō's sally may imply that he recognized the tale had a gravity that would lend itself to being a subject for lectures, as the *Chronicles of Japan* did. Or it may be a reference to Murasaki's views in the tale about the comparative value of genres. Heian culture followed the Chinese ranking: history was best, poetry was good, and fiction did not even belong in the list, so degraded was it. The author herself inserted a "defense of fiction," a passage in which her eponymous hero assures his adoptive daughter (the object of his unrequited desire) that tales really do tell more truth than do histories.[7] Both comments, by the sovereign and by the fictional character Genji, attest to male interest in the *monogatari*. We may read them today as subversive votes in favor of the vernacular produced by women (cannily placed by the female writer in the mouths of men). Historically they have been used to endorse an image of the author as a talented, wise woman (*saijo*). Biographies of notable Japanese women, popular in the Edo period (1600–1868), hold Murasaki up as a model reader of serious works.[8]

We have two well-known accounts from women readers closer to her time that imply a more emotional investment in the tale. The first is by the woman referred to as the Daughter of Sugawara no Takasue (b. 1008), who writes of her youthful longings to acquire the entire manuscript and live a life warranting the attention of one of its male leads. In her *Sarashina journal* (*Sarashina nikki*, c. 1060), she regrets these desires in retrospect, since they kept her from religious devotions, but she cannot suppress the joy the *Genji* inspired in her.[9] A second account is *Mumyōzōshi* (The nameless tale), a narrative of women discussing characters and incidents in the *Genji* and other fiction. The chatty evaluations suggest that these readers, who were still only an elite fraction, typically found pleasure in the book and felt empathy for the plight of favorite figures. The readers also indicate their disapproval of Genji's young wife, who has an affair, and of men who misbehave beyond what their rank entitles, but the enthusiastic recollection of moving scenes implies the readers' close knowledge of and love for the text.[10] The *Mumyōzōshi*'s author, thought to be the Daughter of Shunzei (who was actually his adopted granddaughter, 1171?–1254), focuses on the poetry of the tale and thus stays well within the range of response that we see from male readers at this time, including Fujiwara no Teika (1162–1241), whose name is associated with the production of the standard recension. It is significant for the reception of the tale that literary history recounts the first major canonizer of the text as Teika, a man with interest in it as a source for poetry. As Teika's father Shunzei (1114–1204) states, "Composing poetry without knowledge of the *Genji* is to be greatly deplored."[11] Those who sought to make its poetic riches accessible may have preferred more manageable summaries and handbooks. Such attenuation of the volume of the text was perhaps necessary to allow more of the literate population to become familiar with it, but offering guides began a process that would lead people to accept nubbins in place of the whole. Although the guides are meant to bring all the references alive, their sketches and allusions are by their nature disjointed. Appreciating the text through poetry, one of the chief features of the etiquette of reading the *Genji*, was thus in some ways a path to the eventual undoing of the text's full potential.

The tale is not without its didactic moments; the ideal woman, as described by men in the "Broom Tree" (*Hahakigi*) chapter, should be accomplished in poetry and the domestic arts. Genji teaches his young ward Murasaki calligraphy and the reticence necessary in a noble's wife. Nonetheless, one might expect the *Tale of Genji* to be avoided as a source of moral lessons, given that adultery and incest (or at least the troubling of the imperial line) are central motifs.[12] We may be forgiven for attributing acts of resistance to the tale's unproductive wives and unfriendly women, one of whom flees the hero so completely that he feels compelled to make do with her brother instead. Add to this the Buddhist criticism of false, decorative language incommensurate with truth, and it becomes likely that no amount of poetic value could forestall complaints and even censure of her work. Murasaki Shikibu was not too long in the ground when dedicated Buddhist monks sought to spare her the pain of damnation for the error of misleading the public through words. *Genji ipponkyō hyōbyaku* (Invocation for the one-volume sūtra on *Genji*) of 1168, composed by Chōken (d. 1203), is one example of prayers for her salvation.[13] The role of court ladies in sponsoring such services complicates the notion that this was a purely misogynistic move, however. The ritual redeems the author and points to another way in which the subversive potential of the story survived. In other circles, Murasaki Shikibu was hailed as a bodhisattva who taught through her examples of wickedness the truth that all deserve compassion.[14] Far from locking the tale into a strictly formal etiquette of readings, her medieval audience seems, on balance, to have given the author a lot of credit for using the resources of her mind in the depiction of literary and ethical worlds.

Later medieval writers find it necessary to craft commentaries to explicate the lexicon of the *Genji*. With so much effort required to simply follow the story, they might have focused primarily on the technical aspects. But they do not hesitate to recommend the characters as models for women and for men, extending to members of the warrior class. The foremost champion of the tale is Ichijō Kanera (or Kaneyoshi, 1402–1481), whose commentary *Kachō yosei* (Evocation of flowers and birds) of 1472 is only one piece of evidence we have as to his belief in its efficacy for more than poetic allusions. In the words of Steven Carter, "He wants it to be an encyclopedia of courtly life, a work that shows the courtier what the ideal of the aristocratic life should be."[15] Kanera also lectured often on the *Genji*, and found it helpful in advising Hino Tomiko (1440–1496), who stepped into politics in the vacuum left by her husband, the shōgun Ashikaga Yoshimasa (1435–1490). We might say that up to this time, the *Genji* was a guide in two senses, and many a literary light minded Murasaki's lessons on humanity along with her incomparably rich lyric phrases.

GUIDES FOR THE *GENJI* IN EARLY MODERN AND MODERN JAPAN

When did this change? Why did commentators become less comfortable with the complexities of human interaction and women's take on them? Certainly Hayashi Razan (or Dōshun, 1583–1657) was harsh toward women writers of the vernacular. He wished to build literacy by enhancing education in the native tongue, one of the key ways that Confucianists and the printing revolution transformed society from his day onward. Razan found it unpleasant that women—those untrustworthy creatures—had done so much of the classic writing in that idiom.[16] G. G. Rowley and P. F. Kornicki have documented how some Edo period critics warned women away from the text on account of their presumed special susceptibility to its lewd messages.[17] It is by no means the case that the Edo period brought uniformly hard times to the *Genji*: it was taught at *terakoya* schools for commoners and was a standard part of a bride's trousseau among the elite. But so prominent an author of didactic texts as Kaibara Ekiken (Ekken, 1630–1714) was mindful about this: he felt that Murasaki should not be readily available to feminine readers.[18] The tale continued to be read in digest forms that conveyed the gist of famous episodes, but not their full color. One might know all the symbols for incense that corresponded to each of the chapters, but not the fragrance of the original dialogue in which a character such as his main love, the young Murasaki, subtly rebuked the wanderings of the hero.

The *Genji* appeared in more places over the early modern period, but to somewhat less effect. Parodies and allusions in literature bespeak a broad familiarity with the text (or its commentaries) across the culture, with depth of reference arguably rarer.[19] Primers for women hit the high points while emphasizing a visual approach.[20] *Honchō jokan* (Mirror of women in our country), published 1661, is attributed to Asai Ryōi (c. 1612–1691), a male author of the vulgate *kana zōshi* form. A two-page woodblock illustration shows a typical scene of Murasaki Shikibu looking out over Lake Biwa from a room at Ishiyama-dera temple.[21] There she sees her inspiration (and according to some versions of the legend, composes the tale in one night). The same landscape is depicted in *Onna Genji kyōkun kagami* (Women's mirror of *Genji* lessons), a work of 1713 signed by one "Yama Asako," who is also thought to be a male writer, in spite of the feminine appellation.[22] "The mountains are shallow" is the name's literal meaning, a clue both to the falsity of the signature and to a lack of respect, perhaps, for the achievement (whether of the commentator, the female reader, or the tale itself is not clear). Pages devoted to each chapter combine a brief outline of its happenings with random useful knowledge, as, for example, the illustration of the glaive-wielding heroine of the Noh play "Tomoe" that occupies a square on the page with the tenth chapter, "*Sakaki*" (The Green Branch, in which Genji's stepmother puts herself out of his amorous reach by becoming a nun).

There was no question that the *Tale of Genji* was regarded as a canonical masterwork, and the attention given it by the nativist Motoori Norinaga (1730–1801) only reinforced this. Motoori is well known for christening Murasaki's aesthetic *mono no aware* (the capacity to feel things), and for championing the vernacular as the essence of Japan in contradistinction to Chinese values.[23] His several commentaries took the text into the nineteenth century with full acclaim. Given the aim of universal elementary schooling promulgated at the end of that century, the question of whether this book should be read by all became crucial. The encounter with the West seems to have paradoxically both enforced and shaken the view that the *Genji* was the national representative masterpiece. The more masculine *Tales of the Heike*, with their claim to epic status, took that place in many eyes, domestic and foreign.[24] Descriptions of the hyper-feminine *Genji monogatari* are rimmed with small excuses that seek to diminish its place in the canon. Consider these lines by Suematsu Kenchō (1855–1920), who undertook the first translation into English during the late nineteenth century:

> It was the evening of the fifteenth of August. Before her eyes the view extended for miles. In the silver lake below, the pale face of the full moon was reflected in the calm, mirror-like waters, displaying itself in indescribable beauty. Her mind became more and more serene as she gazed on the prospect before her, while her imagination became more and more lively as she grew calmer and calmer. The ideas and incidents of the story, which she was about to write, stole into her mind as if by divine influence.[25]

This is the archetypal scene of Murasaki at Ishiyama-dera, portraying her with little self-determination. The *Genji* was thus not unambiguously in the vanguard of Japan's efforts to craft a modern national image, and it took the Bloomsbury group's discovery of it in England a few decades later to facilitate the process of moving into the international canon.[26] By the 1920s interest in exploration of the self through literature led to strong favoring of Heian women's writing at home, sometimes with ample appreciation of its profundity, and sometimes in a way that viewed female expression as thoughtlessly natural.[27]

The war years were difficult for the *Genji*. Tanizaki Jun'ichirō's (1886–1965) modern translation was not a joy to the authorities, who were opposed to any breath of indulgence that might distract the populace from the sacrifices of empire.[28] It took the postwar peace to give such a text an opportunity for a comeback, and of course the context had changed. Readers welcomed it as their cultural inheritance from a more pacific time, but with reforms to the writing systems, new generations would lack the ability to read even Tanizaki's version comfortably. New translations were often incomplete, but displaced the original nonetheless. All fifty-four chapters might occupy several volumes of compendia of the classics, marketed by major publishers to fill shelves in libraries and in the homes of the college-educated, but it is unclear how much these were read. Now it was bits and pieces of the tale braided into books used to prepare for examinations to enter the right high school or college. The philosophical content of the text was of relatively little consequence for such cribs, most attention being given to antiquarian details and grammatical analysis that could lead the student to the "right" answers.[29] Manuals that go deeper for junior college and college students still aim to facilitate an educational task, in their case the composition of acceptable graduation theses. They adhere closely to the time-honored approaches of literary critics, focusing on author and character studies, and advising certain topics in background history.[30]

Over time the expectation that one would know something about each of the chapters—be able to recognize an album illustration of a principal scene, or to play a board game incorporating all the favorite characters, such as *sugoroku*, common in the Edo period[31]—gave way to a trend to dwell on Genji's youthful affairs as represented in the first third or so of the book.[32] Even the popular *manga* series on the tale seem to draw from shallow conceptions and specialize in not rocking the Genji-romance boat. Yamato Waki's *Asaki yumemishi* (*Tale of Genji manga,* 1980–1993) presents the spectacle of Lady Rokujō as a jealous threat, and highlights Aoi (Genji's first wife, and the target of Rokujō's rage) as a pathetic, longing, soon-to-be mother.[33] In the didactic vein, a rather clever parody, disguised as a magazine issue that investigates the runaway phenomenon of *Genji monogatari*, draws from multiple fields of popular culture. Titled *Weekly Shining Genji* (*Shūkan Hikaru Genji*), the imitation periodical displays hyper-headlines

(Extravagance Dazzles! Rokujō Love Mansion—a reference to the home that Genji built to assemble all his women on the grounds of the late Lady Rokujō's estate),[34] a glossy "Special Pinup" of Hikaru Genji, and more than two hundred pages of information for the reader, spiced up with wide-eyed comic drawings, banners and bubbles, and such "features" as the "Genji Diet." This last informs us that falling in love with the Shining Genji is a sure-fire way to lose unwanted kilos quickly.[35] A promotional slogan on the front cover promises "extreme weight loss secrets of all the characters." Inside, black-and-white drawings show a full-cheeked woman's face labeled "before relationship with Genji," and a much thinner one claiming "after two months on Genji." Bulleted text introduces Genji's thoughts on each of his lover's "after" look, with extra "skinny" on Kashiwagi, the man who slept with Genji's young wife and wasted away. A lively setting by which to convey the fact that women in the tale tend to pine for the hero, the "Genji Diet" draws attention to the message that romance is the core of the story. The page is rounded out by a box with a pie chart proving that, according to the ancient Ministry of Civil Administration, the number one cause of death in the *Genji* is spirit possession.

The *Tale of Genji* today tends to be prepackaged as the national classic (the martial *Tales of Heike* having suffered a slight deflation in the wake of the failed fifteen-year war), a novel in which women's darker side is displayed in the characters and the narrative, but which is disciplined for the larger culture through multiple-choice exams and predictable renditions of the major story arcs through television and film.[36] The one-thousandth anniversary (*sennenki*) celebrations tend to focus on the public display of artifacts associated with the tale and products derived from them, commercial items as diverse as the usual elaborately designed exhibition catalogues and a rather more unique series of six eyeglass-wiping cloths imprinted with scenes from an eighteenth-century album.[37] Illustrated guidebooks map out temples and sights connected to the text, along with nearby shops and restaurants.[38] A pocket edition directs the fan to sweet-shops that carry a special product commemorating each chapter.[39] A lecture on Genji-era dyeing methods or a hike in the woods to discover flora mentioned in popular chapters reinforce the cultural specificity of the tale and give participants the lesson that this is something rarefied and worthy of special comment.[40] It is unclear, nonetheless, whether the establishment of the "*Genji monogatari Sennenki shō*," a prize to be awarded in the genre of novels tapped out on cell phones, is a sign of cultural legitimacy for these products written mostly by young women, or another affirmation of the slight taint that lingers around the masterpiece that we also call the world's first novel. Fans of the novel-writing nun and selection committee member Setouchi Jakuchō (b. 1922) might find the question puzzling, since her own history includes both scandalous adultery and a full modern translation of *Genji monogatari*.[41] The prize seems to intimate at least a sense of irony.

DANGER REVISITED

The case of the *Genji* may reveal a larger truth about conduct and the manuals that would control it. For an area of conduct or content to deserve controlling, it must be full of possibilities. These always have the potential to reassert themselves in spite of the exhortations of guides. All the scolding in the world cannot assure that an impressionable reader will reject aspects of Genji's behavior that are morally repugnant by conventional standards. Nor can interpretations that deny or minimize Murasaki Shikibu's critique of her society be guaranteed to sway opinions. The structure of vigilance that shapes a guide assumes the danger in the raw material.

Little wonder, then, that society at large is not entirely comfortable with endorsing the powerful currents of meaningful, destabilizing content in this tale, and prefers a tidy etiquette. Why does Genji sleep with his stepmother and chase her phantom in every woman he meets, or even hears of? Why is his self-proclaimed true love, Murasaki, childless? Should women prefer suicide or Buddhist orders to life in society? With the text itself before us, it is hard not to ask these questions, and by doing so to deeply interrogate the role of female desire and male power, or of male desire and female power (more evident when the characters are referred to as "middle captain" or "woman" in the original than in the guidebook nicknames that package them in a sham consistency). The interpretation industry has, over time, surrounded us with distractions, all the while attaching cultural value to hollowed outlines of the conflicts in the text. One might even say that the etiquette of reading constructs the split between surface and depth, form and content, forcing readers to feel that there is a realm of the text that it is proper to be conversant with, and one that is better left hidden. Genji becomes the ideal man, the romantic hero whose gallantry is everywhere welcome.

Murasaki is cast as the perfect wife, forbearing and kind. Rokujō is what women must avoid being, a negative stereotype to embrace temporarily for the ultimate purpose of wholehearted rejection; the dead Aoi the means to understanding her rival's horrible nature. Our lives will be better if we heed Murasaki Shikibu's lessons on love, the seasons, and artistic expression, the books and magazines tell us, but we must mind that the depth of her resistance to the pieties of order not attract unschooled attention. *Genji* guides are consequently often guides to Genji the hero, to his affiliations, to what he does and how elegantly he does it, to the beauty and grace of those he romances, not to the women who refuse his advances, to the costs of policing male and female behavior, or to the very act of telling such a tale. Is this particular minding of Murasaki a gain, or a loss? Although everything about it may not merit "official approval," and every reader may not be a good candidate to explore the whole messy thing, the *Genji* remains a worthy challenge that takes us beyond what we know. The more fitting guide is surely one that raises as many questions as it answers.

NOTES

1. Nihon Bunka Tsū Kenkyūkai, ed., *Nihon bunka tsū shiriizu: Genji monogatari tsū to yobaretai!* (So you want to be a *Genji* expert!) (Tokyo: Micro Magazine, 2008).

2. I would like to acknowledge the critiques of students at the University of North Carolina at Chapel Hill and the University of Pennsylvania, especially the Penn graduate students Beth Tucker, Rachel Epstein, and Frank Clements, who pushed me on this and other aspects of the argument, to the relief of our fabulous editors.

3. Super Dollfie dolls can be constructed to taste by assembling individually sold parts, but the Hikaru Genji model is a package, dressed in a chic black Heian-style court costume and long wig. http://www.volks.co.jp/jp/event/0810tenshikourin/genji.html (accessed October 15, 2008).

4. Murasaki Shikibu's journal, *Murasaki Shikibu nikki*, provides the first datable reference to her tale, which we therefore know was in existence in some form by 1008. The Web site of the Committee for the One Thousandth Anniversary (*Genji monogatari sennenki iinkai*) had a calendar of events all over the country, with the most lavish centered around the November 1, 2008, proclamation of Classic Literature Day (*koten no hi*). http://www.2008genji.jp (accessed October 15, 2008). The Web page for the Bank of Japan branch tour promised hands-on experience with anti-counterfeit measures and information about the two-thousand-yen bill, which has a portrait of Murasaki. http://www3.boj.or.jp/kyoto/kengaku/2008/2008kengaku.htm (accessed June 15, 2008). The pace of events was much slower as we entered 2009, but exhibitions are still

opening, and reading groups will continue to labor when their aim is to work through all the chapters.

5. Richard Bowring, trans., *Murasaki Shikibu: Her Diary and Poetic Memoirs* (Princeton, N.J.: Princeton University Press, 1982), section 38, 95. Ueda Kikan, Kishigami Shinji, and Akiyama Ken, eds., *Makura no sōshi, Murasaki Shikibu nikki* (*The Pillow Book* and journal of Murasaki Shikibu), Nihon koten bungaku taikei (Collection of Japanese classical literature), vol. 19 (Tokyo: Iwanami Shoten, 1958), 473.

6. Bowring, *Murasaki Shikibu*, section 71, 137. Bowring revises his translation to "Lady Chronicle" in *The Diary of Lady Murasaki* (London: Penguin Books, 1996), 57. Ueda, Kishigami, and Akiyama, eds., *Makura no sōshi*, 500.

7. See Chapter 25, "*Hotaru*" (Fireflies), 461. Citations here will be to the superior translation by Royall Tyler, *The Tale of Genji*, 2 vols. (New York: Viking, 2001). Kitamura Kigin, *Genji monogatari kogetsushō* (*Tale of Genji* moon on the lake commentary), annotated by Arikawa Takehiko, Kōdansha gakujutsu bunko (Kōdansha academic library) (Tokyo: Kōdansha, 1982), 2:426–31.

8. Abe Hirotada's (1612–1678) *Honchō retsujoden* (Biography of women in our country), vol. 3, goes so far as to designate Murasaki Shikibu a *saijin* (talented person). Edo jidai josei bunko (Edo period women's library), vol. 85 (Tokyo: Ōzorasha, 1998), n.p.

9. See Edward Seidensticker's translation *As I Crossed a Bridge of Dreams: Recollections of a Woman in Eleventh-Century Japan* (London: Penguin Books, 1975), section 3, 46–47; section 11, 64.

10. Michele Marra, "*Mumyōzōshi*: Introduction and translation," *Monumenta Nipponica* 39, no. 2 (Summer 1984): 115–145; "*Mumyōzōshi*, Part 2," *Monumenta Nipponica* 39, no. 3 (Autumn 1984): 281–305; "*Mumyōzōshi*, Part 3," *Monumenta Nipponica* 39, no. 4 (Winter 1984): 409–434. Fujiwara no Shunzei no musume, *Mumyōzōshi* (The nameless tale), Kitagawa Tadahiko, ann., in *Kodai chūsei geijutsuron* (Theories of the arts from ancient and medieval periods), annotated by Hayashiya Tatsusaburō, Nihon shisō taikei (Collection of Japanese thought), vol. 23 (Tokyo: Iwanami Shoten, 1973), 347–407.

11. ". . . a famous judgment in the *Roppyakuban uta awase* (*Poetry Contest in Six Hundred Rounds*, 1192)," cited by Haruo Shirane in *The Bridge of Dreams: A Poetics of 'The Tale of Genji'* (Stanford, Calif.: Stanford University Press, 1987), xvii.

12. There is debate about whether liaisons in the tale actually break the incest taboo, but they certainly threaten to do so. See Norma Field, *The Splendor of Longing in The Tale of Genji* (Princeton, N.J.: Princeton University Press, 1987), 26; and Doris G. Bargen, "The problem of incest in *The Tale of Genji*," in *Approaches to Teaching Murasaki Shikibu's The Tale of Genji*, ed. Edward Kamens (New York: Modern Language Association of America, 1993), 115–123.

13. Inaga Keiji, "*Genji hyōbyaku* (Invocations for *Genji*)," in *Nihon koten bungaku daijiten* (Full dictionary of Japan's classical literature) (Tokyo: Iwanami Shoten, 1984), 2:405.

14. Janet Goff, *Noh Drama and The Tale of Genji: The Art of Allusion in Fifteen Classical Plays* (Princeton, N.J.: Princeton University Press, 1991), 200.

15. Steven D. Carter, *Regent Redux: A Life of the Statesman–Scholar Ichijō Kaneyoshi* (Ann Arbor: Center for Japanese Studies, University of Michigan, 1996), 163.

16. Hayashi Dōshun, *Tsurezuregusa nozuchi* (*Tsurezu regusa* field hammer), ed. Muromatsu Iwao, Kokubun chūshaku zensho (Complete collection of commentaries on native texts) (Tokyo: Kokugakuin Daigaku Shuppan, 1909), 1.

17. G. G. Rowley, *Yosano Akiko and The Tale of Genji* (Ann Arbor: Center for Japanese Studies, University of Michigan, 2000), 30–32. P. F. Kornicki, "Unsuitable books for women? *Genji monogatari* and *Ise monogatari* in late seventeenth-century Japan," *Monumenta Nipponica* 60, no. 2 (Summer 2005): 155–162. Kornicki indicates that female literacy was much higher than has been assumed, but cautions that we do not have a clear picture yet. Haruo Shirane discusses negative reactions to the tale's eroticism by and for both genders in "*The Tale of Genji* and the dynamics of cultural production: Canonization and popularization," in *Envisioning The Tale of Genji: Media, Gender, and Cultural Production*, ed. Haruo Shirane (New York: Columbia University Press, 2008), 24–31, 38–40. Ii Haruki sees a turn to didactic and political uses for the tale around the time of Ichijō Kanera. He argues that it was seen in the Edo era as "a guide for proper living" and "a text of high moral standards for both men and women," but this may be the flip side of taking the *Genji* as a dangerous text. In either case it cannot be read without instruction. "Didactic readings of *The Tale of Genji*: Politics and women's education," in *Envisioning The Tale of Genji,* ed. Shirane, 167.

18. Kornicki, "Unsuitable books," 158.

19. Two-thirds of the space in Nakano Kōichi's fifty-page listing of Edo period *Genji*-related publications fall into the categories of digest, commentary, encyclopedia, etc.; the rest are secondary literary products, including illustrated books and theatrical appropriations. *Genji monogatari no kyōju shiryō—Chōsa to hakkutsu* (Materials on the reception of *Tale of Genji*—Survey and discovery) (Tokyo: Musashino Shoin, 1997), 365–415.

20. Joshua Mostow discusses the role of illustrations in establishing the "minimum required knowledge" for women in "*Genji monogatari* to jokunsho" (*Tale of Genji* and instruction books for women), trans. Kazuko Kameda, in *Genji monogatari to Edo bunka—kashika sareru gazoku* (*Tale of Genji* and Edo culture—*Ga* and *Zoku* visualized), ed. Kojima Naoko, Komine Kazuaki, and Watanabe Kenji (Tokyo: Sōwasha, 2008), 337–346.

21. Asai Ryōi, *Honchō jokan* (Mirror of women in our country), Edo jidai josei bunko, vols. 11–12 (Tokyo: Ōzorasha, 1994), n.p. Murasaki Shikibu is treated in vol. 12, maki 9.

22. Yama Asako, *Onna Genji kyōkun kagami* (Women's mirror of *Genji* lessons), Edo jidai josei bunko, vol. 1 (Tokyo: Ōzorasha, 1994), n.p. The author may be Yamamoto Joshu, according to the commentary by Tateishi Kazuhiro, 3.

23. Patrick W. Caddeau, *Appraising Genji: Literary Criticism and Cultural Anxiety in the Age of the Last Samurai* (Albany: State University of New York Press, 2006), 3. Consult Caddeau for Hagiwara Hiromichi's (1815–1863) important challenges to the Norinaga orthodoxy.

24. See Tomi Suzuki's account of the valorization of the *Genji* and other feminine texts as precursors of the realistic novel and keepers of native heritage within the context of promoting a phonocentric view of nationality through language. She also argues that modern notions of progress played into "Gender and genre: Modern literary histories and women's diary literature," in *Inventing the Classics: Modernity, National Identity, and Japanese Literature*, ed. Haruo Shirane and Tomi Suzuki (Stanford, Calif.: Stanford University Press, 2000), 71–95. Also see the same author's "*Tale of Genji*, national literature, language, and Modernism," in *Envisioning The Tale of Genji*, ed. Shirane, 243–287. Basil Hall Chamberlain and F. Victor Dickins (1838–1915) were harsh with Murasaki in comparison to martial and recluse literature. The latter's title *Primitive and Mediaeval Japanese Texts* (Oxford: Clarendon, 1906) suggests his relative evaluation of the two works. W. G. Aston, whose *History of Japanese Literature* set a standard, is an exception. He credits her with inventing the novel in Japan (94), defends her styles, rejects the idea that it is a Buddhist or Confucian tract (97), deplores the morals of the tale, but celebrates the decency of it (97–98) (London: William Heinemann, 1908).

25. Suyematz Kenchio [*sic*], "Introduction by the translator," in *Oriental Literature: The Literature of Japan* (1900) rev. ed. (Freeport, N.Y.: Books for Libraries Press, 1971), 5. See John Walter de Gruchy's discussion of Suematsu's 1882 and 1898 English versions in *Orienting Arthur Waley: Japonism, Orientalism, and the Creation of Japanese Literature in English* (Honolulu: University of Hawai'i Press, 2003), 24, 121–123.

26. Arthur Waley's renowned translation appeared in six parts between 1925 and 1933, and as a "complete" novel (lacking a chapter and much finessed) in 1933. See De Gruchy, *Orienting Arthur Waley*, 123–125.

27. See Suzuki, "Gender and genre," 83–89. See Tomiko Yoda for a thorough understanding of the way femininity, as located in these texts, was employed to develop the modern masculine national subject. *Gender and National Literature: Heian Texts in the Constructions of Japanese Modernity* (Durham, N.C.: Duke University Press, 2004).

28. As G. G. Rowley explains, Yosano Akiko's (1878–1942) unexpurgated translation (her second foray) appeared in 1938–1939, while Tanizaki's effort, for reasons that probably included the military's desire to police his publisher, Chūō Kōronsha, suffered cuts of many key sexual elements. *Yosano Akiko and The Tale of Genji*, 154.

29. An example of a high-quality grammar guide is Mitani Eiichi's *Genji monogatari yōkai* (Essential explanations of *Tale of Genji*). The volume on "*Kiritsubo*" is volume 7 in *Bunpō kaimei sōsho* (Grammar explication series) (Tokyo: Yūseidō, 1954). Modern vernacular translations in the postwar period include Tanizaki's uncensored efforts of 1951–1954 and 1965, and Enchi Fumiko's (1905–1986) 1967–1973 project, to which she sacrificed much of her eyesight, and the translation of Setouchi Jakuchō (b. 1922), ten volumes that can be credited with starting the current *Genji* boom. The full range of studies of the text reflected multiple degrees of popular and scholarly interest.

30. These kinds of guides are still available, for instance, Akiyama Ken, ed., *Shin Genji monogatari hikkei* (New *Tale of Genji* handbook) (Tokyo: Gakutōsha,

1997). Each chapter is given a brief "new reading" (*atarashii yomi*), but the tradition of *Genji* studies is more in evidence than a full postmodern approach.

31. More than fifteen varieties of *sugoroku* (Asian backgammon) are extant, but many are based on Ryūtei Tanehiko's parodic *Nise Murasaki Inaka Genji* (Sham Murasaki, rustic *Genji*). Nakano Kōichi, *Genji monogatari no kyōju shiryō* (Materials on the reception of *Tale of Genji*—Survey and discovery), 487.

32. A trend reflected in the English abridgments of the tale. Suematsu offered the first seventeen chapters; Edward G. Seidensticker's Vintage Classics edition (1990) selects from twelve of the first seventeen; Helen Craig McCullough translates only part of ten chapters, but includes numbers 35 and 40 in *Genji & Heike: Selections from The Tale of Genji and The Tale of the Heike* (Stanford, Calif.: Stanford University Press, 1994); even Royall Tyler sticks to portions of the first seventeen in his 2006 abridged edition for Penguin Books (although the excisions are noted).

33. Especially obvious in the portions included in the Kodansha Bilingual Comics edition, Waki Yamato, *The Tale of Genji, Flowers: Part I*, translated by Stuart Atkin and Yoko Toyozaki (Tokyo: Kōdansha intānashonaru, 2001). Yuika Kitamura examines this and other manga versions that focus on sexuality in "Sexuality, gender, and *The Tale of Genji* in modern Japanese translations and *manga*," in *Envisioning The Tale of Genji*, ed. Shirane, 329–357. See Akiko Hirota's "The *Tale of Genji*: From Heian classic to Heisei comic" for a defense of the careful way in which comic artists study the original and achieve meaningful interpretations, *Journal of Popular Culture* (1997 Fall), 31:2, 38–49.

34. "*Gōka kenran! Ai no Rokujōtei*," *Shūkan Hikaru Genji* (Weekly shining *Genji*), ed. Shūkan Hikaru Genji henshūbu (Tokyo: Naapuru, 1998), cover.

35. "*Miru miru gekiyase*" (Extreme weight loss while you watch). Ibid., 222.

36. The notorious film "*Sennen no koi: Hikaru Genji monogatari*" (Genji: A Thousand-Year Love, 2001), directed by Horikawa Tonkō, focuses on Genji's romantic troubles, presented as Murasaki Shikibu's lessons for her charge, the young Shōshi.

37. Offered by Tooray for a rather pricey two thousand yen each (which is nonetheless the price for plain ones as well).

38. A lavish edition, complete with *Genji monogatari sennenki* logo on the cover, is *Genji monogatari o aruku tabi* (A walking tour of *The Tale of Genji*) (El Shuppan, 2008), credited to Genji Monogatari Sennenki Kinen Gaidobukku Seisaku Iinkai (Committee for preparing the guidebook for the one thousandth anniversary of *The Tale of Genji*).

39. Bungei Shunjū, ed., *Genji monogatari no Kyōto annai* (A *Tale of Genji* guide to Kyoto) (Tokyo: Bungei Shunjū, 2008). Every fourth page gives an appropriate treat, some created especially for the celebration, others with long pedigrees (also given).

40. Some events occurred outside Japan, such as "*The Tale of Genji* millennium lecture: Color, design, and ritual in the Heian Court (794–1185) of Japan." The Japan–America Society of Georgia scheduled this lecture on Saturday April 5, 2008, during the Association for Asian Studies annual conference, held

in Atlanta, but attendance by scholars was low. Yoshioka Sachio, a fifth-generation Kyoto dyer, spoke in Japanese about his research and experimentation in reproducing ancient dyes. Nature hikes were featured prominently on the calendar of events mounted by the Sennenki committee.

41. The *Genji* prize category was added to the third year of the "*Kētai shōsetsu taishō*" grand prize competition for this new genre. RBBNavi, May 12, 2008, http://www.rbbtoday.com/news/20080512/51010.html (accessed October 15, 2008). See the competition Web site in "Genji mode" to learn how the new and old go together ("The modern Murasaki Shikibu is you"), http://nkst.jp/pc/index2.html (accessed January 9, 2009). The winner, *LOVE BOX~Hikari o sagashite* (Love Box~Looking for the light), was the work of Yaguchi Aoi, a high school student, http://nkst.jp/award08.php (accessed January 9, 2009). At the prize ceremony, Setouchi confessed that she had written a cell phone novel called *Ashita no niji* (Tomorrow's rainbow) under the name "Purple" (Pāpuru). http://sankei.jp.msn.com/culture/books/080924/bks0809241811003-n1.htm (accessed January 9, 2009).

CHAPTER 2

Box-Lunch Etiquette

Conduct Guides and Kabuki Onnagata[1]

MAKI ISAKA

Masuyama is an ardent admirer of the art of Sanogawa Mangiku. . . . Mangiku has prevented Masuyama from becoming disappointed with him even backstage where things tend to turn topsy-turvy. He always follows "The Words of Ayame" so gracefully. . . . When he has no choice but to take lunch in the presence of visitors in the green room, for example, he will elegantly excuse himself and take his lunch quickly but quietly. Just seeing him from behind, nobody could ever tell that he was actually eating.

—"*Onnagata*," Mishima Yukio (1925–1970)

This epigraph is from Mishima Yukio's short story "*Onnagata*," which portrays one Sanogawa Mangiku, a fictitious contemporary kabuki actor allegedly modeled after an *onnagata* renowned in Mishima's time.[2] *Onnagata* are actors, usually male, specializing in women's roles in the all-male kabuki theater.[3] As the premier *onnagata* of his day, Mangiku is depicted as an actor of talent, beauty, and discipline, whose performances regularly win critical acclaim. And yet, rather than concentrating on the actor's work onstage alone, the text emphasizes Mangiku's way of eating lunch in his dressing room *in order to* illustrate that he is indeed a virtuoso actor. Although this twentieth-century story is mostly about Mangiku's life offstage, that cannot explain why the text associates Mangiku's daily behavior directly with his excellence in theatrical performance. Why is conduct *offstage* made responsible for artistry *onstage*, such as singing (*ka*), dancing (*bu*), and acting (*ki*)? Are well-behaved pianists always maestros? Are all divas well mannered? Or, is this just a whim of the writer?

This offstage–onstage correlation might not have "natural" reasoning of any sort, but seen in the context of the history of kabuki, noting the relationship happens to be perceptive of Mishima. "The Words of Ayame" (*Ayamegusa*), mentioned in the epigraph, is in fact a historical document published in the Edo era (1600–1867),[4] and it instructs *onnagata* to eat a box lunch in a specific way, not to eat a nighttime snack, and so on.[5] Ultimately, the text declares that *onnagata* should act like women all the time, totally erasing the offstage–onstage boundary. The justification for this given in "The Words of Ayame" is that actors cannot switch their identities so quickly. This sounds simple, but there is much more than that to Ayame's advice.

The importance of Ayame's advice here is multifold. To begin with, the performance theory articulated in "The Words of Ayame" in and of itself presupposes the holistic nature of what has sometimes been differentiated in modern times: "natural reality in daily life" versus "performed theatricality onstage," "one's identity" versus "physical appearance," and "mind" versus "body." The Edo-era fusion of offstage–onstage that "The Words of Ayame" demonstrates, however, encourages us to revisit the modern demarcation between "interiority" and "exteriority" of human beings. Another reason the advice is important derives from the societal milieu in which such holistic perception was located. The above-mentioned understanding of people and their lives, which presupposes those kinds of unison (mind and body, for example), was not confined to theater but was rather a basic understanding, common sense taken for granted in Edo-era Japan. For instance, the imperative to keep performing one's designated role "around the clock" applied to people in society at large, not only to theater practitioners.

The two above observations together open the enticing potential for reading treatises about kabuki acting designed for *onnagata* as manuals of conduct for a wide-ranging readership. As we will see, kabuki-related publications boasted a substantial readership well beyond actual theatergoers, not to mention kabuki actors, as they not only provided information for the playgoers but also functioned as a virtual "theatergoing" experience for the broader audience of kabuki lovers who could not afford to go to playhouses. To put it another way, treatises about acting were also pastime reading for those who enjoyed the theater, and it would tell them that *onnagata* should adhere to specific rules of decorum for women, which they say is natural to women's sentiment, and therefore, for example, take lunch quietly. Here we can observe a process by which particular actions (bodily conduct) are not only conjoined with appropriate femininity but are also received as being so conjoined by wide audiences, hence creating the aforementioned potential for *onnagata* treatises to be used as conduct manuals. It is with this in mind that this chapter studies a few *onnagata* treatises, such as "The Words of Ayame."

ACTING AROUND THE CLOCK: ORDINARY LIFE "VERSUS" EXTRAORDINARY PERFORMANCE?

"The Words of Ayame" is a treatise of *onnagata* artistry, its words and ideas attributed to a renowned *onnagata*, Yoshizawa Ayame I (1673–1729). Extant theater reviews of his day demonstrate that Ayame won critical acclaim for his spectacular performances. As we will see shortly, what was most praised was his ability to pass as a woman. Commendation accorded this skill shows us the flip side of the same coin—the understanding that it is actually everyday life that constitutes stage performance. Simplifying to the extreme, there is no essential difference between so-called real life and stage performance. Even such a seemingly trivial action as eating lunch in private becomes subject to scrutiny, for it determines artistry onstage. "The Words of Ayame" makes this point clear in passages such as these:

> It is hardly possible for an *onnagata* to be considered proficient unless he spends his everyday life as a woman.[6]

> An *onnagata* remains an *onnagata* even inside his dressing room. He should take this to heart. When he takes a box lunch, for example, he should do so out of sight of the people in the room.[7]

In other words, *onnagata*'s performance of women should not be limited to acting onstage.

Such an emphasis on offstage acts is not unique to "The Words of Ayame" but is found in many tracts aimed at *onnagata*. "The Secret Transmissions of an *Onnagata*" (*Onnagata hiden*),[8] a treatise attributed to another famous *onnagata*, Segawa Kikunojō I (1693–1749), demonstrates an extreme case of this union of offstage and onstage behavior. According to the compiler of this text, Kikunojō was in full dress on his deathbed, in accordance with the *onnagata* garb code.[9] Likewise, *The Pioneering Analects from Past and Present Actors* (*Kokon yakusha rongo sakigake*, 1772), which includes "The Secret Transmissions of an *Onnagata*," contains another intriguing example to the same effect: "The duty of *onnagata* is first and foremost to imitate women. If an *onnagata* goes to a bad neighborhood after dark, he should take sufficient care to wear a new loincloth. [This is far more important] than carrying a sword. He would look beautiful even when he was stripped."[10] Theories on *onnagata* artistry in these texts are quite similar in their attention to everyday life as the base of *onnagata* artistry, whether it is nocturnal walking, eating, or even dying. These texts do not recognize a decisive boundary between onstage performance and daily conduct offstage but situate the foundation of acting in everyday life.

This leads to an important criterion for the achievement of superb acting, that is, verisimilitude. Many kabuki-related publications in the Edo period present plausibility as one of the most important criteria for acting. In the case of *onnagata*, plausibility involves whether or not he can pass as a woman. To understand this point more fully, let us look at some theater reviews from Ayame's time. A cluster of periodicals called "actor-critique booklets" (*yakusha hyōbanki*) began to be published regularly from the mid-seventeenth century to provide theater lovers (both playgoers and those kabuki lovers who could not go to playhouses) with news concerning kabuki and its actors. A certain actor-critique booklet in 1704 has this to say about Ayame: "A genuine woman from top to bottom, no matter what he has under his loincloth. Regardless of what role he is made to play, whether a high-ranking lady-in-waiting, a warrior's wife, or a maidservant, Ayame completely reproduces the woman as is, without any element of fabrication."[11] In short, Ayame is said to have genuinely looked like a woman, and *The Pioneering Analects from Past and Present Actors*, a theater book, presented Ayame as "peerless in all the three cities" (*sangoku musô*) and "incomparable through all ages" (*kokon murui*).[12]

Kikunojō is also praised in an uncannily similar way. For example, he appears in an actor-critique booklet published in 1746 as "a person who doesn't need the character [of *gata* in the compound noun] *onnagata*."[13] *Onnagata* minus *gata* leaves *onna*: woman. Here, the compound word *onnagata*, derived from *onna*, returns to its "origin" *onna*; the performer of womanliness (*onnagata*) is restored to her "rightful" position, that is to say, "woman as is" (*onna*).[14] Likewise, the aforementioned theater book, *The Pioneering Analects from Past and Present Actors*, describes Kikunojō and his younger brother Kikujirō as follows:

> [Kikunojō] lacked nothing as far as women's technique was concerned.... Most *onnagata* become sexually unattractive as they age, but Kikunojō was extremely good at love scenes in *furisode* [a long-sleeved *kimono* exclusively

> for youth] until he was over sixty years of age [*sic*]. He was not only beautiful but also skillful. He was none other than one of the founders of the *waka-onnagata* [young *onnagata*] tradition.
>
> And his younger brother Segawa Kikujirō was also a master. . . . Kikujirō's acting was in accordance with "The Words of Ayame." It was maestro Ayame who left the thirty-item [*sic*] saying. Also, *for his entire life*, Kikujirō did not act like a man. The Segawa brothers truly mastered the woman's Way, from *everyday life* to mindset, and to various [artistic] techniques suitable for women.[15]

Notice here that Kikujirō's reputation is justified not only by his performance onstage but also by his conduct offstage, as obvious from such phrases as "for his entire life" and "everyday life" above.

Of equal significance is that Ayame and Kikunojō are merely representative of *onnagata* in those days and are by no means exceptional. Kikujirō attests to this in the above excerpt, as does another *onnagata*, called Kokan Tarōji (?–1713), who is associated with a fascinating anecdote himself. While dressed as a thirty-something matron, Tarōji lingered in front of the stage during an interlude in the performance. Nearby audience members moved to make room for him, thinking that he must be a female audience member searching for an open seat. "Sequel to 'The Dust in the Ears'" (*Zoku Nijinshū*), the text that includes this anecdote, presents it as irrefutable proof that "Tarōji was indeed such a maestro."[16]

We need to put this praise for the *onnagata*'s convincing offstage performance of femininity in historical perspective, however. Reputations for such performances are specific to premodern kabuki, and we should not generally apply our knowledge of contemporary *onnagata* to those of the past, and vice versa. When the new government in the Meiji era (1868–1912) adopted Westernization and modernization as state policy, it opened the way for rapid and far-reaching transformations in Japanese society, affecting everything from the status of actors to education systems, and to the epistemological grids by which people made sense of things, including how to understand gender. While it is beyond the scope of this chapter to discuss all the changes the Meiji period brought to theater, suffice it to say that kabuki was not free of transformations.[17] It is thus important to keep in mind that the image of *onnagata* in common currency today (especially the notion that "*onnagata*'s artistic femininity and women's femininity are mutually exclusive") does not apply to the kabuki theater in the Edo period.

While this chapter mainly uses texts on the artistry of *onnagata*, the points discussed here are not necessarily unique to *onnagata*. Consider the following remark an obscure *onnagata* made to the celebrated male-role actor Sakata Tōjūrō I (ca. 1647–1709): "Since I am an *onnagata*, I work hard to imitate women. Because you are a male-role actor, you should work hard to imitate men."[18] This remark takes as truth the idea that acting *is* imitating, regardless of the gender of the character being played. It is in this broader landscape that we should understand the notion that the ability to plausibly pass as a "real woman" constitutes a significant criterion for any *onnagata* performance. And it is in this very landscape that such a seemingly unrelated act as eating one's lunch off-stage in a manner allegedly conceived as womanly is explicitly connected with artistry onstage. In this sense, the offstage–onstage fusion is not so much specific to *onnagata* artistry as applicable to all kabuki dramaturgy. What is more, the significance of such fusion does not stop here. The offstage–onstage correlation is contiguous to another "pair": body and mind. If you cannot help but betray your ordinary life in extraordinary situations, such as in theatrical performance, then, your face cannot help but reveal what you are feeling, which is to say, can we separate the face from feeling so clearly?

KEEPING UP APPEARANCES: EXTERIORITY "VERSUS" INTERIORITY?

"The Words of Ayame" and "The Secret Transmissions of an *Onnagata*" make seemingly endless reference to humans'—in this case, female humans'—behavior, actions, and the like. A relatively short guide, "The Secret Transmissions of an *Onnagata*" consists of ten terse technical instructions. Their specificity, however, shows us that women look, dress, and/or behave in accordance with their specific emotional state or social class. The text includes instructions on the use of props and makeup for a womanly appearance (secs. 1, 2, 6, and 7); the relationship between women's external appearances and their internal states and identity, such as their emotions and their social standing (secs. 3, 4, and 5); and how to use cosmetics to keep an *onnagata*'s face wrinkle-free (sec. 8).[19]

In comparison, "The Words of Ayame" contains much more detail. Nevertheless, the same specificity obtains, that is, the approximation of states and appearances. Ayame requires that *onnagata* keep their appearance mischievous yet their minds chaste (sec. 3), live as women in everyday life (sec. 7), hesitate to perform strong women's roles (sec. 8), avoid purposely trying to make the audience laugh (sec. 9), give the highest priority to chastity (sec. 13), remain *onnagata* even inside the dressing room (sec. 22), hide their wives and children (sec. 23), try not to deviate from women's sentiment (sec. 24), and remain young (sec. 29).[20]

Importantly, the texts greatly emphasize the body, such as its posture and movements. Yet training the body is not an end in itself, because the body carries significance due in large part to its role or its capability to represent the character's state of mind. For example, "The Secret Transmissions of an *Onnagata*" reads:

> When a woman hugs a man while faking love, she will hug him over both his arms, and face sideways. If it is with true affection, she will cling to him, with her arm deeply under his left arm; [by following this principle], then, you will appear realistic.[21]
>
> When they are upset, women cry before [speaking].[22]

When a character in kabuki is in a specific emotional state, be it love or anger, the actor playing the character should copy the external appearance, such as moving his hands in a particular way or becoming speechless. (As for the "speechless" example, see the next section for its toxic implications.) "The Words of Ayame" underlines the mental aspect of a womanly appearance much more than does "The Secret Transmissions of an *Onnagata*," but such is also coupled with practical instruction in body movements (secs. 2, 6, 12, and 24).[23] Here it is presupposed that one's outer appearance speaks of his or her thoughts, attitudes, and emotions.[24]

"The Words of Ayame" and "The Secret Transmissions of an *Onnagata*" make connections on many levels between physical appearances and the "essence" of being. On one level, this is a matter of people's identities. Eiko Ikegami states, "External appearance, as signified by a person's choice of costume, hairstyle, cosmetics, and other decorative accessories, can function as a critical means of expressing as well as classifying a person's categorical identity; in other words, it becomes a powerful human 'identity kit.' "[25] Here I add that the body itself, and how one uses it, is already his or her "identity kit." Even the act of walking illustrates this. In terms of human locomotion, the theater director and critic Takechi Tetsuji (1912–1988) proposes that, from the mid-Edo era onward, there were at least two types of limb combinations. While those engaged in physical labor such as farming and mining employed a walking style in which the right leg and the right hand moved forward at the same time, city dwellers in urbanized areas walked in a style in which the right leg and the left hand simultaneously moved forward.[26] "Don't judge a person by his or her looks," we might be told, but in Edo-era Japan you would certainly be judged by your clothing, coiffure, ornaments, gait, or what have you. This is no wonder, as the master discourse in the society of those days dictated that how you appear *is* who you are.

Appearance and existence are thus interchangeable in this context. Moreover, an *onnagata*'s training of the body as "that which equals what exists inside" goes beyond creating the socially approved identity kit. In other words, the *onnagata* is not concerned merely with surface appearance. Here it is helpful to remember the Buddhist notion of "mind and body as one entity" (*shinshin ichinyo*). This concept of a unified body–mind is of great moment, especially in the context of *shugyō* (cultivation). *Shugyō* refers to the physical training necessary to master artistic techniques perfectly so that the practitioner's body completely internalizes the techniques as second nature. This practice of *shugyō* is prevalent among what is generally subsumed under the name of Japanese traditional culture, for example, Japanese dance, swordsmanship, and tea ceremony, to name just a few. Although *shugyō* has been adopted as a training method in these broad realms well beyond religious communities, Yuasa Yasuo reminds us of the importance of its Buddhist origin, for *shugyō* means "a pragmatic enterprise aiming at spiritual training and improvement of character *through training of one's body*."[27] Not only is the body an identity kit, but it, in effect, *is* the mind.

Shugyō consists of two phases: repeated somatic training (such as that of posture and movements) and internalization of the technique in question as second nature. Thomas P. Kasulis deftly summarizes Yuasa's point about *shugyō* as follows: "Gradually . . . the posture becomes natural or second nature. It is *second* nature because the mind has entered into the dark consciousness and given it a form; it is an acquired naturalness."[28] Accordingly, *shugyō* seeks the way to make something quasi-immediate out of what is mediated.

It is intriguing to compare this understanding ("quasi-immediacy can be created out of what is mediated") with another understanding held by critical theory today. In contemporary critical theory, immediacy is considered highly dubious. For example, no matter how immediate it might sound, a shout of "ouch!" is impossible without an understanding of the meaning of this "word," and no human being projects this seemingly immediate shout without having mastered the language in advance. On the one hand, critical theory asserts that "everything is constructed, hence no such thing as 'the natural' no matter how natural it might seem." On the other hand, *shugyō* holds that "anything can be constructed as second nature if given serious devotion." These are simply the two sides of the same coin: the natural or the immediate. In this sense, contemporary critical theorists and *shugyō* practitioners approach the aporia of immediacy from seemingly "opposite" directions. If, for example, psychoanalysis is to discover, by scrutinizing language, that pure and perfect immediacy is formidably difficult, then *shugyō* is to create the shortcut to such illusionary immediacy by repeated training. Just as many people in English-speaking communities would automatically shout "ouch!" when feeling pain, *onnagata* as *shugyō* practitioners would naturally move their extremities appropriately in accordance with each situation. One might say that while contemporary critical theory reveals that immediacy is theoretically impossible, the notion of *shugyō* proposes its practical substitute, because "quasi-immediacy" might not be "immediacy" in theory, but in practice it functions the same as the illusionary immediacy would. Ultimately, the logic of *shugyō*, according to Yuasa, presupposes that "*the way the body exists controls the way the mind exists*."[29] In this paradigm, the *onnagata*'s faithful imitation of an object (women) and the attainment of what they think is the perfect essence (what might later be called ideal femininity) are by no means mutually exclusive. They are, in fact, one.

To sum up, we cannot take it for granted that an internal identity can be differentiated from external appearances, as people sometimes assume. This might have become widespread popular common sense in modern times, but it is never a natural fact that applies to any society ahistorically. People in Edo-era Japan, including kabuki actors, did not hold this idea; as we have seen, they had another logic instead, one that internalizes the concept of *shugyō*. It presupposes that what appears (externally) creates what exists (internally) and that these should be identical to each other in the ideal state.[30] It is for this reason that such texts as "The Words of Ayame" and "The Secret Transmissions of an *Onnagata*" diligently regulate how *onnagata* physically express womanly sentiment. The former (expressions) creates the latter (mentality), and not the other way around.

Since this idea is not confined to the realm of theater, it is no wonder that it also appears in other types of Edo texts, especially those that purport to tell women how to behave. For example, "The Words of Ayame" shows a great similarity to *Greater Learning for Women* (*Onna daigaku*), a popular book of "precept literature for women" published first in the early eighteenth century, in its approach to ideal femininity. The two texts detail attire, posture, daily conduct, and attitude so that the preachee, the one who is to be preached and thus regulated, can attain femininity as second nature.[31] It is of great significance not only for professional performers of femininity but also for lay women, because how you look is none other than who you are. And who were the putative preachees? According to the texts themselves, *Greater Learning for Women* and "The Words of Ayame" provide instruction for women and *onnagata*, respectively. But can we divide them so clearly?

MÖBIUS STRIP OF CITATIONS: WOMEN "VERSUS" *ONNAGATA?*

In the last two sections, we have seen that the *onnagata* treatises assume no clear boundaries between "mind" and "body," "one's identity" and "physical appearance," and "natural reality in daily life" and "performed theatricality onstage" and that these fusions are in line with the master discourse. I also mentioned that kabuki-related publications boasted an extensive readership that included not only kabuki insiders and actual playgoers but also many other kabuki lovers. This statement itself—about the readership—requires evidence; furthermore, we would like to explore specifically how these ideas reached women in Edo-era Japan, and what they meant to them. Did they take "lessons" from actors, whose social status was made so low in those days?

The first question about the readership is related not only to the theater industry but also to the publication industry and its surrounding culture, such as the well-established business of lending libraries in the Edo period. The phenomenon of kabuki popularity in the Edo era deeply integrated theater and publication. Popular actors' voices, accents, postures, gestures, movements, attire, and accessories were all described in detail in kabuki-related publications such as playbills, theater books, and actor-critique booklets.[32] The historical significance of these publications cannot be appreciated fully without taking into consideration the following phenomenon, noted in an 1829 theater book: "There are many theater lovers in this world these days, but very few theatergoers."[33] So it is that these publications not only provided kabuki information for playgoers but also functioned as virtual theatergoing for those kabuki fans who could not go to playhouses for whatever reasons.

The question of whether or not women took "lessons" from kabuki actors is a little bit more complicated. Kabuki was a theater of people and not of the social elite, and it remained subject to interference by and suspicion of government authorities. Playhouses were categorized as *akusho* (evil places), along with brothels; kabuki was even banned from time to time.[34] The social status of kabuki actors was so low that "no matter luxuriously they might have lived, kabuki actors were not [treated as] 'human beings.'"[35] In short, kabuki was considered, by the government and the social elite, to be depraved theater until the Meiji period, when it transformed itself into classical theater. It is thus not surprising that *Greater Learning for Women* emphasizes that women "must not feed their eyes and ears with such stupid things as kabuki, *jōruri*, and the like."[36] Likewise, *Women's Treasury* (*Onna chōhōki*), a reference book for daily life published in 1692, also admonishes women not to copy the clothing fads of *onnagata*.[37] That women had to be cautioned this way itself reveals that there was indeed such a phenomenon as imitating *onnagata* fashion. For example, there was patterned cloth known as *Edo-kanoko*. In the city of Edo, this textile, however, was called *Kodayū-kanoko*, named after the popular *onnagata* Itō Kodayū II (?–1689).[38] The existence of popular namesake items attests to there being a trend to imitate *onnagata* fashion despite the prohibition found in *Greater Learning for Women* and the contempt revealed in *Women's Treasury*.

These observations of the readership and of vogue *onnagata* present us with a complicated picture of women and *onnagata*. First, the primary preachees of the *onnagata* treatises were undoubtedly the *onnagata* themselves. Considering the broad readership of theater print media, however, some women were likely to have been readers of *onnagata* acting manuals as well. Moreover, we can assume that they were not only observers but also a certain type of preachees themselves. This is related to the Edo-era gender system. While present-day kabuki operates on the basis of the dichotomy between the artistic–artificial femininity of *onnagata* and the natural femininity of women, such a decisive dualism did not exist in the Edo period.[39] Women and *onnagata* shared the concept of femininity as that which is second nature, obtained through training. Accordingly, women adopted the fashion—such as wearing hairpins, sashes, and combs—created by or named after popular *onnagata*,[40] and *onnagata* had to be aware that they were an important part of the chain of citation among the doers of femininity:

> An *onnagata* should not be adored by women. It is bad if a woman wants to be his wife. An *onnagata* must have many male admirers who harbor the wish, "If only there were a woman like this." As for women admirers, an *on-*

> *nagata* should make his fashion—such as combs, hairpins, [forehead] kerchief, clothing, and sashes—be adored by them. You should wish that your fashion be imitated by women at warriors' residences, courtesans, and young ["nonprofessional"] girls. Make them think that you are a woman just as they are. [That is the most important point] when it comes to female admirers.[41]

One may want to say, "*Onnagata* are to women not as copy is to original, but, rather, as copy is to copy."[42] Women and *onnagata* are here transferring and circulating femininity as that which is internalized in, and inseparable from, their bodies. For, we recall, the exterior and the interior cannot be clearly demarcated. It is not that one hands "femininity" to another, as an intact object. Unwittingly or otherwise, each "transaction" involves revisions to one degree or another, and may even involve an accidental mutation. Then, with countless, constant, and mutual "transactions," such an illusionary idea as "origins" vanishes in the aporia of the "chicken or the egg."[43]

And it is via tangible and visible markers (for example, clothing) that women and *onnagata* circulated femininity. Tangibility here echoes the master discourse of "how you look is who you are," which we saw earlier. *Onnagata* treatises thus dictated an influential, if not ultimately ideal, femininity to women as well. *Greater Learning for Women* might have indeed prohibited women from seeing kabuki, and *Women's Treasury* scorned the vogue created by *onnagata*.[44] As Jennifer Robertson effectively puts it, however, "During the Tokugawa period (and beyond), the paragons of female-likeness were *onnagata*."[45] This paragon might not be an officially designated one, but it was nonetheless a powerful, de facto one. It is precisely this labyrinth of gendering that epitomizes how they did femininity at that time. Women and *onnagata* were simultaneously citers and citees to a certain extent.

Given this, it is quite noteworthy that *onnagata* treatises propose what most probably is "ideal femininity" in the disguise of "real femininity" in a tactful and yet insidious manner.[46] The textual mechanism is as follows. These *onnagata* treatises justify *onnagata* instructions with the statement that "real women (*hon no onna*) do it this way." "The Secret Transmissions of an *Onnagata*" bluntly "observes": "When they are upset, women first cry before [speaking]."[47] Likewise, "The Words of Ayame" reads: "[Ayame once advised Jūjirō, another *onnagata*] not to attempt to make the audiences laugh. It is fine if they spontaneously laugh, seeing the action. It is not women's spirit (*onna no jō*) to purposely make [people] laugh."[48] The expression "real women (*hon no onna*) do it this way" is presented as if it were purely an observation of fact. Both texts claim, in other words, that they capture the plain truth about women's spirit.

In technical terms, such a statement is called "constative." A constative statement is a statement in which a speaker removes all the possible variables and simply and objectively describes a fact ("women's spirit is *A*"). Roughly speaking, the concept of constative can be posited vis-à-vis another critical concept, "performative." A performative statement is a statement *in* or *by* which a speaker performs something, such as to promise, declare, and so on. Importantly, postmodern examinations of performativity have revealed the formidable difficulty of constative, and as a result it has been proposed the constative—at least most of them— be considered to be the performative in disguise, whether or not they are intended as such: The *A*-is-*B* type of statement is most likely to assign the *B* attribute to *A*. "Women's spirit is *A*" thus means, "I pronounce that women's spirit is *A*." If we apply this knowledge to the two constative statements in the excerpts above, they will read: "I pronounce that women first cry before speaking when they are upset" and "I pronounce that it is not women's spirit to purposely make people laugh." It is a tactful and yet insidious way of defining the "nature" of others. It might be called gender stereotyping, but stereotypes are arguably a euphemism for this operation to begin with, and more importantly, "defining that you are *A*" and "ordering that you must be *A*" are, as we know, logically just a step apart. In other words, defining that women are, for example, obedient by nature is merely one step away from ordering that women should be obedient.

Other examples in which "The Words of Ayame" defines women include "descriptions" of—thus prescriptions of—women as weak (sec. 8), as likely to flinch in front of many people (sec. 12), and as chaste (sec. 13).[49] Similarly, "The Secret Transmissions of an *Onnagata*" explains how women behave when they are feigning love, feeling true affection, and angered. Kikunojō gives instructions on body movements for *onnagata* based on such "observations."[50]

The implications of such constatives are expectation, regulation, and prohibition. Notice that expectation here includes what is usually regarded as incapability; for instance, when she is upset, a woman cries before explaining her feelings. This is a classic example of "damned if you do, damned if you don't." On the one hand, if you are unable to verbalize your emotions, you have to admit that you are intellectually incapable of it. Should you be capable of such expression, on the other hand, you are not considered a "real woman." In short, women are ("must be") weak, emotional, chaste, timid, and bad at manipulating people, such as by purposefully making them laugh.[51] Bearing this in mind, one can see that when a text dictates conduct, an effective way to do so is to put it in the constative mode. It might even be argued that, while these texts were explicitly binding on the primary preachees (*onnagata*), they were far more implicitly and insidiously binding on their secondary preachees (women). It is in this sense that *onnagata* treatises tactfully propose what "ideal femininity" is—for whomever it is—by claiming that the instructions are derived from observations of "real femininity."

To summarize, these texts point to an understanding that the body is important, that the body signifies the mind, that everyday life is important, that offstage conduct creates onstage performance, and that the ultimate performance generated in such a way is plausible and hence commendable. These kinds of fusions, or, depending on the perspective, blurred and nebulous boundaries, are of great importance.[52] They are considered integral to the artistry of *onnagata*. In other words, the art of *onnagata* is theorized in such a way that the rigorous training of *onnagata* (*shugyō*) unites the body with the mind and the onstage performance with daily life. In addition, prolific publications about kabuki provided people with amusement, but those pastime readings shared with the master discourse the critical premise about humans' conduct, namely, "what you do equals who you are." In this sense, reading theatrical treatises in Edo-era Japan was a multifold experience. You would certainly be entertained with intriguing anecdotes, marvelous descriptions of stage performances, and so on and so forth. You would also absorb, unwittingly or otherwise, a certain idea about the image of a person, that is to say, whom you should be, or, rather, whom you believe you want to be.

NOTES

1. Unless otherwise noted, all translations from Japanese are mine. When introduced for the first time, all Japanese names, except for those of authors publishing their works in English, are given in the Japanese order: surname first, followed by the given name. In subsequent references, a single element is used: the family name for those in modern times (1868 onward), or the given name for those who lived before that. Regardless of the general principle, well-known pen names are used for writers; the given name in their stage name is used for kabuki actors (e.g., Ayame, and not Yoshizawa).

2. Mishima Yukio, "*Onnagata*," in *Hanazakari no mori, Yūkoku: Jisen tanpenshū* ("The forest in full bloom" and "Patriotism": Short stories selected by the author) (Tokyo: Shinchōsha, 1968), 161–186. The epigraph is from pp. 162, 165–166.

3. To be sure, there were women kabuki actors, including women *onnagata*. For female *onnagata*, see my "Women *Onnagata* in the Porous Labyrinth of Femininity: On Ichikawa Kumehachi I," *U.S.–Japan Women's Journal* 30–31 (2006): 105–131. On the same actor, Kumehachi, see also Loren Edelson, "The Female Danjūrō: Revisiting the Acting Career of Ichikawa Kumehachi," *Journal of Japanese Studies* 34, no. 1 (Winter 2008): 69–98, although the article is not about *onnagata*. For women performers, see also Kelly Foreman's chapter in this book.

4. "The Words of Ayame" was included in *The Actors' Analects* (*Yakusha banashi*) published in 1776. See Fukuoka Yagoshirō, "*Ayamegusa*" (The words of Ayame), in Hachimonji Jishō, ed., *Yakusha banashi* (The actors' analects), republished in Gunji Masakatsu, ed., *Kabuki jūhachibanshū* (Eighteen great kabuki plays), Nihon koten bungaku taikei (Collection of Japanese classical literature), vol. 98 (Tokyo: Iwanami Shoten, 1965), 317–326. "The Words of Ayame" had already been published before 1776 in another anthology, but this chapter uses *The Actors' Analects* version, as per convention. For philological information, see my "Gender of *Onnagata* as the Imitating Imitated: Its Historicity, Performativity, and Involvement in the Circulation of Femininity," *positions: east asia cultures critique* 10, no. 2 (Fall 2002): 279. "*Ayamegusa*" is available in an English translation: Fukuoka Yagoshirō, "The Words of Ayame," in *The Actors' Analects*, ed. and trans., Charles J. Dunn and Bunzō Torigoe (New York: Columbia University Press, 1969), 49–66.

5. Fukuoka, "*Ayamegusa*," 318, 323.

6. Ibid., 319.

7. Ibid., 323.

8. "The Secret Transmissions of an *Onnagata*" had long been considered lost, but the contents of it were included in an anthology, *The Pioneering Analects from Past and Present Actors* (*Kokon yakusha rongo sakigake*) published in 1772, and these passages are generally known as "The Secret Transmissions of an *Onnagata*." See Kinjinsai Shin'ō, *Kokon yakusha rongo sakigake* (The pioneering analects from past and present actors), ed. Gunji Masakatsu, republished in Nishiyama Matsunosuke, Watanabe Ichirō, and Gunji Masakatsu, eds., *Kinsei geidōron* (Theory on the way of arts in the premodern period), *Nihon shisō taikei* (Collection of Japanese thought), vol. 61 (Tokyo: Iwanami Shoten, 1972), 482–483. For philological information, see my *Secrecy in Japanese Arts: "Secret Transmission" as a Mode of Knowledge* (New York: Palgrave, 2005), 73–74.

9. "Right before his last moment, [Kikunojō] is said to have taken a bath and arranged his hair, with his forehead shaven. He then dressed himself formally and put an [*onnagata*] kerchief on his forehead. He had *hyakuman-ben nenbutsu* [the million-time Buddhist invocation] chanted around his deathbed and bid farewell to the people in the theater world. Thus [the late Segawa Kikunojō] is said to have passed away" (Kinjinsai, *Kokon yakusha rongo sakigake*,

483). This anecdote concludes the text consisting of Kikunojō's instructions for *onnagata*.

10. Kinjinsai, *Kokon yakusha rongo sakigake*, 489.

11. *Kabuki hyōbanki shūsei* (Collected kabuki actor-critique booklets), ed. Kabuki hyōbanki kenkyūkai (The kabuki actor-critique booklets study group), vol. 3 (Tokyo: Iwanami Shoten, 1973), 548.

12. Kinjinsai, *Kokon yakusha rongo sakigake*, 468, 469, 474, 475. The term "theater book" (*gekisho*) generically refers to books on kabuki published in the Edo era. Along with actor-critique booklets (*yakusha hyōbanki*) and playbills (*banzuke*), theater books were major kabuki-related publications. See also note 32 below.

13. *Kabuki hyōbanki shūsei, dai 2-ki* (Collected kabuki actor-critique booklets, series 2), ed. Yakusha hyōbanki kenkyūkai (The kabuki actor-critique booklets study group), vol. 3 (Tokyo: Iwanami Shoten, 1988), 55.

14. Importantly, by no means is each concept (*onna* and *onnagata*) monolithic and the interaction between them lineal. Such a model of interaction would be far too simple even if bilateral. Instead it is that the interaction happens among multiple concepts of *onnagata* and equally multiple concepts of *onna*, and that such an interaction further keeps creating definitions of *onna* and *onnagata* anew. See also note 43 below.

15. Kinjinsai, *Kokon yakusha rongo sakigake*, 473–474; emphasis added. *Furisode*, literally "swinging sleeve," is adolescent clothing; it was initially for both girls and boys before the initiation to adulthood but later became a "girls-only" item.

16. Tamiya Kōon Shirogorō, "*Zoku Nijinshū*" (Sequel to "The dust in the ears"), in *Yakusha banashi*, 349. There are many similar anecdotes of "*onnagata* who pass" recorded in kabuki discourse; see, for example, my "Women *Onnagata* in the Porous Labyrinth of Femininity," 106–107. One should be careful, however, about the complex implications of the very presence of such anecdotes because, if *onnagata* had been totally successful in passing as women, the anecdotes would not have been preserved.

17. For these changes in the Meiji era, see my "Women *Onnagata* in the Porous Labyrinth of Femininity," 117–121. For a broader history of *onnagata* artistry, see my "Images of *Onnagata*: Complicating the Binarisms, Unraveling the Labyrinth," in Ayelet Zohar, ed., *PostGender: Gender, Sexuality and Performativity in Japanese Culture* (Newcastle upon Tyne, U.K.: Cambridge Scholars Publishing, 2009), 22–38.

18. Kaneko Kichizaemon, "*Nijinshū*" (The dust in the ears), in *Yakusha banashi*, 345. The obscure *onnagata* in question is Sugi Kuhei.

19. Kinjinsai, *Kokon yakusha rongo sakigake*, 482–483.

20. Fukuoka, "*Ayamegusa*," 318–321, 323–324, 326.

21. Kinjinsai, *Kokon yakusha rongo sakigake*, 482.

22. Ibid.

23. Fukuoka, "*Ayamegusa*," 317–320, 324.

24. I recognize that my usage of the words "exterior" and "interior" presumes the existence of a boundary between the two. I use them only for the sake of clarity, and only for analytical purposes, with no intension to endorse

such a demarcation. We should not take it for granted that an internal identity can be differentiated from external appearances. Such a dichotomy is a historical product of modernity, and *onnagata* discourse in the Edo period is not located in this modern episteme. Such a boundary in and of itself is being questioned here.

25. Eiko Ikegami, *Bonds of Civility: Aesthetic Networks and the Political Origins of Japanese Culture* (Cambridge: Cambridge University Press, 2005), 245.

26. Takechi Tetsuji, *Teihon Takechi kabuki: Takechi Tetsuji zenshū* (Takechi kabuki, the standard edition: The complete works of Takechi Tetsuji), ed. Ariki Daisaburō, vol. 1 (Tokyo: San'ichi Shobō, 1978), 168–172. Incidentally, the parallel gait is called *nanba*, which has attracted attention from those who are interested in martial arts.

27. Yuasa Yasuo, *Shintairon: Tōyōteki shinshinron to gendai* (Theory of the body: An Eastern mind–body theory and the present) (Tokyo: Kōdansha, 1990), 101; emphasis in original.

28. Thomas P. Kasulis, "Editor's Introduction, " Yuasa Yasuo, *The Body: Toward an Eastern Mind–Body Theory*, ed. Thomas P. Kasulis, Shigenori Nagatomo and Thomas P. Kasulis, trans. (New York: State University of New York Press, 1987), 6; emphasis in original.

29. Yuasa, *Shintairon*, 153; emphasis in original. This understanding can demonstrate both similarities to and differences from postmodern theorizations of bodies and languages. As for an incisive and productive analysis of the postmodern "assertion that discourse constitutes its object, or that there is no outside of language," see Vicki Kirby, *Telling Flesh: The Substance of the Corporeal* (New York: Routledge, 1997), 149.

30. See, for example, my "Osanai Kaoru's Dilemma: 'Amateurism by Professionals' in Modern Japanese Theatre," *TDR/The Drama Review* 49, no. 1 (Spring 2005): 128.

31. Araki Kengo and Inoue Tadashi, eds., *Onna daigaku* (Greater learning for women), in *Kaibara Ekiken, Muro Kyūsō, Nihon shisō taikei* (Collection of Japanese thought), vol. 34 (Tokyo: Iwanami Shoten, 1970), 202–205. For further similarities between the two texts, see my "Gender of *Onnagata* as the Imitating Imitated," 269–270. For a comprehensive analysis of etiquette books in the Edo era, see Ikegami, *Bonds of Civility*, 324–359.

32. As introduced in note 12 above, these are three important groups of kabuki-related publications. The above-mentioned actor-critique booklets and playbills provided readers with an update on kabuki and its actors. Theater books contain such topics as "introduction to kabuki," "the history of kabuki," "introduction of kabuki plays," "actors, now and past," and "actors' treatises," among other things. For a vivid example of how a theater book describes kabuki actors, see Hachimonji Jishō, *Yakusha zensho* (The complete book on actors), in Gondō Yoshikazu, Munemasa Isoo, and Moriya Takeshi, eds., *Kabuki, Nihon shomin bunka shiryō shūsei* (Collected historical documents of Japanese popular culture), vol. 6 (Tokyo: San'ichi Shobō, 1973), 199–241. *The Complete Book on Actors* was published in 1774.

33. Kimura Mokurō, *Gekijō ikkan mushimegane* (Theater under the microscope), ed. Munemasa Isoo, republished in *Kabuki*, 311.

34. Examples include, but are not limited to, the female performer ban in 1629, the *wakashu* (young boys) kabuki ban in 1652, and the Ejima–Ikushima incident in 1714. The actor Ikushima Shingorō is said to have had an affair with Ejima, one of the highest-ranking female officials in service of the shogun's mother. When the affair was exposed, it resulted not only in the exile of Ejima and Ikushima but also in the punishment of all parties concerned, ranging from banishment to capital punishment, and to the closure of kabuki playhouses. A number of regulations ensued.

35. Ōzasa Yoshio, *Nihon gendai engekishi: Meiji Taishō hen* (History of Japanese contemporary theater: The Meiji and Taisho eras) (Tokyo: Hakusuisha, 1985), 18.

36. Araki and Inoue, ed., *Onna daigaku*, 203.

37. Namura Jōhaku, *Onna chōhōki* (Women's treasury), in *Onna chōhōki Nan chōhōki* (Women's treasury and Men's treasury), ed. Nagatomo Chiyoji (Tokyo: Shakai Shisōsha, 1993), 20.

38. Hachimonji, *Yakusha zensho*, 229.

39. See, for example, my "Gender of *Onnagata* as the Imitating Imitated," passim; "Women *Onnagata* in the Porous Labyrinth of Femininity," 119. As for the birth of the concept of "natural femininity grounded in women's bodies" in the context of Japanese theater, see Ayako Kano, *Acting Like a Woman in Modern Japan: Theater, Gender, and Nationalism* (New York: Palgrave, 2001), passim.

40. See, for example, Hachimonji, *Yakusha zensho*, passim. See also Yoshikawa Yoshio, "*Kabuki-geki no onnagata*" (*Onnagata* in the kabuki theater), in *Engekishi kenkyū, dai-1 shū* (Study of the history of theater, part 1), ed. Engekishi gakkai (Tokyo: Daiichi Shobō, 1932), 80; "*Genroku-ki no onnagata*" (*Onnagata* in the Genroku era), *Engekishi kenkyū, dai-2 shû* (Tokyo: Daiichi Shobō, 1932), 183.

41. Kinjinsai, *Kokon yakusha rongo sakigake*, 483. *Bôshi* (a.k.a. *yarô bôshi*) is a certain kerchief placed at the foreheads of *onnagata*. For a discussion on its origins and epistemological significance, see my "Gender of *Onnagata* as the Imitating Imitated," 250–251, 257.

42. Here I am borrowing Judith Butler's parlance, along with its thinking frame: "[G]ay is to straight *not* as copy is to original, but, rather, as copy is to copy" (*Gender Trouble: Feminism and the Subversion of Identity* [New York: Routledge, 1990], 31; emphasis in original).

43. In other words, the unlimited process of copying creates countless copies not identical to the alleged "original." See also note 14 above.

44. Araki and Inoue, ed., *Onna daigaku*, 203; Namura, *Onna chōhōki*, 20.

45. Jennifer Robertson, "The Shingaku Woman: Straight from the Heart," in *Recreating Japanese Women, 1600–1945*, ed. Gail Lee Bernstein (Berkeley: University of California Press, 1991), 90. The Tokugawa period is another appellation of the Edo era, as it was the period when Japan was ruled by the Tokugawa shoguns, and the shogunate was located in the city of Edo, the site of present-day Tokyo.

46. "Ideal femininity" is bracketed because it requires many clarifications, such as who defined it as ideal and by what criteria, and "real femininity" is bracketed because women's studies and gender studies have already discovered the nonexistence of it.

47. Kinjinsai, *Kokon yakusha rongo sakigake*, 482.

48. Fukuoka, "*Ayamegusa*," 319–320.

49. Ibid., 319–321.

50. Kinjinsai, *Kokon yakusha rongo sakigake*, 482.

51. Although he does so in a different context, Philip Auslander analyzes the non-comical feature attributed to women in terms of the act of exercising power. See "'Brought to You by Fem-Rage': Stand-up Comedy and the Politics of Gender," in *Acting Out: Feminist Performances*, ed. Lynda Hart and Peggy Phelan (Ann Arbor: University of Michigan Press, 1993), 316–325.

52. These kinds of fusion are analogous to the fusion of sex and gender in Shingaku ("heart learning") in the Edo era that Robertson analyzes: "Shingaku rhetoricians . . . sought to fuse sex and gender. . . . Sex was perceived as subordinate to gender" ("The Shingaku Woman," 90).

CHAPTER 3

The Perfect Woman

Geisha, Etiquette, and the World of Japanese Traditional Arts

KELLY M. FOREMAN

In spite of the fact that the majority of geisha do not marry or bear children—something usually expected of good women in Japan—geisha are often cast as the epitome of woman on her best, most feminine Japanese behavior. Perpetually enrobed in kimono, posture and gestures restrained, and apparently at the dedicated service of their male customers, geisha seem to embody flawless female etiquette. They pour sake without dripping or drenching their long kimono sleeves, or without calling attention to the act. She instigates conversation only when needed. While these quiet, elegant, attentive geisha seem entirely to be at their customers' service, they see themselves first as servants not of customers but of their teachers and the arts guilds they populate. The strict rules of deference and humility that define the traditional arts world shape the geisha person into one that the outside world encounters primarily within the geisha parties, known as *ozashiki*. However, even though the geisha demeanor serves and defines the *ozashiki* setting well, it originates instead within the arts world.

The geisha world, known as the *karyūkai* (flower and willow world), has long been famous for its myriad rules for both customers and geisha, learned by observation and assisted by a natural savvy for refinement. During my field studies within the *karyūkai*, geisha used the term "common sense" to describe the often bewildering code that guides human relations in their community. This sense is cultivated within the traditional arts world in which geisha reside, and is transmitted by observation, oral instruction, and teacher–student relationships. This chapter examines how the traditional arts world defines behavior and etiquette within the *karyūkai*, and how both geisha and customers come to understand how it all works.

The term "geisha" has been and continues to be applied rather sloppily and broadly, but true geisha are defined as women who are officially registered as such with a small central office located for each geisha community, called a *kenban*, and who study classical Japanese music and dance and perform it for gatherings in order to pay for their art lessons and public stage performances. The geisha business works today much as it did a century ago: customers host parties in small venues such as teahouses, whose owners call the *kenban* to request the number of geisha appropriate to the party's requirements and the customer's budget. Geisha then join the gathering, classical Japanese music and dance are usually performed by both geisha and customers, and sometimes customers conduct business. After an hour or two, the geisha move on to another gathering or return home. Thus, regular life for geisha focuses on these nightly gatherings in which they perform music, and dance, drink, and converse with customers and devoted patrons.

Geisha spend their days immersed in learning five to six different genres of music and dance, including how to play the *shamisen* (three-stringed plucked lute), three different drums, voice, and the flute. Geisha study each genre the same way that all students of Japanese traditional music and dance—including professional soloists, Kabuki actors, and amateurs—do, and they are expected to memorize all repertoire and prepare for and perform large public recitals. These genres of music and dance are often ill-suited to geisha gatherings because they originated within the elaborate Kabuki theater setting, so daily training does not necessarily prepare these artists to perform the shorter and simpler pieces required for the small teahouse settings. Thus, geisha dedicate themselves to mastering genres that have limited value in their daily work, and they dedicate themselves to pleasing the top teachers of these genres with whom they study.

GEISHA AND THE WORLD OF JAPANESE TRADITIONAL ARTS

Geisha maintain great loyalty to their teachers and live most of their lives close to debt in order to study with them. Studying music or dance in Japan bears little resemblance to studying them in the West, where fees usually cover only lessons and instruments, and students are free to change teachers at will. In Japan, each of the classical traditional arts is transmitted through a socio-artistic guild called *ryū*, which is led by an *iemoto* headmaster. For each genre of music and dance there are several *ryū*, each corresponding to a specific style in which the genre is articulated, transmitted exclusively within the membership of the *ryū* group. Once students begin study, they become *ryū* members—whether they are geisha or not—and they must remain loyal to it and its *iemoto* for their entire life or until they cease to be involved with that genre. The *iemoto* functions symbolically as an artistic parent for the children under them, granting select qualified members of the *ryū* the opportunity to earn the family name.

Both geisha and their customers study music and dance within particular *ryū* for each arts genre (most musical genres, dance, tea ceremony, flower arranging, etc.), and *ryū* culture is saturated in etiquette utterly defined by rules. Teachers (and especially *iemoto*) have absolute authority and are never to be questioned. They must be greeted formally each time by kneeling and bowing before and after each lesson, and everyone under the *iemoto*—students, professional musicians, Kabuki actors, amateurs, students—must obey the *iemoto*, pay all fees (these can be in the tens of thousands of dollars), and oblige in whatever ways the *iemoto* asks. Students must seek official permission from the *iemoto* in order to teach, and they must pay regular fees to the *iemoto* for this privilege. When the *iemoto* decides that the *ryū* will host a recital, all members must participate however the *iemoto* sees fit (submitting to the *iemoto*'s choice of repertoire) and must bear whatever costs it entails. Most importantly, all *ryū* members are obliged to perform the art exactly as it was taught to them because the *iemoto* is the only person allowed to alter the style in any way; no improvisation, personal embellishment, or individual style is to be detected. The student is seen as a vessel into which the *iemoto* and teacher pours the tradition and from whom it can be poured out.

Because geisha bypass teaching, marriage, and (usually) child-bearing in order to devote their lives to art, geisha are held as ideal members of the *ryū* and therefore are expected to be particularly exemplary in terms of ideal *ryū* behavior. They are to be passive children of the parent *iemoto* at his or her complete artistic disposal, completely humble and deferential. Because geisha study five or six different genres, they are obliged to five or six different *iemoto* and *ryū*.[1] Therefore, as geisha (and all other long-term students) spend the bulk of their life within the world of *ryū* and *iemoto*, humility and deferential behavior to the art and the art transmitter slowly merges into the geisha self and over time become inseparable components of their personality.[2] It is this deferential person that the outside world sees in the geisha party context, but it is not one that was developed for that purpose.

Rules of the Geisha World

While the *iemoto-ryū* context informs and defines the etiquette of the geisha world, there are also codes of conduct specific to the *karyūkai*. As I proceed to unravel these codes, I begin first with conduct rules that apply to geisha within the *ozashiki* setting.[3] *Ozashiki* has two purposes; the first and most obvious is that it serves as a venue for wealthy patrons to interact with the highly accomplished artists they support, in a personal salon context completely absent in North America. Performances of classical music and dance are given first by geisha and then also by the patrons themselves, because many patrons take lessons in this music. Geisha and customers speak freely about art matters (including those pertaining to the *ryū* and *iemoto*, a taboo discussion in any other context); topics of conversation are unlimited in the geisha gathering.

The second purpose of *ozashiki* is to provide a quiet, elegant context for customers to conduct serious business matters. Geisha simply assist the process by remaining quiet and unobtrusive when things are proceeding well, and exhibiting quick thinking and cleverness to facilitate dealings if discussions begin to falter. Arts performances take place during these more serious business *ozashiki*, but the mood tends to be more somber, and geisha are seen as secondary to the business being conducted. Therefore, one essential geisha etiquette rule is to know when to be quiet and when to intervene.

Also, since it is a Japanese cultural convention to avoid pouring one's own drinks, another essential rule of geisha etiquette is that geisha must see that cups for beer, sake, or whiskey are always kept full. They must also accept drinks poured for them by customers because, unless under strict doctor's orders to abstain, it is seen as rude for geisha not to keep up with customers' alcohol consumption. However, geisha are neither to eat in front of customers nor to deliver dishes or clear the tables, although they may serve customers from larger communal dishes.

Geisha must also observe etiquette rules related to the choice of music and dance. They must consider a number of factors, including the mood of the gathering, the number of geisha performers, and, especially, the budget of the customer(s), since *ozashiki* fees are based on the number of geisha, their seniority, and how long geisha are in attendance.[4] Because performances are usually quickly put together without rehearsal, and because there is a huge body of music and dances from which to choose, the geisha learn rules regarding how to select a repertoire. Since only the owners of the teahouse know the customers' budget, geisha must learn to read the owners' subtle cues, and they develop a keen second sense about this. Repertoire choices must also match the season, since there are pieces appropriate for each month of the year; a piece from the Kabuki repertoire about snow and pine trees would be completely wrong if performed in July, for example.

Good geisha etiquette also includes a tendency toward artistic selflessness, and the expectation that they put aside personal glory in favor of the good of the group, which includes both the other geisha and the customers. Geisha view each other in terms of a "sisterhood," as is common in most group settings in Japan, in which elder geisha care for younger geisha and younger geisha passively defer to their elders' wisdom. In terms of repertoire, this means that elder geisha choose music and dance pieces that might not be their first choice but that will make the younger geisha shine (as well as ones that hopefully they have studied, since it takes years to master a large collection of pieces). Likewise, any pieces of which the customers are particularly fond or which they are currently studying should be incorporated so that they can participate. Because customers tend to study voice, the customer usually sings and the geisha plays the *shamisen* (although there are cases where the customer has acquired significant skills as a *shamisen* player as well, and if this is the case then the geisha sing, provide *shamisen* countermelodies, play percussion, or simply dance). When customers sing, however, geisha must adjust the tuning of the *shamisen* to the customer's vocal range and cover any mistakes the customer might make. And, regardless of repertoire choices, good *ozashiki* etiquette requires all performers to take the pieces seriously as an art transmitted by an *iemoto*, and all are expected to articulate that art accurately and faithfully to the *ryū*.

Although not an outright rule, another *ozashiki* convention is that for geisha to have to resort to musical notation is seen to be a bit unrefined or rude; therefore, geisha are expected to take seriously the task of committing a huge body of music to memory for several genres and several instruments and dance. I had underestimated how daunting a task this is and was taken by surprise late one evening by an older geisha who asked me to perform a lengthy piece from memory. I faltered because I had only memorized pieces until I had learned them well, but I had not continued to maintain them after moving onto other pieces. Thus it had been more than a year since I had played the requested piece. A kind, motherly geisha sat close to me and whispered the pitch numbers into my ear to help me in case my memory failed. No doubt because of her help and the comfort of her being nearby—and in spite of my having kept up with the group's *sake* consumption—I managed to perform the requested twenty-minute *nagauta* piece "*Echigo jishi*" (Lion Dance of Echigo) to the satisfaction of the geisha who requested it, and my dubious status as a foreign musician (who was nonetheless studying *shamisen* with a well-respected *iemoto)* shifted somewhat as I was recognized as one who apparently understood at least something of the rules of Japanese arts transmission—the way of the *ryū*.

Lastly, despite popular notions to the contrary, geisha are explicitly taught to not sell sex (this is discussed further under "Rules Just for Customers"). Elsewhere I have provided some historical background on the complex issue of geisha and prostitution (including public discourse on the topic),[5] but especially within the walled quarters of the Edo Yoshiwara there were strict rules for keeping tabs on the sexual affairs of geisha, since those who did sell sex encroached upon the domain and money of both courtesans and prostitutes (and the houses that owned them). There were all sorts of regulations for geisha restricting personal mobility, adornment, costume, and relationships. For example, geisha were strictly forbidden to wear excessive hairpins or ornaments and were to maintain a subdued appearance, in contrast to that of the flashy courtesans. The following Kansei-era (1789–1801) edict clarified the appropriate behaviors for geisha of the Edo Yoshiwara:

> When customers request that geisha accompany them outside of the Yoshiwara, geisha should refuse. A geisha union (*kumiai*) should be established, and if geisha have an illicit affair with a customer or behave in an inappropriate manner (since this threatens the business of the brothels) the union should examine each case to determine whether anything inappropriate occurred. Also, for male geisha to have relationships with prostitutes, or for geisha to introduce their frequent customers to prostitutes outside of the Yoshiwara is prohibited, and those geisha, male or female, should be barred from their professions.[6]

Geisha are expected to retain a sense of propriety because anything done will be known by everyone else in the community—there are no secrets in this tightly knit community—and geisha are keenly aware of how they are portrayed outside of their community.

Rules Just for Customers

> A customer who is especially popular among geisha is a person who tells interesting stories and who seems to enjoy food or drink. A customer gets respect if he sings a little *kouta* (elegant classical "short song" written for a solo voice) accompanied by the *shamisen* played by the geisha, but if a customer takes the *shamisen* and plays it for a long time, then geisha become annoyed. Sophisticated customers treat geisha with proper respect in *ozashiki*.[7]

In the arts-saturated world of the *karyūkai*, defined by deferential *ryū* hierarchies and traditional culture, it should not be surprising that rules emerged for customers wishing to spend time there. In Kyoto there is an old and well-known rule that one may not visit a teahouse without an introduction from a seasoned customer of that teahouse. Many view this rule as unnecessarily restrictive and old-fashioned, but the practice came about because there are myriad unspoken rules and ways of doing things. This no-first-timers rule creates a type of apprenticeship between newcomers and experienced customers in order to translate the subtleties of human relations in this community. It prevents teahouse owners and geisha alike the embarrassment of having to openly discuss the details of money, billing, appropriate *ozashiki* behavior, and "whether or not sex is available," because another customer demonstrates all of this to them. Regardless of whether customers choose venues that observe the no-first-timers policy, all customers must maintain sensitivity toward money matters and discuss them only when geisha are not present and with teahouse owners at a time other than the gathering.

Another expectation is that at least serious customers should be acquainted with classical Japanese music and dance and preferably study at least one genre. They do not need to learn an instrument, but joining a *ryū* and studying voice with a well-respected teacher (preferably one of the many teachers with whom geisha study) is highly encouraged. With this participation then comes the obligation for customers to perform in the *ryū*-based recitals and concerts, for which accompanists must be hired by the *iemoto* of the *ryū*. Whenever possible, geisha will be hired for these tasks and should be paid well for these concerts to provide them a badly needed extra source of income.[8] And, because customers' lessons occur within the same *iemoto-ryū* system as those of geisha, customers are similarly expected to submit to the *iemoto*. This, in turn, creates a common bond between geisha and customer, which derives from the performance-art world.

Another rule of customer etiquette—one that sometimes surprises new customers—is the tacit expectation that regular customers and especially committed patrons will purchase a large number of tickets for the many public stage performances in which geisha are involved. All *iemoto* sponsor large recitals and, because all performers must pay to perform, customers are expected to offset these costs by ensuring that the house sells out and that geisha therefore do not have to go into debt. This involvement in the arts serves several functions, but one essential one is to help teach customers that the geisha is not an entertainer. She is an artist denied the privilege and salaries offered through the usual venue for artists who specialize in these types of music and dance—the Kabuki theater—which remains all male. She also does not wish to waste her creative energy teaching students (as non-geisha female members of the *ryū* must do), and so therefore customers underwrite the geisha life of performing as well as to offset the astronomical costs of their being members of several *ryū*.

And, as mentioned previously, an important rule for customers to remember is that in spite of all the misconceptions, *ozashiki* is not a context for soliciting sex from geisha. This does not mean that sex with geisha is completely impossible, but if it happens it occurs only after knowing a geisha for some while, and only if there is mutual interest. Flirting is fine. Dirty jokes are fine. However, men who make overt sexual requests will initially be treated as silly little boys before finding themselves increasingly unwelcome.

Rules, Common Sense, or Learned Instinct?

So how do customers learn all of this? The decline in new customers at the *karyūkai* is due not only to a sluggish economy but to a society-wide lack of interest in the traditional arts. Economics and westernization have discouraged younger people from considering the *karyūkai* a staple of leisure life, and without tutelage from elders, younger would-be customers have little or no exposure to teahouse etiquette, to geisha, and to the arts as a whole. In response to these issues, some geisha communities have instigated a practice *ozashiki*, which advertises a set fee and delineates all features for new customers ahead of time, designed for those with absolutely no prior experience or understanding of this world. Such is the case with *zashiki nyūmon kōza* (introduction to *ozashiki*), offered in the Asakusa community in Tokyo, and the public-style (no introduction required) *ozashiki* offered in Kyoto through the Kyoto Gion Maiko Museum and Café.[9] This lower-stress *ozashiki* is a modern response to the personal apprenticeships that used to comprise the customer base, but it does not replace the experience of decades of interaction, lessons, and arts involvement that former seasoned customers and patrons cultivated.

Given the ease with which one can offend in this highly sensitive community, it would seem prudent to create handbooks or guidebooks for geisha and customer alike. Potential customers of Edo geisha were able to consult guidebooks or directories (*saiken*) to the pleasure quarters in order to learn the hierarchies and fees of (and how to tell the difference between) prostitutes, courtesans, and geisha, and to find hints on the conduct expected of customers. The general public were also avid readers of *sharebon,* whose witty short stories about the pleasure quarters provided some insight into this world of play and fantasy. And, according to Ikegami Eiko, the wide range of Tokugawa etiquette manuals (such as *setsuyō-shū* and *chōhōki*) available to Edoites, including those produced specifically for certain genres of performing arts and poetry composition, contained the foundations for polite behavior that would have crossed over to the formal *karyūkai* settings.[10]

Outright how-to manuals for mastering the geisha world were and continue to be avoided as a mode of teaching within the *karyūkai*, whose members prefer to acquire knowledge more subtly, over time, and without a great deal of obvious or overt devotion to the task. Even though all must learn what it is to be rude, how to recover if one makes a misstep (as one inevitably does), and even how to break the rules, young geisha and new customers are given the same patient tutoring that parents bestow upon children in Japan, gently paddling them into place through a sideways glance, a particular choice of words, a subtle gesture. Many teahouse owners are themselves former geisha and are very effective teachers for geisha and customers alike. Rarely blunt or crass about such matters, they supply proper cues to help all parties know how to behave without causing undo embarrassment or shame. Eventually, such matters become second nature and little further shaping is necessary. Customers who truly master this sensibility are said to develop a sense of *iki*, a term which originated within the Edo *karyūkai* to describe an unconscious and effortlessly chic sense of refinement and good taste. An *iki* person never has to think about or be told how to behave, what to wear, or what to do; such things will always come naturally to them. Indeed, to read a manual in order to learn a code of conduct would be completely antithetical to being *iki*, and therefore the *karyūkai* has always viewed the idea of such manuals with disdain.

Iki is an aesthetic sense, one that originates in color design, and the people who celebrate and exemplify them; *iki* is the nexus of art and human relations in the Edo *karyūkai*.[11] Thus, art and aesthetics played an indispensable role in defining what it meant to embody and perform *iki*, and this in turn shaped what refined behavior was. The power of influence that the arts world had on mainstream societal etiquette was very strong indeed during the Edo period. Arts society, with its *iemoto-ryū* structure, provided a completely separate and autonomous world in which one could climb and rise through the ranks regardless of one's birth rank, in stark contrast to the rigid Tokugawa class structure. Not surprisingly, Edo commoners and merchants eagerly participated in the various arts, and the geisha-*karyūkai* provided a context that facilitated and celebrated this widespread arts participation. The codes of etiquette that defined the arts world then exerted a wider influence on the broader urban society. Ikegami goes even further, when she asserts that "the codes of [Tokugawa] hierarchical civility themselves were heavily influenced by the traditions of performing arts and were thereby aesthetically defined. For these reasons, hierarchical patterns of civility and aesthetic standards of civility were in many ways twin outgrowths of Tokugawa social developments *that cannot be understood separately*" [emphasis added].[12]

What about bad behavior? Geisha, as women who lived a life in the spotlight rather than one devoted to caring for children, husbands, and in-laws, went against societal expectations for women, and therefore were always behaving a bit badly as women.[13] Today the behavior of geisha attracts nowhere near as much attention or scrutiny as it once did, as Edo social moralists were rather vocal in criticizing both the personal and financial freedoms that geisha enjoyed as well as the occasionally shocking fashions they began and which ordinary women then emulated (such as wearing men's *haori*). Kitagawa Morisada's famous and widely distributed 1853 treatise *Kinsei fūzokushi* (Customs of the early modern period) included a barbed critique of geisha (*geiko*) in Kyoto and Osaka whose comportment he found to be insufficiently deferential:[14]

> Geiko of Kyoto and Osaka, both inside and outside the officially licensed districts, are extremely rude.[15] First of all, when they arrive they invariably say, "My, I am exhausted," whether or not they had to walk a long distance. This could not be more than a few *chō*—nobody would be exhausted by this.[16] After that, geisha enter the room greeting their customers with their eyes only, without moving their hands or lowering their heads. They have no scruples about taking the seat of honor. Edo geisha are more courteous than their counterparts in Kyoto and Osaka. When they arrive, they say something like "thank you for calling me today" to the proprietor of the teahouse and to the group, and then before they enter the room, they place their hands on the floor outside of the threshold and say something like *irasshai* (welcome). Edo geisha never fix their makeup with their customers present, but in Kyoto and Osaka they take out their cosmetics bag and mirror (*kagamibukuro*) for no reason and fix their makeup in the presence of customers.[17]

It is not clear whether geisha read these critiques or, if they did, how seriously they took them, but surely geisha heard indirectly about such criticisms and would have been informed about the public discourse about them. However, even if geisha were aware of such charges of insufficient humility within the *ozashiki* context, it is likely that they did not pay them heed because their full loyalties are to *iemoto* and the *ryū* groups from which they derive their names.

For this reason, humility is not really transferred to customers during *ozashiki* because they are not *iemoto*. Geisha are deferential by habit, but there's an aloofness and an emotional distance that usually make geisha polite but not lowly. Only arts immersion make this possible; it is the unique Japanese *iemoto-ryū* system that shapes geisha over the twenty to forty years they spend being involved as *ryū* members, and it is why short cuts in arts training have never taken hold.[18] The commitment in time and finances required in the *ryū* system is very high, but it creates a unique arts-imbued person whose impeccable comportment is effortless and nearly unconscious. It also creates a person who will clearly exhibit her displeasure with crude demands and thus educate anyone who believes that the obedience is easily transferred from *iemoto* to rich customer. Geisha, as well as most *ryū* members, relinquish their autonomy to receive the secret knowledge of the art, not because they take pleasure in serving anyone and everyone. The dedication to archaic music and dance to which the vast majority of the Japanese public has no exposure is an essential selling point for why knowledgeable customers willingly spend so much money on behalf of geisha.

NOTES

1. Geisha never study under more than one *iemoto* for the same genre, however.

2. For further discussion in English about the culture of the *iemoto-ryū* system, see Francis L. K. Hsu, *Iemoto: The Heart of Japan* (New York: Halsted, 1975), and Eiko Ikegami, *Bonds of Civility: Aesthetic Networks and the Political Origins of Japanese Culture* (Cambridge: Cambridge University Press, 2005).

3. I must clarify that this is not intended as a comprehensive list of *karyūkai* rules, nor is it a prescriptive guidebook for navigating this community.

4. Because much of this repertoire derives from the Kabuki setting, it can be quite elaborate in structure; several *shamisen*, several singers, and a full percussion section would all be necessary for certain pieces. Should they be requested (even in excerpted form), such pieces therefore require many musicians and an even higher price tag.

5. Kelly Foreman, "Bad Girls Confined: Okuni, Geisha, and the Negotiation of Female Performance Space," in *Bad Girls of Japan*, ed. Laura Miller and Jan Bardsley, 32–47 (New York: Palgrave, 2005).

6. The first performers referred to as "geisha" were male. Mitamura Engyō, *Karyū fūzoku* (Culture of the geisha community) in *Engyō Edo bunka* (Engyō Edo Culture) series, vol. 27 of *Engyō Edo bunko* (Engyō Edo Collection), ed. Asakura Haruhiko (Tokyo: Chūō Kōronsha, 1998), 203.

7. Iwabuchi Junko, ed., *"Danna" to asobi to Nihon bunka* ("Patrons," recreation, and Japanese culture) (Tokyo: PHP Kenkyūjo, 1996), 31.

8. Further discussion of finances and patronage can be found in Kelly Foreman, *The Gei of Geisha: Music, Identity and Meaning* (London: Ashgate, 2008), 87–103.

9. *Maiko* are girls under the age of eighteen who participate in *ozashiki* but who are considered to be in the initial training phase of their careers. Sometimes called "apprentice geisha," they usually specialize in dance (rather than music), and are limited to Kyoto.

10. Ikegami, *Bonds of Civility*, 327.

11. Kuki Shūzō, 'Iki'*no kozo*, in Nara Hiroshi, *The Structure of Detachment: The Aesthetic Vision of Kuki Shūzō: With a Translation of* 'Iki'*no kozo* (Honolulu: University of Hawai'i Press, 2005).

12. Ikegami, *Bonds of Civility*, 328.

13. See Foreman, "Bad Girls Confined," for a discussion of Japanese perceptions of geisha as transgressive women.

14. Geisha in Kyoto and Osaka are referred to as *geiko*, although the two terms have roughly the same meaning. I discuss the historical development of these terms in detail in Foreman, *The Gei of Geisha*, 44–51.

15. *Burei* means "no courtesy or manners."

16. One *chō* measures roughly 109 meters.

17. Kitagawa Morisada, *Kinsei fūzokushi* (Customs of the early modern period) (1853), cited in Aketa Tetsuo, *Nihon Hanamachi shi* (History of Japan's *Hanamachi*) (Tokyo: Yūzankaku Shuppan, 1990), 221.

18. It would be tempting to assume that a year or so of dance and music training, focused entirely on the genres actually performed during *ozashiki*, should be sufficient and perhaps even ideal vocational training for the job of entertainment. Certainly women could bypass the *iemoto-ryū* system in this way—one need only find an adequate teacher—and I attended a performance at a Tokyo club whose dancers did exactly this. They did not begin to resemble or behave like geisha, however, and they did not (fortunately) use the term "geisha" to describe themselves.

CHAPTER 4

Mortification, Mockery, and Dissembling

Western Adventures in Japanese Etiquette

GAVIN JAMES CAMPBELL

Japan has a reputation for ferociously unforgiving standards of etiquette. And it must be admitted that historically things have not always gone well for visitors. In 1556, for instance, a Portuguese explorer unwittingly became a laughing-stock at a *daimyō*'s party: "Then having caused a table to be covered for us, and on it placed store of good meat and well drest," he reported with chagrin, "we fell to eating after our own manner, of all that was set before us, whilst the jests which the Ladies broke upon us, in seeing us feed so with our hands, gave more delight to the King and Queen, than all the Comedies that could have been presented before them." He was not, he pouted, "accustomed to feed with two little sticks."[1]

The closing of the country roughly a century later had the unexpected advantage of sparing foreigners further disgrace and, if current English-language guidebooks are to be believed, also concentrating the nation's best minds on refining native etiquette to levels of rococo complexity. Thus, when Westerners reopened the country in the 1850s, the opportunities for humiliation abounded. Some early visitors suspected in fact that the Japanese played on this ignorance, sniggering into their kimono sleeves while Westerners made unwitting asses of themselves. The starchy British diplomat Rutherford Alcock, clearly not in the mood for a good joke, observed that because foreigners' knowledge "of the etiquette, forms, and customs of an Eastern court" was "very slight and imperfect," he feared that the Japanese were making foreign dignitaries follow "some mockery of their forms, which is alleged to be in accordance with their customs, while it is, in fact . . . calculated to humiliate and degrade in the eyes of the natives."[2] Alcock enjoyed the imperialist's last laugh, however, living long enough to see the Meiji emperor cumbrously outfitted in European court costume, and Japanese aristocrats fumbling through foreign rituals.

Alcock stood at the vanguard of a rapid turnaround whereby Westerners held the upper hand, bullying and barging their way through the home islands. Opportunities for social embarrassment still loomed, but more often the Japanese became the object of mirth. Travelers tittered at "daintily kimonoed ladies clutching forks upside down in the wrong hand, grasping the body of a tea-cup for fear the handle to which they are unaccustomed will prove too frail," and on and on through a whole list of faux pas, suggesting that the days had passed of being embarrassed for not correctly wielding two little sticks at dinner.[3]

Though Japan's "westernization" has provided modern tourists a constant source of lamentation, a shared transcultural standard of etiquette would at least seem to promise an end to any confusion regarding bad manners, self-inflicted mortification, and native mockery. Nevertheless, there are nearly a dozen books on the market specifically aimed at guiding travelers through all the approved niceties (though still nothing on the customs of an Eastern court). There are an additional scrum of specialized advice manuals targeting business manners, Zendo and dōjō etiquette, tea ceremony propriety, proper bathing techniques, and good behavior for vacationers, in addition to general travel guidebooks that also include sections on how to eat, bow, exchange business cards, and navigate common social pleasantries. What is more, every book expects that readers will be gladly willing to make the effort. "Chopsticks are really not that difficult to master, provided you put in some practice," comes the cheery reassurance.[4]

Whereas Alcock and his Victorian brethren had little compunction in belittling Japanese standards at almost every turn, contemporary guidebooks expect the traveler not only to tolerate but to embrace native ways. "Courtesy requires that visitors in Japan should attempt to follow Japanese customs," reminds one book; it is best, advises another, to demonstrate "that one dissociates oneself from the unfortunate past and really does look forward to building relations with one's Japanese opposite numbers on the footing of mutuality, of equality of respect and consideration."[5] A traveler's sincerity is not for its own sake, however, but is a down payment on a particular psychological investment that only the Japanese have the matching funds to redeem. In return for the traveler's embracing cultural relativism and following Japanese ways, books promise that the "real" Japanese people will open themselves intimately, providing rare authentic experiences and insights tailored to the psychological needs of each visitor. As a result of learning how to use chopsticks or how to bathe, travelers make new discoveries about themselves and return home with a heightened level of self-awareness. The etiquette guides exist, therefore, to provide an entrée into the "real" Japan by unlocking the nation's private semiotic codes. The rest is up to the Japanese, who ought to respond warmly and sincerely.

And yet, sadly, the Japanese fail again and again. Even as guides to native manners promise private access to the "real" Japan, they stir fears that Japanese etiquette is such an all-encompassing labyrinth of fictions as to make Japanese culture and society frigid and impenetrable. Moreover, they agitate suspicions that etiquette introduces into a traveler's experiences the constant possibility of deceit, thus invalidating even those encounters that on the surface had seemed genuine. If, as book after book insists, Japan has from ancient times built its society upon a "culture of lying" enforced by a rigid code of etiquette, the traveler is left wondering when a cigar is in fact a cigar.[6] Guidebooks and travel writers provide no relief, having achieved such a level of self-contradictory consensus that in some cases they quite literally plagiarize each other.[7] The reaction is fierce and deeply personal. Travel guides and sojourner narratives repeatedly berate the Japanese for their inability to appreciate or respond to emotional sincerity. Moreover, they suggest that contact with liberal Western tolerance has dropped the scales from Japanese eyes, leaving them no excuse for refusing a reformation, other than their own lack of moral courage and spiritual honesty. In the end, books that claim to celebrate cultural relativism short-circuit their message by instead simply flattering readers, insinuating that the ludicrous rules for Japanese polite society stand in damning contrast to the psychological forthrightness of the reader's own culture.

"I AM SICK AND TIRED OF TALKING TO YOU"

Sir Rutherford Alcock and his Victorian brethren would no doubt have been amazed at the consternation of our contemporary guidebooks. Despite some quibbles and grumblings, travelers to Meiji Japan were routinely impressed and delighted by the elaborate etiquette they encountered at all levels of society. Summarizing the general opinion, an author explained that "every writer who has treated of the subject, praises the great urbanity, mutual respect, and formal, but real politeness of the people."[8] There was admittedly some sprinkling of ambivalence and confusion. When Richard Hildreth revised his book on Japan for publication in 1860 he combined into one chapter the subheadings "Civilization of the Japanese," "Their Custom of cutting themselves open," and "Animals." Still, overall impressions were almost uniformly positive.[9]

Japan's policy of westernization during the Meiji period not only radically altered the etiquette landscape, but it inflated an already oversized vanity among travelers who believed that they quite naturally deserved this sincerest form of flattery. A *New York Times* correspondent gushed that the Japanese were "willing imitators" of "customs which they esteemed as better than their own."[10] In matters of propriety, travelers conceded that native standards were impeccable and quaint, but the signposts of true civilization and modernity lay in the etiquette manuals of Paris, London, and Berlin, with perhaps a few stray leaves from New York. One sojourner immediately elevated her impression of her Japanese host when he served tea, "*our* kind," she gloated, "*with* cream and sugar, served in cups *with* handles."[11] Travelers enjoyed a kind of parental satisfaction watching their children grow into maturity. With admirable speed and diligence, the Japanese were learning to do things properly.

The wind at their backs, Western tourists, with some notable exceptions, displayed a bracing level of condescension toward Japanese customs and sensibilities. The *Handbook of the Japanese Language*, for instance, suggests committing to memory an array of peppery phrases such as, "No one scolds the cook or servants when necessary" (to be used at a hotel), or "Really this is all nonsense dilly-dallying and waiting here forever!" (useful on the train), or "I am sick and tired of talking to you" (as one might say at a curio shop).[12] The turn-of-the-century tourist's bible, the *Handbook for Travellers in Japan*, includes an even wider selection of dyspeptic gems, promoting the utility of "Why do you do such things?" "Please pay attention," "What a horrid smell!" and "It is so nasty I can't eat it."[13] Guidebook authors suggested that the only time you would want to speak to the natives was in command, complaint or contempt.

Because language remained such a basic hurdle, Western etiquette provided the common grammar for international communication. Entering the gee-gaw-strewn Victorian parlor of the Marchioness Nabeshima, a visitor marveled, "I instantly recognized that we were in the presence of a very great lady indeed."[14] Breakdowns, however, occurred where Japanese standards of behavior still prevailed, most notably at the public inn and in traditional native homes during foreigners' visits. Clara Whitney, an American teenager living in Tokyo in the 1870s, was horrified when a family she visited followed her to the door as she left and bowed deeply, their foreheads touching the floor. "How could a freeborn daughter of America practice such slavish, humiliating customs?" she sputtered in her diary. Looking for a way to extricate herself with republican principles intact, "I merely bowed an American bow, and with no more than American politeness cheerfully said my 'Sayonara,' and while they were all lying prostrate in the dust, I stepped out to my jinrikisha and let them lie."[15] One can only wonder what her hosts made of that.

These sorts of communication misfires did not go unnoticed by the Meiji government and its supporters, determined as they were to win the admiration of the Great Powers. Not only did the aristocracy replicate European manners while ordinary citizens attempted self-reform, but bureaucrats did what they could to accommodate foreign sensibilities by, for example, trying to ban public undress or mixed bathing because "it concerns the national reputation."[16] While many travelers laughed at what they considered the half-baked results, Clara Whitney was smitten. "Mr. Nakahara behaved himself quite gallantly," she bubbled, "carrying my umbrella for me and helping me in every gentlemanly way. His native politeness is heightened and polished by foreign grace which sits on him well." Likewise, when Mr. Murata arrived home after a stay in the United States, Whitney cooed, "At home he seemed to me to be stupid and awkward, but he is quite changed now and has about him the nameless dignity and bearing of a gentleman."[17]

Despite these good marks, Mr. Nakahara and Mr. Murata and their entire nation remained the subject of foreign judgment, making condescension a natural part of the tourist's relationship with native people. Not surprisingly, the Japanese dug in their heels. Ignorance of proper form and the often strong reluctance of tourists to follow local custom placed a heavy burden on public accommodations and disturbed Japanese guests and hosts alike. In response, restaurants and hotels charged foreigners higher prices and often extracted revenge in the form of a substantial, obligatory tip (*chadai*). A guidebook written by public-spirited Tokyo businessmen defended these practices, hinting at a high level of frustration on the Japanese side. "It is a simple matter to apprehend that foreign travellers should have to pay a little more than native travellers," they maintained, "for the very reason that they require more prompt attentions, fresh water in the bath, have to occupy a portion of the kitchen and separate hands to cook special food for them, and likewise several other inconceivable requirements, whilst others all run in one channel." Moreover, rejecting the bruising phrases suggested in Western guidebooks, they promoted instead "many thanks for the trouble you have taken," "I am glad to see you," "please do not trouble," and "excuse me."[18]

Whether such advice helped bring down the level of bravado is unclear, but it seems to have had little effect in convincing tourists that Japanese standards of etiquette deserved the same consideration as their own. Of course, visitors sometimes accommodated themselves to local custom. "I suppose it would look rather queer to our friends at home," Whitney giggled after calling at a friend's house, "to see us all seated as 'Jappy' as possible."[19] But even then Whitney and others considered Japanese etiquette a charming remnant of a fading feudal society, not a compelling alternative to modern Western standards. Their travels only confirmed this conclusion since the Japanese they encountered appeared themselves so bent on adopting Western models and junking their own. Native customs held anthropological and historical interest, but they in no way laid equal claims of authority over a tourist's behavior.[20] It seemed perfectly reasonable, therefore, to rely on phrasebooks heavy with condescension and chastisement for their hosts who were, after all, merely freshmen in the great classroom of civilization.

"A PLACE WITHOUT A SOUL"

Such chauvinism is no doubt unthinkable to the great majority of modern travelers, told by guidebooks that "there are huge benefits to be gained by caring and sharing," and advised to approach foreign cultures with "deference, consideration, and some humility."[21] As a measure of the transformation, one contemporary guide to Japanese etiquette includes subheadings that would have been laughable to many Victorian travelers: "Don't Criticize or Complain," "Be Modest," "Be Calm and Cordial," "Adjust Your Behavior to the Circumstances," and "Don't Act Like You Own the Place."[22] Historically speaking, however, this change in tone is a remarkably recent phenomenon. Aside from two apparently futile postwar attempts by Japanese authors to write guidebooks, until the 1980s there were almost no etiquette guides for travelers, and the material that existed did not flatter the Japanese.[23] *Fodor's Japan* 1977 edition, for example, suggests that norms of Japanese politeness border on pathological, revealing deep-seated problems with the nation's society. "The politeness of the Japanese," the authors explain, "stems as a way of life from the suppression of individuality." The flawless surface masks dark intimacies that, if expressed honestly, "could shatter the fixed social structure."[24] A tourist has little incentive to join such a charade. Thus it was that until quite recently nothing but common decency and personal whim dictated a traveler's emulation of Japanese manners.

The 1980s, however, marked a significant shift in enthusiasm for what Clara Whitney had so indelicately called acting "as 'Jappy' as possible." The overwhelming power of the Japanese economy during the "bubble" years compelled foreigners to study the proper procedure for exchanging business cards, bowing, and eating with two little sticks. At the same time, the rise of Lonely Planet not only as a guidebook but as a traveling philosophy did much to erode Victorian chauvinism and instill cultural relativism as the central tenant of a traveler's outlook.[25] Under this new paradigm, quickly adopted by all of Lonely Planet's competitors, travelers are expected to authenticate their travels by eating at "local" restaurants, meeting "real" people, and staying away from places that are commonly popular. As far as possible they are supposed to enter *into* the society rather than merely evaluate it from a cool Victorian distance. To facilitate this process, guidebooks include special sections devoted to history, politics, arts, geography, religion, language, social structure, and etiquette, all designed to give the tourist a holistic understanding. A mastery of these details allows the traveler to "integrate seamlessly into diverse cultures," or at the very least not disturb their equilibrium, and achieve an "authentic" experience denied to the "mere tourist."[26]

Despite their earnest desire to enrich the Japan travel experience, current guidebooks often encourage the very anxiety and skepticism they seek to dispel. Claiming to simplify travel with insider advice on avoiding embarrassing faux pas, they nevertheless justify their publication and purchase by making Japan's culture seem overwhelmingly—even pathologically—complex. The *Culture Shock! Japan* series, for example, upped the ante by changing the subtitle of its 2005 edition from *A Guide to Customs and Etiquette* to the more daunting *A Survival Guide to Customs and Etiquette* (emphasis added). "Gaining a thorough understanding of a people can take several years of living and working among them," another book warns, "and sometimes not even that is sufficient."[27]

In addition, authors routinely amplify the anxiety and confusion by insisting that Japanese etiquette is a kind of freak-show remnant of rigid feudal pieties "when the social hierarchy dictated how a person spoke, sat, bowed, ate, walked, and lived." Authors admit that things have changed but nevertheless linger over ghoulish tales of retainers who forfeited their lives for a mere whiff of impropriety: "Failure to comply with the rules would bring severe punishment, even death. More than one Japanese literally lost their heads for committing social blunders."[28] The potentially lethal consequences of bad behavior provide a constant leitmotif, but few writers savor the scent of Japan's charnel houses more than Boyé Lafayette De Mente, a one-man Japan publishing industry. In olden times, he relates in any number of his publications, failing to bow with mathematical precision "could result in a death sentence, sometimes carried out on the spot." It seems little consolation that De Mente then tries to buck up the terrified reader by diagramming proper form. Even the Japanese are frightened, and the deadly penalty for failure naturally makes them touchy and unable to bear criticism. "Hardly a year goes by that several ranking executives, shamed by some failure or criticisms, do not take their own lives," De Mente further discourses, and their example is followed by other hypersensitive souls across the nation. "While criticism by foreigners is not likely to bring on a suicide," he cautions, "visitors should nevertheless be careful." And in a chapter on how to apologize, he dusts off a few more feudal corpses, relating that in Old Japan apologies ranged "from the simple *sumimasen* [excuse me] to suicide by a ritualistic slicing open of the abdomen." Readers are surely not much comforted to learn that "some of the more drastic forms of apology are still a distinctive part of contemporary Japanese life."[29] Disembowelment, suicide, apologizing, bowing, beheading, businessmen, and samurai all are jumbled together in a horrifying phantasmagoria of hothouse civility and brutality that leaves alarmed readers in a pitch of wonderment, dismay, and fear.

Rather than generating sympathy and cultural sensitivity, then, guidebooks and travel accounts suggest that the Japanese have distorted etiquette beyond recognition, replacing its benevolent function with a series of malevolent mystifications designed to conceal the truth and to empty human communication of sincerity. "One of the darkest sides of the national soul," writes an English sojourner, is "the habitual lying to preserve appearances."[30] Book after book explains that this culture of fabrication can conveniently be boiled down to a fundamental duality that lies at the heart of all Japanese communication: *tatemae* and *honne*. The former is merely a façade, while the latter is a person's true feelings; the trick is never letting anyone discern the difference between fiction and reality. The natural consequence, however, is a "schizophrenic mental environment," a social and emotional hall of mirrors so discombobulating that not even the Japanese can understand what is actually occurring.[31] More to the point, they do not really care. As a result, they have lost the ability to relate to each other with emotional honesty even in the most intimate settings. One author tells of a female student who confesses that "the most romantic thing she could imagine would be to be kissed in public," yet a merciless code of behavior emasculates her nervy swain and denies her even this crushingly innocent dream.[32] Etiquette has so retarded Japan's emotional maturity that many, such as the widely praised writer Lesley Downer, wonder what capacity the Japanese actually have left to register their feelings at all. "What range of emotions did these people experience?" she ponders. "Different from ours, I suspected."[33] With no way to touch or articulate the profoundest matters of human life, Japan is, writes another, simply "a vast machine without a purpose, a place without a soul."[34]

These shortcomings are, authors explain, compounded and magnified by encountering foreigners whose relaxed, egalitarian approach to human interactions throw their stiff hosts off balance. So acculturated to dissemblance, the Japanese do not know how to respond, making it "of course impossible to impose a Western-style relationship within a Japanese context and assume the same outcomes—especially in matters of the heart." Even those fluent in Western ways of conducting social interactions cannot be fully trusted. It is therefore wise "to remind yourself that, pleasing though it is to be on a positive 'one-to-one' with a Japanese colleague or business partner, the fact remains that this is likely to be purely an intellectual accommodation of Western behavior."[35] More *tatemae*.

Many foreigners convince themselves, however, that their own liberated example will help demonstrate a more authentic way of living, a model the Japanese will then rush to embrace. But we are warned that Japanese etiquette has since feudal times demanded rigidity and conformity and concealment, and this inflexible heritage will not and cannot change. Visitors "should never allow themselves to think that if they persist they can 'break the mold' of centuries-old traditions and mindsets." [36] Instead, readers are reminded that Japanese levels of propriety are an overzealous fiction that they should tolerate while traveling and conducting business but that should not be taken at face value. "Much 'beating around the bush' is done which often leads to misunderstandings and seems like a waste of time to foreigners, but this must be taken into consideration when dealing with the Japanese," sighs one guidebook.[37] The tragedy, of course, is that although the Japanese see an escape route through the West, "our unruliness, our lack of conformity, our ethnic diversity terrify and repel them," as one American sojourner claims, adding, "Yet how they dream of our luxurious freedoms."[38] Even with the unshackled example of the West at their fingertips, even knowing their society "is empty of the individual human content that makes up a much more complete and satisfying emotional and spiritual life," the Japanese remain passive prisoners to their fetid rituals of duty and obedience.[39]

So much for cultural relativism. Ironically, what began as a desire to sensitize readers to differing cultural norms ends up bashing Japan and touting the superiority of the traveler's own society. While all this self-complacent stridency might sound eerily reminiscent of the Victorian era, in fact the deeply personal nature of the frustration with Japanese etiquette, and hence with Japan itself, is quite recent and reflects the historically evolving needs travelers bring to their Japan experience.

For their part, Victorian tourists desired to amass social prestige through travels of comprehensive studiousness. A British guidebook from 1901 noted that "not only is a voyage to the mysterious East . . . essential to complete one's education, but absolutely necessary; for the principal topics and subjects of conversation in all grades of society are often in these days personal reminiscences of journeys to different parts of the world."[40] Not wanting to return home without a stock of charming vignettes, travelers took pride in peering into everything. Their resulting reminiscences and guidebooks were generally expansive compendia of facts about Japanese life rather than self-referential diaries of evolving psychological states. One British account captures the educative nature of travel with its almost comically broad range of index entries; under the letter M, for example, we find: "Mongols," "Monkeys," "Moral Courage, lack of," "Mosquito," "Mothers-in-law, land of," "Mounted infantry," and "Mud, boiling."[41] Etiquette was simply another portion of Japanese life for study and interpretation, not an impediment to a fulfilling travel experience. (E: "Etiquette," "Excitability of the Japanese," "Eyesight, reasons for defective.")[42] Tourists did not feel particularly compelled to gain the intimate confidence of Japanese people, so they rarely concerned themselves with measuring the degree to which politeness or sincerity mediated their encounters. None mentioned *honne* and *tatemae*. Though occasionally speculating that their hosts' disarmingly polite behavior was mere dissembling, they did not much care as long as things went smoothly.[43] "In Japan, as elsewhere, etiquette requires a good many things to be done under feigned pretenses, and on many occasions an affected ignorance of what everybody knows," one author blithely noted.[44] This was considered an occasional bother common to all polite societies rather than a uniquely Japanese problem. In fact, travelers looked forward to the day when Western etiquette would replace Japanese manners not because they thought the little fibs of polite society were so fundamentally damning, but because they hoped that Western manners could provide a common civilized vocabulary to unloose tongues knotted by incompatible languages.

But contemporary travelers want more than mere encyclopedic knowledge. They arrive anticipating an illumination of unseen aspects of themselves, a psychological project they expect the entire nation will take an eager hand in. Japan, writes one traveler, is "where I was always finding out more about myself."[45] The title of Cathy Davidson's widely acclaimed book *36 Views of Mount Fuji: On Finding Myself in Japan*, might more truthfully and economically have been titled *36 Views of Myself*: "I was seeing Japan," she muses, "but I was also seeing myself again."[46] In search of the sword that beheaded the novelist Mishima Yukio, another sojourner writes that the trip would help him "find out things about Mishima, about Japan, and even a little more about myself," and a wandering professor muses that ultimately Japan is about "finding one's way back to oneself."[47] None of their books have an index, tempted though one might be to look under "I."

Hemmed in by rigid rules of etiquette, however, the Japanese are unable to generate the human sincerity required to help travelers find deeper levels of self-awareness. Old women in deeply rural areas who dispense salt-of-the-earth feminism and disdain the polite pleasantries of urban society have achieved a devoted following among some travel writers.[48] Yet they are a small pool of authenticity amid the wide glassine surfaces of polished propriety. The majority of travelers go and return with little assurance that the nice people they met and the moving experiences they had were emotionally sincere encounters rather than merely plastic smiles and canned clichés. The Japanese will not tell them—and even if they did, *tatemae* and *honne* would never disperse the clouds of doubt. This robs travelers of their authentic encounter with the "real" Japanese people because, as the guidebooks ultimately suggest, there *are* no real Japanese people. They are simply actors in a never-ending performance who have forgotten that the proscenium, the props, and the lines are all fantasy. Japan is a flim-flam society.

The deeply charged emotional dynamic created by this lingering psychological drama means that guidebooks and travel narratives often take etiquette as a highly personal affront. The British academic Simon May, for example, laments that "though the Japanese are wonderfully loyal, hospitable, courteous and kind, they seldom reciprocate a foreigner's *love*."[49] Aside from describing the qualities of an ideal servant rather than a friend, May's *cri de coeur* reveals that the central "problem" with Japanese etiquette, and therefore with Japan, is that it refuses to cooperate in the psychological needs of the modern traveling public. But rather than questioning whether tourists have in fact freighted their vacations with excess emotional baggage, they instead collectively blame the Japanese and their entire culture—from feudal times to the present—for denying them "authentic" encounters that stretch the boundaries of self-awareness. Instead, any failures of human communication not caused by a traveler's chauvinistic indifference to Japanese etiquette are ultimately blamed on the dysfunctions of Japanese society.

In the end, Victorians travelers, for all their pig-headedness, nevertheless remind us that Japanese etiquette is a relatively recently discovered "problem," one that reveals more about the modern traveler's anxieties and needs than it does about weaknesses in Japanese society.

NOTES

1. Quoted in Michael Cooper, ed., *They Came to Japan: An Anthology of European Reports on Japan, 1543–1640* (Berkeley: University of California Press, 1965), 195.

2. Sir Rutherford Alcock, *The Capital of the Tycoon: A Narrative of a Three Years' Residence in Japan*, vol. 2 (New York: Greenwood, 1863), 329.

3. Harry A. Franck, *Glimpses of Japan and Formosa* (New York: The Century Company, 1924), 74.

4. Helmut Morsbach, *Customs and Etiquette of Japan*, 3rd ed. (London: Bravo, 2005), 28.

5. Boyé Lafayette De Mente, *Etiquette Guide to Japan: Know the Rules That Make the Difference!* (Tokyo: Tuttle Publishing, 1990), 40; Morsbach, *Customs and Etiquette of Japan*, 9.

6. Simon May, *Atomic Sushi: Notes from the Heart of Japan* (Surrey, U.K.: Alma Books, 2006), 64.

7. See, for example, Sean P. Bramble, *Culture Shock! Japan: A Survival Guide to Customs and Etiquette* (Portland, Ore.: Graphic Arts Center Publishing, 2005), 97–99, and Morsbach, *Customs and Etiquette of Japan*, 40–41, which repeat in form and sometimes exact wording advice on gift-giving. Who plagiarized whom would require further investigation.

8. Charles MacFarlane, *Japan: An Account, Geographical and Historical* (New York: George P. Putnam, 1852), 276. See also Foster Rhea Dulles, *Yankees and Samurai: America's Role in the Emergence of Modern Japan, 1791–1900* (New York: Harper and Row, 1965), 68–69.

9. Richard Hildreth, *Japan and the Japanese* (Boston: Bradley, Dayton, 1860), v.

10. *New York Times*, December 2, 1869, 2.

11. Frances Parkinson Keyes, "From the Land of the Rising Sun," *Good Housekeeping* 82 (January 1926): 140.

12. Quoted in Hugh Cortazzi, *Victorians in Japan: In and around the Treaty Ports* (London: Athlone, 1987), 346–347.

13. Basil Hall Chamberlain and W. B. Mason, *Handbook for Travellers in Japan*, 7th ed. (London: John Murray, 1903).

14. Keyes, "From the Land of the Rising Sun," 140. Here I am relying on John Kasson's observation of the ways in which etiquette helps avoid "semiotic breakdown" amid confusing claims to social identity. John Kasson, *Rudeness and Civility: Manners in Nineteenth-Century Urban America* (New York: Hill and Wang, 1990), 70 and passim.

15. M. William Steele and Tamiko Ichimata, eds., *Clara's Diary: An American Girl in Meiji Japan* (Tokyo: Kōdansha, 1979), 44.

16. Quoted in Satsuki Kawano, "Japanese bodies and Western ways of seeing in the late nineteenth century," in *Dirt, Undress and Difference: Critical Perspectives on the Body's Surface*, ed. Adeline Marie Masquelier (Bloomington: Indiana University Press, 2005), 157. See also Edward Seidensticker, *Low City, High City. Tokyo from Edo to the Earthquake: How the Shogun's Ancient Capital Became a Great Modern City, 1867–1923* (New York: Alfred A. Knopf, 1983), 92.

17. Steele and Ichimata, *Clara's Diary*, 52, 126.

18. Welcome Society of Japan (*Kihin-kai*), *Guidebook for Tourists in Japan*, 5th ed. (Tokyo: Tokyo Chamber of Commerce, 1910), xxix, iii, 230–245.

19. Steele and Ichimata, *Clara's Diary*, 92–93. To be fair, as Whitney extended her stay over several years (1875–1880) her attitudes toward the Japanese and their customs modified into acceptance and often admiration. The quotations in this essay are taken from the period not long after her arrival, reflecting the more common opinion of travelers who spent only limited time in Japan.

20. For an early example of this anthropological and historical interest, see J. M. Dixon, "Japanese Etiquette," *Transactions of the Asiatic Society of Japan*, 13 (1885): 1–21.

21. Paul Norbury, *Culture Smart! Japan: The Essential Guide to Customs and Culture*, rev. ed. (London: Kuperard, 2008), 19.

22. Dean Engel and Ken Murakami, *Passport Japan: Your Pocket Guide to Japanese Business, Customs and Etiquette*, 2nd ed. (Novato, Calif.: World Trade Press, 2003), 44–45, 67–68.

23. Bun Nakajima, *Japanese Etiquette* (Tokyo: Japan Travel Bureau, 1955); World Fellowship Committee of the Young Women's Christian Association of Tokyo, Japan, *Japanese Etiquette: An Introduction* (Rutland, Vt.: Charles E. Tuttle, 1955).

24. Eugene Fodor and Robert C. Fisher, eds., *Fodor's Japan and Korea* (New York: David McKay, 1977), 48.

25. Lonely Planet's first Japan guide appeared in 1981. For more on the rise and dominance of Lonely Planet, see Tad Friend, "The Parachute Artist: Have Tony Wheeler's Guidebooks Travelled Too Far?" *The New Yorker*, April 8, 2005.

26. Bramble, *Culture Shock! Japan*, back cover; David Mura, *Turning Japanese: Memoirs of a Sansei* (New York: Atlantic Monthly Press, 1991; Grove, 2006), 41 [from the 2006 edition]. Here I am relying on Erving Goffman's notion of "bounded regions" of social performance, particularly his division of "front" and "back stage." Erving Goffman, *The Presentation of Self in Everyday Life* (New York: Anchor Books, 1959), 106–140.

27. Engel and Murakami, *Passport Japan*, 7.

28. Both quotes from Beth Reiber and Janie Spencer, *Frommer's Japan*, 9th ed. (Hoboken, N.J.: Wiley Publishing, 2008), 621.

29. De Mente, *Etiquette Guide to Japan*, 35, 77, 87.

30. May, *Atomic Sushi*, 47.

31. Norbury, *Culture Smart! Japan*, 43–44.

32. Bramble, *Culture Shock! Japan*, 37.

33. Lesley Downer, *On the Narrow Road: Journey into a Lost Japan* (New York: Summit Books, 1989), 152.

34. Peregrine Hodson, *A Circle around the Sun: A Foreigner in Japan* (London: Mandarin, 1992), 276.

35. Norbury, *Culture Smart! Japan*, 136.

36. Both quotes are from Norbury, *Culture Smart! Japan*, 150.

37. Scott Rutherford, *Insight Guide, Japan*, 3rd ed. (Singapore: Insight Guides, 2003), 353.

38. J. D. Brown, *The Sudden Disappearance of Japan: Journeys through a Hidden Land* (Santa Barbara, Calif.: Capra, 1994), 96.

39. De Mente, *Japan Unmasked*, 213–214.

40. Frank Charlton, *The Eastern Traveller's Guide* (London: Wm. Clowes and Sons, 1901), xiii.

41. Kate Lawson, *Highways and Homes of Japan* (London: T. Fisher Unwin, 1910), 348.

42. Ibid., 345.

43. For some examples of this suspicion, see G. Waldo Browne, *Japan: The Place and the People* (Boston: Dana Estes, 1904), 62; Pat Barr, *The Deer Cry Pavilion: A Story of Westerners in Japan, 1868–1905* (London: Macmillan, 1968), 193; Steele and Ichimata, *Clara's Diary*, 63, 67. My larger point about the lack of

concern for sincerity among Victorian travelers follows the conclusions of Karen Halttunen, *Confidence Men and Painted Ladies: A Study of Middle-Class Culture in America, 1830–1870* (New Haven, Conn.: Yale University Press, 1982), 153–190.

44. Hildreth, *Japan and the Japanese*, 482–483.

45. Laura J. Kriska, *The Accidental Office Lady* (Rutland, Vt.: Tuttle, 1997), 302.

46. Cathy Davidson, *36 Views of Mount Fuji: On Finding Myself in Japan* (New York: Dutton, 1993), 13.

47. Christopher Ross, *Mishima's Sword: Travels in Search of a Samurai Legend* (London: Fourth Estate, 2006), 146; May, *Atomic Sushi*, 3.

48. See, for example, Downer, *On the Narrow Road*, Davidson, *36 Views of Mount Fuji*; Karin Muller, *Japanland: A Year in Search of "Wa"* (Emmaus, Penn.: Rodale, 2005).

49. May, *Atomic Sushi*, 205–206, emphasis in original.

CHAPTER 5

A Dinner Party Is Not a Revolution

Space, Gender, and Hierarchy in Meiji Japan

SALLY A. HASTINGS

My title is a play on Mao Zedong's dictum that a revolution is not a dinner party. In his 1927 "Report on an Investigation of the Hunan Peasant Movement," Mao wrote that revolution "cannot be anything so refined, so calm and gentle, or so mild, kind, courteous, restrained and magnanimous" as inviting people to dinner, writing an essay, painting a picture, or doing fancy needlework. A revolution, he wrote, "is an act of violence whereby one class overthrows another."[1]

In this essay, I borrow and invert Mao's imagery to discuss international and gender relations in late nineteenth-century Japan. Whereas Mao confidently assumed that dinner parties operated in accordance with well-established (if unimportant) rituals, in the late nineteenth-century encounter between Japan and the great powers of the West, the dinner party was a contested site. Proper behavior at Western-style dinner parties was one of the standards by which Westerners judged Japanese women, and thus the level of Japanese civilization. Official banquets were among the few occasions when Western visitors and residents of Japan could observe Japanese women directly and thus form their judgments about the level of Japanese civilization, for few foreigners penetrated the privacy of the Japanese home. Moreover, it was primarily in dining rooms, both in Japan and abroad, that Japanese men and women learned about gender relations in Western society.

Consideration of the dinner party complicates our understanding of Japanese women's participation in modernity by challenging the binary opposites of home and outside world, private and public life. In the late nineteenth-century West, the dining room and the parlor constituted a third type of space, one in which both men and women had a legitimate place, albeit not on equal terms. Moreover, this was a semi-public space in which a family interacted with non-family members of both genders.[2] Let us use "dinner party," then, as shorthand for what Louisa May Alcott referred to as "dinners, balls, calls, etc."—namely, the social space in which respectable men and women could gather together for food, entertainment, and conversation.[3] Although contemporary observers often commented on the food itself, the utensils with which it was eaten, the national origin of the chef, and whether one sat on chairs or on the floor, my interest is in the gendered social arrangements of these affairs. The Japanese and Western men and women who met in this space were, of course, of the very privileged classes. It was precisely these classes who were engaged in imagining civilization, more particularly Japanese civilization. Moreover, both the Japanese and their Western observers assumed that the elite were the essence of Japan; the miserable conditions of the poor were presumed to be much the same everywhere.[4]

It goes without saying that the Japanese experience of dinner parties took place in a world that was rapidly becoming divided between colonizer and colonized. Although never formally colonized, Japan was subject from 1854 to 1894 (and in limited respects until 1911) to "unequal treaties," or what several historians have termed "informal imperialism."[5] In the 1880s the Japanese government sponsored dinner parties and balls at the Rokumeikan (literally, "Deer Cry Pavilion"), a government guesthouse designed by a British architect. Conventional histories of modern Japan make passing mention of the rise and fall of the era of the dinner party, that is, the social events held at the Rokumeikan. These histories, however, fail to treat the balls and dinner parties as part of the discourse on the construction of gender in modern Japan.[6] Rather, these entertainments figure only as examples of indiscriminate, uncritical imitation of the West. The decline of costume balls and dinner parties is credited to a nationalist reaction.[7] If, however, we take seriously the importance of gender as a category of analysis, the Japanese staging of balls and dinner parties cannot be dismissed as a misguided imitation of superficialities. Rather, Japanese government officials implemented the reforms of social life in the Rokumeikan era precisely because they understood, as recent studies on formal imperialism have demonstrated, how important gender relations were to the Western conceptualization of civilization.[8] The Japanese rejection of the dinner party as a ritual for ordinary couples merits investigation as to exactly what values were being either rejected or preserved. This study of dinner parties, then, allows us to explore how the informally colonized Japanese "refashioned and contested European claims to superiority."[9]

EARLY ENCOUNTERS

The differences between Japanese and Western social customs became apparent as soon as Japan established formal diplomatic relations with the Western powers in the 1850s. Diplomacy required formal dinners, and the residences of Westerners in Japan required dining rooms. Townsend Harris, the first U.S. consul to Japan, had one in his "consulate general" in Shimoda in the 1850s, and William C. Whitney, who arrived in Japan in 1875 to help found Japan's first commercial college, had a dining room in every home his family occupied.[10]

When Townsend Harris arrived in Shimoda in 1857, the governors of the province invited him and his party to dinner. Henry Heusken, Harris's Dutch interpreter, noted with regret that there were no women present:

> The absence of man's angel of mercy gives a sort of emptiness, a certain sadness to the Governors' dinner. Had some noble Japanese matron been hostess at the table, had we been able to dance a polka with the Governors' daughters, what a good time we would have had! What a dismal life the poor Japanese officers must lead, forced as they are by a suspicious and cruel law to forsake that which makes the charm of existence.[11]

When Heusken visited a year later, he was again informed that custom forbade women to be present.[12]

The Japanese who visited the United States in 1860 as part of the first Japanese official mission found American customs equally mystifying. During their stay in San Francisco, the delegates were surprised that women were among those who arrived at their hotel to pay official respects. It had not occurred to the Japanese that the women were the wives and daughters of officials.[13] In Washington, the Japanese delegates were invited to numerous receptions, dinners, and dances where, to their surprise, they found women to be an essential part of the public festivities in their honor. They were astonished to find that their responsibilities as guests at the president's banquet included accompanying a lady to dinner. At a party sponsored by Secretary of State Lewis Cass, one Japanese delegate felt as though he had arrived on another planet when he observed men and women moving about the room on their toes like Japanese dancing mice. Although they admired the women's dresses, the Japanese concluded that dancing was "nothing but interesting hopping about the room."[14]

Even more puzzling than the mysteries of dancing were the expressions of gender hierarchy that the Japanese observed at social gatherings. If both men and women were present in a room, one must greet the women first. On a street, men gave way to women. Men had to remove their hats to greet women. One member of the 1860 delegation concluded, "American ladies are treated in such a way as we respect our parents."[15] More than a decade later, a member of the Iwakura Mission of 1871–1873 expressed similar bewilderment:

> In Japan the wife serves her husband's parents, a child serves its father and mother, but here it is the practice for the husband to serve the wife. He gets a lamp for her, he fetches her shoes, he offers her food, he brushes her clothes. When she sits down, he helps her, when she gets up, he helps her. When she wants to sit, he offers a chair, and when she is about to go out, he offers her what she needs. If he should incur the least anger from his wife, he shows affection, he shows respect, he begs her pardon on bended knees. If she still won't listen to him, he is obliged to leave the room, and it sometimes happens that he does not get anything to eat.[16]

When they were invited into homes, the Japanese delegates were surprised to find that the wife presided as hostess while the husband busied himself with miscellaneous tasks. The wife, said one, "was just like the head of the family."[17] These manners obscured, of course, the fact that married women in the United States had far fewer economic and legal rights than their husbands. Japanese who visited Westerners resident in Japan were equally astounded to be received by a woman. When their host explained to them that "it was the European custom for the ladies to preside and even take the place of honor at table," the Japanese quickly adjusted, so that when other male guests arrived and shook hands with the hostess, "however astonished they might have felt, their countenances betrayed no wonder."[18]

The mutual surprise experienced by Japanese and Westerners at formal social gatherings was the product of differing assumptions about the gendered nature of public space. The Japanese expected that only men would be present at official ceremonies, whereas Westerners assumed that formal celebrations were extensions of the dinner parties they held in their own homes. They expected that the presiding official and his wife would invite appropriate public figures and their wives. It soon became apparent to U.S. observers, however, that Japanese men did not take their wives with them when they went out, either to government ceremonies or to friends' homes. Townsend Harris observed in 1858, "The wives of the upper classes never make visits, not even to relatives."[19] Clara Whitney, an American girl who accompanied her father to Japan in the 1870s, noted that Japanese women seldom appeared in public with men and that they in fact did little calling after they were married.[20]

In these earliest diplomatic encounters, both Japanese and Westerners reacted to the discovery of cultural differences by assuming that their own practice was superior. On being introduced to a daimyō's daughter, Clara Whitney wrote in her diary, "I often wish that some of these narrow-minded women could mingle with and see the delightful freedom in American society and the social gatherings of the sexes where knightly chivalry is shown towards women, and a woman's opinion is held as of much account as that of a man. . . . I'm glad I am an American girl and not a daimyō's lady."[21] The Japanese were no less certain of the correctness of their own position. A U.S. ship captain in Japan invited officials who had taken part in the 1860 mission to the United States to visit his ship together with their wives and children. One of those invited, Muragaki Norimasa, wrote in his diary that "it is because he still does not know the customs of our country that he, in conformance with his own customs, should have made such a suggestion."[22] Shibata Takenaka, an official who took part in the embassy that the Tokugawa shogun sent to Europe in 1864, found Westerners' habit of arriving with their wives "hateful." When two English guests whom he invited to his hotel brought their wives, he concluded that "their only conceivable purpose was to get a look at our party."[23]

In the 1870s the more astute observers on both sides could see that the Western practice of dinner parties was related to patterns of courtship, patterns that were different in Japan. On the one hand, Shibusawa Ei'ichi, when he was among the members of the shogun's delegation to the Paris Universal Exposition in 1867, attended a ball at a French minister's house. He observed, "These gatherings are not solely for the purpose of promoting friendly relations between people; they also enable the young to assess the appearance and, by conversation, the intelligence of potential spouses."[24] On the other hand, Clara Whitney wrote of the Japanese, "Here the youth of the two sexes keep entirely separated and never mingle as we do, and they couldn't very well, for the morals, manners, etc., are so different from those at home. A girl *must* marry whom her parents will and, as she sees very little of other men, she does not know what it is to love until after she is married."[25]

The experiences of the Whitney family illustrate how difficult it was for both Americans and Japanese to change either their thinking or their behavior. In 1875 the Whitney family invited many Japanese friends to their home for a Christmas celebration. Mr. Whitney tried to introduce some of the Japanese young men and women to each other, but he was unsuccessful. Clara wrote in her diary, "Ladies and gentleman in Japan never meet in social circles as they do in America, and it is not propriety for the sexes to mingle in society unless the gentlemen wish to marry. So not even American customs could reconcile this old prejudice."[26] Clara and her mother, for their part, were shocked to find that their friend Mrs. Tomita had agreed to look for wives for two of their Japanese male acquaintances. Clara lectured Mrs. Tomita soundly, terming such behavior "dishonorable" and the practice of having go-betweens "shameful." Clara afterward confided to her diary, "How thankful I am that I received birth and education in dear, free America where such things are never heard of."[27]

There are a few important observations to make about these early encounters. First, the Japanese, especially those who traveled abroad, were aware that Japanese practices with respect to clothing, marriage, and public etiquette affected how Westerners perceived the degree of civilization in Japan. As a member of the 1862 mission to Europe, Ichikawa Wataru was proud of how highly Europeans esteemed Japanese lacquer, but he was embarrassed in Cologne to see a display of pictures of scantily clad Japanese workers.[28] Shibusawa Ei'ichi was disturbed to find that "when foreigners discuss Japanese customs, they say that the Japanese normally have no recourse to activities of the mind, but are solely addicted to pleasures of the flesh."[29] He himself favorably compared the monogamy of the West with the 480 concubines of the Turkish sultans; presumably he ranked Japan somewhere in between.[30] Ichikawa and Shibusawa were correct in their assessment that Westerners noticed nudity and "licentiousness." Western descriptions of Japan were filled with images of nearly naked workers, promiscuous mixed bathing, obscene pictures, concubines, prostitutes, and nude women diving for pearls.[31]

Second, international encounters generated new modes of behavior. The British minister to Japan, Sir Harry Parkes, sailed through the archipelago with his wife. When his ship called at Uwajima in 1866, Prince Date, the local daimyō, gave a dinner for Sir Harry and Lady Parkes.

The officers of the Parkes's ship, *Princess Royal*, were pleased when the princesses and the ladies of the household were introduced, undoubtedly a concession to the presence of Lady Parkes.[32]

The third point is a cautionary note about the sources themselves. Observers on both sides engaged in essentialism, both about themselves and about the "other." In their discussions of gender, writers employed absolutes that were transparently counterfactual. Clara Whitney repeatedly asserts that Japanese men and women "never meet in social circles," "never mingle," and "keep entirely separated."[33] At the same time, her diary is filled with examples of couples who came to dine at the Whitney's home and of Japanese who invited the Whitneys to dinner as a family. Kume Kunitake, in his report on the Iwakura Mission, makes passing mention of Dr. Mary Walker, a Civil War battlefield physician who routinely dressed in men's clothing. He immediately adds, "In the teachings of the Orient, the woman rules within [the home] but she has no role outside it."[34] Kume's assertion that Japanese women had no role outside the home was contradicted by any number of Western reports of Japanese women working in the fields.[35]

Essentialism, hierarchy, and accommodation to the West all figure in the memoirs of Julia Dent Grant. The wife of President Ulysses S. Grant, she made a world tour with her husband in 1879. Mrs. Grant was not an advocate of either equal education or equal rights for women; on the contrary, she had no shame about her ignorance of both Roman numerals and the American constitution. Nevertheless, she was shocked to discover the seclusion of Eastern women. In Cairo the Khedive did not include his wife in the banquet that he gave in honor of General Grant. Mrs. Grant declared that the custom preventing Egyptian women from attending such gatherings was hard and unjust: "In America we would not consent to such an unjust custom. We always were present at the entertainments given by our husbands if any women were.[36]

The Japanese government used the visit of the Grants to display its understanding of the social world of the dinner party and thus its entitlement to a high position in the hierarchy of nations. In her memoirs, Mrs. Grant explicitly mentioned Japanese wives in attendance at a theatrical entertainment and a farewell banquet, and they were probably also present at a number of other festivities the Grants attended. When Minister of War Saigō Tsugumichi met the Grants at the scenic shrine at Nikkō, his wife joined him. The wives of Yoshida Kiyonari and Mori Arinori saw the Grants off when they left Yokohama.[37]

THE ERA OF TREATY REVISION

From the time the Harris Treaty of 1858 came into effect, Japan had sought to negotiate more favorable conditions in its relationship with the Western powers. Treaty revision had been the primary purpose of the Iwakura Expedition of 1871. From the late 1870s on, there was a widely shared understanding in Japan that in order to favorably impress Western observers, the treatment of women needed to be changed. As the educator Hatoyama Haruko recalled the year 1884 in her autobiography, "It was the era of preparation for treaty revision, and for the sake of revision, it was necessary that Japan win recognition that it was civilized in every respect; towards that end, we had to remove every trace of barbarian customs oppressing women."[38]

Some of the efforts of the Japanese government to demonstrate the high level of civilization in Japan were directed toward accommodating the social world of the dinner party. Members of the international community rejoiced in 1879 when Japanese women began to appear at parties, and Minister of Foreign Affairs Inoue Kaoru issued an invitation jointly with his wife to a reception in honor of the emperor's birthday.[39] The birthday celebration became an annual event, as did cherry blossom parties in the spring.[40]

The most striking representation of the government's determination to demonstrate Japanese competence in Western rituals was the construction of a two-story brick building called the Rokumeikan in 1883. Here, Japanese officials could meet with foreigners in dining rooms, parlors, and ballrooms to dine, play cards or billiards, dance, or listen to music.[41] In the spring of 1884, Japanese women held a bazaar at the Rokumeikan to benefit a charity hospital.[42] That fall, when Inoue invited members of the international community to a ball to celebrate the emperor's birthday, he invited them to the Rokumeikan.[43]

In keeping with the increasingly Western style of public celebrations, the empress adopted Western clothing for public events in 1886. The other women of the imperial family, her ladies-in-waiting, and the wives of officials were required to follow suit. This change brought Japanese women's official attire into conformity with men's; the emperor and his officials had adopted Western dress in 1872. In addition, the change to Paris fashions eliminated any question as to whether women should be attired in the court dress of the empress or in the kimono style of samurai women.[44]

In the West the dinner party was an extension into the public realm of a domestic ritual. Western couples dined with their families and apart from their servants in dining rooms within their homes. When they entertained other couples, they incorporated the guests into a more formal (often exclusively adult) version of this ritual. In Japan, meals were served on individual trays rather than at table, a point on which the Japanese prided themselves. The family patriarch did not necessarily eat in the same room or at the same time as his family, and his wife and children might share their meal with the servants.[45] Thus, in staging public dinner parties, the Meiji political leaders were initiating the elite into an unfamiliar rite.

The proliferation of dinner parties and balls in Tokyo in the 1880s did not occur solely at state initiative. During more than two decades of foreign residence, diplomats, merchants, and missionaries provided models of "civilized" social life. Japanese men who had traveled abroad built houses with dining rooms and hosted events with their wives. In her autobiography, Hatoyama Haruko claimed that the party that she and her husband Kazuo hosted in late 1881 was the first Western-style marriage announcement banquet in Japan. The entertainment ranged from American Civil War ballads to Nō chants.[46] About a year later, on December 12, 1883, Minister of War Ōyama Iwao and his wife hosted a ball at the Rokumeikan to celebrate their marriage.[47] The Western-style wing that the statesman Matsukata Masayoshi built onto his Tokyo house included a dining room.[48]

At these many dinner parties, Western visitors met Japanese wives, whom they often found wanting as dinner partners. The German physician Erwin Baelz once sought out his host's eighteen-year-old daughter, preferring her informal liveliness to the company of the distinguished ladies, "who were all slaves of etiquette."[49] In contrast, Baelz declared geisha to be "intellectually and aesthetically the most cultured section of the women of Japan."[50] Other Westerners shared his views on the relative merits of wives and geisha. The American scientist Edward S. Morse described geisha as "good-natured, witty and sprightly girls . . . who earn their living by entertaining at dinners and are far better company than the usual run of girls and women at home."[51]

The number of social events, their novelty, and their link to official policy provoked lively debate. Fukuzawa Yukichi, a noted educator and writer, contributed to these discussions in a number of editorials in the newspaper he edited.[52] Fukuzawa's main emphasis was on establishing equality between husband and wife. He wanted legal reform that would give women property rights and equal access to divorce, plus social reform that would allow them to assume more responsibility in society. He criticized Japanese-style parties, where women were forced to sit separately like attendants, with no opportunity to socialize with men on equal terms.[53] He rejected, however, existing Western practices. "In the West, women's behavior sometimes goes beyond control: they make light of men, their minds are sharp, but their thoughts may be tarnished and their personal behavior unchaste; they may neglect their own homes and flutter about society like butterflies. Such behavior is no model for Japanese women.[54]

In contrast to his eloquence on behalf of equality in marriage, Fukuzawa was rather cynical about how to handle the institutions of concubinage and prostitution. Assuming that it was futile to expect men to reform, he asked that appearances be maintained, "that men hide all traces of their immoral behavior."[55] Such subterfuge was necessary because of the power of the West: "The whole world is dominated by Western civilization today, and anyone who opposes it will be ostracized from the human society; a nation, too, will find itself outside the world circle of nations."[56] At the heart of this cynical approach was Fukuzawa's recognition that the West, which set high moral standards for others, did not live up to them.

Beneath his cynicism, however, Fukuzawa was genuinely in favor of equal, monogamous marriages. His objection to concubinage was that it was often based on a payment to the woman's family, and "a marriage involving buying and selling is not compatible with civilized practice."[57] He wanted concubines concealed. He invoked his specialized knowledge of the West, saying,

> I have visited some of the civilized countries and have seen the actual conditions in each. I have also heard from friends and read books. If I am to discuss the actual truths, there are many points that must be raised, but as far as outward appearances are concerned, there is not a single Western civilized country that exhibits the filth seen in Japan. I cannot bear this shame, for it reflects the total ignorance and backwardness of our citizens.[58]

Fukuzawa knew, however, that the invisibility of prostitutes in the landscape of Western countries was from artifice rather than from purity: "In the West, the number of prostitutes is very large and their business prospers, but the decorative techniques used are very thorough, and nothing is revealed to the public eyes. No one talks about it, and no one hears about it."[59]

Fukuzawa did not share the enthusiasm of the German Baelz and the American Morse for the geisha. He criticized Japanese men who had studied abroad and yet allowed geisha at their parties: "They enjoy the geisha's entertainments or take part in their games, never embarrassed by lewd talk or suggestive gestures, drinking and talking, laughing, yelling, and in extreme cases, lying down and sleeping, not caring if these women, a dozen of them, begin undressing near him."[60] Prostitution, however, he treats as a necessary evil: "Prostitution is indeed lowly, ugly, and for the person who practices it, must be both physically and spiritually degrading. However, in our society today, it cannot be abolished. Rather, society depends on it for the preservation of order."[61] Fukuzawa wanted prostitutes, like concubines, hidden from sight.[62]

Fukuzawa is particularly critical of Japanese men who married former geisha and prostitutes, as a number of officials of the Meiji government had done. There is thus implicit political criticism in Fukuzawa's prescription for parties. First, he wanted to exclude concubines, including those elevated to the position of wife, from polite society. Second, he wanted geisha banned from parties.[63] Erwin Baelz shared Fukuzawa's notion that wives and geisha did not belong at the same party. Baelz was very uneasy when, at the home of a prince, geisha entered a party where the prince's mother, wife, and daughter were in attendance:

> I was really distressed to see these wenches behaving as if they were quite at home, laughing loudly, clapping to applaud the dances, and so on, whereas the ladies of rank were extremely reserved and modest in their behaviour. . . . I was sorry to see these young ladies, in accordance with old Japanese custom, circulating among the guests and pressing sake upon them, tasting it themselves first in the usual way.[64]

Fukuzawa promoted the creation of dining rooms and parlors in Japan, in the sense that those terms designate a space, either in public buildings or within the home, where men and women can meet as equals. He decried the tyranny of Japanese men, who, far from recognizing a separate sphere, "declare themselves the sole masters of their homes, claiming authority over the parlor, the bedroom, and every corner of the kitchen."[65] He pointed out that "even when we say women manage the households, what they truly manage is the innermost part only and their power does not reach out to the part that faces out."[66] He lamented the fact that social oppression kept young men and women apart, and he blamed men's patronization of brothels on "the lack of opportunities for men to enjoy normal and platonic associations with women."[67] Fukuzawa was not alone in these views. Other male reformers, such as the liberal Ueki Emori, the Christian educator Iwamoto Yoshiharu, and the Christian thinker Uchimura Kanzō, all argued for a home in which the wife presided with her husband over the household.[68]

Thanks to diaries and letters, we have some insight into how women of the era evaluated the dinner parties of the 1880s. In 1880 Clara Whitney's family was invited to a private party at a Shinbashi teahouse, where geisha were present. When the entertainers first sang and danced, Clara found them playful and ladylike and so "had a good opinion of the dancing girls and thought they were not so bad after all." In the course of the evening, however, she changed her opinion: "The dance after supper was so disgusting that I lost forever the good opinion I had had of dancing girls, for be they ever so pretty they cannot be good." Her Japanese friend, a Christian married woman, linked the attractions of the geisha to the problems of concubinage and prostitution: "You see now why Japanese young men are so often bad. They like geisha who do bad things."[69]

For the Japanese women who had studied in the United States, the struggle for the dinner party became synonymous with the struggle of wives against concubines, geisha, and prostitutes. Yamakawa Sutematsu, a Vassar graduate and the first Japanese woman to graduate from a U.S. college, showed that she had absorbed the ideal that women should maintain the purity of society when she wrote to an American friend in 1883,

> I refuse all the invitations I possibly [can,] but when I am invited by the Japanese I generally go for as a rule Japanese ladies are so retiring that they never go to parties and consequently when the ladies are not present men are not so careful of their behavior as they might be. I think the women should learn to mingle with men more and use their influence so that men won't go for singing girls and such for their amusement.[70]

When Sutematsu decided to marry General Ōyama Iwao, Sutematsu's friend Tsuda Umeko wrote to an American about what "wonderful good" Sutematsu could do as an official's wife "when all the other great men's wives are former geishas."[71] A few years later (1887), Tsuda wrote in a letter to the United States that she and Sutematsu were dismayed that geisha appeared at social events and that "these women did all the entertaining, leaving nothing to the ladies to do in reality, and by their appearing in society and mingling with men, they become first the mistresses and finally the true wives of the finest and highest ranked gentleman." She added, "Such was the case with Mrs. Ito, Mrs. Kuki, Mrs. Yoshida, and dozens of others, while the young girls are left in the cold."[72]

The concern shared by Fukuzawa, Ōyama, and Tsuda about geisha-turned-wives highlights their ideal of the dining room as a space in which men and women could socialize together, either as married couples or as young adults in search of suitable marriage partners. Enlightened Japanese women perceived the presence of geisha at dinner parties as a threat to male morality and the practice of monogamy in Japan. They may also have feared that they themselves would be categorized as sexual objects to be toyed with. The prominence of former geisha as glittering lights of Rokumeikan life reinforced Japanese suspicions that Western manners forced respectable women to perform in public in roles normally reserved for geisha. Even more frightening, if parlors and dinner parties became the space in which marriage partners were chosen, how would respectable women compete with geisha for positions as brides? Alice Mabel Bacon, a close friend of Ōyama and Tsuda, gave articulate expression to the idea that the geisha was a rival to the respectable woman for the position of wife:

> So fascinating, bright, and lively are these geishas that many of them have been taken by men of good position as wives, and are now the heads of the most respectable homes. Without true education or morals, but trained thoroughly in all the arts and accomplishments that please,—witty, quick at repartee, pretty, and always well dressed,—the géisha has proved a formidable rival for the demure, quiet maiden of good family, who can only give her husband an unsullied name, silent obedience, and faithful service all her life.[73]

The staging of balls and dinner parties declined significantly in the 1890s. The Rokumeikan was sold to a private club, and many Japanese women reverted to Japanese dress, even for public appearances.[74] Dinner parties, which had risen in favor as the Japanese pursued treaty revision, declined in popularity when opponents of the government decried cultural concessions to the West. In 1887 and 1888 there was vigorous debate in Japan over proposals for treaty revision. Minister of Commerce and Agriculture Tani Kanjō severely criticized the proposals that Inoue Kaoru had offered to the Western powers for treaty revision. Tani's resignation from the cabinet forced Inoue to resign and withdraw his proposals, which had included the appointment of foreign judges. In these debates, the Rokumeikan became a symbol of cultural subservience to the West, and the emergence of this conservative critique of westernization marks the end of the Rokumeikan era.[75]

Although it was certainly not the deciding factor in inhibiting balls and dinner parties, we should note that many Westerners reacted negatively to the Rokumeikan activities, particularly to Japanese women wearing Western dress. Edwin Dun was an American who went to Japan as a government employee in 1873, married a Japanese woman, and remained there except for brief intervals until his death in 1931. He considered Japanese women's adoption of Western dress "an unforgivable crime against good taste," and he was not alone.[76] Many Westerners, gazing at Japan as the Oriental "other," wanted it to remain "other." Tsuda Umeko, who in so many other respects was an advocate of reform, echoed these sentiments, saying about the proposal to change the empress's clothing to Paris styles that the Japanese would "make themselves a laughing stock by too much imitation of the foreigners."[77]

Western actions did far more, however, than any reaction to the Rokumeikan to undermine the claims of Western nations to moral superiority. When the English freighter *Normanton* sank, the crew escaped in lifeboats, allowing the twenty-three Japanese passengers to be lost with the ship. Initially, the consular court at Kobe exonerated the captain, although at a retrial he was given a three-month sentence.[78] The retrial can be credited to the vigorous press, which accused the British of treating the Japanese like luggage and which was quick to link the incident to the issue of treaty revision.[79] The Japanese scholar Hirakawa Sukehiro has noted that what really provoked the Japanese public was the failure of the West to adhere to its own standards.[80] Fukuzawa made the same argument when he pointed out that Western condemnations of concubinage and prostitution took no account of the existence of the same institutions in Western society. After the *Normanton* case, there seemed less justification than ever in subservience to such hypocrisy.

CONCLUSION

In and of themselves, dinner parties and balls were certainly not revolutionary. On the contrary, "knightly chivalry" might be termed counterrevolutionary, a turn toward the Western past. Certainly, the Meiji feminist Kishida Toshiko was sharply critical of adopting chivalrous manners without making any change in society.[81] Although dinner parties would not have revolutionized Japan, they would have been an admirable reform. Their institution would have been one step toward marriages centered on the conjugal relationship. Dinner parties and balls declined in popularity both because elite Japanese men were unwilling to give up geisha and because Japanese families were unwilling to let members of the younger generation select their own marriage partners. Thus, the resistance to dinner parties and balls reflected a conscious decision to structure the modern Japanese family along the parent–child axis, with the household head having strong control over decisions such as marriage partner and place of residence.

In retrospect, far more attention has been given to the exclusion of Japanese women from politics in the 1880s than to their exclusion from dinner parties. It is important to human history that when Japanese women learned about the idea of political rights, they wanted such rights for themselves. If Japanese women had secured voting rights in the 1880s, they would have been without peer in the world. Monogamy and respect within their own households were privileges that some Western women already enjoyed. The decline in the popularity of dinner parties could be read as a decision by male members of the Japanese elite that if they could not have geisha at parties along with wives, they would henceforth simply not invite the wives. The scholarly conclusion that the nationalist reaction to the Rokumeikan era was "a genuine appropriation of the best of Japanese tradition" does not place a high value on women's economic, political, or even domestic rights.[82]

NOTES

1. Wm. Theodore de Bary, Wing-tsit Chan, and Burton Watson, *Sources of Chinese Tradition* (New York: Columbia University Press, 1960), 870. This essay originally appeared in *US–Japan Women's Journal English Supplement* 18 (2000): 107–152, and is reprinted here with the permission of Josai University.

2. Daphne Spain, *Gendered Spaces* (Chapel Hill: University of North Carolina Press, 1992), 123, notes that while the dining room was "specifically designed for gender contact," the parlor was a woman's space that was open to outsiders.

3. The quotation is from Erna Olafson Hellerstein, Leslie Parker Hume, and Karen M. Offen, eds., *Victorian Women: A Documentary Account of Women's Lives in Nineteenth-Century England, France, and the United States* (Stanford, Calif.: Stanford University Press, 1981), 339.

4. Rutherford Alcock, *The Capital of the Tycoon: A Narrative of a Three Years' Residence in Japan*, 2 vols. (1863; New York: Greenwood, 1969), 2:73, wrote that the crowded conditions of peasant homes were not peculiar to Japan. Susan Thorne has noted the conflation among British evangelicals of the laboring poor at home with the heathen races overseas. See her "'Conversion of Englishmen and the Conversion of the World Inseparable': Missionary Imperialism and the Language of Class in Early Industrial Britain," in *Tensions of Empire: Colonial Cultures in a Bourgeois World*, ed. Frederick Cooper and Ann Laura Stoler, 238–262 (Berkeley: University of California Press, 1997).

5. See, for instance, W. G. Beasley, *Japanese Imperialism, 1894–1945* (New York: Clarendon, 1987).

6. Historians interested in the construction of gender, in contrast, often fail to mention the social life of the Rokumeikan. See, for instance, Masaki Hirota, "Notes on the 'Process of Creating Women' in the Meiji Period," in *Gender and Japanese History, Volume 2: The Self and Expression/ Work and Life*, ed. Wakita Haruko, Anne Bouchy, and Ueno Chizuko, 197–219 (Osaka: Osaka University Press, 1999).

7. See, for instance, Mikiso Hane, *Modern Japan: A Historical Survey* (Boulder, Colo.: Westview, 1986), 107–108.

8. On the importance of gender in formal imperialism, see Dipesh Chakrabarty, "The Difference—Deferral of a Colonial Modernity: Public Debates on Domesticity in British Bengal," in *Tensions of Empire*, ed. Cooper and Stoler, 383.

9. Ann Laura Stoler and Frederick Cooper, "Between Metropole and Colony: Rethinking a Research Agenda," in *Tensions of Empire*, ed. Cooper and Stoler, 4.

10. Townsend Harris, "Letter to Catherine Ann Drinker, November 21, 1856," in *Some Unpublished Letters of Townsend Harris*, ed. Shio Sakanishi (New York: Japan Reference Library, 1941); and Clara A. N. Whitney, *Clara's Diary: An American Girl in Meiji Japan*, ed. M. William Steele and Tamiko Ichimata (Tokyo: Kōdansha International, 1979), 28, 81.

11. Henry Heusken, *Japan Journal 1855–1861*, trans. and ed. Jeannette C. Van der Corput and Robert A. Wilson (New Brunswick, N.J.: Rutgers University Press, 1964), 92.

12. Heusken, *Japan Journal 1855–1861*, 205.

13. Donald Keene, *Modern Japanese Diaries: The Japanese at Home and Abroad as Revealed through Their Diaries* (New York: Henry Holt, 1995), 36.

14. Yasuhide Kawashima, "America through Foreign Eyes: Reactions of the delegates from Tokugawa Japan, 1860," *Journal of Social History* 5 (1972): 495, 501.

15. Kawashima, "America through Foreign Eyes," 501.

16. Keene, *Modern Japanese Diaries*, 100.

17. Kawashima, "America through Foreign Eyes," 501.

18. C. Pemberton Hodgson, *A Residence at Nagasaki and Hakodate in 1859–1860 with an Account of Japan Generally* (London: Richard Bentley, 1861), 204.

19. Harris, "Letter to Mrs. Sandwith Drinker, July 16, 1858," in *Some Unpublished Letters*. Harris noted there were exceptions, such as mothers visiting daughters or women going as pilgrims to temples.

20. Whitney, *Clara's Diary*, 53, 79.

21. Ibid., 65.

22. Keene, *Modern Japanese Diaries*, 17.

23. Ibid., 74.

24. Shibusawa Ei'ichi, *The Autobiography of Shibusawa Ei'ichi: From Peasant to Entrepreneur*, trans. Teruko Craig (Tokyo: Tokyo University Press, 1994), 160.

25. Whitney, *Clara's Diary*, 97.
26. Ibid., 56.
27. Ibid., 84.
28. Keene, *Modern Japanese Diaries*, 51.
29. Ibid., 86–87.
30. Ibid., 84.
31. These particular phrases are taken from the writings of William Elliot Griffis. Robert A. Rosenstone, *Mirror in the Shrine: American Encounters with Meiji Japan* (Cambridge, Mass.: Harvard University Press, 1988), 10, 93, 105, 109.
32. John R. Black, *Young Japan: Yokohama and Yedo 1858–79* (1883; Oxford: Oxford University Press, 1968), 2:6.
33. Whitney, *Clara's Diary*, 56, 97.
34. Peter Duus, *The Japanese Discovery of America: A Brief History with Documents* (Boston: Bedford Books, 1997), 175.
35. See, for instance, Black, *Young Japan*, 1:118, and Alcock, *Capital of the Tycoon*, 2:70–72, 143.
36. Julia Dent Grant, *The Personal Memoirs of Julia Dent Grant*, ed. John Y. Simon (Carbondale: Southern Illinois University Press, 1975), 38, 106, 231–232.
37. Grant, *Personal Memoirs*, 299–305.
38. Hatoyama Haruko, *Waga jijoden* (My autobiography) (Tokyo: Nihon tosho sentā, 1997), 126.
39. Edwin Baelz, *Awakening Japan: The Diary of a German Doctor*, ed. Toku Baelz (1932; Bloomington: Indiana University Press, 1974), 45, 51.
40. Clara Whitney attended the luncheon and cherry viewing in 1884. Whitney, *Clara's Diary*, 329.
41. There are number of descriptions of this building in English, two of the more detailed being Julia Meech-Pekarik, *The World of the Meiji Print: Impressions of a New Civilization* (New York: Weatherhill, 1986), 145–151; and Edward Seidensticker, *Low City, High City: Tokyo from Edo to Earthquake* (New York: Alfred A. Knopf, 1983), 68–70.
42. Whitney, *Clara's Diary*, 331; and Barbara Rose, *Tsuda Umeko and Women's Education in Japan* (New Haven, Conn.: Yale University Press, 1992), 64–66.
43. Whitney, *Clara's Diary*, 334.
44. Sally A. Hastings, "The Empress' New Clothes and Japanese Women, 1868–1912," *The Historian* 55, no. 4 (Summer 1993): 677–692.
45. Jordan Sand, *House and Home in Modern Japan: Architecture, Domestic Space, and Bourgeois Culture, 1880–1930* (Cambridge, Mass.: Harvard University Press, 2003), 33–39. Anne Walthall, *The Weak Body of a Useless Woman: Matsuo Taseko and the Meiji Restoration* (Chicago: University of Chicago Press, 1998), 135, describes Hirata Atsutane's view that "the Japanese eat correctly, in accordance with the way of the gods, each with his own tray and his food served in individual dishes." Atsutane contrasts this to the "rude and filthy" Chinese practice of sitting at the same table and dipping from the same bowl.
46. Hatoyama, *Waga jijoden*, 90–91.

47. Akiko Kuno, *Unexpected Destinations: The Poignant Story of Japan's First Vassar Graduate*, trans. Kristen McIvor (Tokyo: Kōdansha International, 1993), 151–152.

48. Haru Matsukata Reischauer, *Samurai and Silk: A Japanese and American Heritage* (Cambridge, Mass.: Harvard University Press, 1986), 105–106.

49. Baelz, *Awakening Japan*, 127.

50. Ibid., 56.

51. Rosenstone, *Mirror in the Shrine*, 215.

52. The following discussion is based on English translations of editorials that appeared in the *Jiji shimpo* in 1885 and 1886. Yukichi Fukuzawa, *Fukuzawa Yukichi on Japanese Women: Selected Works*, ed. and trans. Eiichi Kiyooka (Tokyo: Tokyo University Press, 1988), 6–137.

53. Fukuzawa, *Fukuzawa Yukichi on Japanese Women*, 11, 68.

54. Ibid., 35.

55. Ibid., 78.

56. Ibid., 79.

57. Ibid., 82.

58. Ibid., 83.

59. Ibid., 90.

60. Ibid., 85.

61. Ibid., 89.

62. Ibid., 99.

63. Ibid., 100.

64. Baelz, *Awakening Japan*, 127.

65. Fukuzawa, *Fukuzawa Yukichi on Japanese Women*, 46.

66. Ibid., 116.

67. Ibid., 107, 118.

68. Sand, *House and Home*, 23–24.

69. Whitney, *Clara's Diary*, 303–304.

70. Kuno, *Unexpected Destinations*, 144.

71. Ibid., 145.

72. Yoshiko Furuki, *A Biography of Ume Tsuda: Pioneer in Higher Education of Japanese Women* (New York: Weatherhill, 1991), 71.

73. Alice Mabel Bacon, *Japanese Girls and Women* (1891; Boston: Houghton Mifflin, 1896), 288–289.

74. For specific examples, see Hastings, "The Empress' New Clothes," 687.

75. Kenneth B. Pyle, "Meiji Conservatism," in *The Cambridge History of Japan, Volume 5: The Nineteenth Century*, ed. Marius B. Jansen (Cambridge: Cambridge University Press, 1989), 689–690.

76. On Dun, see Fumiko Fujita, "Encounters with an Alien Culture: Americans Employed by *Kaitakushi*," in *Foreign Employees in Nineteenth-Century Japan*, ed. Edward R. Beauchamp and Akira Iriye, 107–113 (Boulder, Colo.: Westview, 1990).

77. Furuki, *Biography of Ume Tsuda*, 78.

78. Donald H. Shively, "The Japanization of the Middle Meiji," in *Tradition and Modernization in Japanese Culture*, ed. Donald H. Shively (Princeton, N.J.: Princeton University Press, 1971), 97–98, and Sukehiro Hirakawa, "Japan's

Turn to the West," in *The Cambridge History of Japan, Volume 5: The Nineteenth Century*, ed. Marius Jansen, 488.

79. James L. Huffman, *Creating a Public: People and Press in Meiji Japan* (Honolulu: University of Hawai'i Press, 1997), 155.

80. Hirakawa, "Japan's Turn to the West," 488.

81. Sharon L. Sievers, *Flowers in Salt: The Beginnings of Feminist Consciousness in Modern Japan* (Stanford, Calif.: Stanford University Press, 1983), 38.

82. The quotation is from Hirakawa, "Japan's Turn to the West," 489.

CHAPTER 6

The *Oyaji* Gets a Makeover

Guides for Japanese Salarymen in the New Millennium

JAN BARDSLEY

"It is the age when men, too, must think of their appearance," proclaims the Japanese men's style guide. In 2008 a major Kyoto bookstore devotes two shelves to books on style and manners for men. Although this collection pales in comparison to the two bookcases devoted to similar books for women, it reveals a market niche for instruction on masculine comportment. Written by Japanese men, the three guides selected for discussion here target the reader as a salaryman (*sarariiman*), a white-collar company man. Although men work in diverse occupations in Japan and various forms of masculinity are alive in popular culture, it is the salaryman who is most commonly seen as representing typicality. The guides depict salarymen as eager to climb through the corporate ranks and concerned about navigating transnational business. If only he can win over the young Office Ladies (OLs) who snicker at him, master Western table manners, and use English appropriately, success is his. To do this, he must overcome all the negative traits commonly associated with the salaryman, including his arrogant sense of entitlement and his provincial tastes. If he falls short, the salaryman must resign himself to becoming just another down-market oldster (*oyaji*), as outmoded as the corporate system he represents. Yet the men's guides are exuberant in their belief that this type *can* be saved. All he needs to do is lose the stubbornness, practice some easy tips, and adjust that *oyaji* attitude.

By examining how men's guides attempt to rescue the Japanese man from his own worst habits, this chapter locates the salaryman in a prickly narrative of race and gender. Although the guides use humor to win over the recalcitrant reader, all are serious in pointing to the same sort of gentlemanly figure as the model to emulate. As numerous anecdotes make clear, this model is imagined as an upper-class Anglo male associated with such powerful financial and fashion capitals as London, Paris, and New York. There is an unmistakable spectrum of racial cool operating here. At the low end stands the *oyaji*, drawn as such a hick that he has no clue about the frumpiness of his clothing or how offensive others find his behavior. Near the high end, we find the successful gentleman, who is so adept at speaking English, international etiquette, grooming, and interacting with others that one would hardly recognize him as Japanese at all. He comes closest to the Anglo model, the pinnacle of masculinity. Comics in the men's guides exaggerate the distance between the two models: *oyaji* figures are drawn in bold strokes that caricature East Asian features, while the gentleman passes as a blandly pleasant Anglo character or as a fantastic male beauty of indeterminate race. Japanese women play an important role in this schema because they are seen as more westernized, and thus more accomplished than Japanese men. Women's greater proficiency with English, their comfort with travel and study abroad, and their cosmopolitan tastes align them with the fantasy image of the Western gentleman. It is this cultural capital that allows them to mock the salaryman, even though he is often their boss.[1] The way these men's guides employ humor, however, points to some resistance, or at least unease, with this narrative of *oyaji* failure.

The *oyaji* figures as a comic character in all three men's guides examined here. The guides are widely available inexpensive paperbacks.[2] *The Classy Guy and the Low-Rent Guy* (*Jōryū otoko to karyū otoko: Shinia kaizō kōza, 37 renpatsu!* 2005) by Obuse Makoto, subtitled "Makeover Lessons for Seniors: 37 Sure-fire Tips," targets middle-aged and retired men concerned about presenting a youthful, less *oyaji*-like demeanor. Shutō Shinchirō's *Good Grooming for the Popular Man* (*Moteru otoko no midashinami*, 2008) is directed to the young, single salaryman who wants to impress the OLs and get ahead at work. Shutō makes his point with humor by presenting *manga* of an *oyaji* who serves as the prime example of what *not* to do. Yamasaki Takeya's *Men's Etiquette: The Refined Adult's Style* (*Otoko no sahō: Senren sareta otona no sutairu*, 2007) addresses those with aspirations to becoming—or, at least looking like—a high-powered corporate executive in the global market. For all his hopes of becoming the cosmopolitan gentleman, Yamasaki confesses to his *oyaji* moments and insists, though in a jovial tone, that he will not give up all his pleasures, especially his love for slurping Japanese noodles. Taking each guide in turn, we begin with a closer look at definitions of the *oyaji* and then examine the advice designed to prevent men from becoming him. In conclusion, an overview of recent U.S. men's guides enables a comparative analysis of Japanese and U.S. manuals. Although there are many similarities between the two country's manuals, it is the Japanese man who is expected to perform both Western and native etiquette equally well, while the American man is held to standards of good conduct in numerous spaces both outside and inside the company. Finally, to go beyond this specter of either/or, we take up the phenomenon of the young Japanese men dubbed "grass eaters," noting trends that suggest how many in the new generation may be rejecting both the *oyaji* and westernized cosmopolitan models in favor of adopting more of the behaviors and pleasures associated with Japanese women.

THE *OYAJI* GETS A NEW LOOK IN RETIREMENT

The word *oyaji*, a descriptor for older men, carries a range of connotations these days, from "dad," a term of endearment, to the derogatory "geezer." At best, the *oyaji* inspires fond respect. A scene between a compassionate father and his lovelorn son in a recent TV drama, for example, depicts the young man pouring his heart out as he cries, "*Oyaji*!"[3] Japanese films from *Early Spring* (*Sōshun*, 1956) to *Shall We Dance* (1996) have offered sympathetic views of salarymen, who fear they have no recourse but to follow the company path that will inevitably turn them into cranky *oyaji*. But at worst, the *oyaji* is seen as the butt of jokes for his comically dowdy suits, his liberal use of pomade, his crude habits (spitting, loudly slurping soup, public drunkenness), and his "aging body odor" (*kareishū*)—all of which are at odds with his enormous sense of entitlement. Unflattering characterizations of *oyaji* as poor supervisors turn up everywhere in books and *manga* about the OL experience, as the chapter by Hiroko Hirakawa in this volume explains. In the extreme, disrespect for older men led to the crime dubbed *oyaji gari* (geezer hunting), a phenomenon in which teens attacked and even killed older men on their way home at night, which attracted attention in the 1990s, Japan's "lost decade" of economic recession.[4] The suicide rate among older men skyrocketed in the 1990s as expectations for lifetime employment evaporated and many lost their jobs, a factor contributing to the *oyaji*'s down-market and down-at-the-heels image.[5] In 2001 the debut of the men's fashion magazine *Leon* introduced a completely new image—the *choiwaru oyaji* or "the middle-aged man with a bit of bad-boy charm." Every cover of this best-selling magazine features Girolamo Panzetta, an Italian celebrity in Japan who is in his mid-forties and embodies "Euro chic." *Leon* promotes luxury-brand fashion, skin care products for men, spa treatments, and advice on how to attract younger women. At a time when concerns about Japan's rapidly aging population dominate discussion of the nation's future, and the ideal of maintaining a stylish physical appearance is ever more important, the figure of the outmoded *oyaji* embodies both personal and collective fears about growing old. And that's where Obuse Makoto comes to the rescue.

The author of several books on economics and the arts, a self-described "anti-aging producer," a lecturer, and a Web site instructor, Obuse Makoto, whose birth date is not given, directly addresses readers as *oyaji* in his humorous guide *The Classy Guy and the Low-Rent Guy.* Large, satirical cartoons of the *oyaji* in the book and on its cover establish the light-hearted tone of this guide. They capture the *oyaji*'s foibles and his fashion faux pas, depicting him in unflattering ways as a Japanese man with a wrinkled face, thick eyebrows, puffy eyes, thinning hair, and a pudgy body. Completely unlike the Anglo-looking businessman who illustrates proper behavior in *Men's Etiquette* or the fantastic male beauty in *Good Grooming for the Popular Man* discussed below, Obuse's *oyaji* reads as ludicrous in every way and serves as an example of behaviors to avoid. Cartoons lampoon the *oyaji*'s lack of style. His white briefs, as baggy now as diapers, his see-through nylon summer shirts that reveal the half-moon of his old-fashioned undershirts, his ill-fitting slacks, his stuffed-to-overflowing shoulder bag, and his pretentious attempts to model the *Leon* ideal prompt recognition while inciting laughter and discomfort at the same time.

Chapter titles in *The Classy Guy and the Low-Rent Guy* add to the humor, describing the *oyaji*'s worst traits as syndromes or diseases. These traits include barking at restaurant employees, jabbing his finger in the air to make a point, excavating his teeth with a toothpick, and exhibiting unrelenting negativity. (See Laura Miller's chapter in this volume for a comic of this hapless character that captures him in jabbing-finger mode.) Obuse writes in a conversational manner, including many bad jokes, puns, and parenthetical insertions of humor. For example, he imagines an *oyaji* mistaking the term for aging-body odor, given above, for the fragrance of Japanese curried rice (*karēshū*), which is a cheap, odor-producing dish adored by *oyaji*. Japanese aesthetics make a brief debut, too, but are used for comic effect. When Obuse tells his reader not to let his mind wither, he emphasizes that he does not mean "wither" (*kareru*) in a *wabi-sabi* way that appreciates the beauty in decay. He just means, "You're all dried up, Dad!" He advocates that Japanese men enjoy opening presents in front of the giver just as Americans do, adding, "If you think you shouldn't have to follow American customs, Pops, it's too late! How about that Christmas cake you eat every December 25th?" Obuse's comically didactic tone anticipates his reader's resistance.

The point that Obuse seriously intends to drive home is that older men should enjoy a vibrant life in retirement. For all his effort to make the *oyaji* see himself as others see him, Obuse earnestly wants older Japanese men to adopt a new, more optimistic vision of themselves as retired men. He also makes an appeal to class consciousness, most boldly in his title, and on the inside of the book jacket. He states that class actually has nothing to do with one's finances, academic pedigree, upbringing, or neighborhood. Rather he uses "upper class" and "lower class" to delineate people: the "upper" make an effort to live youthfully by having a positive attitude, are willing to try new things, exhibit kindness and empathy toward others, maintain their curiosity, and can look at themselves objectively, while the "lower" have lost interest in everything, become crabby, and give in to a wretched old age. Obuse explains that one's attitude is more important than anything else to calculating age, observing that while some seniors project exceptional youthfulness, there are those still in their thirties who already act like "lower-class" fuddy-duddies.

By dislodging class from its usual markers and age from years, Obuse proposes that all his readers have the chance to become classy and vital *if* they are willing to take a critical view of themselves and strive to change. This strategy reveals a conservatism commonly found in self-improvement guides. Readers are not asked to scrutinize the social environment that has created certain standards of performance and appearance but to manipulate them to their best advantage. Doing so becomes a matter of individual effort and pride. Moreover, in these guides, the actual income levels that determine how individuals may spend their retirement, and whether or not they must return to work, disappear in a framework that imagines all the *oyaji* as comfortable, middle-class men with adequate funds. Addressing his reader light-heartedly, Obuse constructs his reader as one of "us old guys."

What changes does Obuse advise the *oyaji* reader make? He needs to let go of the past—chuck the stuff that has been cluttering his house for years and lose the look he adopted in the days of the 1980s bubble economy or at folk concerts in the 1970s. Long before the *oyaji* ends his career, he needs to develop interests outside his work, such as volunteering in the community and cultivating hobbies. As Shibamoto-Smith describes in her chapter, in this volume, on newspaper-advice columns, "action is where it is at," and the *oyaji*, too, will be happier when he finds his passion. Obuse also urges his reader to undertake some of these activities jointly with his wife so that they have a companionate relationship when they find themselves increasingly together in retirement. Using popular slang that expresses a wife's frustration with a retired husband suddenly home all day and in her way, Obuse warns his readers that they do not want to become "oversize garbage" (*sōdai gomi*) or "wet, fallen-leaves master" (*nureochiba teishu*). Obuse also observes that older men can learn from their female counterparts, whom one sees enjoying themselves in groups on excursions and participating in activities of all kinds. (He pokes fun, however, at older women who frequent tanning salons and dress like their daughters in cheap, skimpy Shibuya 109 teen styles.) Advocating more conventional wisdom, Obuse suggests that all seniors (he uses the loanword *shinia*), men and women alike, maintain their health through proper exercise and nutrition and endeavor to keep their memory in shape. Even though he satirizes the *Leon* style, Obuse does recommend that men try getting their hair cut at a salon and experiment with skin-care products. They also need to "liberate themselves from that 'aging-body odor' inducing hair tonic," a sure sign of *oyaji* frump.[6]

Like the other guides discussed in this volume, *The Classy Guy* emphasizes self-surveillance. Old age begins, states Obuse, when one no longer cares about what others think when they look at you.[7] This may bring a certain pleasurable sense of freedom, but it leads to using age as an excuse to be rude. At the same time, one should not hesitate to ask younger people politely for assistance or directions—a classy senior does that. *The Classy Guy* concludes by discussing the benefits of moving to the countryside in retirement, advising that one try the country life first on the weekends to see if it feels right before making any drastic moves. It may turn out that the reader prefers proximity to Starbucks and department stores to the rural life. With humor and authority, Obuse directs *oyaji* to a graceful old age, one that allows them to shed their former sense of entitlement in favor of being more pleasing to those around them and happier with themselves.

AN URGENT MAKEOVER FOR SALARYMAN OYAMA

The cover of *Good Grooming for the Popular Man* (2008), by the fashion consultant Shutō Shinchirō (b. 1967), declares: "These days, there's nothing strange about men looking chic. In work and romance both, it's the first impression that determines your success!" As for what's inside the book, the *manga* beneath this proclamation says it all. Prominently featured is a handsome young salaryman, a *manga*-style beautiful boy (*bishōnen*) who has large, expressive eyes; sports a full, trendy hairstyle; and wears a purple tie. As it turns out, this is Kimura, the new advertising executive in the office who is stealing all the OLs' attention. Behind Kimura stand three girlish, uniformed OLs clasping their hands in adoration. Farther behind and smallest of all is the comic figure of a nerdy *oyaji* whose facial and body language reveal that he does not understand what Kimura has that he does not. This is the unfortunate Oyama, a manager in the much less hip operations section and the guide's protagonist, whom we follow through many *manga* as he tries to learn all the ins and outs of good grooming from his subordinate Sasaki. In big *manga*-style characters on the book's first page, Oyama asks his reader: "Haven't you ever wondered, 'Why is *that* guy so popular?' Perhaps this means that the women in your office find your appearance NG (no good). Well, once there was a guy just like you. . . ."[8]

These lines are prelude to an over-the-top two-page *manga* that begins the book. Here, the handsome Kimura, drawn with a sparkling aura about his head and shoulders, so gorgeous that he is unreal, seems almost unaware of the attention he has caused among the OLs and the grief he has stirred in Oyama. Oyama's panic over the attention that the OLs lavish on Kimura dramatizes the frustrations that ordinary men can feel when, to their minds, OLs hold them up to unrealistic standards of masculine beauty. They cannot become Anglo men, nor can they become fantastic *bishōnen*. Graphics caricature Oyama's pain, exaggerating it for comic purposes, but reveal a sore point in office politics all the same. When Oyama overhears the OLs praising Kimura for his tidy appearance and chic suits, but scoffing at Oyama as dumpy and unkempt, Oyama literally falls to the floor in despair. Once he commandeers his subordinate Sasaki into showing him the ropes, however, Oyama is so full of enthusiasm about his decision to learn better grooming that he literally soars like a superman, nearly strangling Sasaki in his over-excitement as he grasps him about the neck. There is a way to achieve this masculine beauty after all!

Such comedy makes this men's guide approachable and fun to read. Its exaggeration of Oyama leaves room for the reader to take comfort—while he may need to pick up some tips, there's no way he is as clueless as that *oyaji*. At the same time, the *manga* gets across the main themes of the guide: cleanliness is the key to good grooming; OLs are picky, westernized critics who will gossip about you mercilessly; and, most optimistically, you do have the opportunity to change yourself. With practice and attention, even Oyama can lose his offensive *oyaji* look and become closer to the Kimura ideal. Surprisingly, the guide does not resolve Oyama's quest for coolness, instead ending with a straight-laced essay explaining the author Shutō's fashion philosophy and establishing his credentials as one experienced in the sophisticated circles of New York City's high culture, where he has worked for such luxury-brand firms as Hugo Boss and Prada. It is the New York connection rather than his work in Japan that gives Shutō his cache here.

In the afterword Shutō explains his mission as showing Japanese salarymen, both newcomers to the company and established executives, how they can achieve the elegance embodied by men in Manhattan. Shutō states that many Japanese women have come closer than Japanese men to achieving this kind of elite, cosmopolitan chic. Over his eighteen years in the fashion and cosmetics advertising industry, and while dividing his time between Japan and New York, Shutō believes that he has benefited most from learning New York men's fashion. He appreciates the way these gentlemen (linguistically blending the cultures, he uses the loanword *gentoruman* followed by the Sino-Japanese *shinshi*) cultivate an unblemished appearance that neglects nothing, from their groomed nails to their polished shoes. They are committed to "total grooming."[9] Putting forward what he understands as their definition of *midashinami* (generally translated as "appearance" or "deportment"), Shutō explains the concept as "taking care so as not to be embarrassed in front of others." This is an attitude that displays as much self-respect and self-love, he argues, as concern for others.

Turning the lens from this New York ideal to his Japanese readers, Shutō urges them to ask themselves, "Am I presentable?" He writes the question in English with a *katakana* transliteration alongside—in essence, pushing his reader to catch up with global chic through use of

English. Repeating this English expression, would the Japanese man hear his own voice or the imagined voice of the fantasy Anglo woman or stylish Japanese woman, and would he see himself through their eyes? Shūto explains that behaving as a gentleman requires attention to speech, etiquette, and attitude. Although he finds that Japanese men, especially younger men, display more interest in style news than do their American and European counterparts, and have more access to men's fashion magazines and trendier clothing, most fail to understand how to cultivate an overall image of polish, stopping at a concern only for clothes. He hopes that his guide, by presenting grooming tips in an approachable manner, will help Japanese men achieve the global standard (*gurōbaru sutandādo*), and he assures his readers that by putting his advice into practice little by little they will not only look better but will feel more vital as well. Shutō's guide also promises that a man's corporate career success depends on turning out a polished façade and a can-do attitude. The fact that the young advertising exec Kimura, the OL heartthrob, serves as the catalyst for Oyama's self-improvement project implies that some young Japanese men have already attained this global cool. The Japanese *oyaji*, however, is in need of serious help.

How does Shutō guide his reader via the protagonist Oyama's mishaps? Most of the book's nine chapters are divided into several short sections, each devoted to some relatively minute aspect of body care and each beginning with a four-frame *manga* of Oyama getting it wrong and Sasaki wondering if he will ever get it right. When the guide offers that both men and women can benefit from skin-care products and that even the same ones will do, for example, Oyama goes off to buy a "starter kit" for women and ends up at home with a fully made-up face and a startled expression. He mistakenly thinks that avoiding too much sun means being covered head to toe and that anti-aging strategies equal acting childishly. He applies a full facial masque at the office and irritates everyone by dousing himself with perfume. When Sasaki prods him to think how embarrassing it would be to show up at his girlfriend's house with dirty socks, Oyama simply responds that he does not have a girlfriend so there's nothing to worry about. (The *manga* depicting steam rising from Oyama's socks leaves no doubt about their condition.)

At other times, Sasaki, a younger man who realizes he needs to make his own efforts not to become an *oyaji*, shares painful memories of romantic possibilities foreclosed by his own failed grooming. In one *manga* he sits dejectedly at a bar with Oyama, relating the tale of his happiness at finding a "cute girl" eyeing him until he realizes she was staring at his nose hair. Another *manga* depicts Sasaki fleeing the scene when he realizes that a girl he just met will be put off by the bad breath left by his garlicky lunch. Most often in Oyama's case, too, the offended are young women. We see tears streaming down Oyama's cheeks in one comic, his face contorted with anger in another, and even his breakdown in one frame. All this angst is generated by the capricious preferences of young OLs who, for example, prefer men without much body hair but recoil at the thought of hirsute men taking pains to remove theirs.[10] The *manga* depict the women as interchangeable, uniformly critical, and quick to ridicule men. Such behavior recalls the sociologist Ogasawara Yuko's 1990s research on how OLs exert influence over male bosses by threatening to damage their reputations at the office, most often by gossip.[11] Moreover, the men's response underscores rising anxiety over "their status as objects of aesthetic and sexual appraisal," as the anthropologist Laura Miller has discussed.[12]

In contrast to the sympathy for men-as-victims that these *manga* may induce in the reader, Shutō's prescriptions take women's preferences as a matter of course. He teaches the techniques of body care in a straightforward fashion, always with the understanding that this aim toward "a sense of cleanliness" or *seiketsukan*, a term that carries connotations of purity and neatness, is a trait valued not only by OLs but by others as well. The guide includes several instructions on the correct way to wash one's face, shave, shape nails, remove excess body hair, defeat body odors, manage dental hygiene, eat properly, and choose and care for clothing. *Good Grooming for the Popular Man* is less concerned with manners than with appearance, serving up every part of the body for attention. Although the guide positions young women as the most callous critics, there is no advice about how to ask a woman for a date, how to develop an intimate relationship, or even how to negotiate collegiality at work with colleagues or your boss. Of concern is avoiding the harshness of their westernized gaze. The first order of business is to protect oneself from humiliation by correcting offensive appearance and behaviors.

THE JAPANESE MAN AS EXECUTIVE AT HOME AND ABROAD

The most sedate of the three manuals discussed here, *Men's Etiquette: The Refined Adult's Style*, concentrates on instruction in masculine behaviors appropriate to specific social situations. Although appearance is important here, too, *Men's Etiquette* emphasizes performance. Active verbs (underscoring the importance of conduct) serve as the titles for each of the book's chapters—to wear, to meet, to speak, to gather, to ride, and to visit—with separate chapters devoted to eating and drinking in the Western and Japanese styles. Subtitles connect all the action to men: men's deportment, men's courtesy, men's etiquette, and so on. The book's overleaf proclaims: "Elegance and Wisdom. What are the essentials you need to become your best self? A visual explanation of the 'savvy guy's' (*dekiru otoko*) keys to success."[13] The author Yamasaki Takeya (b. 1935) is a business consultant, prolific author, and patron of the prestigious Urasenke School of the Tea Ceremony. Like Shutō, Yamasaki bases much of his advice on his many years of experience working abroad and interacting with non-Japanese.

For Yamasaki, good manners are simply good business, and thus a polished demeanor gives the Japanese executive entrée into a kind of elite, global men's club. He accentuates the positive, finding much to commend about both Japanese and Euro-American manners. Rather than brandishing the possibility of humiliation, as Obuse and Shūto do, Yamasaki likens the pleasures of becoming adept at etiquette to the fun of playing a game where everyone knows and abides by the same rules. Like Shutō, Yamasaki observes that those ignorant of these rules will never achieve corporate success, no matter how good they may be at their job, for others will perceive them as uninterested in self-improvement. In a particularly masculine moment, Yamasaki promises that those who do choose to follow etiquette will have knowledge that they can wield in their favor like a sword (*katana*). Reading Yamasaki's book, one can easily imagine the classy Japanese executive as a samurai in a tennis sweater handling business with the same manly grace with which he pops a ball over the net.

Men's Etiquette reads somewhat like a travelogue. Yamasaki recounts parties in the United States and Europe, and wedding banquets and bullet-train trips in Japan. But he also adds a "high/low" panache, describing in one section how delightful it is to wear a tux, and in others, how comfortable to change into casual clothes or enjoy a backyard party in blue jeans, as Americans do. The theme of adapting to new situations recurs throughout *Men's Etiquette*, often with the suggestion that novel experiences and even the effort to move out of one's comfort zone by adopting different manners bring fresh pleasures. Through these vignettes, Yamasaki implicitly pays tribute to the imagined figure of an elite businessman who possesses a global savoir-faire.

The cartoon figure that pops up throughout *Men's Etiquette* underscores this desire for a kind of post-race neutrality. The young businessman, who exemplifies Yamasaki's advice and sometimes gets caught making mistakes, is simply drawn and would probably strike many readers outside Japan as Anglo if he were not in a Japanese book meant for Japanese readers. Drawn in the same bland fashion, women, who appear infrequently, are distinguished from the men mainly by their longer hair. These women may wrinkle their noses at smoke or bad breath, but they are not the malevolent, comic creatures of Shutō's guide. One cartoon of a man labeled as a foreigner (*gaijin*), however, depicts a huge man with thick brows and a prominent nose that towers over the "Japanese" businessman with whom he is talking. Interestingly, it is the foreigner rather than the Japanese who is more graphically described as unique.

Despite its allegiance to a degree of elitism, *Men's Etiquette* offers intriguing moments of resistance, often related with humor, when the *oyaji* either cannot or will not follow Western etiquette. At times Yamasaki presents himself as this befuddled Japanese man, and at other times he addresses his reader in a knowing way as one who possesses typical shared anxieties and preferences. Like Obuse, Yamasaki attempts to build camaraderie with his reader through noting commonalities. Unlike the post-race, nondescript cartoon figure genially willing to conform to all the rules, the man who emerges in these narrative moments is fully aware of his Japanese body and its Japanese urges and must choose whether or not he wishes to bend his body to foreign etiquette. At times Yamasaki suggests internalizing new behaviors, advising readers to "learn through the body" or, more literally, "attach to the body" (*mi ni tsukeru*) the new modes. In other instances, however, Yamasaki resists or takes a modified approach to Western etiquette, as we shall see by examining what the guide has to say about dining and interacting with women and foreigners.

Much of Yamasaki's advice about table manners in Japan and in the Euro-American West, such as seating, use of utensils and napkins, ordering in restaurants, and choosing wine can be found in almost any guide to modern manners. Remarkable in *Men's Etiquette* are the personal digressions, chiefly the unabashed joy and occasional embarrassment that memories of drinking and dining situations rouse in Yamasaki. Advising his readers to try a cocktail before dinner rather than their usual beer, Yamasaki recalls how much fun it was to try all kinds of cocktails when he worked in New York. Real conversation starters they were, too! He laughs at himself when recounting how a formal Parisian dinner party ended with dessert and delicious champagne. Not realizing that the dessert course was considered the appropriate point to serve champagne, he regretted that it had not appeared earlier in the meal so he could have enjoyed more. Commenting on what clothing to wear for dining events reminds him that friends in the United States wear casual clothes at dinner parties in their home while his Dutch and Parisian friends never fail to don jackets and ties when entertaining. Yamasaki does not evaluate one way as better than another but recounts the cultural differences as charming. But not all his recollections are happy ones. Memories of the time he went without a jacket to a Manhattan restaurant that required them still causes him embarrassment. Yamasaki could not fit in the large ones available to borrow and spent the entire dinner in his overcoat. Men's socks level the playing field, however, offering equal opportunity for mortification to Japanese and foreigners alike: Yamasaki explains that so few social situations require removing one's shoes in public these days that even Japanese men, like men from abroad working in Japan, need to take care to avoid the discomfiture of having one's old, torn socks suddenly revealed.

Soup, *soba* (buckwheat noodles), and the topic of slurping earn special attention in *Men's Etiquette*, revealing a body politics fraught with tension between the natural urge and the demands of etiquette. The deliberate humor in these chapters is worthy of Itami Juzō's 1986 comedy *Tampopo*, a film that takes viewers through an adventure to find the perfect ramen-noodle recipe and along the way pokes fun at pretentious food manners and revels in the sheer sensuous pleasures of eating, playing with, and touching food.[14] Like *Tampopo*, Yamasaki pays special attention to the issue of slurping. He acknowledges soup, particularly Western-style soup, as a challenge for the Japanese man, but lets his reader in on the little-known secret that Western men, too, are apt to slip up during the soup course. Yamasaki observes that his reader may be surprised to learn that, as with the problem of finding perfect socks, the Japanese and Western man can find more common ground than one might expect when it comes to prohibitions against making noise while eating. In such moments, Euro-American men are depicted as equally coerced to uphold manners, now understood as universal, that conflict with natural, boyish desires to enjoy their food.

The politics of constraint in the face of soup comes together in the chapter, "To Eat and Drink (Western Style): Men's Manners Common to All Nations." In the section, "The Sound of Slurping Soup" (*Sūpu o susuru oto*), Yamasaki explains that as Japanese are used to making noise when drinking hot miso soup, they feel constrained when trying to sip Western-style soup silently and end up making slurping sounds as soon as they let down their guard. This reminds Yamasaki of the time five or six friends at a dinner party were waiting for the guest of honor, a European friend of impeccable educational background and a much-respected businessman, to arrive. The guest came just in time for the soup course but stopped the party cold when he began loudly slurping his soup. Quickly realizing everyone's horror, he immediately corrected himself and began sipping quietly. Yamasaki still remembers how time stopped during that moment of shock but advises his reader that this incident shows that one should not assume that Westerners never slurp. Indeed, most Westerners he has queried confess that not only do they prefer to slurp, and in fact do so in private, but they also like to raise the bowl directly to their lips as Japanese do, when no one else is around. This leads Yamasaki to surmise that although the more one practices such table manners, the more natural they become, there is no necessity for one to stress over forcing perfect behaviors. Moreover, he counsels that when in a Japanese inn, for example, surrounded only by other Japanese, it is fine to slurp even Western soup in Japanese style.

"The Sound of Eating *Soba*" (*Soba o taberu oto*), a section in the chapter, "To Eat and Drink (Japanese Style): Japanese Men's Stubborn Devotion to Tradition," is as delightful as it is tongue-in-cheek. The chapter covers the proper use of *oshibori* (a small towel to clean one's hands before eating) and chopsticks, how to pour sake, how to sit in a tatami-mat room, and how to order at a sushi bar. A section on ordering Chinese food comes in here, too. But it is the section on *soba* that allows Yamasaki to wax poetic, and even though he smiles at his own enthusiasm for the noodles, he offers the most positive approach to food ritual as a way to heighten sensual pleasure. Yamasaki fondly recounts how, as a student, he even invented his own *soba* rituals. Whereas other contemporary conduct literature discussed here and elsewhere in this volume endorses maintaining vigilance over one's appearance for fear of offending, or inviting ridicule, Yamasaki shows how enjoyable it can be to turn a romantic lens on oneself, doubling one's pleasure. He describes the scene with a wry humor, slightly embarrassed about relating moments of unabashed gratification and vanity.

Yamasaki sets the scene by commending *soba* as an unpretentious but healthy dish that is best eaten quickly. Since it is neither gorgeous nor gourmet, it does not encourage overeating. Among *soba* dishes, it is the humble *zaru soba* (buckwheat noodles with dried seaweed sprinkled on top) that has genuine *kiosa* (cleanness, purity) and is most appealing to Yamasaki. Whenever Yamasaki shows up for lunch at his local shop, the employees bring him *zaru soba* without his having to say a word. In a passage reminiscent of *Tampopo*, Yamazaki playfully instructs the reader in how to eat *soba*: It comes as a mound on a wooden tray, and one must be careful always to draw the noodles from the top. Pulling from the side does not allow you to pick up noodles skillfully as it causes too many to "straggle indecisively." You must take just a few strands of *soba* at a time in a neat bunch that has made a "definitive farewell" to those that remain, and eat them after dipping them in the *tsuyu* or broth. Yamasaki also observes that servers should bring the *sobayu* (hot water in which *soba* was cooked) to the customer only at the end of the meal, as this should be consumed after eating the noodles; when the *sobayu* sits on the table too long, the flour settles. As for Yamasaki, he never mixes the *sobayu* with even a little *tsuyu*, as the saltiness makes him thirsty.

Ah, the memories *soba* brings back! When he was a school boy, Yamasaki got all his friends to experiment with a method he christened "the formal protocol for eating *zaru* and *morisoba* [*soba* alone, without seaweed]" that called for dabbing *tsuyu* on one's lips after taking a bite of noodles in order to let the full flavor of the noodles shine on its own. Yamasaki also remembers how, as a college student, he used to stop in at a local *soba* shop on his way home from the public bath close to the room he rented near the university. He recalls the pleasant sensation of his body, warm and relaxed from the bath; the delicious taste of warm sake and *zaru soba*; and the *wabishisa*, an aesthetic sense of melancholy piqued by having this experience as he sat all by himself. Reflecting on himself in this situation made him feel quite sophisticated. Wearing Japanese *geta* (wooden clogs) made the experience even cooler, he says. Yamasaki's "Sound of Eating *Soba*," again much like the film *Tampopo*, calls on Japanese high aesthetic culture to gently satirize pretentious ceremony but also to imbue the ordinary with exotic and sensuous pleasure.

Bringing noodles down to grassroots culture, Yamasaki concludes the section with some last words of praise for enjoying the delicious Japaneseness of *soba* as a liberating experience:

> *Soba* is a dish that brims with Japan's common folk (*minzoku*) sensibilities. So, don't hold back—go ahead and make all the noise you want when you eat it. These days, even among the Euro-Americans who are not used to making any sound when eating, there are many who follow this "chic Japanese" (*iki*) way of making noise when eating.[15]

Invoking the *minzoku* and the Edo-era aesthetic of *iki* born in the merchant culture of the pleasure quarters of the Yoshiwara, Yamasaki connects noisy noodle eating to a fundamentally Japanese way of life that is so much fun that even foreigners want to try it. For all Yamasaki's cheerleading, however, this call to slurping reads as comic, as though there is still something *Tampopo*-funny and laughably unreal about the image of all kinds of foreigners and contemporary Japanese getting into noodle noise. In contrast, scenes of Japanese or foreigners failing to live up to Western etiquette is cause for embarrassment, and although this may lead to humor, it is always the failed performance and not the practice itself that is held up for ridicule.

When it comes to his chapter on speech, Yamasaki addresses such topics as body language, the use of Japanese honorifics, injecting humor, and skillful ways to say "No" (given in *katakana* as *nō*) and to express appreciation and thanks. He also includes two sections about interacting with foreigners: "How to Converse with a Person from Abroad" and "Putting Foreigners First." Yamasaki admits that situations in which Japanese have to speak with those from abroad can put them in a panic—what if they do not know the other's language? What if their English is not sufficient? In these cases, Yamasaki suggests simply addressing the other in Japanese, as many from abroad are studying the language now; especially those who stay in Japan for some length of time are quite good at speaking it and expect to do so in Japan. Thus, there is "nothing rude about speaking to the other in Japanese." If your fellow businessman does not understand Japanese, he will use hand gestures and you can try a few words of English. In the end Yamasaki assures his reader that in a conversation between a Japanese and non-Japanese, both men making an effort and being sincere (as an illustration shows) will foster communication. Interestingly, although Yamasaki begins by discussing how men may deal with "foreign language," this quickly slips into his identifying English as *the* second language to know.

In "Putting Foreigners First," Yamasaki states that while some believe that it is politically incorrect to use the word *gaijin* (which he problematizes to a degree by writing it in *katakana*), as it lumps all from abroad in one undifferentiated group, he finds it a convenient term, one that he considers to come with all the positive meanings of "guest." This position ignores, of course, all those who come from overseas to live and work permanently in Japan, the problems faced by Korean Japanese and other minorities, and the numerous workers from poorer countries who labor in "dark, dangerous, and dirty" jobs. Except for some mention of Chinese businessmen he has met in Singapore and Hong Kong, all Yamasaki's references to the foreign businessman tend to point to the figure of a Euro-American executive. As we have seen, he is the model to emulate. Yamasaki believes one must be tolerant when *gaijin* are bewildered by Japanese customs, and he insists on putting the *gaijin* first, even when the person is much younger and seeks to be deferential to Yamasaki. Remember that when you're overseas, others will treat you as the guest, he advises. Despite this assurance of reciprocity, Yamasaki's policy of "*gaijin* first" uncomfortably recalls the days of the Allied occupation of Japan, and how Americans took joy in what they saw as Japanese politeness while being oblivious to how the country's occupied status forced Japanese into a relationship of servitude—"*gaijin* first"—to the occupier.[16]

Women and a new twist on "ladies first" come into the picture briefly in *Men's Etiquette* in the section "Ladies First" (*redei fāsuto*), in the chapter "To Gather: Men's Decorum for Parties and Ceremonial Occasions." Yamasaki explains that there is a movement to tone down expressions of "ladies first," as it is chauvinistic and demeans women as the weaker sex. Even so, he knows that Japanese men, especially those in the countryside, where courtesy holds that men come first, will find any expression of "ladies first" hard to abide. But a good way to get used to this, he advises, is to think more broadly about putting the other first. He suggests that if one practices "ladies first" etiquette in this light, then women will not be offended. Trying this in the Japanese context can create confusion, however. Yamasaki relates how he surprised a Japanese woman once by standing aside so that she could enter an elevator first, and she insisted on waiting until he entered. Yamasaki suggests that this scene should not be read as a battle over Japanese or Western customs, but as a situation in which codes become confused as each tries to show deference to the other. As with his advice on soup, Yamasaki makes explicit that his reader may stubbornly resist performing "ladies first" behavior of any kind because it is un-Japanese and unmanly—and most of all, not "Japanese manly." Thus, he nudges his reader by connecting men-first Japanese behaviors to the provincial and the outmoded *oyaji*.

In this and other respects, *Men's Etiquette* gives the impression of trying to win over a Japanese male reader imagined as somewhat recalcitrant. Yamasaki's guide is most fun to read when memories of pleasing events or embarrassing moments derail his otherwise prosaic instructions. The negotiation between the *oyaji*'s natural body and the cultivated, westernized one described in *Men's Etiquette* ends up in many ways as a testimony to Yamasaki's own unfinished struggle to blend these dichotomies. Yamasaki realizes that there is something of the Oyama in him and his reader that leads to frustration, resistance, and shame. At the same time, there are moments of perfect performance when he is the champagne-sipping gentleman in the tux in Paris, the casual fellow in jeans at the backyard barbeque in the United States, or the noodle-slurping, *geta*-shod poet in Tokyo. Recounting these scenes redoubles his delight as he tastes the drink and food once again and enjoys imagining himself at the center of these events. Yamasaki might well have titled his book *Memoirs of a Japanese Gentleman.*

CONCLUSION: COMPARISON WITH MEN'S GUIDES IN THE UNITED STATES

Despite the veneration of New York savoir-faire evident in Japanese men's guides, messages abound in the United States about how American men could use some lessons of their own in masculine deportment. *Queer Eye for the Straight Guy*, an American cable TV show that became a sensation when it debuted in 2003 showed how five gay men could transform a different style-challenged straight man into a chic one each week. Men in the United States can consult men's etiquette and fashion guides as well.[17] Such guides have much in common with their Japanese counterparts in terms of their advice on grooming, table manners, encouragement of confidence and positivity, and most of all, in their optimistic belief that, with a nudge in the right direction, any man may reinvent himself as a gentleman. U.S. guides, too, prize accessibility and easy-to-digest lists of tips, and lighten their didactic tone by revealing the blunders of the authors or Oyama-like figures, and there are many manuals that promise to guide the reader from dowdiness to dash.

But there are obvious differences between the two sets of guides as well. U.S. men's guides reveal many more public spaces in which a man must be on his guard. Not only must he observe etiquette in business settings, but also at the gym, at sporting and arts events, on the Internet, at weddings and parties, when invited to address public audiences, and when unexpectedly speaking with authorities such as a traffic cop. Notably, the U.S.

men's guides offer advice for getting along with women bosses, in-laws, and women as potential lovers, wives, and paramours-turned-just-friends. The ideal man should be able to mix a cocktail, select wine, and cook a dish or two with expertise. Although U.S. guides regularly include a short paragraph on respecting others' customs when abroad, nothing here comes close to the attention paid to negotiating foreign travel or languages that one finds in Japanese guides. Manners in the United States are neither tagged as American nor contrasted with a set of rules elsewhere. The assumption is that the reader should consult a country-specific guide for travel, and there is little mention that customs devised elsewhere obtain in the United States, except perhaps for the guidebook that includes a foreword by an English butler and those that make some nod to English or European usages of eating utensils and Japanese ways of eating sushi. But customs arising in other cultures do not define the American gentleman. Bad manners or ill-chosen attire do make the American man laughable, and to some extent provincial.

This brief look at U.S. guides suggests some concluding remarks about contemporary conduct literature for Japanese men. At the office, formal dinners, and in other business settings where behavior is carefully calibrated, the mannerly Japanese man must make an effort to look pleasing, act pleasing, and keep up with changing gender codes. This will get him ahead in his career, give him self-confidence, and bring the unique delight of a performance well done. But when off-duty, unlike the ideal man imagined in U.S. guides, he's relatively free to act as he likes. Although he must take care to avoid the minefields that heartless OLs establish for him at work, he is on his own in matters of romance. As he ages, however, the Japanese man needs to make efforts to keep up in modified ways with the styles of the times. Should he fail to exhibit manly etiquette at appropriate times, the Japanese man becomes a comic figure, the *oyaji*. Revealed as hopelessly provincial, the *oyaji* understands no English, no global standard of cool, and no post-race universalism. In the first decade of the twenty-first century, manners guides for Japanese men position them as navigating an ideal that seeks to protect an essential Japanese masculinity, imagined as defined by the body and conditioned through centuries of history, while displaying an agility that enables them to embrace Euroamerican-centric standards coded as aristocratic and presented as cosmopolitan. This is not to say that "do" means Western and "don't" equals Japanese, but that cultivating both selves will lead to a man's ultimate success and prevent him from becoming an *oyaji*.

The panic in Japan over the emergence of "grass-eating or herbivorous men" (*sōshokukei danshi*), however, suggests that young men may be rebelling against both the *oyaji* and cool-exec models.[18] The term was coined to indicate the opposite of "carnivorous women" (*nikushokukei joshi*), women who actively seek adventure and career success. In contrast, grass-eaters favor a quieter, more insular life. Viewed as single men in their twenties and thirties who may live with their parents, enjoy homemaking, and do not smoke, drink, or maintain the slovenly rooms associated with bachelors, they exhibit little interest in sex, romance, or corporate advancement. The grass-eaters are perceived as a population ripe for new products that have not been previously marketed to men in Japan, such as sweets and colorful underwear. Their tastes suggest that these younger men are aiming to expand the pleasures of a beautiful private life through consumerism and making more time to putter at home. Given Japanese anxiety over the nation's low birthrate and women's reluctance to have children, men's pursuit of their "feminine side" has increased the panic over the new generation's ability to reproduce. Neither *oyaji* nor cool execs, the grass-eating generation of men may look to men's guides for advice, but probably in hopes of increasing their own pleasure rather than to advance the cause of Japanese men as the proud *oyaji*.

NOTES

1. See Hiroko Hirakawa, this volume, and Karen Kelsky, *Women on the Verge: Japanese Women, Western Dreams* (Durham, N.C.: Duke University Press, 2001).

2. Obuse Makoto, *Jōryū otoko to karyū otoko: Shinia kaizō kōza, 37 renpatsu*! (The classy guy and the low-rent guy: Makeover lessons for seniors: 37 sure-fire tips) (Tokyo: H & I Kenkyūjo, 2005); Shutō Shinchirō, *Moteru otoko no midashinami* (Good grooming for the popular man) (Tokyo: C & R Kenkyūjo, 2008); Yamasaki Takeya, *Otoko no sahō: Senren sareta otona no sutairu* (Men's etiquette: The refined adult's style) (Tokyo: PHP Kenkyūjo, 2007).

3. The program is *Dan Dan*, which means "thank you" in the Izumo dialect. Aoki Nobuya, director and producer, *Dan Dan* (Tokyo: Nippon Hōsō Kyōkai, 2008–2009).

4. Citing the Japanese criminologist Fujimoto Tetsuya, L. Craig Parker observes the media has exaggerated instances of *oyaji-gari*, making the public believe that this violence against older men is a growing trend. While there were about twenty-five hundred cases reported in Japan per year in the 1990s, most involving middle-class youths who lived with both parents, the 1950s saw more than ten thousand incidents yearly, most involving impoverished, troubled families in the years following the war. L. Craig Parker Jr., *The Japanese Police System Today: A Comparative Study* (New York: East Gate Book, 2001), 182. Roland Kelts gives youths'

boredom as the most common motive for the assaults. Roland Kelts, "Witch Women and Father Hunters: Japan's New Generation Gap," *Doubletake* (Spring 2002): 75–79.

5. James E. Roberson and Nobue Suzuki's introduction to their edited volume *Men and Masculinities in Contemporary Japan: Dislocating the 'Salaryman' Doxa* (London: RoutledgeCurzon, 2003), 1–19, deftly explains the rise and fall of the modern salaryman, discussing how the economic problems of the 1990s affected many older men's self-esteem and sense of masculinity. Romit Dasgupta's essay in *Asian Masculinities* presents an excellent overview of the salaryman's image in popular culture. Romit Dasgupta, "Creating Corporate Warriors: The 'Salaryman' and Masculinity in Japan," in *Asian Masculinities: The Meaning and Practice of Manhood in China and Japan*, ed. Kam Louie and Morris Low, 118–134 (London: RoutledgeCurzon, 2003).

6. Obuse, *Jōryū otoko to karyū otoko*, 121.

7. Ibid., 132–33.

8. Shutō, *Moteru otoko no midashinami*, 3.

9. Words from English, French, and other European languages are rendered in Japanese via the katakana syllabary. Gentleman becomes *gentoruman*, for example.

10. Laura Miller argues that "women's preference for nonhairy men must be considered a primary reason for [hair removal treatments'] growing popularity," Laura Miller, *Beauty Up: Exploring Contemporary Japanese Body Aesthetics* (Berkeley: University of California Press, 2006), 135.

11. Ogasawara's study *Office Ladies and Salaried Men: Power, Gender, and Work in Japanese Companies* (Berkeley: University of California Press, 1998) revealed that consignment to clerical jobs with no hope of advancement gave these women a certain power over their young male bosses, whose promotions depended on convincing others of their ability to manage. To prove this, the men needed the OLs' cooperation. In turn, OLs' gossip, refusal to do work on time for certain men, and ability to turn other women against a man or subject him to devastating "silent treatment" were all geared to making male managers show appreciation for the women and their work.

12. For contemporary views of masculinity, men's beauty, and products and services aimed to help men improve their appearance, see "Male Beauty Work," in Miller, *Beauty Up*, 125–158.

13. This translation uses the terms of American pop psychology. A literal translation is "In order to equip yourself for outstanding humanity, what is it that you most need?"

14. *Tampopo*, directed by Itami Jūzō (Tokyo: Itami Productions, 1986).

15. *Iki* is a Japanese aesthetic term associated with Tokugawa-era pleasure quarters, and thus related to a kind of sensibility that predates Western encounter.

16. For discussion of the way that U.S. and Japanese relations played out in the etiquette of occupied Japan, see Naoko Shibusawa, *America's Geisha Ally: Reimagining the Japanese Enemy* (Cambridge, Mass.: Harvard University Press, 2006).

17. English-language men's guides consulted for this paper were available on the shelves in North Carolina bookstores in spring 2009. Sherrie Mathieson's

guide, *Forever Cool* (New York: Clarkson Potter Publishers, 2006), comes closest to Obuse's manual for seniors in its focus on teaching fiftysomethings how to project a more youthful appearance. E. Jane Dickson's volume, *Debrett's Manners for Men: What Women Really Want* (Surrey, U.K.: Debrett's, 2007), depicts young men of various ethnicities squiring women in such places as casinos, ski resorts, villas, and yachting clubs; *Manners for Men* reads like a manual for James Bond on his best behavior, and teaches how to flirt, seduce, propose marriage, live, and possibly break up with a woman. Sam Martin's guide, *How to Live Like a Gentleman: Lessons in Life, Manners, and Style* (Guilford, Conn.: Lyons, 2007), is similar to Shutō and Yamazaki's books, advising on grooming and behavior, but also giving advice on romance, birth control etiquette, etc., in Chapter 4, "The Fairer Sex." Peter Post's *Essential Manners for Men: What to Do, When to Do It, and Why* (New York: HarperResource, 2003) offers the most extensive range of advice, recommending behaviors for everything from attending a children's game to dating to succeeding as a house guest, a businessman, a driver, and a parent.

18. "'Herbivorous' Men Changing Japan's Consumer Society," Kyodo News Service, *Chicago Shimpō*, July 10, 2009.

CHAPTER 7

The Dignified Woman Who Loves to Be "Lovable"

HIROKO HIRAKAWA

In 2005 a book advocating nationalistic sentiments entitled *The Dignity of the Nation* soared to the top of the charts, becoming a million-volume seller.[1] Creating a "dignity book" boom, its success prompted the publication of other volumes that featured *hinkaku* (dignity) in their titles. Among these subsequent dignity books, however, only one has become a best-seller: Bandō Mariko's *The Dignity of the Woman* (2006), a collection of how-to tips on conduct, etiquette, and philosophy that is supposed to enable readers to realize the life of a "dignified woman."[2] *The Dignity of the Woman* was even more successful than the original dignity book, selling so well that it caught the attention of media abroad.[3] Reportedly, 80 percent of *The Dignity of the Woman*'s readers are women, most of them in their twenties and thirties, an audience that Bandō has expressed particular interest in reaching.[4] Given that few conduct books have achieved the status of a million-volume seller, the phenomenal success of *The Dignity of the Woman* makes it especially intriguing, leading us to ask: What is it about this book that makes it stand out from the profusion of dignity books and women's conduct books? Why do so many women (and perhaps men as well) feel compelled to read this guidebook?

This chapter considers these questions, analyzing both *The Dignity of the Woman* and its reviews, primarily those posted on the Japanese site Amazon.com.jp. As I will show, the book is characterized by a peculiar gap in that, while selling exceptionally well for a conduct book, the majority of readers find it disappointing because it simply repeats the same advice readily found in the existing array of conduct manuals for women. I will argue that it is this gap between the book's status as a million-volume seller, on the one hand, and its overwhelming unpopularity among readers, on the other, that makes this book unique, and that this fissure should be understood in the context of the collective insecurity over the fate of post-bubble Japan that the dignity book boom has successfully exploited.

The book owes its success, at least partially, to the fact that the author possesses the glamorous image of the woman who "has-it-all," thus promising that the book will reveal the secrets that women need to know to do well in both career and family life. However, many readers experience disillusionment when they find that the book's advice is mainly about becoming adept at pleasing men in power. Moreover, they are irritated to find that this art of "lovability" is presented as a matter of feminine virtue, rather than as a strategy for surviving discriminatory conditions. Readers are acutely and palpably frustrated that the book is blind to what many readers perceive as the reality of post-bubble Japan—that the prolonged recession seems to be making the dream of "having it all" for women increasingly beyond their reach. One can only imagine how the financial calamity of 2007 has exacerbated their sense of insecurity.

THE DIGNITY OF THE NATION AND THE "DIGNITY BOOKS" BOOM

It was toward the end of the Koizumi administration (2001–2006) that *The Dignity of the Nation* made the news. The major claim of its author, Fujiwara Masahiko—that Japan risked losing its dignity as a consequence of its Americanization in the name of "globalization"—was promoted with passion. Apparently, as the *New York Times* reporter Norimitsu Onishi suggests, the book resonated with the negative sentiments percolating in Japan.[5] Public opinion was rising against then prime minister Koizumi Jun'ichirō, who emphasized "free markets, deregulation and competition," and who had thus helped create an atmosphere that hailed "brash American-style entrepreneurs . . . as role models for a new Japan."[6] Fears of what many saw as unchecked Americanization prompted Fujiwara to claim that Japan was unique because its people had long valued form and feeling over materialism. Moreover, he advocated that the entire world could benefit by following Japanese ideals. Although his book never defines form and feeling, Fujiwara appealed to the public's desire to find an ineffable and essential site of resistance. Fujiwara proudly assured his readers that this alleged Japanese heritage was far superior to Western "rationalism" and "logic," that *bushido* trumped democracy any day, and he zealously called on the nation to restore its core values. By doing so, asserts Fujiwara, Japan can save itself (and even the globe!) from the degrading control of "savage" America.

Fujiwara's smug bluster immediately reminds us of the infamous best-seller of two decades earlier, *The Japan That Can Say No* (1989).[7] Published during the heyday of Japan's bubble economy, the book was co-authored by Ishihara Shintarō, the current governor of Tokyo, who is known for his xenophobic and misogynistic stance, and Morita Akio, then chairman of Sony. As the scholars Harootunian and Yoda argue, when Japan's bubble economy of the 1980s burst at the end of the cold war, the United States began "progressively detaching itself from Japan" as Japan lost its strategic value.[8] Moreover, they contend that post–9/11 developments, in particular, have exposed Japan's "semicolonized position" vis-à-vis the United States, revealing the fictitious nature of the two countries' purportedly "equal" partnership.[9] Furthermore, the post-bubble recession and the recent rise of China and India in the world market have significantly undermined Japan's national identity as an economic power. *The Dignity of the Nation* reproduces the familiar rhetoric of nationalistic *nihonjinron* (discourse of the Japanese), which is based on a crude and essentialist binary of Japan versus the West. Considering, however, the changes that have occurred since the publication of *The Japan That Can Say No*, the emptiness of Fujiwara's bravado becomes acute, even poignant. Indeed, many readers of *The Dignity of the Nation* cynically laugh at the absurdity of the author's claims. Nevertheless, the very fact that such a book sold 2.5 million copies, attracting many online reviews (591 as of June 2008 on Amazon .com.jp), reflects the Japanese citizen's broader anxiety over the fate of post-bubble Japan in the post–cold war global system. The book's success even allowed Fujiwara himself to publish more books along the same line.[10] Further, Fujiwara's volume led to the publication of a spate of books similarly praising traditional Japanese values, such as *Incredible Japan* (2007), authored by the former prime minister Aso Tarō (2008–2009), and *To the Beautiful Country,* by another former prime minister, Abe Shinzō (2006–2007).[11]

The promotional blurb on the book's cover hails *The Dignity of the Nation* as "an epoch making proposal that gives every Japanese person pride and confidence." While there is nothing "epoch making" or even new about its "proposal," the book is certainly "epoch making" in that it created a "dignity book" boom, making the term *hinkaku* (dignity) the buzzword of the year for 2006. In April 2008 a *Yomiuri Shinbun* reporter visited Maruzen Bookstore in Tokyo and found approximately one hundred books that featured "the Dignity of Such and Such," including *The Dignity of the Japanese*, *The Dignity of the Company*, *The Dignity of the Hospital*, *The Dignity of the Parent*, and even *The Dignity of the Tippler* and *The Dignity of the Fujoshi* (female fans of male–male romance in anime and manga).[12] Three years after the publication of *The Dignity of the Nation*, the dignity boom showed no signs of dying down. According to the aforementioned reporter, as many as thirty dignity books were published in the first four months of 2008 alone!

Apparently, these dignity books have all been attempts to piggyback on the success of *The Dignity of the Nation*, but none has become a best-seller except for *The Dignity of the Woman*. Subtitled "From How to Dress to How to Live," Bandō's slim volume is easy-to-read advice. Each of her book's seven chapters includes "dignity" in the title: "Manners and Dignity," "Dignified Language and Speech," "Dignified Ways to Dress," "A Dignified Lifestyle," "Dignified Interpersonal Relationships," "Dignified Behaviors," and finally, "A Dignified Way of Living." Thus, *The Dignity of the Woman* provides concrete how-to advice in a friendly, sometimes chiding, fashion. Taking up the issue of "keeping promises," for example, Bandō advises: "A dignified person is one whom you can trust. . . . Let me be specific: Keep deadlines; make sure you show up or call when you say you will."[13]

Bandō often adopts a self-deprecating tone and is quick to admit her own faults. Becoming a woman of dignity is clearly a lifetime effort, and one of its hallmarks is having the modesty to realize that one's self-project must always remain in progress. Like a kindly grandmother, Bandō expresses her suggestions in the inclusive manner one finds in public signs all over Japan: "Let's stop applying makeup when we're on the train," and "Let's show our gratitude by writing thank-you notes." Published in September 2006, *The Dignity of the Woman* has been even more successful than Fujiwara's book: as of April 2008 it had sold 3 million copies, while Fujiwara's *The Dignity of the Nation* had sold 2.64

million.[14] The dignity boom thus owes its momentum to the success of Bandō's book, as much as or more than it owes it to Fujiwara's original volume.

THE DIGNIFIED WOMAN AS A "HAVING-IT-ALL" SUPERWOMAN

As a proponent of gender equality, Bandō apparently felt the need to explain why she had written a book aimed only at women. She lists three reasons for focusing on what she sees as women's unique role in creating the life of a dignified nation:[15]

> First, [I wrote this] because many women are confused about how to live in modern society, where their lifestyles and roles have greatly changed and where the old moral standards have become obsolete. Women do not have to get caught up in male chauvinistic ideas of femininity, but that does not mean they may act rough, use vulgar language, and bully the weak. In other words, new virtues are called for in women. Second, women should not make the mistake of following the same path taken by men, who have single-mindedly identified themselves with the organization or the company and, hence, are deeply trapped in power and money games. I believe it is necessary for women to successfully advance in society, but this is because I want women to bring to society and to the workplace different values from those held by old-fashioned men, or rather, to bring the feminine virtues that respect humanity. . . . Third, it's time to reconsider our ways of being as a society and as individuals, given that we are confronted with pressing issues such as environmental destruction [and] the problems faced by the people in the third world. . . . We can no longer afford to care about the happiness of only our own families. The dignity of the woman on a global scale is needed.[16]

Bandō's philosophy, as outlined in this statement, promotes ideas about gender that are hardly new in Japan. Since the era of postwar reforms pursued first in the 1950s, and again even more vigorously around the enactment of the EEOL (Equal Employment Opportunity Law) in the mid-1980s, the media, in describing gender issues, have often used rhetoric that suggests that while the Japanese women find their consciousness rapidly changing, Japanese men are still weighed down by their own traditional thinking. Cleverly manipulating this worn gender-gap rhetoric in ways that make it only seem fresh, Bandō emphasizes the need for "new" guidelines for women, many of whom she sees as acting like "old-fashioned" men. To justify her book's spotlight on women,

Bandō simultaneously draws on the equally familiar rhetoric that women can (and should) save the world with their gender's purportedly unique virtues. In the meantime, she makes sure to include the trendy concept of "global," pointing to women's responsibility to tend to world environmental problems rather than narrowly focus on their own homes. Bandō thus presents herself as an instructor in contradictions. In other words, while she proclaims that women need to develop certain qualities because these are required to meet the challenges of our increasingly globalized world, she simultaneously argues that these are the very characteristics women have always possessed by virtue of being women. Bandō, then, proceeds to describe what these virtues are.

As a woman living in the modern world, the dignified woman has a career. Unlike the majority of female workers in Japan, however, her career requires more than a nine-to-five schedule performing menial clerical tasks; therefore, she is one busy lady. Her rational approach enables her to stay cool and on top of things; for example, she does not hesitate to consider "outsourcing this proofreading to a printing company, changing that weekly meeting to a biweekly one, reading the minutes of this conference rather than actually observing it";[17] she also makes maximum use of "the time spent waiting in a hotel lobby, a train station, or an airport" to take care of small, but necessary tasks.[18] The dignified woman is a successful professional woman. She is totally together.

The dignified professional woman has a "global" (read: Westernized) consciousness. She learns to practice what she observes in her overseas travels: in Australia, she learns to promptly write a thank-you letter after every reception and business lunch she attends; if she is too busy, she sends at least a ready-made thank-you card, as Americans do. A manual written by a fashion critic from France teaches the dignified woman the value of "determining a personal basic color" for her wardrobe.[19] She makes sure to walk with her chin up and her back straight, modeling herself after the *Parisiennes*, whom she finds "much more cool and attractive" than their Tokyo sisters, despite the latter's "impeccable skin care" and their "newer, more expensive, trendier attire."[20]

As a professional, the dignified woman believes that "as long as one has a career, one must place it ahead of everything else."[21] Unlike many professional women in Japan, however, the dignified woman is married and has kids, and is devoted to her family. How does she manage the stress of excelling both in her career and at home—a task many female workers find almost impossible? Bandō to the rescue!

> Some women think housework is their responsibility even if they work outside the home. You should not try to do it all by yourself. Instead, make maximum use of a dishwasher, fully automatic washer and dryer, and microwave. When you are too busy or tired, employ a maid or professional cleaner, and don't feel guilty about it. Tell yourself that you have simply bought the time, and relax.[22]

As the Japanese government's Bureau for the Society of Gender Equality, for which Bandō served as its first general, is well aware, the upward trend of Japanese women delaying marriage and having fewer kids is due, at least partially, to the fact that they know too well that they will not be able to count on their husband's participation in the housework and childrearing: he is simply too exhausted and stressed out from his long commute and overtime work. Bandō, therefore, agrees that you "cannot expect someone at home to share your housework."[23] She therefore proposes taking a "rational" approach, that is, investing in expensive home appliances and professional domestic workers. Too bad if you cannot afford, let alone find, maids. The dignified woman has a successful career with an "international" flavor, which she puts ahead of everything else, yet she manages her home beautifully without her husband's help. Apparently, she is wealthy enough to do so.

As Bandō attempts to clarify, however, the dignified woman is not like the "nouveau riche" woman, who "leads a wasteful life without doing any housework."[24] For her family or friends, the dignified woman can "quickly fix delicious meals with the ingredients available in the kitchen."[25] She uses only "high-quality seasonings" and the "best-quality ingredients" because the dignified woman's well-developed taste buds "can tell an authentic flavor" from an artificial one.[26] Similarly, unlike "many Japanese, who have become affluent only within half a century,"[27] and whose homes are cluttered with unnecessary knickknacks and souvenirs, the dignified woman purchases only carefully selected items, including top-quality furniture. Her aristocratic taste is also reflected in the fact that she not only can recite passages of the Japanese literary classics, but can identify the names of the flowers that appear in them. Her prudent behaviors prove that she is a refined lady: she does not apply makeup on the train, and she makes sure that she "has well-taken-care-of skin and uses only light makeup."[28] The dignified woman does have her guilty pleasures, however. Bandō confesses that she herself takes delight in wearing "high-quality, new underwear."[29]

Thus, the dignified woman is a "has-it-all" superwoman who projects an upper-class aura while remaining ever modest and grounded in an appreciation for the old-fashioned values of frugality, respect, and sentiment. Bandō's impeccable credentials give her credibility as the advocate of this ideal. Born in 1946, Bandō went on to graduate from Tokyo University and entered the prime minister's office in 1969. She trod the path of a successful career bureaucrat, serving not only as the first general of the Bureau for Gender Equality, but also the first female consul general abroad, when she was assigned to Australia. She also became the deputy governor of Saitama Prefecture and is currently the president of Showa Women's University. In June 2008 she was also appointed the CEO of Asahi Beer Co. Simultaneously, true to her "dignified woman" ideal, Bandō has managed housework while raising two daughters with virtually no assistance from her spouse: as Onishi, the *New York Times* reporter cited earlier, writes, "Her husband, a salaryman, did not object [when she did not give up her career after the marriage] but told her flatly that he 'wouldn't help at all' at home."[30] In short, as Marie Iida, a writer based in Tokyo states, "Bandō perfectly embodies the kind of woman that tickles the fancy of young successful career women."[31] She has done it all and lived to tell the rest of us her secrets.

THE LOSER DOGS, THE DIGNIFIED WOMAN, AND THE POLITICS OF LOVABILITY

Three years prior to publication of *The Dignity of the Woman*, a book entitled *The Howl of the Loser Dog* (*Makeinu no tōboe*, 2003) had become a best-seller.[32] The book's popularity made the term "loser dog" a buzzword for unmarried career women. Its author, Sakai Junko, a professional writer twenty years junior to Bandō, humorously and self-mockingly describes the life of single women in their thirties (and older) who have a moderately successful career but no mate. She calls this group of women—herself included—the "loser dogs." Sakai writes:

> These days it has become taboo to talk about someone in terms of winning and losing. But such avoidance has prompted the very trend that has pushed us to get ever more caught up in a competitive frame of mind, pressing us to be always on the lookout as we try to size up, though silently to ourselves, whether we are winners or losers. In the case of a woman, people still make this judgment based on her marital status and whether or not she has kids. Thanks to the prevalence of self-censorship, however, it is now rare for people to make blatantly discriminatory remarks to our faces. They can no longer say to us single women in our thirties things like, "What? Still unmarried? Why? You may be OK now, but you will be lonely as you get older, you know." Instead, we receive an unspoken verdict that says, "Oh, I see, she is a loser."[33]

Even if married, however, not all women are equal. On the hierarchy among the married women, Sakai writes:

> On one end of this spectrum is the stay-at-home mom who found a rich husband and whose kids are successful in *ojuken* [the competitive educational race of "examination hell"]. At the other end is the housewife who has to work part-time to supplement her husband's low income, and whose kids end up becoming delinquent as a result.[34]

Yet, according to the logic of the loser dog, even the woman at the bottom of this hierarchy can console herself with the knowledge that she is better than those who remain unmarried. For Sakai, however, fighting such a prejudice does not accomplish much, but merely exhausts one. It is much wiser to save oneself the grief and just give in. Tongue in cheek, Sakai tells the unmarried woman to just "cower" and "expose [her] belly in a gesture of surrender, such as a loser dog does." Face up to the fact that this is the most realistic "way to get on in life."[35] It is a survival strategy.

It is not clear where Sakai would place the *married,* elite career woman such as Bandō (and her dignified woman). Is she below or above the rich stay-at-home mom, or is she beyond the spectrum? At any rate, given the sarcasm in evaluating the (real or imagined) competition among women for higher social status, Sakai would no doubt "cower and expose her belly" if she encountered a dignified woman. Of course, she would be secretly chuckling to herself all the while about the absurdity of the whole ranking game.

This generation of unmarried Japanese women were also scrutinized by the feminist psychologist Ogura Chikako. Her book *Conditions for Marriage (Kekkon no jōken*, 2004) delves into the unrealistic dreams harbored by many of today's single women in their thirties—or, to put it in Sakai's terms, the "loser dogs."[36] Many still dream of being the most enviable of all the top dogs, that is, a wealthy, stay-at-home mom. As Ogura argues, however, this desire, which she calls the "new housewife orientation," is a compromise for, in reality, it reflects women's cynical sense of resignation that "having it all"—a successful career, a husband, kids, and an elegant life—is not really a dream so much as a mirage well beyond their reach. It is in this context that *The Dignity of the Woman*, written by someone whose credentials seem to embody this impossible dream, sold phenomenally well—ten times as well as *The Howl of the Loser Dog*.

As noted earlier, Bandō sees the dignified woman as embodying the new virtues required of women living in a modern, globalized world, yet she contradicts herself by simultaneously stating that women already possess these virtues simply by being female. Not surprisingly, therefore, almost all of the reader reviews on Amazon.com.jp suggest, in one way or another, that the book's advice is nothing but old-fashioned common sense. While some criticize the book precisely because it serves up old homilies as new, others state that the book is still worth reading since it motivates them to improve themselves by reminding them of the old wisdom.

In fact, some readers respond very favorably to Bandō's nods to the past, expressing a sense of nostalgia for the good old days. A few reviewers self-identify as men (7 out of 149 as of June 2008), either in their response or by the handle they use in lieu of a name. Interestingly (but not surprisingly), it is these "male" reviewers who nostalgically look at the (imagined) past. One of them, for example, states that he bought the book because he was "frowning upon the ways women on TV speak and behave these days," which he contrasts with "the old days when a woman learned, as part of her bridal training, [what the book teaches] from her grandmother and mother, or at a finishing school" (Amazon hiroshi, 8/25/2007). Another "male" reviewer also recalls "the Japanese of the good, old days—the image that we modern Japanese tend to forget" (hideny, 8/1/2006). Another "male" reader explicitly argues that, in his opinion, "the main problem . . . is Westernization of the Japanese," and claims that "the author's message is that the Japanese should not forget their pride in being Japanese, the pride of having the heritage of *bushido*." (This reviewer seems oblivious to the fact that Bandō never touches on *bushido* and that she often praises "Western" sensibility as something we should emulate.) In short, these self-identified male reviewers pine for an imagined past when the Japanese were properly Japanese, men were properly men, and women were properly women.

For the majority of the reviewers, however, the book's old-fashioned advice is obsolete at best, and discriminatory and harmful at worst. One reviewer, for example, criticizes the way that Bandō "unquestioningly applauds the image of [subservient] Japanese womanhood (*yamato nadeshiko*)," a stance that she finds "hypocritical," in that this image "completely contradicts Bandō's credentials" as an elite career woman. In fact, reviewers repeatedly use such terms as "elitist," "pushy," "condescending," and "patronizing" to describe Bandō and her book despite Bandō's frequent use of a self-deprecating tone and her readiness to share faults and failures. One reviewer even describes Bandō as "simply pretending to be modest" and says that her "super-condescending gaze" nevertheless reveals itself (Mokutenryou, 10/2/2007).

Some readers point out that elite women like Bandō tend to end up identifying with men in power as a result of their own efforts to succeed in a male-dominated society. For example, one reviewer states, "After all, women like her who scold other women's attitudes and behaviors have had to carefully maneuver in a conservative [privileged] world to secure a place for themselves" (skinhead-f, 3/5/2008). Given the already cited positive reviews by "male" readers, it is particularly interesting to note how aptly this reviewer anticipates the book's appeal for men, when she writes that *The Dignity of the Woman* "will certainly be welcomed by those conservative folks who believe that 'men should act like men, women like women.'" Calling these men *oyaji* (dad or old man) and Bandō an "*oyaji* manipulator" (*oyaji korogashi*), another reviewer eloquently expresses her strong sense of irritation at conservative society, which is dominated by such men and the women who fawn on them:

> As I read the book, I became extremely frustrated without knowing why. Then it occurred to me, "Oh, this book is about how to be loved by *oyaji*, who are everywhere you look in Japan." After I realized this, I had no problem finishing the book. It is true that it will be easier to go about life if we know how to please *oyaji*, but I will have none of it. Without the author's impeccable academic and career credentials and her status as a wife and mother, this book would never even have existed or sold so well. Anyway, I am sick of the *oyaji* society that attaches too much importance to the type of "dignity" preached in this book. I am also sick of the women who cater to the needs of such a society. (Satsuma-imo, 2/22/2008)

Unlike Bandō, the majority of the alleged readers of her book—women in their twenties and thirties—are office ladies (OLs), low-paid clerical workers who have virtually no prospect of promotion. Many conduct books for OLs teach the "proper" ways of serving tea, bowing, greeting others, and so on. Not surprisingly, the manuals in this category do not question what is expected of OLs but instead seek to teach readers how to meet these expectations, calling it being "lovable" (*aisareru*).[37] More than twenty years after the passage of the EEOL, such manuals remain easy to find.[38]

It is in this context that it is worth noting that Bandō chooses to entitle one section of the book "Become a woman who loves (*aisuru*) rather than the one who is lovable/loved (*aisareru*)." Criticizing women's tendency to cling to the belief that happiness depends on one's lovability,

Bandō advises instead, "Let's love people around us as much as possible," and explains: "As the saying goes, 'Kindness is not done for the sake of others.' As you help and love others, you, too will become helped and loved, even before you realize it."[39] In short, Bandō is saying we should be lovable in order to be loved. And here, as the above reviewer who calls Bandō an "*oyaji* manipulator" succinctly points out, becoming "lovable" means accommodating "*oyaji* society." The term "oyaji society" is shorthand for Japan's postwar system of lifetime employment for the majority of salarymen. This system assumes that the male employee is willing to work endless hours of overtime, to accept transfers to other parts of Japan and abroad, and, importantly, that he has a wife who competently manages their home in his absence. Bandō's dignified woman makes sure her male bosses' and coworkers' needs are accommodated in the office, too.

The dignified woman that Bandō promotes is particularly obliging in this system, because, like her male counterparts, she puts work ahead of family, yet, unlike him, she does all the housework for the family. But what if she becomes pregnant or her kids or in-laws fall ill? Bandō advises:

> When it is time to exercise the rights guaranteed for workers, let's not forget to express our gratitude. The Maternity and Family Care Leave Act grants the female worker such rights as taking leaves and working reduced hours. These rights are indispensable if a woman wants to keep working while raising kids. Many women desired and fought for these rights for a long time. So when we exercise these rights, let's not forget to express our thanks to our colleagues and boss, and say to them, "I apologize in advance for the inconvenience," or "Thanks to your cooperation, I am able to have and raise my children."[40]

While the dignified woman is "grateful" to her boss and colleagues for their "cooperation," she never considers asking her husband to be "cooperative" in raising their kids and caring for sick family members. Lovability clearly has its costs.

As lovable as she may be to the "*oyaji* society," the dignified woman does not seem to be well loved by her readers. Some typical expressions that readers use to describe Bandō include: "She is such a 'nice' person that she seems to come straight from a textbook, but a society full of such people would be dull. . . . I find her unnatural, suspicious, and unapproachable" (nyan, 2008/4/16); "She has no human face, and what a bore! . . . She is way too nice but not appealing at all" (Micchan, 12/11/2007); "A woman who is too perfect . . . who almost feels like a machine" (nekomura shizu,

2007/12/8); "Cannot feel her human-ness, sweetness, warmth" (daisy, 10/29/2007); "A mean, unpleasant woman" (sasako, 10/11/2007); "An arrogant woman who must be hard to get along with" (yumi, 8/24/2007); and "Though anybody would find her pleasing, I can't imagine that she has any real friend" (tomosaru, 8/10/2007). In short, many readers feel that the dignified woman is a "teacher's pet" (*yūtōsei*) whom they cannot trust.

To be fair, Bandō does indicate that lovability is a strategy for survival in a male-dominated society, thus implying that the dignified woman is more than a mindless Goody Two Shoes. For example, after the quote cited above on taking a maternity leave, Bandō continues:

> Even if the law guarantees it, when you take a maternity leave, it will often burden others. Because of this, there are still many people who would say to themselves in disgust, "That's why women are useless." You might want to respond, "Hey, taking a maternity leave is our right." But that kind of attitude will unnecessarily provoke and upset such people. The same thing can be said about the EEOL. When [young people] find out that "male only" want-ads were normal prior to the EEOL, they might scream in disbelief, "You are kidding!" Yet various forms of discrimination persist. . . . Discrimination should not be tolerated. It is a fact that those who discriminate are wrong. Yet at the level of an individual, things will go much more smoothly if you silently make efforts and prove your ability while showing your gratitude to the people around you rather than screaming, "My rights, my rights, my rights!"[41]

Similarly, Bandō cites, as an example of the "undignified" woman, a female boss who addresses her *male* subordinates by *kun* (an informal title used to address one's equal or subordinate) or who uses informal speech when ordering them to do something for her. While use of this type of informal language by a male boss is usually regarded as perfectly normal, Bandō claims that it is "undignified" if used by a female boss (to *male* subordinates). She explains this double standard:

> She might intend [the informal speech] to express affection and closeness, but her [male subordinates] would simply regard this as a sign of haughtiness. If you politely ask them, "Would you please file this for me?" or "Would you please call so-and-so for me?" they will follow your orders more willingly. . . . There are still many men who are sensitive about being respected by women, and these men feel upset if they are spoken to as equals. All of this is ridiculous on their part. But I don't think that we should bother making waves about it.[42]

As mentioned earlier, many OL conduct books seek to teach female employees how to act properly feminine in the office, and hence "lovable" to their male colleagues and boss. While these manuals take for granted the expectation of such lovability, Bandō at least acknowledges that it is "ridiculous." As a woman who long struggled in the virtually all-male world of elite national bureaucrats, Bandō knows too well that, in order to succeed in such a world, it is often more efficient to go along with the double standard rather than loudly protesting it: the success of any woman depends on her being found "lovable" by the elite men for and with whom she works, and who continue to hold power over her. For Bandō, therefore, the lovability of the dignified woman is a survival strategy; it does not emerge as a result of her mindlessly identifying with the elite male world.

Nevertheless, as seen above, the image of the dignified woman fails to win sympathy from Bandō's readers; one reader explains:

> It must have been tough for a woman of the author's generation to pursue a successful career while raising kids. The challenges that the author encountered must be beyond comparison with the situation today. . . . Her book communicates well with regards to the difficulties she encountered and the strategies she took to overcome such difficulties. But it does not tell us much about how she was feeling in each of the processes and how she has grown as a result, which makes it hard for us to empathize with her. Because of this, the book gives us the impression that it is written by a successful, older woman who lives in a world different from ours and who talks down to us, which is most unfortunate. (pata, 7/24/2007)

As this reviewer perceptively notes, *The Dignity of the Woman's* readers cannot identify with Bandō's model of the dignified woman because they feel that she has not been honest enough to share her own struggles navigating *oyaji* society. While Bandō's advice amounts to pleasing the men in power, she acknowledges that having to do so is absurd. Yet Bandō makes this criticism in a cursory manner, without elaborating or sharing how she felt when complying with this double standard. Nor is she ready to laugh at the absurdity, the way that the "loser dog" Sakai, who pokes fun at the prejudice against unmarried women and at herself for going along with it, does. Instead, Bandō solemnly and without any sense of irony or sarcasm calls the act of pleasing a prejudiced, male-dominated society "dignified."

While Bandō works at the top of the business world and now enjoys the privilege of being at the other end of the spectrum from the OL in the organizational hierarchy, both she and the female clerical workers share a similar duty. Both are expected to be lovable to all the men around them, all of the time. Paradoxically, the OL is actually the one who can act much more freely than Bandō, the CEO. As the sociologist Yuko Ogasawara details in her 1996 book, contrary to the stereotype of subservience, many OLs engage in various acts of covert and overt resistance, sabotaging their male bosses and colleagues while laughing at the rat race they must run.[43] As Ogasawara points out, the OLs are able to engage in such sabotage because they are excluded from this race, and hence have nothing to lose. In contrast, as a participant in the race, Bandō cannot afford to offend elite men by confronting or ridiculing their chauvinism. Of course, as a former career bureaucrat who championed the "gender-free" society, Bandō has to make some token disapproving remarks about male chauvinism. But a lady remains diplomatic, never strident. She knows she catches more bees with honey! One reviewer describes how she had witnessed Bandō acting like "a typical tactful bureaucrat" at a reception she attended (so.b.it, 8/11/2007). A super-elite career woman, Bandō needs to be "tactful" not only at the reception: she must please everyone, which, unfortunately, makes her advice sound "half baked" (tuurukku, 8/7/2007).

CONCLUSION

One reviewer states that Bandō's book, which she sees as often making discriminatory statements against women, gets away with such remarks "thanks to the abuse of the term 'dignity'" (aja, 12/23/2007). Indeed, the success of *The Dignity of the Woman* (and *The Dignity of the Nation*) seems partially attributable to the fact that the term "dignity" has captured the collective imagination in the face of Japan's diminished status in the world and many individuals' sense of their new place in the nation. The term *hinkaku*, the combination of *hin* (refinement, classiness) and *kaku* (rank), conjures an aristocratic aura, suggesting one's superiority in tastes and virtues. In the context of Japan's losing its status in terms of economic power, the intangible concept of *hinkaku* may have provided some hope to citizens concerned with Japan's status in the world. Similarly, in the context of the prolonged recession, the term *hinkaku* may have given some solace to those who have been excluded from the dream of material success.

For many readers, however, the advice in *The Dignity of the Woman* is outdated because, in their eyes, it fails to adequately address the conditions of post-bubble Japanese society. For example, the reviewer who called Bandō "a typical tactful bureaucrat" writes:

> If you work in the private sector, you will not be able to succeed no matter how faithfully you follow the author's advice. The fact that this book became a best-seller may indicate that bureaucratic propriety is still valued in Japanese society. In this sense, this book may be very useful for women who are working for government offices or similarly old-fashioned organizations. (so.b.it, 8/11/2007)

Likewise, another reviewer speaks of the gap between privileged bureaucrats and the majority of Japanese:

> The book's advice may be useful for those who, like the author, have high academic credentials and work for the government. But it is not helpful for the majority of us, who work in diverse environments. This is particularly true now that competition has become more intense and our jobs have become unstable. (newsheep, 10/21/2007)

As Yoda notes, the prolonged economic recession in post-bubble Japan "became identified with the breakdown of the nation's unique economic system: the growth machine supported by the iron triangle (industry, bureaucracy, and single-party politics) as well as by the ethos of harmony and formidable work ethics of a homogeneous and highly disciplined population."[44] This sentiment about Japan during recession is a shared one, as is well reflected in the readers' quotes above. The readers speak to the sense that "the breakdown of the nation's unique economic system" is exposing the illusion of a "homogeneous" population, widening a gendered gap between those who have (i.e., elite, full-time workers, the majority of whom are men) and those who have not (i.e., the part-timers or temporary workers, the majority of whom are women). It is the sense that elite bureaucrats like Bandō are sheltered from this harsh reality that hits ordinary women particularly hard. As mentioned earlier, many OLs take advantage of their exclusion from the promotion track to exert a certain degree of informal power over their salarymen bosses and colleagues. To some extent this is possible because OLs are traditionally hired for full-time work: they know they cannot be easily fired on the basis of their job performance. Due to the prolonged recession, however, an increasing number of employers, big corporations in particular, have ceased to hire full-time OLs, replacing them with temporary workers (*haken*).[45] This trend, of course, could significantly undermine the subversive power that OLs have long been able to wield as full-time employees with a degree of job security. After all, anyone can fire an uppity temp!

Or, can they? A recent TV drama series entitled *The Dignity of the Temp* (*Haken no hinkaku*, 2007) gives a different picture. I close my discussion of Bandō's book by reading this drama as yet another line of advice to women. *The Dignity of the Temp* became popular approximately two months after the debut of *The Dignity of the Woman*.[46] The TV show's heroine, Omae Haruko, is a *haken* worker, but an exceptional one. Her salary is ranked "Special A"—she earns three thousand yen per hour, a salary that only 0.1 percent of *haken* workers surveyed by the Ministry of Health, Labor, and Welfare in 2004 were fortunate enough to earn.[47] In many ways, Omae is the antithesis of Bandō's ideal of the dignified woman. She is in her mid-thirties and remains unmarried—a "loser dog" in Sakai's terms. She used to work at a bank as a full-time OL but was fired due to the bank's restructuring. After the layoff, she worked at a fish market in Tsukiji, dismantling tuna (!), but she was again fired, out of the blue, which led to her present job working for a food company on a three-month contract. A lone wolf, Omae refuses to settle down: she works only for three months, spends the next three months traveling, and intends to maintain this work–travel cycle. She is remarkably unconcerned with being seen as lovable by the men in her workplace: she refuses to do any overtime work; does only what is specified in the contract, never assisting people outside of the section she is assigned to; and takes orders only from her immediate boss, ignoring those from other superiors, including the top executives. Her salarymen bosses and colleagues are initially put off by her assertiveness, but they somehow come to accept and even admire her by the end of her three-month contract.

The Dignity of Haken, thus, cleverly combines the realistic with the fantastic. It highlights the type of employment that many women in post-bubble Japan find themselves in—laboring as a *haken* worker. Yet its heroine's portrait is completely unrealistic. Omae possesses extraordinary skills that bring her exceptional earning power for a *haken* worker. She started her *haken* career in a cashier's job at a grocery store, earning only six hundred yen per hour, but she somehow managed to obtain more than twenty licenses and certificates of various kinds, including ones for operating crane trucks and handling nuclear fuels! Her extraordinary abilities cause her to be accepted and admired by her bosses and colleagues despite the fact that she obviously makes no effort to be lovable. Interestingly, as the quotes above show, readers of *The Dignity of the Woman* feel that being lovable is not enough to survive in post-bubble Japan, where "the nation's unique economic system" is breaking down. Many women seem to sense that this breakdown is undermining the conditions that traditionally allowed them to flaunt the stereotype that demanded they be lovable but that also allowed them to exercise subversive power over their salarymen colleagues. Bandō and Omae may have credentials that are equally out of reach, making them nothing but "fantasy" role models for many OLs. Yet women can at least empathize with Omae and enjoy the vicarious thrill of her acting with indifference because, instead of preaching about being lovable, she does not give a damn and still is loved in the end.

NOTES

1. Fujiwara Masahiko, *Kokka no hinkaku* (The dignity of the nation) (Tokyo: Shinchō Shinsho, 2005).

2. Bandō Mariko, *Josei no hinkaku* (The dignity of the woman) (Tokyo: PHP Shinsho, 2006).

3. For example, see Makihara Kumiko, "Japan's Subtle Etiquette Code," *International Herald Tribune*, July 10, 2007; Onishi Norimitsu, "Japanese Author Guides Women to 'Dignity,' but Others See Dullness," *New York Times*, March 29, 2008; Bruce Wallace, "Japan Talks Dignity, or Lack Thereof," *Los Angeles Times*, September 22, 2007.

4. http://www.j-cast.com/tv/2007/12/29015146.html.

5. Onishi, "Japanese Author Guides Women to 'Dignity.' "

6. Ibid.

7. Morita Akio and Ishihara Shintarō, NO *to ieru Nippon* (The Japan that can say "no") (Tokyo: Kappa Books, 1989).

8. Harry Harootunian and Tomiko Yoda's "Introduction" to their edited volume *Japan after Japan: Social and Cultural Life from the Recessionary 1990s to the Present* (Durham, N.C.: Duke University Press, 2006), 2.

9. Harootunian and Yoda, "Introduction," *Japan after Japan*, 3.

10. See, for example, Fujiwara's *Kono kuni no kejime* (The distinction of this country) (Tokyo: Bunshun Bunko, 2008); *Sokoku towa kokugo* (The motherland is the national language) (Tokyo: Shinchō Bunko, 2005).

11. Abe Shinzō, *Utsukushii kuni e* (To the beautiful country) (Tokyo: Bunshun Shinsho, 2006); Aso Tarō, *Totetsumonai Nihon* (Incredible Japan) (Tokyo: Shinchōsha, 2007).

12. http://www.yomiuri.co.jp/book/news/20080423bk04.htm.

13. Bandō, *Josei no hinkaku*, 196.

14. http://www.yomiuri.co.jp/book/news/20080423bk04.htm.

15. Interestingly, six months prior to the publication of *The Dignity of the Woman,* a book entitled *The Dignity of the Man* was published, but did not sell well at all.

16. Bandō, *Josei no hinkaku*, 5–6.
17. Ibid.
18. Ibid.
19. Ibid., 74.
20. Ibid., 80.
21. Ibid., 176.
22. Ibid., 177–178.
23. Ibid., 175.
24. Ibid., 107.
25. Ibid., 108.
26. Ibid.
27. Ibid., 116.
28. Ibid., 88.
29. Ibid., 70.
30. Ibid.
31. Iida Marie, "Dignity of Women," on the blog NeoJaponisme, http://neojaponisme.com/2007/10/23/dignity-of-women/.
32. Sakai Junko, *Makeinu no tōboe* (The howl of the loser dog) (Tokyo: Kōdansha, 2003).
33. Ibid., 9.
34. Ibid., 8.
35. Ibid.
36. Ogura Chikako, *Kekkon no jōken* (Conditions for marriage) (Tokyo: Asahi Shinbun-sha, 2004).
37. Interestingly, as Bardsley's analysis in this volume shows, some manuals for men guide young men to be lovable to their OL colleagues, if not their older female boss, and *oyaji* men to both their stay-at-home (old) wives and to their young OL subordinates.
38. Look, for example, at Nishide Hiroko's *Aisare OL no isshūkan oshigoto jutsu* (The art of being a lovable OL from Monday through Friday) (Tokyo: Sōgō Hōrei Shuppan, 2006). In fact, when you "google" conduct books for OLs on Amazon.com.jp, the majority of the books that come up on the first page do contain the term "lovable" (*aisareru*) in the titles!
39. Bandō, *Josei no hinkaku*, 190–192.
40. Ibid., 211.
41. Ibid., 211–212.
42. Ibid., 49–50.
43. Yuko Ogasawara, *Office Ladies and Salaried Men: Power, Gender, and Work in Japanese Companies* (Berkeley: University of California Press, 1998).
44. Tomiko Yoda, "A Roadmap to Millennial Japan," in Yoda and Harootunian, *Japan after Japan*, 2.
45. According to the Ministry of Health, Labor and Welfare, approximately 80 percent of corporations with five hundred or more employees used *haken* (temporary) workers in 2004. http://www.mhlw.go.jp/toukei/itiran/roudou/koyou/haken/04/index.html.

46. The information about this TV drama series is based on its official Web site, http://www.ntv.co.jp/haken.

47. According to the Ministry of Health, Labor and Welfare, 50.7 percent earned between 1,000 and 1,500 yen, 24.1 percent earned 1,500 to 2,000 yen, and 21.2 percent earned 1,000 yen or less in 2004. http://www.mhlw.go.jp/toukei/itiran/roudou/koyou/haken/04/index.

CHAPTER 8

Making and Marketing Mothers

Guides to Pregnancy in Modern Japan

AMANDA C. SEAMAN

> After several days, I already had forgotten there were pregnancy magazines in the house. However, my husband hadn't. "Hey! Have you read the pregnancy books I bought?" he suddenly asked me. I vaguely replied, "I think that I've already read them." Hearing me sidestep the issue, he saw through me. "I'm not a liar. I read them but I already forgot them. I'm just not a reading person."[1]

Amid falling birthrates and talk of Japan as a "childless society" (*shōshika*), there has been a marked increase in the marketing of goods and services to pregnant women. Among the products in this "boom" are advice and how-to books and magazines for expectant mothers. To be sure, advice manuals, particularly pregnancy-advice manuals, are not unique to Japan. Moreover, the twenty-first century Japanese version of such manuals, with its full-folio pages, glossy paper, color photographs, and guides to trendy baby names, reflects only the latest stage in a history reaching back to the Tokugawa era (1603–1868). In this chapter, therefore, I wish not only to explore how manuals and magazines for expectant women have changed from their beginnings in the Tokugawa period, when they were created for a literate and moneyed minority, to the present day, when they address a socially and economically diverse audience, but also to demonstrate the degree to which this body of works has consistently served as a medium for the representation and (just as significantly) the regulation of the pregnant female body. The genre of pregnancy manuals represents a curious mixture of social practice, folk beliefs, and medical advice, and reveals the more general expectations of and attitudes toward women held by the societies that produce it. Examining these manuals thus sheds light on how pregnancy has been perceived not only in the past but also now, when birth rates are plummeting and anxieties about the future of the "Japanese people" itself are expressed in editorials, at think tanks, and on the floor of the Diet.

Pregnancy-advice manuals reflect change both in scientific and medical knowledge, and in social and cultural practices. They do more than provide a means for women to learn about their bodies and the changes they will undergo; they also offer a window into how women's reproductive bodies have been perceived by society, and how knowledge of pregnancy has been transmitted to women. For instance, a manual that teaches women what to do in order to gestate a child would seem to be simply a variation on the generic "how-to" guide—how to cook, how to build a patio, how to change a car's oil; as Robbie Kahn has noted, the pregnancy-advice manual aims to "instruct and guide a woman through pregnancy, childbirth and lactation."[2] Unlike the examples described earlier, however, the techniques being taught in the pregnancy guide are not directed at some external physical object—chicken gizzards, lumber and nails, the oil pan. On the contrary, childbirth literature is fundamentally a literature about the body and how it acts. These guides thus must create what Kahn has called "a textuality for life itself, and . . . could be said to be written in lifeworld language," a language "concerned in a unique way with how to live and what to do."[3] Kahn notes, "Childbirth literature also accepts the prevailing medical language as its own—often resorting to statistics and technical language rather than plain speech."[4] As a result, the "lifeworld language" of the pregnancy manual, in Japan as much as in the United States, is in fact a kind of diglossia—one language is chatty and informal and the other clinical and detached—and these languages are juxtaposed in uncomfortable and off-putting ways or segregated within entirely different sections of the text. This duality says volumes, I would suggest, about the way in which elite and everyday discourses both have a place in the process by which pregnancy is represented and regimented within any social milieu.

In the rest of this chapter, therefore, I will explore the changing attitudes, emphases, and languages that defined pregnancy manuals from three historical periods: the Tokugawa (1603–1868), during which Confucian principles of social regulation and behavior shaped the ideal relationship between a mother and her fetus; the early Showa (1926–1940), in which issues of public health and hygiene dominated approaches to pregnancy and the pregnant woman's body; and the contemporary Heisei period (1989–), in which pregnancy has come to be seen in terms of "lifestyle" and the pregnant woman has been refashioned as a fertile consumer of material goods and a fruitful producer of human life. In each case, I will discuss how pregnancy manuals have been used by society to create, discipline, and define women, their bodies, and their choices.

THE TOKUGAWA ERA: THE AGE OF COMPORTMENT

The era of the Tokugawa shogunate (1603–1868) marked the birth of the genre of the "instructional manual," books and pamphlets meant to guide an individual's conduct and behavior in a variety of social contexts. The appearance of this genre was the result of a series of interrelated economic, political, and technological changes in the early seventeenth century. The first of these was the rise of a new social stratum, that of the *chōnin* ("townspeople"), who owed their influence and power to money and mercantile activity rather than to high birth and the possession of landed property. The growth of a consumer economy brought with it the expansion of goods and services to a broader population, one that required guidance as to their proper use and enjoyment. A good example of this phenomenon is that of the "floating world" or "pleasure quarters" of Edo. There, an increasingly non-samurai clientele, often satirized for its social *faux pas* by writers such as Ihara Saikaku, sought guidance in a variety of texts containing rules for appropriate conduct.[5] In turn, with the rise in importance of the mercantile class, the ruling class elaborated and disseminated a neo-Confucian ideology of hierarchical order and obligations, both to maintain social control and to manage the potentially dramatic changes that the rise of the *chōnin* might bring to the traditional political and social order. Rules of etiquette, once the purview of high-ranking samurai families, were adopted by and applied to wealthy commoners as they moved up the social hierarchy.[6] Finally, the rise of printing and print culture in the early seventeenth century made it possible not simply to codify and standardize social rules and mores but to make them available to a broader audience, namely, in the form of the printed manual or pamphlet.[7]

A particularly important segment of this audience was women. The growing affluence of merchants and craftsmen brought with it ever-larger households and social obligations, whose management required wives to master a broad array of economic, personal, and moral skills and expectations. While these skills and expectations had deep roots within high-born samurai society, there was concern among traditional elites that commoners lacked the "moral education and internal discipline to comport themselves with prudence and wisdom."[8] To address this concern, a variety of guides to proper behavior and morals were published and revised over the ensuing decades—the so-called *jokun* or "women's training manuals," written in the *kana* syllabary and addressing topics such as moral values, proper deportment, and home management.[9]

One of the most important and widely read of these *jokun* was the *Onna chōhōki* (Record of women's treasures), first published in 1692, which offered *chōnin* women a synopsis of the female rituals, behaviors, and duties followed in the warrior households of earlier centuries. William Lindsey indicates that this manual in particular follows the Ogasawara rituals, which came into being in the Muromachi period (1333–1573).[10] While a number of recent studies have been devoted to this rich and complex text, it is most significant for our purposes because of the guidance it contains regarding pregnancy and childbirth, including a series of drawings depicting fetal development in utero.[11] As Yuki Terazawa has pointed out, this material was drawn directly from a medical handbook of the time, *Fujin kotobukigusa* (The book for a woman's auspicious moment, 1692), which, along with the *Inagogusa* (Grasshopper manual, 1690–1691) was a popular text in its own right.[12] As the practice of medicine shifted from dependence upon Chinese cosmological principles to the observation of bodily symptoms, competing schools of physicians created handbooks to circulate their ideas, texts that, despite their paucity of practical guidance, became handbooks for lay people. In particular, birth manuals such as the *Inagogusa* and the *Fujin kotobukigusa* were especially long-lived because, unlike earlier texts on childbirth, they offered detailed accounts of the entire cycle of pregnancy, childbirth, and "lying-in."

The *Fujin kotobukigusa* reflected the Neo-Confucian pro-natalist rhetoric that advocated large patrilineal families and the birth of a male heir. Moreover, in keeping with the philosophical tenets of the day, it assumed that one's moral behavior affected not only the social world but also one's physical well-being.[13] As a result, it was filled with practical, behavioral advice meant to protect the development of the pregnant woman's baby. The expectant mother, we are told, should avoid "taking too much medicine, excessive drinking, inappropriate moxibustion and acupuncture, urinating in inappropriate places, carrying heavy things, stretching [herself] to grab something out of reach and walking up a steep path."[14] In addition, she was supposed to guard herself from improper foods, music, and scenes.

To a degree, this association between maternal behavior and fetal well-being was consonant with the notion of "maternal impressions" found in other cultures, including those of Western Europe and the United States; pregnant women thus were supposed to avoid certain foods because consuming them would leave a physical impression on their children (strawberries, for example, would leave a red mark on the infant).[15] In the Tokugawa era, however, maternal impressions were thought to be not only physical but also behavioral in nature. The proper comportment of the pregnant mother-to-be was critical, since it would produce a visible outcome: both physical behavior and proper mental attitudes were consolidated under the rubric of *taikyō* or "fetal education." As the *Fujin kotobukigu*'s author, Katsuki Gyūzen, noted, a mother who wanted to have a handsome and virtuous child should say only righteous things, avoid indecent gossip, wear pearls, and keep herself looking beautiful, while at the same time avoiding the company of ugly women, cripples, and the physically inferior.[16]

In these texts, the womb was defined as the central locus for both the mother's and the fetus's bodies. As a result, the mother's body acquired special significance, since her treatment of it became what Lindsey has described as "the prime initiator of her and her fetus's health."[17] This sensibility was reflected in the *Onna chōhōki*, which drew upon the medical tradition as the basis for its own advice on maternal behavior. For instance, sexual intercourse during unusual weather events (e.g., high winds, typhoons, or earthquakes), or in front of religious statuary, was strongly discouraged for its potentially deleterious health effects, such as fetal damage, difficult delivery, and shortening of the child's life.[18] Diet was a particular focus of the *Onna chōhōki*, which discussed four broad categories of food—two of them to be sought after (foods that would enrich the fetus and mother, and foods that would increase breast-milk production), and two of them to be avoided assiduously (foods that could damage the fetus or the mother, and foods that could cause moral failings in the child). Some foods were to be avoided outright: crab and ginger, for example, were said to cause lateral births and gnarled digits. In other cases, it was combinations of food that posed a danger, and not only to the fetus's immediate, physical well-being: eating sparrow together with rice wine, the text warned, made it more likely that a woman's child would fall into lascivious ways.[19]

The *Onna chōhōki* remained the main guide for women throughout the Tokugawa era. It was revised and reprinted a number of times, with the last significant revision occurring in 1847. While it continued to adhere to the teachings of Gyūzen, it gradually came to incorporate the insights and methods of the Kagawa School of medicine, which relied much more upon deductive analysis and experimental observation than on earlier, Chinese-influenced thought. This new approach resulted in more detailed descriptions of the in utero fetus, and a far less Buddhist perspective than was found in the original version of 1692.[20] Despite these often sweeping changes in medical theory and practice during the course of the Tokugawa period, however, the belief in the "critical role a pregnant women's behavior played in the destiny of her body and the fetal body" remained unchanged—a fact reflected in the persistent use of the term *mimochi* (behavior) to describe not only the woman's personal conduct but also her pregnant body (one shared, notably, with the fetus).[21]

FROM MEIJI TO PREWAR JAPAN: THE AGE OF CLEANLINESS

The changes in medical and scientific practice that began to pick up speed during the last years of the Tokugawa era were only intensified by the Meiji reforms of the late nineteenth century. This transformation had an equally profound effect upon women and childbearing. One of its earliest manifestations was that midwifery became the purview of the state. Midwives now were required to obtain official licenses in order to facilitate, or even attend, childbirths; in turn, new regulations for midwifery substituted Western, "modern" techniques for traditional Japanese ones, imparting them through textbooks written by both government hygiene officials and obstetricians.[22] As a result, the use of devices such as the "birthing chair," in which new mothers were required to sit for a week after childbirth with their legs tied shut, was abandoned in favor of the contemporary Euro-American practice of "lying-in."[23] These changes in pre- and post-partum practice, however, were prompted by the Meiji government's broader campaign of "modernization" and national aggrandizement, summarized under the rubric "enrich the country, strengthen the military" (*fukoku kyōhei*).

Women's health, and particularly maternal well-being, occupied an increasingly important place within this campaign. Hygiene and health were seen as critical building blocks for a modern, growing state, an association already emphasized by European reformers in the nineteenth century. As had been the case during the Tokugawa period, elite concerns about the role, behavior, and health of women were expressed through the dissemination of information and advice given directly to women. In place of the Tokugawa guides to conduct, the dominant medium for such communication in the Meiji and Taisho periods was the new and flourishing genre of women's magazines. *Fujin sekai* (Women's world) started featuring advice columns and question-and-answer sections on women's health as early as 1906, a trend that grew during the subsequent decades.[24]

Yet, while these efforts were initially broad in scope, emphasizing bodily knowledge and general health, the reproductive role of women increasingly became paramount as Japanese politicians and military leaders saw demographic growth as essential for national power and expansion, an attitude that became dominant after the Manchurian Incident in 1931 and the onset of active military activity on the Chinese mainland. As Sabine Frühstück has noted, "When politico-economic activities decisively shifted toward imperialist actions in East and South-East Asia, the expansive qualities of the (fertile) female physique appeared in the foreground of the discourse on sex, revealing a preoccupation with the womb, the uterus, fertility and race . . . [feeding] efforts to elevate the value of women's reproductive organs for empire building."[25] As a result, "women's health" now began with menstruation and centered upon pregnancy and childbirth, epitomized by the official slogan, "Let's give birth and increase our population!" (*Umeyo fuyaseyo!*).

This consciousness found its way into the pregnancy manuals of the time, which reveals profound changes in the discourse on pregnancy and birth. Rather than offering cultural admonitions about what foods or activities might cause the fetus to become an immoral young man or woman, the new manuals embraced a far more objective, scientific tone, treating the woman's body as a site both of production and of potential disruption by illness and infection. This fresh approach can be seen in the new emphasis on eugenics and what might be called (somewhat anachronistically) "reproductive science," and on cleanliness and hygiene. The 1932 *Complete Guide to Marriage and Childbirth* (*Kekkon to shussan zenshū*), for example, provided a long and quite technical discussion of Mendelian genetics, while the 1930 manual *Pregnancy, Childbirth, and Fetal Education* (*Ninshin yori ikuji made to taikyō*) suggested the potential benefits of "artificial fertilization" (*jinkō jusei*, presumably a reference to artificial insemination) for humans, pointing to its proven value in livestock breeding.[26]

Clearly, this emphasis reflected the policy interests of the Japanese state, which saw population growth and the elimination of "undesirable" traits as crucial elements for the establishment of Japanese hegemony within Asia. The pro-natalist ideology of the 1930s, for example, informed the manuals' cursory, and often hostile, treatment of abortion. The 1932 *Complete Guide to Marriage and Childbirth* has a section with the heading "Don't Have an Illegal Abortion!" (*Yami shujutsu wa ikenai!*), containing four pages of warnings about the dangers to the mother's health and concluding with an admonition to avoid abortion at all costs. Nevertheless, it is worth noting that Japanese feminists had been early advocates for hygiene laws and eugenics. Hiratsuka Raichō and Ichikawa Fusae, for instance, argued that men should submit documents before marriage stating that they were free of venereal diseases. Sumiko Otsubo has argued that the Eugenic Marriage Popularization Society (*Yūseikekkon fūkyūkai*) and its magazine *Yūsei* (Eugenics), both established in 1935, offered an important forum for activists such as Hiratsuka to advocate for the "protection of mothers" (*bosei hogo*). Indeed, much of the information provided in *Yūsei* focused on positive eugenics and how to achieve this through marriage.[27] Likewise, the inclusion of detailed information on "family planning" (*katei keikaku*), including multiple methods of birth control—condoms, pessaries, sponges, and the rhythm method—indicates that pro-natalism and population enhancement, while significant influences on the prewar discourse on reproduction, were neither absolute nor monolithic in nature.

Eugenics concerns, however, were overshadowed in early Showa pregnancy manuals by issues of health and hygiene. *The Complete Guide to Marriage and Childbirth* thus began with the chapter "Marriage and Hygiene," and throughout the genre the topic was presented in prophylactic terms. Pregnancy, the manuals suggested, was a minefield of potential illness and "women's diseases" (*fujin no kakariyasui byōki*), which had to be negotiated carefully to ensure successful childbirth and a healthy baby. Most pregnancy manuals thus were devoted to defining potential diseases during pregnancy, describing their symptoms, and prescribing hygienic techniques designed to prevent their onset.[28] Such solicitude was not confined to pregnancy, to be sure. One pregnancy manual described each stage of female sexual maturation in terms of its accompanying diseases and potential health problems; under the heading "young women's ailments" (*shōjo no byōki*), for example, were included sections on candida and trichomoniasis in addition to putatively more serious ailments, such as the inability to grow body hair. Nevertheless, the attainment of childbearing age was accompanied by a tenfold increase in potential afflictions, each of which required special care and attention. Entire sections were devoted to the treatment of flu, pneumonia, and a range of other ailments (running the gamut from tooth decay to heart disease) during pregnancy.

Prewar pregnancy guides, however, did not simply contain a long list of illnesses and lectures on breeding; they also provided extensive information about nutrition, exercise, bathing, and even beauty, with sections addressing hair and skin care during pregnancy. In order to serve all women in Japan, *From Pregnancy to Childbirth* (published in 1928) included a special section on farm life, explaining how to balance the demands of agricultural labor with pregnancy, and how to maintain proper nutrition in rural areas.[29] Since most births occurred at home, there was extensive discussion of how to prepare the home birth room. Moreover, while the manuals took the presence of a midwife for granted, they also provided information on how to wrap the belly (with bands similar to *hara obi*) after birth, suggesting that in some cases midwives were either rare or unavailable. Once the baby was born, there also was information about how to cope with the afterbirth, and the various illnesses that commonly afflicted newborns.

In general, then, pregnancy and childbirth were treated during the Meiji and early Showa periods as scientific matters, amenable to management through the provision of proper information, due vigilance, and hygienic conditions. Yet while the moralizing discourse of "maternal impressions" found in the Tokugawa women's manuals had no explicit place in this modern language of birth, it is important to note the deeper resonances between them. As in the *Onna chōhōki*, it was the mother who bore the ultimate responsibility for the success or failings of her offspring, a responsibility tied intimately to the way in which she managed and protected her body, defined as the matrix for fetal growth and development. In the words of the postwar edition of *The Complete Guide to Marriage and Childbirth*, "From the time she is pregnant, the mother's everyday words and action create a beautiful feeling and have an effect of the fetus."[30]

POSTWAR JAPAN: FROM PATIENT WIFE TO SAVVY SHOPPER

In the aftermath of the war, Japanese society was focused both upon rebuilding a shattered country and, just as importantly, on regaining the sense of normalcy that had been lost during the long decades of conflict and deprivation. Marriage and family life were critical elements of this process of normalization: on the one hand, the return of men from army service and the establishment of a peacetime economy made possible a new focus upon family life, while stable households made possible daily (male) labor and the raising of a new generation of postwar Japanese citizens and consumers. The valorization of parenting and family life, which marked the postwar period, was epitomized by the marriage in 1959 of the crown prince, Akihito, to the commoner Shōda Michiko. Their carefully cultivated embrace of quotidian familial activities and relationships was set before the Japanese public as an example to which all young Japanese couples might aspire. More to the point, Michiko's decision to nurse and raise her own children, rather than place them in the care of imperial household staff, established "mothering" as the proper and most valuable contribution that Japanese women could make to the process of recovery and normalization.[31]

The conservative nature of this reemphasis upon motherhood and family was reflected in the continued popularity of prewar pregnancy manuals. Although sections were added to reflect new vaccination and other requirements, some of them prompted by the occupation government, in large part the texts available to women in the late 1940s and 1950s were identical to those that had been used by their counterparts two decades earlier. In the 1960s, however, the ascendancy of new obstetric procedures and technologies, in addition to the introduction into Japan of new theories of child development and childrearing, produced a sizable change in the focus, organization, and content of pregnancy literature. While the fundamental identification of pregnancy and childbirth with marriage and the nuclear family continued to hold sway, the new manuals reflected a shift in childbirth away from the home (where most routine births had occurred before and immediately after the war), to the hospital, and from participation by a midwife to supervision by physicians. In a fashion similar to that seen in the Meiji period, pregnancy and childbearing were being reframed, with the process now defined as a series of medical, technological procedures in which the woman was as much passive patient as active participant. This reframing was performed by the manuals themselves, which were arranged in terms of hospital protocols and demands, such as the monthly series of standard obstetric examinations, shaving, episiotomy, monitoring, and so forth.

This format, with occasional updates reflecting new technology (and new hairstyles), held sway until the arrival of the Internet age in the 1990s. Today, Japan is awash in information for women having children, with computers and cell phones enabling instant, around-the-clock access to chat rooms, discussion groups, nonprofit databases, and company Web sites. The traditional print media has grown apace, with multiple companies publishing advice manuals for pregnant women, monthly magazines targeting pregnant women and their children, and educational resources addressing every aspect of the child's life and development. In addition, when a woman begins her prenatal care, many of the larger hospitals, which publish their own information on pregnancy and delivery, distribute these materials to their own patients.

The most notable element in this new body of pregnancy literature is the genre of pregnancy magazines. A leader in this field is the Shufu no Tomo Company, which, in addition to its "Balloon" series of pregnancy guides, publishes the glossy monthly magazine *Pre-Mo* (short for "premotherhood") and a spinoff set of pamphlets. Recently, the Recruit company launched its own line of magazines geared toward wealthier readers, heralded by the March 2004 appearance of *Nin-sugu* (a neologism created from the words *ninshin*, meaning "pregnancy," and *sugu*, meaning "soon"). The most overt integration of consumer culture and pregnancy can be found in the so-called mooks (book-length materials in a magazine format), one of which is published by Gakushū Kenkyūsha under the title *Pregnant Living* (Ninshin seikatsu). These mooks combine catalogues of seasonal maternity fashion with health and lifestyle content for expectant women. Two such mooks were released in the summer of 2006, one for women in the first through fifth months of pregnancy and the other for those in the fifth through tenth months of pregnancy. Each came with free gifts for the reader: maternity underwear (complete with a picture of a dog) for those early in their pregnancy, and a decorative cover for the *boshi techo* (the mother–child health record issued by the local government) for those nearing their delivery date.[32]

Each of these three magazines is aimed at a different audience, defined in terms not only of age but also of social class. Notably, these distinctions are encoded in consumerist terms—namely, by the country of origin and cost of the goods being advertised in each magazine, and (to a lesser extent) by the age of the real-life female models who appear in them, as well as the professions of their husbands.[33] Women who are having children in their later twenties and thirties often have a higher education level and have worked longer, and have more money to spend on baby goods and clothing for themselves. By these criteria, Gakushū Kenkyūsha's mooks are aimed at the wealthiest and most high-status group of readers. The products they advertise are comparable in price and exclusivity to those found in high-end general women's magazines, while their models represent, in attire and surroundings, a level of material well-being possible only for the wealthiest segment of Japan's population. In their own way, however, *Pregnant Living*'s counterparts are driven by the similar goal of guiding pregnant women in the creation of miniature consumers, wrapped in designer baby clothes from birth and driven around in Italian strollers.

This agenda is reflected in the editorial content of the magazines. To a degree, each attempts to address its target audiences with specially crafted content: feature articles on prenatal sources of stress (and methods of relaxation), the costs and benefits of childbearing in one's thirties (a relatively new phenomenon in Japan), and ways to reduce stretch marks (in particular, through the use of various name-brand creams and ointments). In other cases, however, the editors tap into recent consumer trends and recast them for pregnant women. In magazines from 2005 to 2007, for example, aromatherapy, yoga for stress reduction, and fashions were adapted for the expectant set, while the standard women's magazine litany of nutrition and menu-planning advice made its appearance as well, with day-by-day diets including recipes and calorie counts for each dish.[34]

Moreover, whatever the target demographic of the various magazines, each relies upon time-tested tools of niche marketing in order to maintain and cultivate its readership, in particular, soliciting reader information via response cards at the back of each issue and offering monthly freebies (such as music CDs) as incentives.[35] Such information gathering has editorial value, insofar as it provides potential real-life models for the magazines, in addition to personal stories and details that can be mined for future content. Just as importantly, however, the reader-response cards allow the media companies to generate a large database in order to market both baby products and merchandise for older children.[36]

These efforts are supported and advanced, finally, by the synergistic use of magazine Web sites, where featured items are offered for sale, and by a range of other services—most notably, baby-naming guides, which provide up-to-date lists of trendy names and *kanji* (Chinese characters) suitable for boys and girls. The authors of *Pregnant Living* even provide advice on name selection to help parents avoid names that would be considered embarrassing or confusing in foreign countries. For example, a reliable girl's name such as Mariko is a bad idea for the globetrotting woman-to-be, since *maricón* means "homosexual" in Spanish. In turn, naming your son Katsuo could lead to his being the victim of jibes on business in Italy (due to the name's similarity to *ragazzo*, Italian for "little boy").[37]

Taken as a whole, therefore, the various magazines devoted to pregnancy and childbirth reveal striking continuities with the broader patterns of consumer culture and consumer marketing in Japan, imbricating pregnancy tightly within the web of consumerism and capitalist commercialism that defines so much of contemporary Japanese life, particularly in the urban centers. Pregnant women still are valued as producers, but now the product of their labor(s) is perceived less as future soldiers, workers, and wives than as future consumers. At the same time, this recent pregnancy literature treats pregnancy itself as a kind of "lifestyle" and casts its participants as a niche market. As a result, the media approach to pregnancy has shifted, blending counsel with commercialism to frame pregnancy not only as a process of physical and emotional transformation culminating in the baby's arrival, but as a ten-month-long shopping binge.

In contrast to the magazines, with their pop-journalistic tone and focus upon what might be called the ephemera of pregnancy, the newer generation of pregnancy manuals represents a more traditional and ostensibly professional source of guidance to the expectant mother. In particular, while the content and editorial decisions of the magazines are made by nonmedical writers and journalists (in consultation, they hasten to add, with "professional advisers"), the manuals continue to be written by medical experts such as doctors and nurses who hold high positions in maternity hospitals around Japan.[38] One of the most popular of these texts comes from the publishing company Benesse, which was founded in 1955 and promotes itself as "Caring for your well-being and creating it with you."[39] In addition to offering educational and language instruction materials (Berlitz International is a subsidiary), Benesse produces a number of products and resources under the Tamahiyo Club label aimed at women who wish to "enjoy their own lives and remain socially active while caring for homes and children." Among these are magazines, books, and various Web sites where visitors can post information about products and services that they like. In addition, a baby-naming service called *Nazuke Hakase* has been created to provide parents with "individualized expert baby naming advice that incorporates the parents' particular preferences and ideas."[40]

Until recently, Benesse's *Big Encyclopedia of Pregnancy* (*Tamahyo ninshin daihyakka*) was the most popular pregnancy-advice book on the market.[41] This folio-sized volume opens with color photographs of the fetus developing in utero, accompanied by text describing each stage of the process, from the division of the fertilized egg to implantation to fetal growth to birth. The next section presents another color-photo spread showing a woman giving birth in a hospital, with her husband and doctor beside her. The text for this section describes the stages of labor and approximately how long each lasts. While the more graphic details of labor have been erased from this version, another manual—*The First-Time Mother's Guide to the Ten Months of Pregnancy and Childbirth* (*Hajimete mama ni naru hito no ninshin to shussan jukagetsu*)—is more explicit, providing diagrams depicting episiotomies, forceps deliveries, and Caesarian sections.[42]

The manual then goes on to discuss pregnancy in three-week stages, with each stage illustrated by an ultrasound picture of the developing fetus, drawings of the fetus inside the mother's body, and (in the 2003 edition) a piece of fruit comparable in weight to the fetus (cherries, melons, watermelons, etc.).[43] The bulk of the book is geared toward the pregnant woman, with sections on morning sickness, weight maintenance, procedures at normal prenatal doctor's visits, and exercise, each illustrated with color photos and realistic pictures. Aside from one glossy section on food, complete with recipes giving calorie counts and salt-content information, the manual discusses only problems in pregnancy—including premature labor, miscarriage, and gestational diabetes—before concluding with a brief guide for new fathers and information on baby names. These latter sections are illustrated with cartoon figures and often follow a question-and-answer format.

As this brief survey of the contents of the Benesse *Encyclopedia* suggests, the general categories of information found in pregnancy manuals have remained quite consistent over the years. While modern manuals reflect that medical knowledge about the female body and the mechanics of pregnancy have grown significantly, certain cultural ideas and advice found in the Tokugawa manuals can still be found in modern manuals. The dangers posed by stretching to reach things in high places, described in the *Onna chōhōki*, are prominently featured in the *Encyclopedia*, nicely illustrated with the proper way to get items down from shelves. The *hara obi* (now containing Lycra!) has likewise remained a focus in manuals over the centuries, although recent texts advise against tying them too tightly, unlike popular Tokugawa manuals that admonished women to bind them up in order to keep the fetus from growing too large.[44] Moreover, while Confucian ideas about incorrect behavior damaging the fetus no longer have much (if any) currency, the term "fetal education" (*taikyō*) continues to be used in the twenty-first century. The mother's actions still are seen as critical to the future of her fetus; now, however, it is "stress" rather than impropriety that is the enemy. Instead of wearing pearls to guarantee a beautiful baby, women are encouraged to take part in aromatherapy, avoid arguments with their husbands, and play Mozart to calm themselves and their fetuses.

There are, however, important ways in which today's manuals differ significantly from their predecessors. Perhaps most noticeably, contemporary examples of the genre emphasize weight gain, diet, and physical fitness, issues that received far less attention in the Tokugawa or even earlier Showa periods. In part, this reflects salutary changes in the material conditions of female life, since, until relatively recently, malnutrition was a problem for the general population, making increased caloric intake and other dietary requirements for expectant mothers an often difficult goal. A similar interpretation is possible for the increased attention modern manuals give to morning sickness, a problem that receives only the barest of mentions in the Tokugawa guides or in the 1932 *Methods for Safe Birth and Childrearing* (*Ansan to ikujiho*).[45] The fact that morning sickness is now addressed in far greater depth, and includes advice on dietary and lifestyle means to combat it, likely reflects the infrequency of more dire threats to pregnancy, allowing what were once dismissed as minor or marginal discomforts to take on greater importance.

Nevertheless, food and body issues, which already had begun to play a significant role in pregnancy and childbirth manuals by the mid-1990s, have become even more prevalent concerns in the pregnancy literature of the last decade. Detachable charts now allow women to measure their weight gain over the course of the pregnancy, while the standard illustrations of fetal development are accompanied by photographs (usually featuring real-life models) demonstrating the shape of the mother's stomach and describing her weight gain. One manual even includes a sidebar for each month in which an expectant mother discusses how her weight and body shape have changed, and her reactions to it. Of course, such materials reflect a sensible concern with prenatal health, and therefore the recent refashioning of *taikyō* (fetal education) in terms of body maintenance and stress reduction is a response to the physiological hazards that stress-related ailments such as high blood pressure pose for mother and fetus. At the same time, the popularity and ubiquity of special diet guides and cookbooks for pregnant women, the emphasis on avoiding "excessive" weight gain, advice on how to minimize (and later efface) pregnancy-specific body changes such as stretch marks, and guidance on how to dress in a stylish and even chic way all speak to a profound ambivalence about the physical manifestations of pregnancy itself.[46]

In part, this ambivalence stems from the degree to which pregnancy as experience and as cultural signifier has been shaped by consumerism. While the commodification of the female body is not a new phenomenon, its recent iteration has taken the iconic form of the so-called *bodikon gyaru*, or "body-conscious" girl, which came into prominence in the 1980s. While the enactment of the Equal Employment Opportunity Law (EEOL) in 1985 acknowledged, at least in principle, the professional aspirations of young Japanese women, those aspirations quickly were linked to a physical ideal (slim, narrow-waisted, toned) that required its own level of dedication. As Laura Miller has observed, "[The] fitness and diet craze produced a new aesthetic in which independence and achievement were presented through bodies that were the result of attention, labor, and of course money."[47] As has been the case throughout the twentieth century, moreover, the pursuit of the "appropriate" body was mediated, encoded, and facilitated by the mass media, which served a pedagogical function by teaching its (female) audience how to recognize the ideal and, just as importantly, what goods and services might allow it to be attained. The message transmitted by these media, in short, is that female bodies are sites and objects of consumption, dependent for their well-being on the continuous acquisition of "necessary" information and commodities.[48]

The degree to which this imperative shapes pregnancy in millennial Japan is most evident in popular media products such as *Pre-Mo* or *Pregnant Living*, which explicitly define the pregnant woman as the sum of her consumer choices—the dress and shoes she wears, the spa she visits, the nursery furniture she chooses, and so forth. It can be seen as well, however, in the manuals. To a degree, this is a result of the synergy that defines modern media conglomerates: the Benesse *Encyclopedia*, for example, features advertisements for the company's other lifestyle products (offering advice on nutrition, early childhood education, etc.), and for its catalogues of pregnancy and infant-focused consumer goods. At a more structural level, however, the manuals are shaped by the exigencies and paradigms of consumer marketing, a congruence seen most clearly in their exclusive focus upon the period between conception and birth, and upon matters relating only to fetal development and maternal well-being. Unlike guides from the Tokugawa era, or even from the prewar and immediate postwar periods, recent manuals contain no mention whatsoever of birth control, much less abortion. Similarly, whereas the manuals of the 1930s were focused upon female sexual health and hygiene from menstruation onward, those of the twenty-first century confine themselves to the period of gestation itself. Manuals and other related pregnancy literature conclude with the birth of a child; while babies serve as props in the photos, they are silent and docile, and little if any attention is devoted to what happens after the child is born. "Pregnancy" and "the pregnant," in other words, have been tightly defined and bounded as a niche market separate from young (unmarried) women on the one hand, and older women, both with and without children, on the other. When a woman becomes a mother, her reading materials and her duties and responsibilities change. The earlier emphasis on fashion is replaced by advice on rearing the child, a demographic-cum-marketing delineation emphasized by Benesse's inclusion of advertisements for a markedly distinct category of child- and mother-centered lifestyle products at the end of the *Pregnancy Encyclopedia*.

This segregation of pregnancy from the rest of female life and experience, however, also suggests the anxieties that surround pregnancy at the beginning of the twenty-first century. As we have seen, the literature of pregnancy in earlier centuries reflected contemporary definitions of the woman's place within society, and the contexts within which her role should be exercised. In the Tokugawa period, comportment and moral rectitude were the imperatives that shaped contemporary expectations of mothers and motherhood, with pregnancy seen as a physical process whose successful outcome depended upon the woman's proper comportment as well as deportment. During the early Showa period, health replaced morality, as the imperative now was expressed in terms of productivity: the mother was an agent of and contributor to the growing nation and empire and needed to keep her body free from disease in order to do her duty. In the twenty-first century, while the medical danger faced by mother and baby is far lower, and the moral fitness of the mother no longer linked in a direct, unmediated way to the physical fitness of her fetus, the physical consequences of pregnancy are still at the heart of popular and professional literature. Now, however, the trouble that expectant mothers confront has to do with the changing body itself.

The new generation of pregnancy manuals, therefore, is informed not by concerns about women's morality or health, but rather by women's anxieties about their changing bodies, bodies that they have been taught must be controlled and managed in order to guarantee their economic, social, and emotional success. In part, these anxieties are quelled through materialism: the discomforts of pregnancy are salved by the pleasure of having the best stroller or a cute Italian maternity outfit. More generally, however, the goal seems to be to allow a woman to be a mother, with her new child as the ultimate "benefit," but at the same time to save her from the bodily transformations that pregnancy works upon mothers, thus minimizing the unwanted "costs" that come with motherhood. This impression is strengthened by the way in which the manuals address sexuality and intimacy during pregnancy. Each acknowledges the physical exigencies of the woman's growing body, describing various sexual positions that might accommodate it. The pictures that accompany these discussions, however, feature semi-clad models who clearly are *not* pregnant.[49] The implication, in other words, is that sexual activity during pregnancy, while possible, challenges the imagination and defies representation. Again, it is the non-pregnant body that represents what linguists call the "unmarked" category, the norm against which pregnancy is measured and to which each woman will soon return. Paradoxically, then, the literature of pregnancy in contemporary Japan is one that, by compartmentalizing and containing "the ten months of pregnancy and childbirth," helps minimize its liminal potential. In turn, it may be the case that this reconfiguration of pregnancy, and its integration within the body and lifestyle discourse of young womanhood, is part of a broader transformation in the significance and nature of motherhood itself as Japan faces the looming dilemma of declining fertility.

NOTES

1. Sakura Momoko, *Sō iu fū ga dekite iru* (That's how I did it) (Tokyo: Shinchō Bunko, 1995), 12.

2. Robbie Pfeufer Kahn, *Bearing Meaning: The Language of Birth* (Urbana: University of Illinois Press, 1995), 76–77.

3. Kahn, *Bearing Meaning*, 77.

4. Ibid., 78.

5. On these developments, see William Lindsey, *Fertility and Pleasure: Ritual and Sexual Values in Tokugawa Japan* (Honolulu: University of Hawai'i Press, 2007), 10.

6. See Eiko Ikegami, *Bonds of Civility: Aesthetic Networks and the Political Origins of Japanese Culture* (Cambridge: Cambridge University Press, 2005), 324–362.

7. For a nuanced discussion of this issue, see Peter Kornicki, "Manuscript, Not Print: Scribal Culture in the Edo Period," *Journal of Japanese Studies* 32, no. 1 (2006): 23–52.

8. Lindsey, *Fertility and Pleasure*, 9.

9. Ibid., 10.

10. Ibid., 12.

11. On the *Onna chōhōki*, see, e.g., William R. Lindsey, "Religion and the Good Life: Motivation, Myth, and Metaphor in a Tokugawa Female Lifestyle Guide," *Japanese Journal of Religious Studies* 32, no. 1 (2005): 35–52, and Marcus Rüttermann, "Urbane Schreib-Anleitungen zu femininer Sanftheit (*yawaraka*): Übersetzung und Interpretation eines Abschnittes aus dem japanisch-neuzeitlichen Frauen-Benimmbuch *Onna Chōhōki* (Urban written instructions for feminine "softness": A translation and explication of an excerpt from the early modern Japanese women's manual *Onna chōhōki*)," *Japonica Humboldtiana* 6 (2002): 5–56.

12. Yuki Terazawa, "Gender, Knowledge, and Power: Reproductive Medicine in Japan, 1790–1930," (PhD diss., University of California–Los Angeles, 2001), 80–83. As Susan Burns has noted, "The 'grasshopper' [*inago*] of the title is an allusion to the Chinese *Poetry Classic* (*Shijing*) in which the inset appears as a symbol of fecundity and family harmony." Susan L. Burns, "The Body as Text: Confucianism, Reproduction and Gender in Tokugawa Japan," in *Rethinking Confucianism: Past and Present in China, Japan, Korea and Vietnam*, ed. Benjamin A. Elman, John B. Duncan, and Herman Ooms (Los Angeles: UCLA Asian Pacific Monograph Series, 2002), 181.

13. Sugitatsu Yoshikazu, *Osan no rekishi: Jōmon jidai kara gendai made* (A history of childbirth from the Jōmon era to the present) (Tokyo: Shūeisha Shinsho, 2002), 132–133.

14. Terazawa, "Gender, Knowledge, and Power," 111.

15. For a comparative view, see Cristina Mazzoni, *Maternal Impressions: Pregnancy and Childbirth in Literature and Theory* (Ithaca, N.Y.: Cornell University Press, 2002), 11.

16. Terazawa, "Gender, Knowledge, Power," 112.

17. Lindsey, *Fertility and Pleasure*, 121.

18. Terazawa, "Gender, Knowledge, Power," 99.

19. Lindsey, *Fertility and Pleasure*, 130.

20. For more on the role of Buddhism, see Lindsey, *Fertility and Pleasure*, especially 106–118.

21. Ibid., 130.

22. As Aya Homei cautions, however, the Meiji promotion of "new midwifery" was not simply a matter of "westernizing" Japanese medicine, but instead a process that integrated European practices with older, indigenous ones. See Aya Homei, "Birth Attendants in Meiji Japan: The Rise of a Medical Birth Model and the New Division of Labour," *Social History of Medicine* 19, no. 3 (2006): 407–422.

23. On the "birthing chair," see Sugitatsu, *Osan no rekishi*, 134. This device was common throughout the pre-modern West as well; on its history, see Amanda Carson Banks, *Birthchairs, Midwives, and Medicine* (Jackson, Miss.: University Press of Mississippi, 1999).

24. Ryuichi Narita, "Women and Views of Women within the Changing Hygiene Conditions of Late Nineteenth- and Early Twentieth-century Japan," *U.S.–Japan Women's Journal English Supplement* 8 (1995): 69.

25. Sabine Frühstück, *Colonizing Sex: Sexology and Social Control in Modern Japan* (Berkeley: University of California Press, 2003), 4.

26. Moriyama Yutaka, *Kekkon to shussan zenshō* (Complete guide to marriage and childbirth) (Tokyo: Shufu no Tomo-sha, 1932), 75–79; Yamazaki Kiyoshi, *Ninshin, bunben, sanji no chōsetsu* (The regulation of pregnancy, labor, and childbirth) (Tokyo: Bunka Seikatsu Kenkyūkai, 1927), 145–146; Fukui Masahyō, *Ninshin yori ikuji made to taikyō* (Pregnancy, childbirth, and fetal education) (Tokyo: Kaibunsha, 1930), 9, 242–244. As with other topics in the latter manual, Fukui's discussion of "artificial fertilization" focuses upon how it might be achieved, rather than why, although he ultimately cautions against trying it at home.

27. Sumiko Otsubo, "Feminist Maternal Eugenics in Wartime Japan," *U.S.–Japan Women's Journal English Supplement* 17 (1999): 43–49.

28. This information was also published in women's magazines, which offered their readers admonitions from medical officials to use properly trained and licensed midwives (this latter qualification was emphasized), who would be sure to sterilize their hands before delivering a baby. See Narita, "Women and the Views of Women," 71.

29. Yasui Shuhei, *Ninshin kara shussan made* (From pregnancy to childbirth) (Tokyo: Handbook-sha, 1928), 25.

30. Moriyama Yutaka, *Kekkon to shussan zenshū* (Complete guide to marriage and childbirth) (Tokyo: Shufu no Tomo-sha, 1950), 179.

31. See, in particular, Jan Bardsley, "Fashioning the People's Princess: Women's Magazines, Shōda Michiko, and the Royal Wedding of 1959," *U.S.–Japan Women's Journal English Supplement* 23 (2002): 57–91.

32. *Ninshin seikatsu kōki* (Pregnant living in the later stages) (Tokyo: Gakushū Kenkyūsha, 2006).

33. *Pre-Mo*, June 2006; *Tamahyo Kurabu*, June 2006. *Tamahyo Kurabu* typically features "regular women" as its cover models. *Pre-Mo* also uses readers as models, inviting them to fill out an application form found in the back of each issue of the magazine. Both magazines feature numerous interviews with pregnant women.

34. *Pre-Mo* (May 2006). While yoga and aromatherapy were trends in 2006, by 2007 they were not so popular. In the area of menu planning, *Pre-Mo* featured a winter feast of Chinese cabbage and daikon, while *Tamahyo Kurabu* supplied soup recipes with winter vegetables that were supposed to help ensure a safe birth. *Pre-Mo* (December 2007): 99–105; *Tamahyo Kurabu* (December 2007): 111–115.

35. *Tamahyo Kurabu* is the magazine with CD giveaways.

36. *Pre-Mo* (December 2007): 177–178.

37. This advice is contained in the "Name Book for My Sweet Baby," a supplement included with *Ninshin seikatsu kōki*; see, in particular, page 5.

38. This is not unique to Japan, as a perusal of the pregnancy magazines in most obstetric waiting rooms indicates. Although magazines such as *Pregnancy and Newborn, Fit Pregnancy,* and *Pregnancy* each have a medical advisory board, they are written largely by journalists and feature a substantial fashion component.

39. See the Benesse Web site at http://www.benesse.co.jp (accessed May 30, 2007).

40. Ibid.

41. *Tamahyo Ninshin Daihyakka* (Big encyclopedia of pregnancy) (Tokyo: Benesse Corporation, 2005). This book does not enjoy the iconic status of Eisenberg and Mursoff's *What to Expect When You're Expecting*, a *New York Times* best-seller. Nevertheless, according to Amazon.jp sales rankings, it was among the top overall titles (at 4,722) through last year. The women whom I have interviewed confirm *Tamahyo Ninshin Daihyakka*'s popularity, naming it as the guide they used while pregnant. Although its sales have declined in recent years, it continues to be the leading seller among such manuals.

42. Takayama Tadao, *Hajimete mama ni naru hito no ninshin to shussan* (The first-time mother's guide to the ten months of pregnancy and childbirth) (Tokyo: Seibido Shobō, 1999), 170–171. The title refers to the Japanese reckoning of pregnancy as a ten-month period.

43. *Tamahyo Ninshin Daihyakka*, 36–68.

44. Sugitatsu, *Osan no rekikishi*, 113. As Susan Burns has informed me, popular wisdom during the Tokugawa era dictated tying the *hara obi* tightly, although medical professionals advocated binding it more loosely. The *hara obi* remains popular even today, and Tokyo's Suitengu Shrine, long associated with childbirth and pregnancy, publishes monthly full-color spreads in *Tamahyo Kurabu* listing the days of the dog and urging readers to "tie one up and discover the value of the *hara obi*!" See, e.g., *Tamahyo Kurabu* (December 2007): 145.

45. While brief, the manual's reference to morning sickness is memorable, since it is accompanied by a drawing of a kimono-clad woman vomiting into a pan; see *Ansan to ikujiho* (Methods for safe birth and childrearing) (Tokyo: Shufu no Tomo-sha, 1932), 5.

46. On diet and nutrition, see, e.g., Takashima Keiko, *Ninpu wa hutocha ikenai no?* (Pregnant women shouldn't get fat, right?) (Tokyo: Shinchōsha, 2004); cf. the lengthy discussion of stretch marks in the October 2007 issue of the magazine *Pre-Mo* (at pages 91–96).

47. Laura Miller, "Mammary Mania in Japan," *positions: east asia cultures critique* 11, no. 2 (2003): 273.

48. Yumiko Iida, *Rethinking Identity in Modern Japan: Nationalism as Aesthetics* (New York: Routledge, 2002), 182.

49. See Takayama, *Hajimete mama ni naru hito no ninshin to shussan 10 kagetsu*, photo insert. In later versions of this manual and others, the photographs have been replaced by more discrete line drawings.

CHAPTER 9

When Manners Are Not Enough

The Newspaper Advice Column and the "Etiquette" of Cultural Ideology in Contemporary Japan

JANET S. SHIBAMOTO-SMITH

There exists a plethora of published material on etiquette or conduct available in literally every bookstore in contemporary Japan. One may find etiquette guides for ceremonial occasions,[1] etiquette guides for women,[2] codes of conduct for *sarariiman* work life,[3] conduct codes for corporate life,[4] and on and on. Representative titles include Shimizu's *Encyclopedia of Important Ceremonial Occasions [So You] Will Know Everything*, Shiotsuki's *Advanced Level Manner Lessons for Attractive Women*, and Kawaki's *Collection of Men's Fashion Techniques to Make Women Take a Second Look*. And many messages about how people are supposed to act and, indeed, to be, are delivered in other direct and indirect ways. The most explicit messages come from "official" sources, such as the "Survey on National Characteristics of the Japanese People" sponsored by the Institute of Statistical Mathematics and updated every five years. Results are widely summarized in the major news media. Less official but equally explicit messages come from popular magazines aimed at particular demographic niches. These tell various targeted groups of readers (women, men, young, old, career-oriented, or domestically inclined) how to be the "best"—or at least, how not to be the "worst"—at being whatever sort of Japanese person they are. Laura Miller's work on media representations of both *un*satisfactory and satisfactory ways of being is particularly important in this regard.[5] Messages about "how to be" that are even more implicit circulate through media representations of folks acting and speaking in certain ways.[6]

Despite the ready availability of seemingly all manner of advice about what to do in every circumstance, however, it is often the case that people face problems that they do not know how to handle. As other chapters in this volume make abundantly clear, the terms of interpersonal engagement are undergoing what can at times be a bewildering series of changes. These changes affect the playing out of gender roles in the face of conflicting expectations, decisions about appropriate workplace and family relations, the constitution of satisfying friendships and romantic partnerships, and just in general, how to be a better person. Notably, they affect all segments of Japanese society. Under certain conditions, then, it is hardly surprising that people find their lives not fully satisfactory despite their mannerly adherence to advice gleaned from the general conduct literature. They seek something more, and especially something more specific to their particular situations. These individuals may, in such cases, turn to advice columns, the Japanese counterparts to Dear Abby, Ann Landers, or the more current Caroline Hax's *Tell Me about It* in the United States for guidance through difficult terrain. There they often find advice about another set of "rules," the often unspoken yet ever-present rules laid down by dominant ideological constructions of the good person, the good family member, the good lover or friend—in short, they are often advised to undertake a project perhaps best described as "ideological etiquette." How or why they might be advised in specific ways is the subject of this chapter.

I offer an analysis of the content and form of letters sent to *Asahi Shinbun*'s Life Advice Room (*Seikatsu no sōdanshitsu*) between June 2005 and December 2006. These letters provide insight into the types of concerns advice-seekers raise and common themes in the responses. My analysis links these to the contemporary social concerns that serve as their backdrop, including changes in assumptions about appropriate family relationships, shifts in long-standing norms for gender relations, and ideologies of what makes a "good" person.

THE NEWSPAPER AGONY COLUMN: A BRIEF BACKGROUND

Asahi is not the only major newspaper to offer an advice column. *Yomiuri Shinbun* pioneered such a column in 1914[7] and, except for a brief period during the war, has offered one ever since.[8] It was for long the only one of the three major newspapers (*Asahi*, *Yomiuri*, and *Mainichi*) to run one (Kato 1992),[9] but today many daily newspapers offer an advice column; the *Asahi* column runs weekly in the Life section, the former Women's section of the paper.

At the *Asahi*, letters are sent to the column, and one of several candidate respondents undertakes to advise the writer. Despite the individuality (and even quirkiness) of the advisers, the responsibility to offer a response accessible to an unseen general audience makes these columns a barometer of a commonsense etiquette of being. Naturally, the problems raised by the correspondents in this study do not represent the entirety of Japanese personal or interpersonal problems. Yet this snapshot of the struggles that exceed conduct literature etiquette and prompt the troubled to seek advice in this fashion allows us unique access to the nature of some contemporary concerns. A previous study of letters from the 1986 *Yomiuri* Life Guide column suggests that the letters serve "as anonymous appeals to the wisdom of a kind of community Dutch uncle" and thus are "useful indicators of the common mentality of a society."[10] Richard Hall, writing about U.S. "agony columns," recommends the use of such columns in English-language classes for that very reason—"they offer capsule narratives on a wide spectrum of human problems, *with a strong cultural slant*."[11] We turn, then to an assessment of the cultural slant that may be detected concerning dilemmas of the twenty-first century in advice-column letters in one Japanese newspaper.

Confused? Troubled? Alone? Asahi *to the Rescue*

Sixty letters appeared in the Life section of the international edition of the *Asahi* newspaper over the period of the study. A rotating series of eight "experts" from a range of professional fields served as respondents. They include well-known writers, television personalities, and the like. No professional therapists are included in their ranks, nor are well-known etiquette mavens such as Nishide Hiroko. Instead, the advisers were the fashion critic and celebrity Piiko;[12] the mountain climber Tabei Junko; the romance novelist Yuikawa Kei; the attorney Hotta Tsutomu; the singer, writer, and radio personality Akikawa Tetsuya; the former model and hostess-turned-writer Muroi Yuzuki; and—later in the year—the two members of the *manzai* comedy team *Asakusa Kiddo*, Tamabukuro Sujitarō (Akae Yūichi) and Suidōbashi Hakase (Ono Masayoshi). These advisers ranged in age from their mid-thirties to their early seventies.

The age and occupation of letter-writers varied, too. By far the most letters (fifty-one of sixty) were from women. Writers ranged in age from fourteen to sixty-five, but the majority were baffled Japanese in their thirties. Letters came from housewives, students, and company or store employees. There were also letters from temps or *furītā*,[13] the unemployed, and the retired. There were no letters from self-identified professionals such as lawyers, doctors, or teachers.

What were the letters about? Considered together, the largest number of letters addressed what one might call "intimate" relationships: romantic, marital, or familial relationships, and friendships. The remainder of letters concerned dissatisfaction with the self. While these letters addressed an assortment of interesting topics, such as a gay man's coming out or the difficulty of making a living as a librarian, some were excluded from the analysis because of their rarity or specificity.

Troubled Romance

Six letters relating to romantic relationships came from those free to fall in love, while four had to do with *furin* ("adulterous affairs"). The first group includes a letter from a high school boy who is repeatedly approached by young women then dumped after he has fallen in love. He is told that he must "taste all aspects of love before [he] can know what it is."[14] A fortyish divorced man studying at a vocational school wonders about asking a teacher out. He is brushed off with a simple "grow up," an admonition that offers a glimpse into the accepted norms for being an adult (man) in Japanese society. The respondent Piiko bluntly tells him, "When you fall in love with someone, you lose interest in your studies. Forget love until you get your life in order."[15]

Other letters, all from women, ask how to handle rejection. A twenty-three-year-old company worker is in love with a man she is dating, but he says he's on the rebound and only dating because he's lonely. Yuikawa, tells the writer to accept that the young man doesn't love her (and isn't going to). But she also offers some insights into the common-sense understandings of the gendered etiquette of Japanese dating. First, "real" men should come to terms with their past before they ask someone new out. Manly men wouldn't lead someone on as this young man has! But then, men "essentially" take for granted what is offered easily. So the writer herself should be more elusive. Turn down some of his invitations; allusions to competition may pique his interest. If he shows no interest, however, Yuikawa is clear; the writer should move on quickly to someone else.

Other writers describe similar frustration and pain at being rejected, with words that speak to their distress: I cannot get over the shock of being dumped, I want to ask the reason for the sudden breakup, and so on. One writer worries about her inability to move on and find a new lover. She wants to find someone to love and marry "in order to please her aging parents," a sentiment dismissed by Piiko as simply an excuse. She is probably just tired of playing around and leading a selfish life, he says. So she should stop doing so immediately! But her parents will only be happy, he goes on, if whatever she does is done earnestly. His final advice, "Do everything earnestly." In all these cases of troubled romance, however, responses are consistent: Your heart is broken? Here's what to do.

First, they advise, do not fear the painful (or the happy) aspects of romance.[16] Second, make your own life before you enter a romantic relationship (this is, perhaps, more important for men than for women). Third, do not dwell on your sadness after breaking up. "It's a waste of time to mope," says Tabei. You should take some action (find another boyfriend, throw yourself into your studies, take up a new interest). But whatever that action is, it must be taken up earnestly (*shinken ni*). If you follow this advice, you won't need to look for love; it will find you.

Four women submitted letters about illicit love affairs. One twenty-nine-year-old writer hovers at the edges of an affair; she's married but in love with her boss. He's married, too, so she cannot declare her love to him. Her situation is painful and sad, yet she cannot help loving him. What should she do? Another woman in her twenties who had an affair with a married coworker has already broken it off, but her feelings for him linger. To the first woman, Yuikawa suggests just enjoying the heart-warmingly sad (*setsunai*) feeling of unspoken love, echoing, even more positively, another respondent's advice not to fear experiencing both the sad and the happy aspects of romance. To the second, Piiko says, disabuse yourself of the idea that you and your coworker experienced a kind of "pure love" (*jun'ai*) because affairs with married people aren't pure. To get over your feelings (which were false, anyway), find someone younger—and available—and act; the only way to get over your feelings is to take action. Again, action is key to the resolution of the problem.

The other two letters about illicit love were from women in their forties. One had divorced her husband for a much younger lover. The mother of three children, she saw no marriage in the offing but nonetheless wanted her relationship with the young man to continue forever. Another, still-married woman was rejected by her lover of five years; he had divorced his wife but refused to marry her. Their relationship, he said, just wasn't enough. The writer asks, Is it pointless to chase after him? These last two letters offer their respondents (Muroi and Piiko, respectively) a fairly fertile field for airing some additional "common-sense" notions about love and other matters. First, there are no guarantees that a lover will be there "forever," whether one is married or not. So one might as well just enjoy a lover while he's around, just as one would enjoy a stray cat that came to visit, and not worry about permanency. However, since we *are* permanently connected to our children, it is with them that we are obligated to maintain a permanent relationship. In other words, priority goes to children over romance. And in the second case, Piiko takes the opportunity to expound on the difference between real love (*ai*), which is the desire and ability to fulfill the other's needs, and a lesser kind of love (*koi*), which is simply desire.[17] Obviously, the writer had never really loved (in the sense of *ai*) her lover, so it was not just chasing after him that was pointless, but their entire affair. In these responses we see two additional norms for romance: put your children ahead of your romantic desires, and when you love, do so with other-privileging *ai* rather than the more selfish *koi*. It is unclear whether these same two pieces of advice would be offered to men.

Marriage: Troubles in the Land of "Happily Ever After"

Very few letters came from wives complaining about their husbands—only four, in fact. Two were from women in their sixties. One woman's retired husband, back home after years of *tanshin funin* (a job transfer to another city unaccompanied by a spouse), calls her *anta*, an informal and somewhat dismissive form of "you." When she objects, he dismisses her, saying, "What's wrong with that? Who do you think fed you all these years?"[18] The writer would like him to respect her wishes. What should she do? Her adviser, the attorney Hotta starts by describing some regional and age differences in the acceptability of using *anta* toward a wife.[19] But he also addresses the main issue—the husband is not respecting his wife's wishes. "Since your husband appears to be one of those old-fashioned guys enmeshed in past traditions of patriarchal authority," Hotta says, "you'll probably have to do something drastic. Stop making meals, showing him that *you're* the one feeding *him*. If that doesn't work, leaving wouldn't be a bad idea. Don't go back until he gets lonely and admits defeat." Hotta offers no support for patriarchal authority, no admonitions to patience or to silent suffering, as was routinely advised in the past. What *is* advised is action, a motif seen previously. The call to action is even more striking here. Married women, formerly the ideological vessels of patience, endurance, and an unlimited will to nurture family members (encapsulated in the term *tsukusu*, meaning "to exhaust oneself in service to others"), are now expected to be decisive and to act on their own behalf.

The theme recurs in a letter from another forty-year-old wife, who after only a year and a half of marriage is already fed up with her "self-centered husband." In his response, Piiko lays out her choices. The couple is older, so set in their habits. There is no point in expecting the husband to change. The wife needs to decide between two ways of spending the rest of her life: alone (*sabishii*, which more literally translates as "lonely") but untroubled (*wazurawashiku nai*), or not lonely but bothered (by the husband's inconsiderate behavior). In addition, he cautions "the sooner [you decide], the better. As your husband ages, you might end up having to take care of (*kaigo*) him." Piiko does not advise the writer which course to take, although he admits that he himself would leave. Again, there is a complete absence of advice centered on wifely patience, and a marked shift toward advice to think, decide, and act in terms of the writer's own best interest.

A last spousal complaint comes from the thirty-one-year-old mother of an only child who wants more children. The problem? Her husband thinks one is enough and will not listen to her arguments for more. And this introduces a new theme. Whereas the advice so far has been for people to think about what they want, make decisions, and act on them, we see here the first sign that solo decisive action won't always work. Sometimes it is necessary to *inter*act. Yuikawa advises, "In either case, this is not something you can decide alone. You'll just have to talk this over together thoroughly until you come to an agreement." The notion that thoroughly (and earnestly) talking over a problem will inevitably lead to a satisfactory conclusion will appear again in advice about other issues. When this view of the interpersonal is invoked in the form of advice, the potential for failure is not addressed.

Flawed Families

There are other family members, beyond husbands and wives, and troubles arise between or among them as well. In this section, we examine a range of family issues, with letters from children, siblings, and parents. We begin with children writing about their parents.

One young man is worried about his mother, who is prone to hysterical outbursts. Yuikawa offers two pieces of sensible advice: see a mental health professional, and engage your father in this problem. She then offers her own "sense" that the son's feelings for his mother will be strained if he remains close to the situation; perhaps he could leave the parental home (he is a university student) or otherwise distance himself. The central concern in Yuikawa's advice is not the resolution of the mother's problems but the protection of the emotional relationship between the mother and the son. The privileging of the emotional bond over the material conditions of the parent–child relation will be seen in a more extreme form momentarily.

Another young person writes that her mother favors her siblings. She resembles her paternal grandmother, whom her mother disliked, and surmises that this is the cause. Her letter offers our first encounter with a phrase we will see again and to which the advisers typically do *not* respond: "Frankly, I have come to want to die." She concluded her letter asking, "How can I be loved as much as my siblings? Or is this selfish?" Hotta suggested some steps for ameliorating her relationship with her mother over the long term, but concluded by noting that children like the writer have better relations with their parents as adults than do overly doted-upon children, another implicit plug for a life lived on one's own terms rather than one subordinated to others' behaviors or opinions. Anyway, he continues, the problem between the writer and her mother is one of compatibility, not love. Of course the mother loves the writer as much as she loves her other children. A parent (mother) is emotionally obligated to her children—for life.

Two letters from slightly older women also address issues with parents. One woman "cannot stand" the way her mother treats her daughter-in-law, the writer's sister-in-law. Should she cut off all contact with her mother? No, Tabei advises, because she will regret it later. Children, one sees, need to stay as bonded to their parent (or mother) as much as mothers need to stay bonded to their kids. The second, and more serious, letter is from a forty-two-year-old woman, married with children, who cannot completely overcome her anger toward her mother and stepfather, who abused her both physically and verbally in her childhood. She asks, "What can I do about my anger at my parents, who aren't sorry?" The lawyer Hotta begins by praising the writer's fortitude for having lived through the abuse and made a happy family for herself. He suggests professional counselors and other agencies that can help her work through her memories and feelings. He then turns to the issue of the mother–child bond, the reification of which we see continually invoked. He says, "Tell some trusted person everything you remember about these past painful events. Or write things down and have the person read it. You may see new things as you speak or write these memories. *Then*, how would it be to have that trusted person talk these things over thoroughly with your mother? You can think about how to deal with your stepfather after that."

Well, maybe this will work. Whether it does or not, however, the regular reader of the column will have another chance to appreciate two key themes. First, the emotional bond between parents (particularly mothers) and children should be preserved at all costs. And, second, earnest and thorough discussion of problems will inevitably lead to a satisfactory conclusion.

If children sometimes have problems with their parents, so it is that parents sometimes experience problems with their children. Only two letters in this corpus were from worried parents, one from the mother of a teen who had suddenly become sullen and rebellious, another from a woman whose adult daughter lived at home, did not help out, and had no social life. Tabei and Piiko had essentially the same advice to these mothers: "Stop worrying about your daughters. Get your own life." Even in the case of the obligatory mother–child bond, the *tsukusu* concept, which has had a long run throughout the twentieth century, is, apparently, passé.

Siblings also have issues with each other, but so few letters appeared in this corpus that we may move on directly to the last outpost of "family" problems—in-laws. Three women complain about their mothers-in-law. One woman, who lives with her mother-in-law, dislikes her constant bad-mouthing. Unfortunately, her complaint gets sent to Piiko, who is not filled with sympathy. "Marriage isn't just a compact with a man you love," he admonishes, "it means you join a new family. If you really love your husband, you have to learn to love his mother, no matter what kind of person she is." Anyway, instead of just complaining—which Piiko says just shows a lack of creative imagination—the writer should think of ways to divert the barrage of unpleasant remarks. You're not doing that, he tells the writer, you're just wearing yourself out hating your mother-in-law. Piiko did suggest some clever diversionary tactics, but the message about what is necessary when one marries *into* a family dominates. This is the only response in which the old structures of the patriarchal *ie* "household" system were invoked in a positive way.

The final letter about in-laws is actually about prospective in-laws; in fact, it is about the prospective in-laws of the writer's younger brother. The forty-year-old brother wants to marry his younger girlfriend, but her parents object. They harass him with telephone calls and are pressuring him to break up with their daughter. What to do? Muroi says she would advise that the couple elope. They are both mature adults. Why is a full-grown man tolerating all this hassle? He should just marry the girl. He may be nice, but from Muroi's perspective, he's unmanly. We have here, then, another description of the manly man: he does not equivocate but acts decisively.

Friends: Getting Them and Keeping Them

Nine letters concerned friendships. Some letters came from writers who had friends but whose friendships were problematic, and other letters were from writers who had no friends. Letters about imperfect friends included complaints about hypercritical friends, boring and long-winded friends, or overly familiar (*betabeta*, or "clingy") friends. These all got the same treatment: do what is best for you. One letter directly addresses etiquette of a nuts-and-bolts sort: a complaint about friends who did not respond to her marriage announcement. This woman, whose letter appeared in early December, wanted to know whether it would be appropriate to cull her *nengajō* (New Year's card) list of these nonresponsive friends. Or does etiquette dictate sending them cards? Response (from Tetsuya): "No, it doesn't."

Letters from the lonely complain about the difficulties of making and keeping friends. Responses share with responses from earlier eras[20] a tendency to blame the writers themselves for their friendlessness. A college student writes that she can never make friends; in any new situation, she sees others making friends, but she is left alone. Can she have a normal social life after finishing school? She can only imagine a dark future and has even considered suicide. Teach me, she asks, how to make friends. Tetsuya responds with a lengthy analogy between the sun versus the moon and people surrounded by a large group of friends versus those who have a quieter life with a smaller circle of friends. He surmises that the writer is a "moon" type; it may take time but she will ultimately have friends who bask in the softer light of her moon. The bottom line: don't be impatient. He concludes with an unusual gesture acknowledging the writer's suicidal comment: "Don't disappear, please.

It's enough for you just to be here." As we move into the next category of letters, those asking for help fixing an unsatisfactory self, we will return to the theme of suicide and the responses such remarks evoke.

Another friendless writer introduces herself as a *sabishigariya* ("a person who tends to loneliness"). She notices that she is always the one reaching out to potential friends. If they do not respond, she falls into self-loathing. She wants to feel less dependent on others and be able to live more "strongly." Self-loathing is certainly a serious problem, but Tetsuya responds quite light-heartedly. "Become a melon-bread maker," he says. "Make lots of different kinds of melon bread and give them away. Everyone will be happy and so will you. If you do this, your head will be filled with melon-bread recipes and you won't have time to worry about losing friends. Walk the path of melon-bread making [Tetsuya admits that it need not be melon bread; it could be strawberry bread or banana bread]. If you do this, there will be friends that you haven't yet met at the other end of the path." What can we make of all this bread-making advice? One notices, underneath all the warm, yeasty happiness of sweet breads, a familiar theme: find something outside yourself and throw yourself into it; your troubles will not loom so large, and may even resolve, when you are not so focused on yourself. Being a happy, engaged person is the key to smoothing relationship problems. This advice makes a sharp break with a past that has emphasized, especially for women, a normative self-sacrifice to the interests of others. When it comes to advice about getting along with others, we seem to see here a new (to women, at least) etiquette of selfhood.

There's Something Wrong with Me

Some of the letters in this sample discuss personal flaws that do not seem so very serious. One woman, for example, writes that she has no interest in nature—there are no potted plants on her veranda. She looks at her veranda, bare of greenery, and wonders whether there is something wrong with her. Tetsuya seems untroubled and says, quite simply, "No."[21]

Flaws distressing young writers tend to reflect the fairly ordinary struggles of the teen years. One teen writes about her "pride," which prevents her from being pleased at other people's talents or accomplishments. She wants to "fix" herself. Piiko tells her that her main problem is not pride but jealousy. After an abstract discussion of the individual worth of all people, he reassures her that she will ultimately be just fine, especially since she has already, at fifteen, seen her jealousy for the problem it is.

Of course, if that advice is not followed, the outcome may be less favorable, and one may end up writing a similar letter later in life, as did one thirty-one-year-old office worker jealous of the beautiful women she sees on television. She's also jealous of people with talent. She sees such people and cannot help thinking of herself as a dull sort. Tetsuya advises her to stop attacking herself and to recognize her own accomplishments. "In fact," he says, "give yourself a reward." What kind of reward? Become #1 at something. And here, Tetsuya falls back on the advice we have heard from all the advisers: find something outside yourself to fall in love with. His example here is white clouds. Fall in love with clouds, learn all there is to know about clouds, take pictures of clouds. Become the "go-to" person for cloud questions. You won't have time to be jealous of others. And at the end Tetsuya offers readers a catchphrase to describe this line of advice, which, as we have seen, is a common one: "the liking strategy" (*suki sakusen*).

But let us return to the problems of youthful self-dissatisfaction. Several teen letters have to do with the rigors of study. Two letters come from young women facing college-entrance exams. Their complaints about themselves can be subsumed under the single term "obsessing" (*kangaesugi*; literally, "thinking too much"). Both have failed academic tests. Both find their studies for upcoming exams going poorly. Both complain that they cannot concentrate on their studies because their past failures continue to haunt them. Piiko responds to both of these writers. First, he says, stop fooling yourselves. You're not entrapped in *kangaesugi*; you're just making excuses for not studying. Stop with the grumbling and start studying. He offers, if you don't want to study, go out and find something you really want to do, and do it. The message in both cases is clear: quit making excuses and *act*.

Sometimes, "growing pains" can be more painful than usual—occasionally much more painful. A letter that speaks to the current social problems afflicting youth in Japan comes from an unemployed nineteen-year-old woman who has been a *hikikomori* for four years.[22] She has even suffered from clinical depression. She has found a dream—becoming a comic book (*manga*) artist—but has many self-doubts. Advisers dealing with these more serious problems of young letter-writers tend to offer fairly straightforward advice, but gingerly.

Yet not so gingerly as they do another set of letters from troubled selves.

These latter writers exhibit even more deep-seated unhappiness. Four letters in my sample come from writers at desperate points in their lives. All mention suicide, the wish to die, or the possibility that even dying is too much trouble. A middle-school girl lists all the reasons she has for hating herself: she's bad at her studies, bad at sports, clumsy, indecisive, and, as if those were not enough, a scaredy-cat and a cry-baby. She concludes, "I'm in pain. I hate myself and want to die." A high school girl writes in the same vein. People call her "creepy." Partly it's because she's ugly, but mostly it's because she has a dark (*kurai*) personality and is a bundle of "complexes." She is so unhappy with life that she's considered suicide. She wants to be more like other people. In neither case does the adviser respond to these thoughts of or wishes for death. Instead, in the first case, Tabei praises the student for being so analytical; the writer herself should think of this as a strong point. But the larger part of Tabei's response describes her own feelings of self-hatred as a young woman until—here is the *suki sakusen* again—she discovered mountain climbing. If you find something you love, she concludes, you won't be so frightened and unhappy. In the second case, Tetsuya rejects the notion that the writer should try to be more like others; rather, he suggests that she express all of her personality, including the "bad" parts, in some artistic form. Surely, someone will stop to appreciate the world she creates. It is critical, however, to abide by the rules of the *suki sakusen*: the writer must "throw herself into" this artistic world. Tetsuya prays for the writer's success in her lonely fight.

A twenty-six-year-old temp cannot produce a pleasant enough smiling expression for people; she's trying at her new workplace, but no one acknowledges her efforts. She has no confidence in herself and even thinks she would like to die soon. Lawyer Hotta responds to this letter, beginning by saying, "A woman who wants to please other people with her smiles but is still told she looks angry becomes so unhappy that she wants die. That alone [makes her] cute, lovable, and fantastic."

While wanting to die over a facial expression does not fit widespread Japanese notions of the cute or fantastic, Hotta does have a practical suggestion. It is not, as the reader might by now expect, simply to adopt the *suki sakusen* strategy, although there are some similarities. Rather, he suggests that the letter-writer start a novel—maybe something more like a journal—about herself, but in the third person. Writing her frustrations about her facial expressions and her reactions to people's misrecognition of her smiles or their failures to appreciate her efforts might make her smile, or even laugh. And this smile probably will not be a forced one, but a natural, charming smile, at last. After trying her best smile for a customer, for example, Hotta imagines that she might write, "When she did that, [someone] said, 'Are you showing that twisted face to customers on purpose?' So she spent the day dejected and wanting to die, but when she got home, looked in the mirror and shouted, 'What's twisted is your heart!' suddenly a smiling face appeared. And it was an unstrained smile, a charming smiling face." That's the way to write, Hotta suggests. And in a while, you'll come to like your heroine and can write in your novel–journal about an even more fantastic you. Just how the process of writing in this fashion will translate into the young woman's life outside her journal is not specified.

And, finally, a college student writes that she does not understand the meaning of life. She says she has an ordinary-seeming life, but inside is unfulfilled. Even dying is too much trouble. She is afraid of herself and does not have the confidence to go on living. At the end of the letter, the writer asks, "Why are we alive? Why is life so heavy?" Yuikawa responds, "I still don't have an answer myself." Disheartening, indeed, but Yuikawa goes on to guide the writer not just to ask those questions but to try to answer them. She proposes that even one answer can provide a first clue, and the writer may come to see something, as if the mist had cleared.

CONCLUSION: CLEARING THE MIST

What can we learn about cultural understandings of "mannerly" personhood and proper interpersonal relations from our letters? First of all, the problems addressed in the letters examined above seem to be more tractable than those of earlier eras. Letters from the 1950s and 1960s concerned very serious issues indeed. From a man with a pregnant wife: "If my wife has to take off from work, the whole family will starve to death—is an abortion possible?" From a former tuberculosis patient: "My tuberculosis is finally cured—but I'm always turned down for jobs." A war widow asks: "I'm a widow with a mentally retarded daughter—is death our only [hope of] happiness?"[23] Post-reconstruction, the letters become less desperate, but both the letters and the responses suggest a highly constraining orientation to two fixed notions of happiness and success. For men, this is walking the path to career advancement; for women, "happiness is in the home."[24] These two clear paths guided advisers' responses to letters and enabled them to offer fairly concrete guidance. But in the 1980s, when individualization and diversification became cultural watchwords, the kinds of problems appearing in letters called for more variety in response, and it became more difficult to offer clear-cut, concrete advice.[25] And by the 1990s, responses to letters had become more abstract and tended to throw the decision about what to do back onto the reader, reflecting the difficulty of giving specific advice.[26] At the same time, with the loss of singular, definite life goals, people found themselves with a more pressing need for others' reassurance that their goals were reasonable or their problems real. And this need is certainly seen in the present data, as is the tendency of respondents to offer quite abstract "advice," sending the problem back to the letter-writer herself or himself for resolution.

There are, nonetheless, some definite clues to cultural understandings to be gleaned from the responses to the letters. The primary directives appear, in the early twenty-first century, to advise that one think about and know oneself and not brood about a given problem but instead act decisively to resolve it. "Grumbling" and "hesitating" is out. Suffering in patient, stoic silence is out (*taeru*, meaning "endure," was not seen in these responses, and *gaman*, meaning "patience," appeared only once). Action is where it's at.

There is also more specific guidance offered: problems may resolve themselves if you find something about which you can be passionate and throw yourself into it wholeheartedly (the *suki sakusen*); alternatively, if the problem is interpersonal, thorough and earnest discussion will (inevitably) bring about mutual understanding. Above all, in undertaking whatever course you choose, be sincere.

Gender-differentiated themes in the responses offer hints at cultural images of the manly man and the womanly woman. Men should not, these days, be afraid to experience emotion, but they should put work ahead of feelings (especially romantic ones). The elite career path may not be the only path to success and happiness, but work still figures strongly. Men need to be decisive, for example, by putting a clear end to past relationships before starting new ones, and they need not to futz around. Women, these days, are freed from the old dictates of patient suffering; they, along with their male counterparts, are supposed to act, and to act in their own best interests. They do not need to find happiness only in the home and family; all women writing about career goals are urged to pursue their dream. Two elements of the old "good wife, wise mother" etiquette for female personhood are, however, retained.

When in love, make sure it's other-oriented *ai* rather than self-oriented *koi* or desire. Women should not be romantically selfish. And, too, motherhood is privileged over love, career, and other pursuits, even if this is not the all-sacrificing motherhood of the past. Women's path to happiness is, if not at home in the kitchen, still oriented around a giving stance and a responsibility to children.

These, then, are the remnants of older ways of being that are carried, in muted form, into the twenty-first century. Their undertones complicate the advice offered to the various letter-writers, even as the "experts" attempt to empower writers; indeed, they urge that the writers resolve their own problems by introspection, frank and sincere communication, and decisive action. If, however, the writers want affirmation of their goals or reassurance that apparent impediments to a happier life are reasonable, then the advisers have provided feedback on that score, albeit not always positive feedback. A given letter-writer may not be offered a clear path to the resolution of his or her problem, but when the mist clears, he or she will surely know whether it is a problem of cultural relevance—a problem, that is, that bows to the "ideological etiquette" of being Japanese in the early twenty-first century.

NOTES

1. Katsumi Shimizu, *Subete ga wakaru kankonsōsai manā-daijiten* (Encyclopedia of important ceremonial occasions [so you] will know everything) (Tokyo: Nagaoka Shoten, 2005).

2. Yaeko Shiotsuki, *Suteki na josei no tame no jōkyū manā ressun* (Advanced manner lessons for the attractive woman) (Tokyo: Shogakkan, 2005).

3. Hiromi Inoue, Kazuo Koike, Kyōji Tanaka, and Kenji Matsuoka, *Shakai-jin no tessoku 2001: 21-seiki o ikinuku bijinesuman no shin-jōshiki* (Iron-clad rules for the adult 2001: The new common-sense for the businessman's survival in the 21st century) (Tokyo: Takarajimasha, 2001).

4. Jun Kawaki, *Josei ga furimuku menzu fasshon tekunikkushū* (Collection of men's fashion techniques to make women take a second look) (Tokyo: Daisan Shokan, 1997).

5. Laura Miller, "Bad Girls: Representations of Unsuitable, Unfit, and Unsatisfactory Women in Magazines," *U.S.–Japan Women's Journal English Supplement* 15 (1998): 31–51, and "You Are Doing *Burikko*!" in *Japanese Language, Gender, and Ideology: Cultural Models and Real People*, ed. Shigeko Okamoto and Janet S. Shibamoto-Smith, 148–165 (Oxford: Oxford University Press, 2004).

6. See Shigeko Okamoto and Janet S. Shibamoto-Smith, "Constructing Linguistic Femininity in Contemporary Japan: Scholarly and Popular Representations," *Gender and Language* 2 (no. 1) (2008): 87–112; Janet S. Shibamoto-Smith,

"Changing Lovestyles: Fictional Representations of Contemporary Japanese Men in Love," *positions: east asia cultures critique* 16, no. 2 (2008): 359–387.

7. Katarogu Hausu, ed., *Taishō jidai no minoue sōdan* (Life counseling in the Taisho period) (Tokyo: Chikuma Shobō, 2002).

8. Yomiuri Shinbun Fujinbu, ed., *Nihonjin no jinsei annai* (Japanese people's life guide) (Tokyo: Heibonsha, 1998); a collection of eight hundred letters selected from among those published 1949–1987.

9. Hidetoshi Kato, *Media, Culture, and Education in Japan* (Chiba: National Institute of Multimedia Education, 1992); also available at http://homepage3.nifty.com/katodb/doc/text/2606.html (accessed August 3, 2007).

10. John McKinstry and Asako Nakajima McKinstry, *Jinsei Annai: Glimpses of Japan through a Popular Advice Column* (Armonk, N.Y.: M. E. Sharpe, 1991), 4.

11. Richard W. Hall, "Ann and Abby: The Agony Column on the Air," *TESOL Quarterly* 5 no. 3 (1971): 247–249, 247, emphasis added.

12. *Much* more could be said about Piiko and his twin Osugi, but space limitations preclude even getting started; his twin, it should be noted, contributes to a similar column in the morning version of the *Asahi*.

13. *Furītā* are people between the ages of fifteen and thirty-four who are not in school, lack full-time employment or are unemployed, and who, if female, are unmarried.

14. Including painful love.

15. Piiko is by far the most acerbic respondent, more reminiscent of Caroline Hax than of Dear Abby or Ann Landers. Tetsuya is the most whimsical.

16. But they add that one must not wallow in heartbreak. The *Asahi* respondents have no patience with letter-writers' lingering over love troubles.

17. Janet S. Shibamoto-Smith, "From *Hiren* to *Happii-endo*: Romantic Expression in the Japanese Love Story," in *Languages of Sentiment: Pragmatic and Conceptual Approaches to Cultural Constructions of Emotional Substrates*, ed. Gary Palmer and Debra J. Occhi, 147–166 (Amsterdam: John Benjamins, 1999).

18. That is, financially supported you; *tabesaseru* ("to feed") or the more condescending *kuwaseru* ("to feed") has been commonly used by both men (as here, in the husband's *kuwasete yatta* "I fed you") and women (*tabesasete morau* "to be fed") to refer to the gendered norms of marital structure, where the man "brings home the bacon" and the woman "fries it up in a pan" or, in the Japanese case, "eats" it.

19. *Anta* is more acceptable in the Kansai region than in Tokyo, and it is more acceptable to older women than to younger women.

20. McKinstry and McKinstry, *Jinsei Annai*, 93–94.

21. She is, of course, breaking the *nihonjinron* rule of identity, if not etiquette, that stipulates a special relationship and closeness to nature for Japanese people.

22. *Hikikomori* is a kind of social withdrawal, where young people shut themselves in to their parents' homes and refuse to participate in school, work, and so on.

23. Yomiuri Shinbun Fujinbu, *Nihonjin no jinsei annai*, 32, 73, 85.

24. Tomoka Ikeda, "*Komyunikeeshon to shite no minoue sōdan: Minoue sōdan ni arawareru kachi-ishiki no henka* (Life advice as communication: Changes

in the values that appear in advice columns)," *Ritsumeikan sangyō shakai ronshū* 35, no. 1 (1999): 103–123; quotation is from 103.

25. Nancy R. Rosenberger, *Gambling with Virtue: Japanese Women and the Search for Self in a Changing Nation* (Honolulu: University of Hawai'i Press, 2001).

26. Ikeda, "*Komyunikeeshon to shite no minoue sōdan*," 109.

CHAPTER 10

A Community of Manners

Advice Columns in Lesbian and Gay Magazines in Japan

HIDEKO ABE

This chapter sheds light on how Japanese sexual minorities, mainly lesbians and gays, create community principles through advice-giving in four magazines. *Anise* and *Carmilla*, for lesbians and bisexuals, and *Bádi* and *G-men*, for gay men, are post-1990s commercial publications that provide a forum for the sharing of knowledge and experience in navigating sexual identities.[1] The four magazines feature *sōdanshitsu* (advice column) sections of varying scales and quality, spaces where readers seek advice for various issues—both sexual and social. These advice columns assume an imagined community where sexual minorities live, interact, exchange, and negotiate their everyday lives. By building a sense of community or imagined *family*, they provide the individual (and perhaps isolated) readers a place to belong and to share.

By analyzing these publications, I investigate the messages these magazines carry for lesbians and gays concerning etiquette and social norms, the roles these mediated messages play in their identity construction, and the way in which advice on behavior and manners symbolically creates meaning for everyday life. By examining these questions, I argue that advice columns create space for Japanese lesbians and gays to build a sense of membership in the community where they interact, cope, share, understand, and navigate among themselves for individual maturity and growth, and to present the openness of the community toward the straight world, where social rules and etiquettes overwhelmingly take over the lives of average Japanese. I argue that the four magazines for lesbians and gays ultimately challenge social norms and attitudes as they help gays and lesbians pursue their individual desire and happiness. These magazines thereby address a gap in the historic trajectory of gay and lesbian media. Homosexuality is quite visibly celebrated in pre-modern Japanese art, poetry, and literature. For instance, canonical authors such as Ihara Saikaku (1687) described gay relationships in the *samurai* class and the transgender or homosexual behavior of young actors in Kabuki.[2] In contrast, same-sex behavior and interactions between women are rarely represented in history. We may find traces in art (particularly in *shunga*, erotic woodblock prints known euphemistically as "spring prints") and literature,[3] but they were mainly private or hidden. This imbalance between the representations of male and female homosexuality is still apparent in modern Japan. As a child, I remember asking my mother about a transgender person in my hometown of Tokushima. This *okama*, as my mother called the person, was often seen in public. *Okama* literally means "rice pot," and it is generally considered a derogatory word for male homosexuals, except when used self-referentially.[4] My mother expressed a typically "tolerant" attitude when she described this transgender person as strange but harmless. Some argue that the treatment of homosexuals in Japan differs from that in many Western societies, such as the United States,[5] because legal constraints are nonexistent (i.e., there are no sodomy laws in Japan). Likewise, Japan has no religious or moral institutions forbidding transgender or homosexual behavior, so gay and transgender people have been left alone and "tolerated."[6] The legal expert Taniguchi Hiroaki argues that "no laws in Japan legislate either for or against sexual minorities."[7]

It is important to note that recently the issue of transgender and transsexual identity has received enormous attention from within and outside the lesbian and gay community. Not only did sex-reassignment surgery become legal in 1996, but individuals with gender identity disorder (GID) can now change their sex in the Official Family Registry (*koseki*) if five conditions are met (one has to be over twenty years old, single at the time of application, not have children, have no gonad function, and have received a sex-appropriate organ through surgery). While the GID Act acknowledges the needs of transgender and transsexual individuals, many argue that these five conditions are severe and unrealistic. Nevertheless, the GID issue mirrors the reality of how Japanese accept sexual minorities. GID is a medical problem that needs to be "fixed," while homosexuality is not. While people have become more aware of issues related to sexual minorities, and these minorities have gained some legal protection through the courts, the status of homosexuality is very much unknown and/or unstable. It is true that gay men are seen in public, especially in media (TV and newspapers); that there are hundreds of gay bars in Tokyo alone; and that there are groups of supporters and organizations that help sexual minorities with medical, social, and legal problems.[8] It is also true, however, that most lesbians and gays are very much in the closet and that issues related to sexual minorities are hardly discussed in public media. Moreover, despite their occurrence, attacks on gay men rarely surface in the media.[9] Magazines for lesbians and gays, therefore, play a crucial role in establishing their visibility and enhancing awareness inside and outside the homosexual community.

This chapter reveals the lives of lesbians and gays through analysis of advice columns in four magazines with a special focus on lesbian magazines because of the richness and length of their advice columns in comparison to those in gay magazines. But first I will provide background on how these magazines are planned and structured, and how they appeal to the lesbian and gay communities. Second, by briefly comparing the style and structure of each magazine, I will discuss the role of editors and writers, and then show how advice seekers and givers achieve their goals by seeking and sharing advice and wisdom. Lastly, I will analyze advisers' perspectives by examining their styles, narrations, and positions. In conclusion, I will argue that the positions of advisers are not judgmental but rather tactical. They solve issues not by suggesting that one follow heteronormative rules, but by suggesting that one pursue his or her own desires and happiness.

MAGAZINES FOR ESTABLISHING LESBIAN AND GAY COMMUNITIES

Mark McLelland's extensive research on Japan's "perverse press" shows that it was not until the 1950s that homosexuals felt comfortable talking about their experiences as *tōjisha* (literally defined as "one involved") gay-community authors.[10] The first flowering of postwar gay writing was restricted to privately circulated magazines, such as *Amatoria* and *Fūzoku kitan*,[11] which targeted both female and male homosexuals.[12] Ironically, while these queer magazines continued to focus on homosexual men's lives, lesbian behavior more narrowly became an object of (hetero) male pleasure. As lesbians were increasingly "coopted as a fantasy genre for heterosexual men," publishing by *tōjisha* lesbians became exceedingly rare.[13] Lesbian subjectivity became lost to history.

Joseph Hawkins and Mark McLelland trace this lineage of publishing through to more recent gay men's magazines that have a longer and storied history.[14] *Barazoku* (Rose tribe) (1971–2004) is the best-known among these and is also the most unusual, having been published by a straight man, Itō Bungaku.[15] Although the critic Fushimi Noriaki credits *Barazoku* as having been enormously influential in fostering queer community over its thirty-three-year run, he maintains that as a hetero, the editor Itō cannot be considered a true spokesperson but merely a supporter of gay communities.[16] The issue of insider status or *tōjisha* suggests a strong barrier, one that differentiates non-gay people from gay people (a function that subtly slides between differentiation and discrimination).[17]

The theme of *shōnen-ai* (boy love) was enjoyed not only by *Barazoku's* male readership but also by straight and lesbian women, who sent fan letters to the magazine. This resulted in the establishment of a special section of the magazine, entitled *Yurizoku* (Lily tribe), in which female readers solicited gay husbands. The phenomenon of hetero women loving homosexual men, often referred to as *okoge* (fag-hags; literally, "burned bottom of cooked rice"), receives visible expression in the contemporary field of *yaoi* media, an acronym created from the expression ya*ma nashi* (no climax), o*chi nashi* (no punch line), and i*minashi* (no meaning). *Yaoi* usually refers to male–male romance in texts made for and often by women. While *yaoi* constitutes the latest wrinkle in the publishing history of representation of male homosexuality, many gay activists such as Saitō Masaki argue that "*yaoi* girls were unfairly coopting the 'reality' of gay men and selfishly transforming it into their own masturbatory fantasy."[18] In other words, *yaoi* is far from the representation of the gay man's actual life.

As an adult, my awakening moment concerning lesbian issues occurred when I was drinking in a bar in the early 1990s. It was there that Kakefuda, the very first lesbian to come out in a highly public way, told me how Japanese feminist organizations ignored the issue of sexuality and the role of lesbians in their fight against Japanese patriarchal society.[19] Kakefuda had written a well-known mainstream book entitled *What It Means to Be a Lesbian* (*'Resubian de aru' to iu koto*).[20] A few decades before the debut of her 1992 book, a small lesbian group called *Wakakusa no Kai* (Young Grass Group) had started its own activities.[21]

Along with the birth of this first lesbian group in Japan, various small-scale media began to appear (called *mini-komi*, mini communications). There were newsletters produced by various lesbian groups, with titles such as *Wonderful Women* (*Subarashii onna-tachi*, in 1976), *The Dyke* (*Za daiku*, 1978), *Wheel of Light* (*Hikariguruma*, in 1978), and *Lesbian Newsletter* (*Rezubian tsūshin*, in 1982).

In 1992 *LABRYS*, a self-published magazine produced by Kakefuda and her friends, became the first to attract a substantial (1,700-strong) lesbian readership before it was discontinued in December 1995.[22] Three years later, the first commercial magazine, *Furiine* (Phryne), appeared—and then abruptly disappeared after only two issues. After the failure of *Phryne*, the next commercial magazine for lesbians and bisexual women, *Anise*, came out in 1996, but it too ceased publication the following year. (It resumed irregular publication later.) Meanwhile, another magazine, *Carmilla*, appeared in 2002 but disappeared in 2005 after only its tenth issue.[23] The publication of both *Anise* and *Carmilla*, in spite of their short lives, was a long-awaited welcome for the lesbian and bisexual community, especially because they were sold in large chain bookstores such as Kinokuniya. The gay magazines *Bádi* and *G-men*, on the other hand, are not found in mainstream stores in spite of the fact that *Carmilla* is as explicitly sexual as gay men's magazines. I argue that this suggests that lesbianism is either not as threatening and/or that lesbian sex is still an object of the heterosexual male gaze.

The reality of the lesbian magazines' history of failure in comparison to the success and longevity of gay male media is related to both the financial and political context of the community. Gay men are much better off financially than most lesbians and are highly visible in the public domain in Japan. An example is Fushimi Noriaki, a significant player in the queer community who actively writes and organizes various events and panel discussions on the current social and political issues facing gay men. In fact, he writes about gay men's magazines regularly to ensure the continuity and strength of the gay community as a whole. While some gays criticize the content of these magazines as overly pornographic, Fushimi emphasizes the necessity of such an approach or guiding principle, especially for those who do not live in cities and have no easy access to the gay community. Fushimi himself edited two magazines, *Queer Studies* (*Kuiā sutadīzu*) in the 1990s, and *Queer Japan Returns* (*Kuiā Japan ritānzu*) in the next decade, both of which target politically oriented and educated gay men. In contrast, the lesbian community has only a few public figures, such as the politician Otsuji Kanako,[24] but there is no leader similar to Fushimi.

THE ROLE OF EDITORS AND WRITERS

Before turning to the advice columns found in *Anise, Carmilla*, *Bádi*, and *G-men*, I would like to consider the larger editorial context in which they are embedded. In the mid-1990s, the lesbian activists Hagiwara Mami and Koshimizu Yū asked Ogura Yō, a makeup artist and supervisor for *Bádi*, for help in launching a new lesbian magazine after the failure of *Phryne*.[25] Ogura agreed, and emphasized the importance of Tara Publishing being involved in this mission for the purpose of creating a Japanese gay and lesbian community, thus enhancing the new magazine's claim to membership in a larger family. The resulting publication was *Anise for Womyn* (1996–97).[26] The content of *Anise* reflects this mission to engender community consciousness; the magazine features roundtables of both lesbians and gays exchanging opinions about issues facing the community as a whole.

Ogura explains that the core of gay men's magazines is *sex*. That, he asserts, is the *kushi*, referring to the skewer that pierces the chunks of *yakitori* (grilled chicken). Everything else may be meat, but it's all strung together by the phallic skewer. In other words, everything is designed to help readers understand, interpret, appreciate, and enjoy sex.[27] In addition to having this clear objective, gay men's magazines target specific types of gay men. *Bádi*[28] shoots for *waka-sen* (younger types), *jani-sen* (idol types, from the singing group *Janīzu*), and slim gay types, while *G-men* targets more masculine, athletic, and muscular men.[29] These different orientations are reflected in the images used on their covers.[30]

Bádi and *G-men* were launched a year apart, *Bádi* in 1994, and *G-men* in 1995. *Bádi: Gay Life Magazine* claims to be "No. 1 best-selling, with the most color pictures and pages." The covers feature twenty-something men with stylish, short hair. Fushimi once stated that the popularity of *Bádi* (with a circulation of 80,000)[31] is due to a younger generation of editors and that he himself sometimes feels lost in the magazine.[32] In contrast, *G-men for Guys* (with a circulation of 30,000)[33] claims to be the "No. 1 adult gay magazine," with covers featuring thirty-something, well-built, short-haired macho types, their bodies often ornamented with tattoos. *Bádi* and *G-men* are similar in terms of styles and content; both include many color pictures of naked men having sex, the "skewer" structure, comics, short stories, social and political event information, letters from readers, horoscopes, advertisements, and supplementary adult DVDs. However, they are different in size (*Bádi* is close to 600 pages; *G-men* has about 500 pages) and a few other features. *Bádi* includes approximately two hundred pages of advertisements for everything from bars, restaurants, clubs, and host clubs, to adult variety shops, massage parlors, and hotels, to saunas and beauty salons in all parts of Japan serving gay clients. The amount of advertisements, which occupy one-third of each issue, is the reason that *Bádi* (costing 1,500 yen) is cheaper than *G-men* (which costs 1,800 yen). *G-men* carries fewer advertisements and has about a hundred pages of content similar to that of *Bádi*; however, it also includes practical information on medical and counseling facilities. Fushimi once stated that *G-men* presents good-taste eroticism (at least as he defines it) with occasional political statements on HIV and other issues. He also argued that *G-men* was the first magazine to endorse the idea that its contents were fantasy, while actual unprotected sex carries a risk.[34] The chief editor, Tomita Itaru (who is in his forties), states that readers of *G-men* span all ages, although the majority are in their thirties and forties.[35] The interesting difference between the two magazines is that only *G-men* has a section featuring personal advertisements,[36] in which gay men seek friends, partners, cultural clubs, and organizations.

Lesbian magazines are much shorter (*Anise* has an average of 224 pages, *Carmilla* an average of 168 pages), with advertisements comprising about 10 percent of each issue—far less than found in their gay counterparts. While the gay men's magazines have a clear objective, *Anise* does not. Instead, the editors invite readers to create such an objective on their own. They claim that *Anise* targets women who are conscious about their sexuality "to a certain degree," whereas *Phryne* attempts to target all women. The cover of the magazine usually displays *manga* of two cute, short-haired adolescent girls against a bright, colorful background.[37] This shows that *Anise* targets young, middle-class women, mainly students and Office Ladies (OLs). These are the women that populate the magazine's photographs, which deploy the codes of art photography when displaying nude bodies. In contrast, the drawings in *Anise* all display the *kawaii* (cute) aesthetic of *shōjo manga*. Because of this demographic (young, unsure of herself, financially dependent), the editors take a nonthreatening position in relation to straight society. Another important fact is that all four editors of *Anise* are also in their twenties and inexperienced.[38]

The other lesbian magazine, *Carmilla*,[39] has a clearer motivation. Because it began in 2002 in the wake of *Anise*'s failure, it is apparent that *Carmilla* takes *sex* as its starting point—not unlike gay men's magazines. If sex is a sort of skewer in the gay men's magazines, it is soup stock or *dashi* for the lesbians. *Dashi* is the core of Japanese cuisine, including soups and *nabe* hotpots (made with fish, meat, and vegetables). Common wisdom has it that with a good *dashi*, one can create great-tasting dishes. Like *Anise*, *Carmilla* also targets OLs and students, but there is a marked shift toward explicit discussion and visualization of sex (sometimes sadomasochistic) in *Carmilla*. The chief editor, Inoue Meimy,[40] conceptualizes her audience by saying that she started *Carmilla* specifically targeting future "lesbian reserve troops" (*rezubian yobi gun*), whom she conceives as single, living in small cities, and hungry for information, especially about lesbian sex.[41] *Carmilla* is distinct from *Anise* in two major respects. First, it covers more sex-related topics, and there are numerous sexually explicit illustrations.[42] The initial subtitle of *Carmilla* was "A book of side dishes for girls with girls." Significantly, the editors changed this to "An erotic book for girls with girls" after two issues. Second, they decided to give greater visibility to feminine-type lesbians, as the fashion, hairstyles, and poses of the cover girls attest.[43]

SEEKING AND SHARING ADVICE AND WISDOM

People of almost every age turn to these magazines for advice and wisdom. The majority of those seeking answers in both lesbian and gay magazines identify as people in their twenties, with the exception of *G-men*, which attracts a more expansive group of advice seekers, ranging from their twenties to late fifties.[44] Advice seekers in the four magazines come not only from urban centers but also from Okinawa and Hokkaido.

Unlike lesbian magazines, which include numerous questions with a mixture of practical, social, and political content, gay magazines lack the depth and the multiplicity of issues that face gay men today. There are no questions about the family responsibilities many gay men face, the coming-out issue, HIV-related concerns, or the sexual-identity issues some lesbians have expressed in their publications. None of these is discussed or shared in their advice column. This lack may thus contribute to the fact that more socially aware and politically inspired gay men prefer other types of gay magazines, such as *Queer Studies*.

Anise and Carmilla: Types of Questions

The size of advice columns in lesbian magazines is much larger than those in gay magazines, perhaps suggesting that lesbians have limited access to other lesbians with whom to discuss their lesbian experience, especially regarding sex.[45] This fact is also reflected in the type of questions they ask, such as "Where can I meet other lesbians?" (*Anise*) and "How do I find a love hotel?" (*Carmilla*). Unlike gay magazines, lesbian magazines include limited information on love hotels or other facilities. Other types of questions lesbians ask seek knowledge about lesbianism in general. Such questions touch on the categorization of lesbians into types (*Anise* and *Carmilla*), ambivalent feelings about being lesbian or transgender (*Anise*), marriages of convenience (*Anise*), and medical treatments for taking hormones or having sex-change surgery (*Anise*). These types of questions, the very core issue of lesbian identities, are not found in gay-magazine advice columns.

Lesbian magazines come closest to magazines for straight people when readers talk about their relationships, such as sharing the excitement of sex—"How do we use sex toys?" (*Carmilla*); concerns—"My partner is so jealous that I am scared of her. What can I do?" (*Carmilla*); frustration toward partners—"My partner lied" (*Anise*); and tactics—"How can I leave my partner?" (*Anise*). The last type of question, though relationship oriented, is more lesbian specific, as are those concerning marriage—"What shall I do? I found out that I am lesbian only after I married my husband." (*Anise*); having a family—"Is it OK to have a child outside of marriage?" (*Anise*); attraction toward straight women—"How can I avoid being attracted to a hetero woman?" (*Anise* and *Carmilla*); and coming-out issues—"My mother found *Carmilla* in my room. How shall I handle this?" (*Carmilla* and *Anise*).

Bádi and G-men: Types of Questions

Bádi's advice column is differently styled and structured than *G-men*'s. The former's advice column (which is included in a section titled "Life Tips") is a verbal exchange between a counselor and his young "pupil" (*deshi*) exclusively discussing the relationship of a gay couple. Every month, the *deshi* discusses a different problem facing him and his partner. Most of them are practical (e.g., "How should two men divide housework?") and not gay specific (e.g., "When do we know it's time to live together?" or "How can we spice up our sexual relationship?"). On the other hand, the advice column in *G-men* has quite a different structure. Entitled "Back Room," it is included in the reader's opinion pages, where there are four topic sections: (1) readers' opinions on the previous issue; (2) "I have done it," where readers report their recent activities and experiences; (3) "Let me speak, too" (*Ore ni mo iwasero*), which lets readers state opinions on various issues; and (4) "I am confused" (*Watashi, nayande imasu*). It is this last section that is equivalent to advice columns in other magazines. It is interesting to note that *ore*—a masculine first-person pronoun—combined with the rough imperative form *iwasero* ("let me say") is used in the third column, where readers express their opinions. By way of contrast, *watashi*—a more polite first-person pronoun—is used with the distal ending *masu* in the fourth column, where readers ask for advice. This linguistic imbalance reflects a power negotiation where the one seeking advice is in a subordinate position. *G-men* exhibits a wide variety of questions, including "How can I lose weight with a five-minute exercise?" "Am I perverse?" "How do I get more response letters via personal ads?" "How can we distinguish between *ikanimo-kei* ("obvious gay type") and *nonke* ("hetero")?" "I am worried about my old age. What is life like for two men?" Since readers of *G-men* are generally older, they tend to be concerned about aging and often share feelings of anxiety and fear, and about living alone without a family or children. However, all the questions asked in *G-men* are short and do not seem to be an important part of the magazine.

ADVICE GIVERS AND THEIR STYLE

Among the four magazines, *Bádi* deploys the most formal style, with a serious attitude and linguistic politeness in its advice column. It is interesting to note that the linguistic features of respondents in gay magazines reflect specific gendered social identities compared to those in lesbian magazines. In other words, it is the group of gay men who maintain imagined gender norms in the form of language usage. On the contrary, respondents in lesbian magazines seem to challenge the rigidity of binary gender categories often reflected in linguistic features. Their linguistic style is a mixture of all three forms stereotypically categorized as feminine, masculine, and neutral. Thus, if it is possible to assess the human relationship from a purely linguistic point of view, lesbians sound more egalitarian among themselves than gays do.

Anise and Carmilla

Anise assigns one specific respondent to letters, while *Carmilla* has a group of editors, guest editors, and specialists to address questions. Nogi Sumiko, the primary *Anise* respondent, is described as an optimistic, relaxed, and happy lesbian who calls herself the "ultimate wanderer." Her specialty is relationship problems. *Carmilla* does not have a main respondent. Instead, a group of three "sisters" (unrelated in real life), named Ubazakura, Ikue, and Omeko,[46] representing different generations and types of lesbians, offer their wisdom. Ubazakura is the oldest and has some wrinkles on her face. Ikue is a long-haired self-proclaimed femme (*neko*). The short-haired Omeko self-identifies as a butch (*tachi*). It is significant that both Ikue and Omeko identify themselves with the older binary gender roles (*tachi/neko*), while the older Ubazakura feels uncomfortable being categorized. Unlike *Anise*, whose respondents are all much younger than *Carmilla*'s respondents, *Carmilla* follows the more traditional pattern of having an older woman with more experience advising her junior. Instead of answering the queries directly, the three hold a discussion inspired by the question and thus provide a spectrum of positions on a given issue. The teamwork of the three advisers works quite effectively, with each maintaining her respective persona and role.

Bádi and G-men

Bádi's advice column is answered by the prominent gay artist, writer, activist, and bar owner Ōtsuka Takashi. The section entitled "Training Hall on Human Relationships by Ōtsuka Takashi"[47] usually takes up two pages. Ōtsuka discusses a problem with a "pupil" by placing issues in a broader perspective. Ōtsuka himself lived with a man for eleven years (until his partner's death) and was in another relationship for three years at the time of writing.[48] Due to the master–student framework, the power relationship between the two is clear and represented linguistically. The pupil speaks formally while the adviser answers in an informal, nonthreatening, and inclusive way with soft-sounding endings and expressions.[49]

In *G-men*, advisers are a group of editors and writers for the magazine who represent different types of gay men. This is reflected in their use of language. Some sound more casual and masculine;[50] some polite, sincere, and formal;[51] and some simply casual.[52] Responses are relatively short, a few sentences with no discussion among the advisers. As in other magazines, those giving advice are inclusive and nonthreatening.

Respondent's Standpoint

Lesbian and gay magazines have the goal of creating or/and presenting a community based on shared interests. Advice seekers initiate narration, while respondents send mediated messages with their version of narratives, through which advice seekers construct a new reality for themselves. Walter Fisher defines "narration" as "symbolic actions," that is, "words and/or deeds—that have sequence and meaning for those who live, create, or interpret them." He adds:

> Narration has relevance to real as well as fictive creations, to stories of living and to stories of the imagination. . . . Human communication should be viewed as historical as well as situational, as stories or accounts competing with other stories or accounts purportedly constituted by good reasons, as rational when the stories satisfy the demands of narrative probability and narrative fidelity, and as inevitably moral inducements.[53]

Sharing and exchanging "fantasies" (Ernest Bormann's term in symbolic convergence theory) in the form of narratives among advice seekers helps create a cohesive group, thus building a common culture.[54] In *Anise* several married women seek advice regarding their involvement with other women. Nogi, the main respondent, suggests a divorce, a strikingly different approach from that of other columnists, who urge divorce as the last resort.[55] Nogi, however, adds that divorce has to be done without hurting the husband's feelings. How is it possible? Nogi counsels that women take an approach that entails *uso mo hōben* (telling white lies). She argues that lying is better than hurting someone, especially if a wife cares for her husband. Another woman seeks similar advice, although she is engaged rather than married. Nogi advises her to tell her fiancé that she met someone else but to hide the person's sex, a tactic easily accomplished in Japanese, which typically leaves out pronouns. Nogi's *hiding the truth* or *lying* approach coincides with a Japanese proverb, *shiranu ga hotoke* ("Not knowing is best"). More striking is Nogi's opinion of false marriages. She counsels women not to live a sham life and says that a marriage of convenience is rarely acceptable. She directs them to the personals in the back of magazines, usually posted by gay men looking for wives. Nogi believes that a marriage between a lesbian and a gay man can work, as both can live their own lives honestly. Curiously enough, another solution not suggested in *Anise* is legal adoption. Ōtsuka Takashi argues that legal adoption in Japan is one solution for gay couples wanting to create a family. Adoptions are rather simple in Japan as long as two conditions are satisfied: the adopter must be more than twenty years old, and the adoptee must be younger than the adopter and not a lineal ascendant of the adopter.[56] In fact, Yoshiya Nobuko, a well-known writer, adopted her lover Kadoma Chiyo and lived with her until her own death. The advice regarding marriage among lesbians presents a slightly different picture, for a gay man is often pressured to carry his family's name by producing offspring. Men are not considered fully adult unless they are married.[57] It is therefore culturally more problematic not to be married if you are a man.[58]

The approach Nogi presents strikes a decisive position in relation to straight society. She does not criticize the married women or *shufu* for being in love or in a relationship with a woman. Rather, the criticism is directed to (hetero) society, which assumes that everyone should get married. As long as (straight) society is not ready to accept lesbianism, it is fine to lie. When these women write about their anxieties regarding their change of lifestyle and desires, Nogi assures them that what heterosexual society thinks does not matter—but at the same time they cannot hurt their loved ones. In this sense, *Anise* is quite unruly.

Another decisive position is seen when *Anise*'s guest adviser Mayuki, who has a hetero fetish, advises a young woman who fell in love with her straight best friend. Mayuki tells her to come out and confess her love. She adds, "Don't give up if you want to live as a lesbian," ending her sentence with the strong "Don't give up" (*akirame cha dame*). Mayuki explains why lesbians should not give up with straight women as a possible partner or lover. Most straight women have never imagined or thought about lesbianism, a state that Adrienne Rich terms "compulsory heterosexuality."[59] They do not think of it as an option or a possibility, which means that lesbianism is forbidden. Thus, it is a lesbian's job to bring straight women to the "wonderland," where the former can lead the latter. Both Nogi's and Mayuki's advice presents training grounds for challenge. Mayuki's decisive position toward the issue of coming out is shared by the three advisers in *Carmilla*. When a reader asks for advice about her mother finding *Carmilla* in her room, the advisers counsel that she should reveal her sexuality to her mother. This *see what happens* approach is found often in *Carmilla*.

While Mayuki (in *Anise*) and the three sisters (in *Carmilla*) encourage the reader to reveal her sexual orientation, the chief editor Hagiwara (in

Anise) takes an ambivalent and non-decisive position. She argues that coming out is not a political but a personal issue and that lesbians should think hard about the pros and cons of coming out. Hagiwara recommends reflection and thoughtful examination of books and newsletters, which may help women decide what is best for their particular situation. Hagiwara takes a non-decisive position again when she counsels two women in a relationship who are confused with their *sei-jinin* (sexual identity). Without explaining and/or affirming the ambivalent nature of human sexuality, she advises that it is up to them to *decide* whether they are lesbians or not. As Butler argues, gender is "a normatively constructed, discursively performed social category,"[60] and gender identities are not something we own, but something we achieve, being neither ready-made nor complete. Becoming a woman or a man is a never-ending process.

The concept of sexual identity as something unclear, fluid, ambiguous, and even negotiable is never expressed or discussed in advice columns in the four magazines, but it is hinted at in the mediated messages. Both *Anise* and *Carmilla* receive multiple inquiries about the butch/femme (*tachi/neko*) dichotomy.[61] *Tachi* has the literal meaning of *katana* (sword) and *neko* (cat) and is used as "a historical nickname for unlicensed geisha."[62] A number of columns in *Anise* reveal that some lesbians want to identify themselves in the framework of these roles, whereas others criticize this false and impossible binary. Facing the question of how one ought to fit into this categorization, Hagiwara (in *Anise*) answers in a very general way, suggesting that women do what is most comfortable. When a reader claims that this role categorization is destroying her lesbian relationship, Hagiwara asserts that lesbians do not have to follow the division of dichotomized heterosexual gender roles. She adds, however, that it is fine if there are lesbian couples who feel natural in the binary relationship. In short, her people-pleasing approach and desire to not be judgmental are clearly shared by Nogi, the main adviser.

A slightly different approach toward *tachi/neko* roles is found in *Carmilla*. The most fascinating aspect of the advice column here is the structure and the context of the discussion. Usually Ubazakura, the oldest sister, plays the role of master of ceremonies, asking questions, rephrasing, and summarizing. The three respondents often talk or answer questions from their own experiences, using authority based on age and experience. This provides readers with more specific answers, sometimes enhanced by historical, social, or political nuances. For instance, Ubazakura asks a question about the *tachi/neko* dichotomy in relation to actual lovemaking. In her generation, she claims that such a distinction was never heard of. Both Ikue's and Omeko's contributions provide historical background (how the distinction started), a social context (which is more popular), and a political spin (one has to claim herself *riba* "reversible" or "AC/DC" in order to meet more lesbians). Their answers are well informed and thorough. They also add that the *tachi/neko* roles are confusing, reversible, and less applicable to many lesbians since the introduction of new terms. A few of these are *sukadachi* ("skirt butch)" and *zuboneko* ("pants femme"). Each respondent's linguistic tone is also slightly different. Ubazakura, being the oldest, uses more polite and feminine forms when she is asserting something,[63] whereas Omeko, who self-identifies as a *tachi,* uses both strong stereotypical feminine- and masculine-sounding endings (e.g., *Heso sawatta gurai de aegu ka, tte,* meaning "Nobody breathes like that by being touched on her belly button"). The linguistic characteristics of these three women are not restrained by the binary "genderlect" (gendered speech), whose original meaning assumes that there are two clearly defined opposite gendered varieties.

The criticism against straight society found in *Anise* becomes harsher in *Carmilla.* For instance, the three sisters dish out criticism of hetero society by complaining about the unrealistic "lesbian" sex toys found in commercial videos, most of which are fabricated for straight men. There are occasionally etiquette questions in *Carmilla* (e.g., "My girlfriend's vagina smells bad. What can I do?"), or proscriptions regarding behavior (e.g., women must clean and cut their fingernails before sex). However, what is significant is their openness and basic position that people must be true to themselves.

While not from the column, an article on finding a date is a prime example of how *Carmilla* offers advice. The article isolates five kinds of lesbians and makes suggestions about change: "lose weight," "be clean," "don't be snobbish." At the same time, it concludes, "There's no trash thrown away in 2-chome."[64] In other words, no matter who you are or how you look, you will always find someone. Likewise, this article is paired with an essay on how to write submissions to the personal-advertisement section. It advises not to simply state what you desire (body type, for example). Rather, one should express *who one is* and *what one does.* Write that and they will find you. As this example shows, these advice writers are assertive, confident, open, eccentric, and entertaining.

G-men takes a similar approach to *Carmilla* in providing advice, as several editors express their opinions and suggestions. Each respondent is a little different, almost always providing alternatives as a matter of course. For instance, when a reader asks for a way to lose weight by doing only five minutes of exercise per day, one adviser says "Don't talk like a stupid woman who keeps failing on her diet! Do one hundred sit-ups a day!"[65] Another responds, "I would like to lose weight as well, but it is tough. But even when you do get fat, there is always a demand for such a type. Go ahead and get fat." There are more serious questions about relationships: "I am basically happy with my partner, but still feel unsatisfied. How can I fulfill my life?" Or "What does it mean to live with a man?" One respondent rephrases the question by saying, "Imagine your life without your partner. Don't you think that you are lucky to have someone with whom you can share your life?" Another bit of advice states, "It is wonderful to have a partner. Be positive!" Their responses are primarily based on encouragement, assurance, and affirmation, without presenting an alternative position, such as, "Why don't you talk with your partner about it?" Because these responses are so short, they invariably fail to penetrate the depths of a given issue. This type of exchange is also seen in *Anise*, where respondents do not give advice but rather rephrase the issue and avoid more specific and direct responses. This is totally different from Ōtsuka's approach in *Bádi*. Ōtsuka emphasizes the importance of talking about the issues until the two feel satisfied. For instance, the protégé seeks advice concerning infrequent sex with his partner after living together for a year. This is probably an experience common among many readers; a recent study found that, of twenty-six countries, Japan has the largest number of sexless married couples.[66] Ōtsuka explains that it is typical for a couple to lose interest in sex and that this is the crucial moment for them to work at the relationship very seriously and openly. The bottom line for a couple is to talk it out. The topic of sex is something Japanese couples rarely discuss, but Ōtsuka is asking gay men to attempt it.

NEGOTIATING PROBLEMS, NOT BEHAVIOR

It may be surprising to discover that lesbian and gay advice columns are not really about etiquette, a main concern of this volume. Thus, the issue becomes the very absence of conventional advice and the usual obsession with questions of manners, customs, and decorum. Perhaps this is not unexpected, given that etiquette is all about social rules—something complex and confusing that demands advice in how to navigate the many hazards of being human. Lesbian and gay communities are anxious about protocol and propriety and do not consciously reject such social relations. Advice columns are built on a foundational, self-conscious commitment to openness and affirmation.

At the same time, the openness of the lesbian and gay communities is primarily evident alongside the potentially threatening commitment to propriety in the straight world. The lesbian advice columns come closest to a conventional etiquette column when they discuss the interface between the rules of straight society and the private lives and desires of lesbian women. Significantly, their positions are rarely judgmental and tend toward the tactical, peppered as they are with practical snippets of advice. How one negotiates a particular predicament becomes the problematic, rather than how an individual's behavior needs adjustment. Put another way, these teachers advise students that they cannot resolve problems by following rules. Instead, one should be true to one's desires and identity, whatever they may be. At the same time, the writers never lose sight of the ethical dimension to their advice, appealing to readers not to hurt others—lying might be better in the end. Thus there is the phenomenon of multiple advisers, because their individual opinions imply an open and manifold positionality in their given communities. It is significant that none of the advisers are trained professional counselors, or medical specialists. Even questions regarding sex-change surgery and hormone therapy are answered by non-professional, in-group members of the community. The maturity of the community requires a stable, continuous exchange, encouragement, and empathy in addition to warning and criticism among members. Magazines provide such a space. They attempt to reinforce the existence of imagined communal linkages. This is why the core of the circulated advice comes via an adviser's personal experience and knowledge as lesbian or gay, rather than as a social actor mandating norms and expectations. Advice columns are therefore a kind of training ground for understanding, sharing, coping, and building the sense of what it means to live in the community—even when geographical distance may separate readers from the hot spots of the urban areas. Advice columns, therefore, are not about etiquette per se but about the creation of community based on a common sense of shared principles, agency, incentive, and action.[67] Advice seekers who have a limited history as members of the community contribute dramas and fantasies, while advisers interpret the values, attitudes, and motivations attached to these inquiries and attempt to be as helpful as possible.

NOTES

1. The reason I selected these is that *Anise* and *Carmilla* are the only magazines targeting this market, and *Bádi* and *G-men* are the most popular among several magazines. One of my consultants states, "Because *Barazoku* is out of print recently, it seems that *Bádi* and *G-men* are the only two giant political parties, don't you think?"

2. It prominently includes the relationships between Buddhist monks and young child acolytes during both the Heian period (794–1185) and the Edo period (1603–1868), relationships known as *nanshoku* (male color/eroticism). It is also called *danshoku* (male color). Gregory Pflugfelder, *Cartographies of Desire: Male–Male Sexuality in Japanese Discourse, 1600–1950* (Berkeley: University of California Press, 1999); Gary Leupp, *Male Colors: The Construction of Homosexuality in Tokugawa Japan* (Berkeley: University of California Press, 1995).

3. *Shunga* is a compound word (*shun* + *ga*), *shun* meaning "spring," which signifies eroticism in Japanese language, and *ga* simply meaning woodblock prints.

4. *Okama* is a term used since the 1900s to refer to homosexual men with effeminate behavior, so it can be viewed as a derogatory word for some gay men. The more recent term is *gei* (gay) for (younger) male homosexuals. Lunsing Wim, "What Masculinity? Transgender Practices among Japanese 'Men'" in *Men and Masculinities in Contemporary Japan: Dislocating the 'Salaryman' Doxa*, ed. James E. Roberson and Nobue Suzuki (London: Routledge Curzon, 1998), 280.

5. Sharon Chalmers, *Emerging Lesbian Voices from Japan* (New York: RoutledgeCurzon, 2002); Mark McLelland, *Queer Japan from the Pacific War to the Internet Age* (Lanham, Md.: Rowman and Littlefield, 2005); Mark McLelland, Suganuma Katsuhiko, and James Welker, eds., *Queer Voices from Japan: First-Person Narratives from Japan's Sexual Minorities* (Lanham, Md.: Rowman and Littlefield, 2007).

6. Chalmers uses the term with irony.

7. Taniguchi, Hiroaki, "The Legal Situation Facing Sexual Minorities in Japan," *Intersections: Gender, History and Culture in the Asian Context* 12 (January 2006). Online at http://wwwsshe.murdoch.edu.au/intersections.

8. The most well-known TV program is called *Onē Mans*, on Nihon TV broadcasting. It is a variety show run by sexual minorities whose areas of expertise include makeup (IKKO), flower arrangement (*Kariyazaki*), and fashion (*Uematsu*) and food (*Maron*) topics. The majority of the audience is female.

9. In 2000, a man in his thirties was murdered in Tokyo after he had been repeatedly hit with a wooden pole. Three men were arrested, two of whom were under fifteen years old. According to the police report, they confessed that

together with friends they had been attacking gay men for money, thinking that the victims would not report crimes to the police in order to hide their sexual identities. Interestingly, the media never mentioned that the victim was a gay man. *Ugoku gei to rezubian no kai* (Moving gay and lesbian organization) reports that there have been thirty-four cases of similar attacks (not murder). Kazama Takeshi and Kawaguchi Kazuya, *Dōseiai to iseiai* (Homosexuality and heterosexuality) (Tokyo: Iwanami Shinsho, 2010), 127.

10. The notion of *tōjisha* is crucial to understanding the history of the gay and lesbian movement. Vincent, Kazama, and Kawaguchi strongly argue that gay studies in Japan have to be developed only by members of the movement themselves. Keith Vincent, Kazama Takashi, and Kawaguchi Kazuya, *Gay Studies* (Tokyo: Seidosha, 1997), 2.

11. *Amatoria* started in 1951 and ended in 1955, while *Fūzoku kitan* started in 1954 and changed its name to *SM fantajia* (SM fantasia) in 1975. At that time the topic of male homosexuality disappeared, while lesbianism as an object of hetero men's object took over. There were many more private magazines circulated during the same period for gay men, cross-dressers, and other sexual minorities. McLelland, *Queer Japan*, 69, 127–128, 138–139.

12. Ibid., 128–129.

13. Ibid., 138.

14. Joseph R. Hawkins, "Invisible People: An Ethnography of Same-Sexuality in Contemporary Japan," (PhD diss., Department of Anthropology, University of Southern California, 1999).

15. Ito Bungaku was a successful publisher of books about masturbation and lesbians written by Akiyama Masami. Because of the success of these magazines, he launched a new magazine for gay men. McLelland, Suganuma, and Welker, eds., *Queer Voices*, 142–143.

16. Fushimi Noriaki, "*Fushimi gei shimbun* (Fushimi's gay newspaper)" in *Gei to iu keiken* (Experience as gay), ed. Fushimi Noriaki (Tokyo: Potto Shuppan 2004), 245.

17. There are many gay men's magazines published in the 1970s targeting specific nooks and crannies of the gay community. As for the magazines before 2000, see McLelland, *Queer Japan*, 150. Fushimi Noriaki, *Queer Studies 96* (Tokyo: Nanatsumori Shokan, 1996), 19–35. New and more stylish and fashionable magazines appeared in 2000, including *Faburasu* (Fabulous), *SM-Z* (for S&M fans), and more political and academic journals.

18. Quoted in Keith Vincent, "A Japanese Electra and Her Queer Progeny," *Mechademia*, 2 (2007): 70. Wim Lunsing gives a different perspective on *yaoi* in "*Yaoi Ronsō*: Discussing Depictions of Male Homosexuality in Japanese Girls' Comics, Gay Comics and Gay Pornography," *Intersections: Gender, History and Culture in the Asian Context*, 12 (January 2006). Online at http://wwwsshe.murdoch.edu.au/intersections.

19. There was a party for her publication at a bar in Shibuya in 1993. When I later told my friend, who was president of *Nihon Josei Gakkai* at that time, about Kakefuda's comment, she disputed it strongly. The history of the conflict between mainstream feminists and lesbians is discussed in detail in Chalmer's *Emerging Lesbian Voices*, 34–36.

20. Tokyo: Kawade Shobō Shinsha, 1992.

21. It started in 1971 and ended in 1986. It was often criticized for dividing women into *tachi* (masculine) and *neko* (feminine) roles. Izumo Marō et al., "Japan's Lesbian Movement" in *Queer Voices from Japan*, ed. McLelland, Suganuma, and Welker, 205, 213.

22. Fushimi, *Queer Studies 96*, 28.

23. Between the two commercial magazines, there were two issues of *Love Revolution: Sexuality Studies Book* published by Girlish, a private group of lesbians, in 1999.

24. She ran in the upper-house election in the summer of 2007 and, according to the gay and lesbian community, she could have been a powerful leader if she had won the election.

25. There are two other editors, Takahashi Kyōmi (nicknamed Kozō) and Tsuru Mitsuru (nicknamed Tsuru). Koshimuzu Yū later changed her name to Koshimizu Tora. Hagiwara states that she felt responsible for doing something for the readers, who sent five hundred letters to *Furiine* (Phryne). She realizes that there is a strong need for a lesbian magazine. *Anise* 1 (1996):80.

26. The title of the first issue (1996) was *Anise for Womyn: Onna o aisuru onna tachi e* (For women who love women); the name was then changed to *Anise for Womyn: For Lesbians and Bisexual* in the second issue. The title *Anise* has no particular meaning and was a merely a whimsical coinage. *Anise* 1 (1996):i.

27. *Anise* 1 (1996):81.

28. The name came from the word "buddy." The most recent issue (October 2007) has 588 pages and is published by Tera Shuppan in Tokyo.

29. Fushimi, *Queer Studies 96*, 31–33.

30. Fushimi, *Gei to iu keiken*, 134–254.

31. McLelland notes that it sells an average of forty thousand issues a month (*Queer Japan*, 171), but the publisher informed me that it sold about eighty thousand copies at the time I called in 2008.

32. The editors include Saitō Yasuki, the chief editor; Ogura Yō, a writer and artist; and Junchan, an artist and one of the committee members who organized the Tokyo Lesbian and Gay Parade of 2001. He resigned from his position at *Bádi* in 2007 (Fushimi, *Gei to iu keiken*, 157, 176).

33. Telephone conversation with the publisher in 2008.

34. Fushimi, *Gei to iu keiken*, 134, 167.

35. Other editors include Ron (age 31) and Watagashi (age 26). *G-Men*, no. 139 (October 2007):446–447.

36. The personal advertisement includes one's (1) residency, (2) nickname, (3) height, (4) weight, (5) age, (6) e-mail address (optional), and (7) a message label that indicates your physical type and your preferred partner's ideal physical type and sexual preference (there are seventeen labels to choose from: old, young, mustache, beard, well-built, short hair, S [sadistic], M [masochistic], *tachi* [active], *uke* [passive], friends [want platonic friends], fetish, international [prefer foreigners], sex friend [want sex friends], skinny [physically skinny], heavy [physically heavy], and SG [*sūpā gattchiri*, "physically super masculine and fat"]).

37. The author of the *manga* figure is Takashima Rika.

38. The contents of the magazine include a *tokushū* (special feature), *manga* (usually three to five stories per issue), short stories (usually three), *Anise Essence* (introduction to new books, movies, etc.), *Anise Avenue* (introduction about lesbian bars and events around Japan), *Mix Juice* (panel discussion with other sexual-minority groups), occasionally *Anise Gallery*, where they introduce lesbian arts, and lastly *tsuushin-ran* (personal ads). In the last issue (the fifth), the four editors apologized for the publication being abruptly discontinued. When *Anise* was restarted in 2001, they explained there had been financial reasons for its abrupt cancellation.

39. The title of the magazine came from the British gothic novel *Carmilla*, written by Joseph Sheridan Le Fanu in 1872.

40. She used to work for a publisher for erotic magazines targeting heterosexual women. There are two other editors, Kawanishi Yukiko, who is mainly in charge of novels, and Sato Chisa, an editor working for the publishing company Pot Shuppan.

41. http://bian.nabeshirt.com/repo1/Carmilla.htm (accessed November 2007).

42. Because of this, many of my lesbian friends do not read *Carmilla*. One calls it merely a porno magazine.

43. Inoue mentions this on her Web site.

44. *Anise* readers ranges from fifteen to thirty-five years old, with early readers in their twenties comprising the majority (48%), followed by those in their teens (28%), late twenties (16%), and thirties (8%). The average age of *Carmilla* readers of the first five issues was 24.4 years old, which is slightly older than readers of *Anise* (23.9 years old). After the fifth issue, *Carmilla* did not supply information on readers' ages.

45. The size of the advice column in *Anise* is between two and eleven pages per issue; *Carmilla* is between three and nineteen pages; *Bádi* is two pages; *G-men* is one to two pages.

46. In *Carmilla*, cartoon-like drawings are used in place of the respondents' real faces. Ubazakura (mature/old beautiful woman) is the oldest of the three. Because she refers to Yoshiya Nobuko by saying that she is in the same generation, I assume that she has to be over seventy. She claims that she has "graduated" from sexual activities. The second oldest, Ikue, claims that she has been a lesbian for thirty-four years and that she is a *neko yori riba* (more femme than butch, but either way is fine). The name Ikue suggests *iku* (to come/orgasm). The youngest, Omeko, states that she has been a lesbian for twenty-five years and specializes in oral sex. She says that she lives with a *yome* (bride), hinting that she is *tachi* (butch). But she later mentions that she has tried both. She personally does not care about the categorization. She says that the *neko* lesbian is more popular, but because of her work as a host/hostess in a bar, she switched to *tachi*. The name Omeko literally means "female sex organ." *Carmilla* 2 (2003):159–163.

47. The term *tūman*, created by Ōtsuka, means a continuous and friendly relationship. It was taken from the word *tsuma* (partner) in classical Japanese, which was originally pronounced as *to-u-ma*. *Bádi* (August 2007):334.

48. http://tuman.cocolog-nifty.com/blog.

49. You can read Ōtsuka's advice column on the Web (http://tuman.cocolog-nifty.com/blog/cat1030590/index.html). *Bádi* also has an advice column on the Web (http://www.badi.jp/editors/index.html) in which questions are answered by several editors, including Saito, the chief editor of *Bádi*.

50. An example is the use of *su* in *yarussu* (I will do it).

51. An example is the frequent use of *ikaga desuka* (How about?).

52. An example is the frequent use of *nā* in *boku mo yaritai nā* (I want to do it as well).

53. Walter R. Fisher, *Human Communication as Narration: Toward a Philosophy of Reason, Value, and Action* (Columbia: University of South Carolina Press, 1987), 58.

54. Ernest G. Bormann, "Fantasy and Rhetorical Vision: The Rhetorical Criticism of Social Reality," *Quarterly Journal of Speech* 58 (1972): 396–407.

55. John McKinstry and McKinstry Asako Nakajima, *Jinsei Annai: Glimpses of Japan through a Popular Advice Column* (Armonk, N.Y.: M. E. Sharpe, 1991).

56. Ōtsuka Takashi, "*Baipasu to shite no yōshi engumi* (Adoption as a bypass)," *Bessatsu Takarajima: Gei no gakuen tengoku* (*Takarajima special issue*: Campus heaven for gays) (Tokyo: Takarajimasha, 1994), 142–143.

57. Mark McLelland, "Live Life More Selfishly: An On-line Gay Advice Column in Japan," in *Internationalizing Cultural Studies: An Anthology*, ed. Ackbar Abbas and John Nguyet Erni, 344–360 (Malden, MA: Blackwell Publishing, 2005).

58. Marriage is an easier transition for men than for women. It is a transition of being taken care of by his mother to being taken care of by his wife. Men usually do not participate in building a family except for supporting the family financially. But for women, marriage brings more work and responsibilities. When women are single, typically they live with their parents, so they are not responsible for any housework. Therefore, Japanese people tend to think that there is no reason for men not to marry.

59. Adrienne Rich, "Compulsory Heterosexuality and Lesbian Existence," *Signs* 5 (1980): 631–661.

60. Heiko Motschenbacher, "Can the Term 'Genderlect' Be Saved? A Postmodernist Re-definition," *Gender and Language* 1, no. 2 (2007):255–279.

61. Chalmers traces the history of these binary gender categories. Chalmers, *Lesbian Voices*, 33.

62. Jennifer Robertson, *Takarazuka: Sexual Politics and Popular Culture in Modern Japan* (Berkeley: University of California Press, 1998), 58.

63. This fact that women become more assertive when speaking in a more feminine-sounding style is found in my earlier study with professional women as well.

64. 2-chome is a district in Shinjuku where there are more than two hundred bars for lesbians and gay men. Hideko Abe, "Lesbian Bar Talk in Shinjuku, Tokyo," in *Japanese Language, Gender, and Ideology*, ed. Shigeko Okamoto and Janet (Shibamoto) Smith, 205–221 (Berkeley: University of California Press, 2004).

65. Due to the linguistic nuance and the use of strong feminine sentence-final particle, I assume that he is an *o-nē type* (feminine).

66. "The Room of Dr. Kitamura," *Mainichi Shinbun*, October 18, 2007. Online at http://mainichi.jp/life/love/kitamura.

67. Ana Garner, Helen M. Sterk, and Shawn Adams, "Narrative Analysis of Sexual Etiquette in Teenage Magazines," *International Communication Association* 38 (1998): 63.

CHAPTER 11

Behavior That Offends

Comics and Other Images of Incivility

LAURA MILLER

The eye-catching "Manners Posters" began appearing in April 2008. Placed along the corridors and near the ticket dispensers and gates of the Tokyo Metro, a new poster was pasted up every month for several consecutive months. The theme was "Do it somewhere else." The most common admonishment found on five of the posters was *uchi de yarō* ("Why don't you do it at home!"), targeting those who irritate other passengers by splaying themselves over the seats, putting on makeup, speaking loudly on cell phones, cranking up iPods so loudly that others can hear, and engaging in drunken behavior.[1] The posters were striking and somewhat comical, with a bespectacled man appearing in each as the unfortunate witness to the behaviors.

In Figure 1, women are urged not to put on makeup while on the train. We see a young woman squeezing an eyelash curler, an implement that seems to cause special anxiety for onlookers. Jumbled cosmetics are jutting from her gaping purse, also considered inappropriately revealing of private matters.[2] There have been similar public service efforts in the past. In 2005, Japan Railways sponsored a *manā appu* ("manners improvement") poster campaign that used images of bunnies, penguins, and other animals to promote better etiquette among passengers.[3] These train and subway posters are notable because the images, not the text, are the core of the communication. In one glance they tell the story.

Contemporary advice literature likewise allows readers to learn manners by processing not only textual instruction but also visual images

家でやろう。
Please do it at home.

FIGURE 1. Don't apply makeup in the train (Tokyo Metro poster).

that illustrate rules. Although various acts of social behavior are not uniformly attended to by all members of society, and may differ by subculture, generation, class, or region, graphic representation changes these acts into behavior that everyone ought to recognize as rude. This is one reason images are so powerful. Another key aspect of a visual mode of instruction is that it allows writers to present behavior that appears to be scientifically dissected and classified. The images take on a life of their own, with the author disappearing and the image itself assuming authority.

This chapter will survey a range of misbehaviors that have been the subject of visual representation. Taken from a variety of books and magazines, the images discussed here illustrate how painstaking diagnosis of manners encodes both aesthetic and ideological canons of taste. Some images might be aimed at a specific audience, age cohort, or gender, while others pinpoint events or locations that could involve anyone. Most often the incorrect behavior is lampooned, drawing attention to the outcome of sociocultural gaffes. These images are not simply dressing for the text, but work to discipline our focus and expose in a concrete way the ideology of manners. Thus, they possess their own type of mandate as an equal, or even a more powerful supplement to the written texts they accompany.

WHAT NOT TO DO

Although conduct literature has a long history in Japan, many recent expressions that are encoded in visual imagery represent new forms of social anxiety. Even so, the use of visuals to illustrate decorous behavior is found throughout Japanese history. Scrolls with drawings and paintings were pressed into service as instruction and Buddhist proselytization during medieval times. Itinerant nuns and others used *etoki* (picture explanation) to explain right conduct and the dangers of wrong behavior.[4] *Etoki* reminds us that the illustrations of manners that we find today are the legacy of a powerful form of pedagogy.

According to Eiko Ikegami, codes of etiquette during the Tokugawa era emphasized the social position of the interactants, or what she terms "hierarchical civility."[5] In her analysis of Tokugawa conduct literature, she notes three distinguishing traits. The first is the careful attention to status differences. The second is documentation of methods for displaying the body for social communication, often accompanied by copious woodblock illustrations. A third characteristic is that the manuals contained little or no negative discipline. Rather, these early etiquette guides provided positive prescriptive formulas to push the reader to strive for an "aesthetic maximum."[6]

One of the most widely read texts during the Tokugawa era was *Onna daigaku* (Greater learning for women, c. 1729), which provides rules for upholding patriarchal norms.[7] The text is based on lectures by the curmudgeon Kaibara Ekiken (1630–1714), a scholar who was a firm supporter of the Confucian belief that society functions best when everyone adheres to strict hierarchies determined by age, status, and gender. The book was a best-seller for decades, and various editions included illustrations, poems, excerpts from literary classics such as the *Tale of Genji* (ironic, given Kaibara's stance on women reading *Genji*; see Chance, this volume), beauty advice, and models for letter writing.[8] A woodblock edition printed in 1843 contains thirty-five pages with numerous drawings that illustrate such things as how to fold gift envelopes and how to arrange ritual offerings on a platform tray. Figure 2 from this version depicts parents and a maid giving the first lesson on

FIGURE 2. First eating etiquette for children (1843 woodblock printed edition of *Onna daigaku*).

eating etiquette to a child. This image accords well with Ikegami's analysis, showing ideal rather than incorrect behavior.

By contrast, today's etiquette advice often includes models of what not to do and other prohibitive formulas.[9] For example, we find many instances in which linguistic ideology—the abstract rules and beliefs people hold about language—is linked to body management through the use of illustrations of how ill-behaved people look when they say displeasing things. Readers are invited to condemn them with the help of drawings, photos, and comics that expose every nuance of the uncivil. In some cases a model may act out an interpersonal scene, which is photographed and accompanied by explanatory text. Points for attention might be visually represented with small, annotated photo tableaux with the strategic placement of the English word "bad" or "NG" (for "No Go" or "No Good"). Originally, NG was used in youth slang, but now it is commonly found in mainstream media as well.[10] In books and magazines, NG is a code that is understood as indicating the forbidden.

An example of the use of the English word "bad" is found in a magazine etiquette column that regularly included visual representations of correct and incorrect manners, either in comic form or as a series of photographs. One month the lesson was on how to properly wait for or to greet someone you are expecting to meet, and readers were coached on how to conduct themselves when tardiness is an issue. Precise information was given for speech, facial expressions, and body language that one should *not* exhibit. For instance, in situations in which the other person is late, it is unseemly to greet them with a scowl when they finally do arrive. A model in the accompanying photograph glares, arms crossed, at an unseen tardy person, behavior that cancels out any proper verbal greeting she might deliver. A large bubble with "bad" written in capital letters floats next to the photo.[11]

Another difference seen in much new conduct literature is its focus on personal development and the beautification of the self, which have come to be considered aspects of etiquette. In recent decades the concept of good manners has been broadened and appropriated by capitalist industries that sell not only many types of courtesy literature, but also general self-improvement services and products in which the upgrading of appearance is reframed as an etiquette problem. For example, one method companies use to sell hair-removal services or products is to position body hair as a social problem related to public propriety. To enter public spaces with body hair sprouting out would be rude. Therefore, the properly denuded body that does not offend others' sensibilities becomes a form of social etiquette.[12]

The prevalence of a new curriculum that contains models of "what not to do" illustrates the notion that unless we know what constitutes the offensive and unbefitting we will not know where the borders are or when we are crossing them. Complaints about manners may also function as a type of lament about current bad times. Schemas for behavior illustrate concern or friction over larger issues than just surface demeanor. In Deborah Cameron's examination of popular writing on taboo English-language use, she suggests that the "fetish of communication" is really a cover for anxiety over social and cultural change.[13] Similarly, the new Japanese etiquette guides are not just about rules for friendly civility but are also about struggles to address changes in social relations and cultural understandings. For example, the celebration of Valentine's Day was introduced to Japan by a chocolate company in 1958, and by the 1970s it had taken the form of female-to-male gifting. Contemporary teen magazines often provide guides to when, where, and how to give chocolate to boys. In one piece, girls are advised not to present the chocolate in the classroom in front of others, and never to turn up at a boy's home with the gift. A photo of a schoolgirl doing the NG-marked behavior is provided for each taboo. Teddy bears, mufflers, and very expensive items are not to be given, but small towels, cell phone straps, and key chains are acceptable.[14] The existence of Valentine's Day manners indicates that it is both a new type of gift-giving and an example of modification in how girls relate to and interact with boys.[15]

Past guides for good behavior most often called attention to methods for marking differences in social position, and this concern continues to

FIGURE 3. "Thanks for your hard work" (Okuaki Yoshinobu, *Keigo no goten*, 22).

be a core aspect of the advice industry. Worry about social hierarchy is prominent in many books on the workplace.[16] Linguistic styles that expose social status are a cornerstone of anxiety for many people, and most guides have sections on the proper use of honorific speech.[17] Not surprisingly, the inability to use correct linguistic forms is a common target for spoofing. In Figure 3, a male underling extends appreciation to his section head, but uses an unbefitting expression.[18] He says *gokurōsan* "Thanks for your hard work," rather than the preferred expression, *otsukaresama deshita. Gokurōsan* is reserved for thanking someone who performs an expected service, and is most often said to delivery people and those in service industries who are just doing their job. As it implies evaluating another's behavior, it should not be said to superiors, and therefore the supervisor in the comic shows his disapproval at being the recipient of this phrase. The section head's crossed arms, his pouty facial expression, and a big sweat drop, together with his exclamation of disgust, all tell us of his displeasure.

At other times, however, individuals might talk with an exaggerated courtesy that will also open them up to rebuke or spoofing. In Figure 4, from *Manual of Deportment and Manners*, two women are shown using highly formalized honorific speech at the threshold of a toilet:[19]

FIGURE 4. A bit *too* respectful (Chiteki Seikatsu Kenkyūjo, *Gyōgi, sahō no benrichō*, 59).

Visitor:	*Tsutsushinde toire o okari itashimasu.*
	I will respectfully step in to borrow the toilet.
Hostess:	*Dōzo, kokoro okinaku otsukai kudasai.*
	Please, make use of it without hesitation.

Their formality suggests that anxiety about correctness in language use nevertheless has its limits. The use of extravagant politeness in such a context, one that juxtaposes high language with a crass situation, also contributes to the comic's funniness. In the illustration, the women are performing the most polite type of bow, the kneeling *saikeirei* (most respectful bow), palms emplaced flat on the floor and turned slightly inward and their bodies tilted a requisite thirty centimeters from the ground.[20] Normally, this level of formality is reserved for important ritual occasions and abject apologies for serious mistakes. Such ceremonial speech and body deportment adjacent to a toilet door with the lowbrow WC written on it (an acronym for water closet, an archaic English loanword for toilet), perfectly captures the absurdity of hyperformality.

FIGURE 5. Ask if you are not sure how to read the Chinese characters for a person's or company's name (Tsuda Hideki, *Me kara uroko no kanji no hon*, 135).

Not only spoken language but also written language may generate embarrassing social mishaps.

Seated Salaryman:	*"Baka da" sangyyō-sama ni wa nani ka to . . .*
	To your esteemed firm "Baka da" we owe . . .
Standing Salaryman:	*Uchi wa Umashikata da!*
	Our company is UMA-SHIKA-TA! [enunciated loudly]

In Figure 5, a cheerful salaryman mistakenly reads the name of his visitor's firm (Umashikata) from his business card as *Baka da*, which means something like "You idiot." [21] The seated salaryman is trying his best to be polite as he begins to utter a formulaic expression of gratitude, yet his gaffe results in a "suspension of transactions" because of the insulting nuance. This comic is a visual reminder that interactional snags may occur even in situations where one is consciously attempting to present the best manners possible. It also points to the way that negotiating written texts, especially in high-stakes business encounters, can be loaded with problems, and it encourages readers not to assume their knowledge of *kanji* (Chinese characters) is always up to snuff.

GENDERED MANNERS

A primary function of conduct literature is to serve as a vehicle for gender training. As gender norms change, up-to-date etiquette books and articles are released to keep readers abreast of new rules. These syllabi for femininity and masculinity address all aspects of interaction in lapidary commentary and with amusing graphics. Feminist scholars often describe prescriptive literature as elitist and conservatively resistant to social change.[22] In contrast to this assumption, contemporary Japanese advice-writing often grapples with transformations in roles and identities, accommodating some changes although rarely disrupting the fundamental gender hierarchy. This uneven advice-writing is not capricious but rather is guided by pragmatism.

For example, Imai Tomoko's *Words One Should Say, Words One Should Not Say to the Wife*, illustrates some minor shifts that have occurred in gender politics.[23] Imai directs her remarks to backward men, explaining how they might talk to their partners and other women without upsetting them. She gives examples of language that is guaranteed to provoke women, together with acceptable alternative phrases to express the same sentiment. For example, rather than say "your style sucks" or "that's nerdy," a man should offer "that's unusual" or "that's interesting." Expressions that can be substituted for "shut up" (*urusai*), "unfeminine" (*onna rashikunai*), and other terms that are no longer considered fitting things to say to women are provided for the clueless reader. The text is liberally sprinkled with tiny drawings of furious women in sidebars entitled "NG" and "What not to say." Imai's book insinuates that while women are no longer willing to tolerate sexist language, the men in their lives lag in this shift in attitude. The expected result of Imai's lexical proposals is that men's social relationships will be less fraught with tension and misunderstanding if only they make some attempts to clean up their surface act.

A huge genre of conduct literature targets the Office Ladies (OLs), the corps of generally young, unmarried clerical workers. The science of language and body management for female clerks includes some material identical to that also directed at the male white-collar worker in the "how-to-do-business" book market. Similar instructions are given to women and men for many office behaviors, such as exchanging business cards, negotiating seating arrangements in reception areas and meeting rooms, and standing in the appropriate place when riding in an elevator. However, there are cases in which business etiquette becomes highly gender-specific. In addition to being given general rules for business decorum, women are instructed in conduct deemed critical to feminine gender performance and are advised on everything from putting on makeup in the office to using the correct voice pitch and intonation.[24]

FIGURE 6. Even when alone, an Office Lady must have good manners (Zennikkū Eigyōhonbu Kyōikukunrenbu, *OL tabū shū*, 171).

In *Anthology of Office Lady Taboos*, comic-like figures illustrate untutored clerks who not only fail to give proper greetings or leaving-takings, but who pass male coworkers or office guests without even bowing, leaving them blistering with anger.[25] In Figure 6, we see a woman who thinks she is alone. She leans back in her chair in contemplation with both feet up on her desk. A pencil is stuck in her mouth and her hands are linked behind her neck. However, a male visitor pops his head in the doorway and catches a glimpse of her unladylike infringement. *Anthology of Office Lady Taboos* advises the OL to be aware of how easy it is to make such a mistake. If one acts in a slovenly manner when alone, the behavior may become habitual and even automatic. Thus, one might inadvertently exhibit the private behavior at the wrong time. Guides, such as this one for OLs, routinely use the terms "others," "coworkers," and "superiors" to refer to men. The visuals, however, are unambiguous as to which gendered person occupies these categories. It is also apparent that many of the nasty OL behaviors held up for censure by male authors do not often bother other women. As well, the male perspective is clearly depicted in these conduct guides. If an OL does not say, "Yes, I understand," or confirm instructions when a male pontificates, she is described as a cheeky miss.[26]

When they are outside the office, women continue to be monitored.[27] Newspaper editorials, letters to editors (see Shibamoto-Smith, this volume), and TV news coverage often deride women's supposedly worsening public manners and outrageous behavior.[28] Those who apply makeup and do other types of beauty work in public are harshly sanctioned, and their deeds are often cited as examples of the deterioration of society. One foreign journalist wrote a detailed description of a woman performing an elaborate beauty regime on a bullet train.[29] He reports that she washed her face in the onboard lavatory (one wonders how he knows this) then returned to her seat, where she applied a thirty-minute facial mask. Japanese critics also grumble that they see women on trains and in public areas doing such things as curling their hair with portable styling wands, plucking their armpit hair with tweezers, or rolling down their socks and shaving. Admonishing readers to never put makeup on in restaurants or in trains is now common in many conduct guides.[30] Women who commit acts of spatial transgression are blurring the boundaries between public and private spaces, and their exploitation of the exterior environment challenges a long-standing male prerogative.[31] In public places young women can be seen not only putting on makeup but changing their clothes, talking on cell phones, and eating snacks as if nobody else were there.[32]

In *Medicine for Somewhat Hideous Women*, Otawa Fumie presents conduct rules in a novel format.[33] Each chapter is devoted to specific types of women who have psychological problems or lack manners. The illustrations are cute and show pretty women in an amusing manner exhibiting wacky behaviors. A few of the types who require reform include the e-mail addict, the girl with a Cinderella complex, the shopaholic, the divination-dependent woman, the somewhat agoraphobic woman, and the *bihaku* (white skin) maniac. Every case includes a checklist of behaviors for the reader to use to determine if she is that type, in addition to prescriptions from Otawa to cure her. One awful type is the woman who puts on makeup while on the train. Otawa relates the case study of Miss G, who has the same daily routine. She boards the train and, once seated, whips out her cosmetic case and begins by applying foundation with a sponge, moving on to eye shadow, blush, and lipstick. Finally, she applies mascara to her top and bottom eyelashes. Within fifteen minutes of boarding the train, Miss G is completely transformed from barefaced to flawless perfection. The subway Manners Poster (Figure 1) is testimony to the fact that many women these days believe they have the right to use public space in a new way. While elders complain that such behavior is absurd or lacking common sense, young women themselves see nothing wrong with behaviors that are not hurting anyone. Many of them claim that for decades the wretched public behavior of men has been ignored or covertly condoned.[34]

FIGURE 7. What one must do to be an elegant lady (Nōmachi Mineko, *O-kama dakedo OL yattemasu*, 65).

Men who openly read explicit pornography in public transportation areas are not as severely condemned as women who apply foundation, lipstick, and blush outside their homes. Women's bodies are openly on view on trains and subways, not only smiling up from the pornographic images in newspapers and *manga* being read by male passengers, but also hanging from the rafters in advertisements featuring nude models. Perhaps there is unease about women's public beauty work because it exposes the degree to which gender performance is culturally achieved behavior, one that requires ongoing effort and shoring up. There is an expectation that a truly feminine woman never reveals the cost and energy that contribute to her gender performance, a view that surfaces in many comics and drawings. The hidden nature of this gender work may also pose problems for transgender people.

For those who switch their gender, navigating the rules of gender performance can be particularly difficult. Nōmachi Mineko's book *I'm Queer but I Am an Office Lady* relates the physical, emotional, and

FIGURE 8. Use your palm, not your finger (Obuse Makoto, *Jōryū otoko to karyū otoko: Shinia kaizō kōza, 37 renpatsu!* 20; reproduced with permission of H & I Kenkyūjo).

psychological transformations that the male-to-female transgender author underwent as she tried to pass as an unremarkable OL.[35] The book has numerous comic-style drawings that show Nōmachi's failed femininity displays. These drawings make it clear that any conception of manners is dependent on normative performance of clearly male or female gender. Nōmachi's unladylike behaviors seep into the realm of bad manners because they flout gender expectations. The cute drawing in Figure 7 shows potential gender slips that Nōmachi worries about. She must think not only about her physical appearance, such as making sure that leg hair does not stick through pantyhose, but also about female-coded speech and body language. She understands that acceptable speech is intertwined with gendered body movements. She wants to make sure that when she uses so-called *onna kotoba* (women's speech), that she does not sound too much like an old lady or a gay man (see Abe, this volume). She ends up overcompensating nevertheless. Her narrative contains a few too many feminine-marked sentence particles, and she squiggles overmuch, as indicated by the sound word *kune kune*. Her interlocutor wonders, "What's wrong?" after seeing this ersatz display.

Men not planning a gender change are also held to new standards of presentation and beautified conduct. In *The Classy Guy and the Low-Rent Guy*, by Obuse Makoto (see Bardsley, this volume), older salarymen are instructed in less dictatorial mannerisms that they ought to strive to adopt.[36]

Frame 1: Senior fellow: *Kimi, wakatteru no ka na?*
Are you sure you got that? [condescending tone]
Junior guy: *Mu!*
Aargh! [irked by condescending guy]

Frame 2: *Sonna shinia ni yubisaki kyōsei gibusu!*
Pita! Batchiri kotei
For an old guy like you, Pops, a finger cast is a must-have!
Smack! These digits aren't going anywhere now!

Frame 3: Senior fellow: *Wakatta ka na?*
Did you understand that?
Junior guy: *Ho!*
Ah!

In Figure 8, male readers are advised to use inoffensive hand gestures, such as indicating something with the entire hand, called the "tour guide" palm, rather than pointing with the aggressive index finger. The drawing drolly suggests that a finger brace is one way to stop oneself from rudely pointing with the finger.

In addition to gestures, speech is also monitored for conformity to gender and status norms. One linguistic mannerism that has been singled out for rebuke is young women's faddish use of the prefix *chō* (super, ultra).[37] Rules about correct language can be found in Higuchi Yūichi's book *Favorite Sayings of Smart People and Stupid People.*[38] The comic in Figure 9 contains the advice: "Don't use too much trendy language or too many popular expressions." In this case, two men in

FIGURE 9. Don't try to be cute or cool (Higuchi Yūichi, *Atama ga ii hito, warui hito no kuchiguse*, 59).

salaryman attire are using young female teen slang, most markedly the prefix *chō*. They exclaim:

First Older Guy:	*Sono nekutai chō kawaii*
	That necktie is super cute.
Second Older Guy:	*Ē ussō*
	Hey, no way.

Their use of *chō* is comical not only because it is not age appropriate, but because it is so closely linked to young female speech habits. The comic also mocks the obsession for fashion thought to characterize girls.

Paragons of desirable female conduct have included kabuki *onnagata* (see Isaka, this volume) and successful career women such as Bandō Mariko (see Hirakawa, this volume). The difficulty of navigating gender identity is clear from the enormous range of counsel available. Guidance for gendered comportment also intersects with other identities as well, so there may be specialized advice for readers from various subcultures (to be discussed shortly).

MANNERS FOR SPECIAL OCCASIONS

Some events in a person's life occur infrequently, yet are subject to so many expected conventions for behavior and speech that most people feel insecure at these times. In addition to weddings and other angst-ridden rituals, unusual social occasions such as going to a geisha party or visiting a boyfriend's parents for the first time will prompt many to seek advice.

Funerals, in particular, are surrounded by a mix of folk beliefs intertwined with Buddhist and Shinto proscriptions. One book on funerals includes material about how to wrap and present condolence money, how to prepare home shrines and altars, how to behave at memorial services and rites, where to place the deceased's portrait and mortuary tablet, what rules govern mourning periods, how to behave at wakes, and how to give gifts to the bereaved.[39] In Itami Jūzō's acerbic film about how family members handle the death of a relative, protagonists watch a "How to Have a Funeral" video for tips on the proper expressions to deliver at the service.[40] The film and the advice literature demonstrate that the ability to comfortably navigate mourning and funeral amenities rests on knowing the expected routines and scripts.

It is not only sad occasions such as funerals that unsettle people. Auspicious times or even unique entertainment events may also cause anxiety. For example, most people will never have the experience of partying with geisha at an *ozashiki*, an evening entertainment gathering in an exclusive teahouse (see Foreman, this volume). In the past it was primarily men from elite backgrounds, themselves connoisseurs or students of traditional dance and music, who patronized these geisha performances. Even so, the upscale lifestyle magazine *Sarai* carried a feature article on "How to play while at an *ozashiki*."[41] The need for instructions in a mass publication indicates that the upwardly mobile who lack this form of cultural capital, but can nevertheless afford to pay for an expensive *ozashiki* event, desire some concrete guidance.

Manners for geisha are marketed to non-geisha as well. In earlier decades JAL manuals for female flight attendants served as textbooks for proper language and behavior in women's secretarial courses.[42] It is not surprising, then, that the allure of the perfectly mannered geisha led to the publication of an etiquette guide intended for anyone seeking tips on how to be ultra-refined.[43] The book was written by a *maiko* (geisha in training) named Ichimame, who became a media sensation in 2007 when she launched an Internet blog on the Ichi Tea House Web site.[44] Figure 10 from Ichimame's book illustrates some *maiko* taboos at an *ozashiki* event. These include placing one's hands on the table, pouring sake with one hand or with wrist flexed back, drinking from a cup held in one hand, and using the hands to balance oneself while sitting. The

FIGURE 10. Taboos at the *ozashiki* (Kamishichiken Ichimame, *Maiko no osahō*, 86; reproduced with permission of Daiwa Shobō).

non-*maiko* can study her guide and refashion themselves into suave connoisseurs of elegance and sophistication.

A bad-mannered *maiko* who pours sake one-handed adumbrates general advice we later find given to all women. One section in the *Book for the Manners You Want to Know and Master Further* concerns the Western-adopted buffet-style party (for the politics and meanings of the Western dinner party in the Meiji era, see Hastings this volume).[45] In an illustration for the piece, we see a female guest grabbing a bottle of wine and helping herself to another glass. The waiter winces at her boorish behavior, insisting that such fine wine should be treated with more delicacy. In other words, the wine is not for guzzling by uncouth women, and the buffet table is not so casual as she imagines.

A new social situation that young women may experience is a visit to the home of their boyfriend's parents for the first time. Conduct writing offers tips on navigating this stressful event. For example, one magazine told readers that, when paying such a visit they should never bring cheap gifts.[46]A comic illustration next to this advice depicts a woman holding out bulging plastic bags from a 100 Yen Shop while saying, "How do you do? Here, please take these, they were cheap, so . . ." His parents look at her with shocked expressions. The reader is advised to think of quality rather than quantity, because a small but elegantly wrapped gift reflects refinement and thoughtfulness. Gifts must not appear to be careless or sloppy, and therefore beautifully wrapped ones indicate care and respect toward the receiver.[47]

Ritual events and transitional times in the lifecourse create a particularly charged atmosphere in which attention to language and decorum take on added weight. There is a category of speech called *imi kotoba*, taboo words and expressions to be avoided on auspicious occasions. In a book of manners featuring Hello Kitty as the model, two pages are devoted to *imi kotoba*, and much advice is given for various circumstances in which one should be careful not to inadvertently use taboo words.[48] For, example, during pregnancy or delivery (see Seaman, this volume) one should avoid verbs such as *ochiru* (to fall down) and *nagareru* (to wash away), and when starting a new job, speakers must steer clear of verbs such as *kuzureru* (to collapse) or *yameru* (to resign).

In Figure 11, taken from a different guide, an anthropomorphic cat giving a speech at a wedding uses the verb for cutting (*kiru*), represented as both a torn sheet of paper and a ghostly bubble emanating from his mouth.[49] This bulliform shape also has a gash in it and a teardrop falling from its eye. Cat-guests turn and gape at the speaker with astonished expressions. Verbs for ideas like "cut" are not supposed to be uttered at a wedding because they might bring about marital breakup through magical association. For example, "cut" brings to mind the concept *en o kiru* "to sever a relationship." Wedding guests are advised to avoid this and many other words, including *wakareru* (to part) and *akiru* (to become bored).

As in the 2005 Japan Railways Improve Manners poster campaign that used animals in order to defuse the preachiness of the admonishments, this conduct book substitutes cats for humans. The use of animals is a form of displacement that renders potentially dangerous or sensitive domains and topics safe and acceptable. In etiquette media, animal surrogates for humans are common because they permit greater reader, audience, or consumer inclusion by erasing or abating such traits as gender or class from the imagery.

FIGURE 11. Taboo words and expressions at weddings (Tanaka Toshiyuki, *Hatachi kara no manā*, 131; reproduced with permission of Shōbunsha).

MANNERS FOR NEW SOCIAL RELATIONS AND NEW SOCIAL IDENTITIES

In addition to a demand for advice that targets people of different socioeconomic backgrounds or gender groups, there is also demand for counseling other groups. Members of subcultural groups and individuals facing new social situations, particularly younger people, also desire guidance.

A foreign journalist believes that young people in Japan have become contaminated by global modernity and have lost their native manners. He says, "Exposed to the corrosive crudeness of Western popular culture, young Japanese are abandoning the sometimes stifling codes of politeness for which their country is famous, while older people look on in horror."[50]

The journalist characterizes Japanese etiquette as both oppressive and unchanging (see Campbell, this volume). There is no doubt, however, that codes for behavior have changed and that members of different generations now have radically different standards. Yet, is it really true that young people completely lack manners or ideas about proper decorum? On the contrary, rather than "abandoning" manners, we may detect an increased concern among young people about how to negotiate new types of social relations and new social situations. Dating and relationships with boyfriends and girlfriends is one arena in which they gladly seek advice.

Dating as a form of heterosexual courtship is a largely postwar phenomenon. During the 1990s one form that dating took was the *gōkon* or "group date." As a new type of social interaction, *gōkon* receives media attention, addressing anxiety about how one should behave in order to make the best impression. Many magazines list tacky behaviors to watch out for. For example, on group dates some men hate to see women whispering secrets to friends, acting or looking bored and shunning conversation, being overly tactile, or dominating the floor in an obtrusive and overbearing manner.[51] In one article on ghastly *gōkon* behavior, a man interviewed for the piece complains about a woman who protests that since she does not drink alcohol, she should not have to pay part of the tab, yet she goes on to drink her share anyway.[52] Other things that one should not do on a first date are outlined in the same piece:

> Don't keep saying "anything is okay."
>
> Don't make your guy look at all the *purikura* (print club photos) in your pocket album.
>
> Don't keep using expressions such as *maji* (seriously) *omae sa* (as for you).
>
> Don't talk about other boys.
>
> Don't use your cell phone for long conversation in the middle of a date.
>
> Don't fart.

Once a girl has reeled in a boyfriend, advice on how to manage the relationship is also available. One teen magazine published a "Master Manual" that included such instructions as: When you are in a peevish mood, don't hang around his friends; don't make a cantankerous face when your boyfriend talks to his female friends; and don't make eyes at two boys at once.[53] Finally, a teenaged girl is also sometimes advised on correct and incorrect ways to present her face to the boy for a kiss.[54]

Recent conduct advice additionally targets specific micromarkets or subcultural identities. A new fashion identity is that of the *gosu rori* or Gothic Lolita, whose laced bodices, pinafores, and puffy skirts mix Victorian frilliness with retro gothic darkness. Among the specialized Gothic Lolita mooks (magazine-books) is *Maizon*, a publication that showcases trendy shops, hairstyles, and accessories for this market. In 2004 *Maizon* published a feature article on Gothic Lolita etiquette, with instructions on everything from table manners to how to sit, stand, and walk beautifully while wearing one's black lace gloves and black satin bolero.[55]

FIGURE 12. Even Gals have rules! (*egg*, "Māchin Sensei ga kataru NG na gendō, kōdō").

As a form of hyper-cuteness and imagined elegance, the Gothic Lolita's concern for manners is not surprising. Yet even working-class subcultural types have their own notions about correctness in language and speech. One subcultural category encompasses *gyaru* (Gal) and *ganguro* (blackface) types, evolved forms of the 1990s *kogyaru* (Kogals).[56] One of the core texts in Gal culture is the magazine *egg*, a monthly that contains a mixture of fashion advice, reader photos, and reader stories about everyday activities. This periodical often carries editorial and "expert" advice for readers. In one issue, someone identified as Professor Martin tells readers that when they are with their boyfriends, they should never say such things as "It would be great if you were like Mr. X" [57] Figure 12 is an illustration that appeared next to his advice.

Girlfriend:	*Anta mo ikemen dattara nā.*
	If only you were a cool dude.
Boyfriend to self:	*Dōse ore wa. . . .*
	What'll I do?

The girlfriend is admiring a cute male singer on TV, comparing him to her less attractive boyfriend. She uses the term *ikemen*, a hybrid English–Japanese coinage created in the *kogyaru* subculture in the 1990s, but now spread to the general population and used in mass media as well.[58] When she wistfully speculates about how nice it would be if he were better looking, the boyfriend shows signs of distress and wonders what he should do.

Another subcultural type that seems to be especially inept at social interaction is the *otaku* (nerd); they are predominantly men who are obsessive fans of video games, comics, and anime. Beginning in 2001, businesses known as Maid Cafés, directed at *otaku*, began appearing. They feature young women dressed in French maid outfits who are ostensibly subservient in serving patrons. In *Moe Rurubu Cool Japan Otaku Nippon Guide*, would-be nerd customers are given a list of "Maid Café taboos."[59]

> Don't touch Miss Maid.
>
> Don't ask Miss Maid for contact information. Stop asking for her e-mail address, telephone number, and so on.
>
> Don't take photos with your cell phone or digital camera.
>
> Don't bring drinks or food from convenience stores or vending machines to the café.

The existence of this list tells us that there must be great numbers of oblivious customers who require explicit training in how to behave properly in this setting. However, it is not only in Maid Cafés that people require such location-specific rules of decorum. There are countless other places that each have norms for appropriate behavior.

LOCATION-SPECIFIC MANNERS

As seen in the debate over women putting on makeup in public, ideas about the difference between public and private space, and behavior appropriate to each, are in flux. A timely example of this is the recent increase in pet-lovers who take their dogs with them onto trains and into stores and restaurants. Although forty years ago few people kept pets inside their homes, pets are now considered valuable members of many households. The modern pet boom is estimated to have begun in the early 1990s, resulting in an enormous industry that includes pet funerals, pet home altars, pet aesthetic salons, pet amulets sold at shrines, dog coffee shops, and dog clothing lines. According to one journalist, there are now more cats and dogs than children under the age of fifteen.[60] In

FIGURE 13. Don't brush pets in public (Shufu to Seikatsusha, *Gambaranai!* 74; reproduced with permission of Shufu to Seikatsusha).

Figure 13 a woman vigorously brushes her dog in a café, while a woman seated nearby, sipping her coffee, looks on with distaste.[61] This drawing and the advice that goes with it, "Don't groom your pet in public," are testaments to the fact that not everyone views pets positively or as adorable pseudo-humans who should have the same access to public space as their owners.

Cafés, restaurants, and trains are places visited frequently by most people in their daily lives, and even with changes in attitudes about what behavior might be appropriate, most conduct literature includes advice about proper decorum when in such settings. There are also locations that might be less mundane for certain groups of people, such as travelers to other parts of Japan. For contemporary travelers to Kyoto, advice on the Kyoto dialect, Kyoto eating customs, and special Kyoto directional orientation can be found in guidebooks.[62] Visitors to Kyoto's many famous shrines and temples, for example, are advised to use good manners when they buy protective amulets (*omamori*) as souvenirs, and to limit themselves to carrying no more than two at a time. Perhaps there is concern that young women will use the amulets to adorn cell phones and bags in the same manner in which they attach numerous Hello Kitty charms and other decorative straps to everything. Additionally, there are some locations that are so specific that rules for appropriate conduct may never be written down or are only found in highly specialized media. One of these unique situations is the religious pilgrimage.

FIGURE 14. Don't use your walking staff on a bridge! (JTB Publishing, "O-henro-san dōchū hiki komogomo taikendan," 11; reproduced with permission of JTB Publishing).

There are many famous pilgrimage types, including circuit ones, in which pilgrims visit a series of sacred sites. The famous pilgrimage around the island of Shikoku, which entails stopping at eighty-eight temples, is deeply associated with the revered Buddhist monk Kōbō Daishi. Over the centuries many etiquette norms that reflect symbolic understandings of this pilgrimage and its lore have developed. Most first-timers learn these on the road from fellow pilgrims, bus drivers, and other participants (often as a result of breaking the proscription). Novice pilgrims might not know beforehand about the numerous conventions associated with the requisite walking staff. Because the staff is said to represent Kōbō Daishi, pilgrims are expected to wash the base of the staff (symbolic of the Daishi's feet) before retiring in the evening. Pilgrims who forget to do this get stern lessons from innkeepers.[63] There is also a story about a time when Kōbō Daishi was not able to find lodgings and so slept under a bridge. This led to the understanding that pilgrims should never let their walking sticks tap on the surface of a bridge as they are crossing, since it may disturb the spirit of the sleeping monk. One must therefore hold the staff off the ground whenever going over a bridge.

Many pilgrims commit faux pas when they first begin their journeys. In Figure 14 a seasoned pilgrim, steaming in anger, yells "*Gorua*!" (Hey!) at a clueless pilgrim tapping his staff on the bridge as he crosses it.[64] The surprised recipient of the sanction looks back in bewilderment. The artist drew the experienced pilgrim larger and in the foreground and the novice pilgrim smaller, as if off in the distance, emphasizing that even from afar, established members of the pilgrim community are on the lookout for violations. This type of breach reminds us that many rules for correct behavior are actually extremely location-specific.

CONCLUSION

From the sacred to the profane, all aspects of a person's life are governed by rules. Although deeply rooted in social practice, manners are also commodified and packaged for profit. One interesting development in this market is books and articles written by *hosuto* (hosts), men who are paid to flirt with and pay attention to female customers in host clubs and bars. These books are intended for a general audience as tips for smoother social interactions. One example is a book on the art of conversation, in which a successful host describes how to use talk to make the most out of relationships and how to deliver refusals in the most inoffensive ways, including other secrets from his craft as well.[65]

Manners and etiquette are beautifully melded into the business of personal identity construction, as seen in advice tailored to Gals, Gothic Lolitas, *otaku*, and other groups. Etiquette advice is pervasive in Japanese media and is dispersed in many places besides the obvious formats for conduct instruction. As shown above, pilgrimage guides, magazines for subculture members, and books on Chinese characters might include the topic of decorum. *Hot Pepper*, a free monthly coupon magazine and restaurant guide, often includes pieces on public manners. Most issues carry tips for good behavior when one is at an "all you can eat and drink" restaurant. For example, advertisements for restaurants that offer such deals have sidebars concerning *nomi hōdai tabe hōdai no manā* (manners for all you can drink, all you can eat) that advise party-goers to make sure that when ordering food they order enough for everyone.

Spending time alone with lovers or dates is also subject to evaluation. An interesting development in advice given to women about bedroom manners concerns their use of cell phones. Cell phones have penetrated all areas of Japanese life and are now restricted or banned in schools nationwide. Numerous articles provide explicit advice for sexual relationships

FIGURE 15. What not to do in bed (*Sign*, "Ettchi no toki otoko ga kizuku Sex igai no aishō").

and for how to act properly in the bedroom.[66] It is rarely a woman's sexual behavior that is rebuked or censored, but rather her increased cell phone use that seems to irritate others the most.

Men carp that their girlfriends sneak a peek at their cell phone address books when they are in the toilet, or do other unforgivable things. The men gripe, "When we are at a love hotel, she uses her cell phone to call other guys while I'm in the shower," and "She checks her phone messages right after we finish having sex."[67] One boyfriend had this to say: "I'm in the hotel with a beautiful, hot girl, and her cell phone's corny ringtone starts. So she answers and starts a long conversation. Then she plays a game on it!"[68] Figure 15 is a drawing illustrating one man's protest to a magazine's open reader's forum that his date had the gall to answer her cell phone *while* they were having sex.[69]

Man to self:	*Ge!*
	Damn!
Woman to telephone caller:	*Moshimoshi? Yadā! Hisashiburi jan!*
	Hello? Oh my God! It's been a long time!

Suspended between the woman's legs, the man juts his head forward in disbelief, his eyes bulging in dismay as she cheerfully chats on the phone.

Etiquette is not a static object existing apart from the reader as a form of pristine knowledge, and readers are not passive consumers of standards and suggestions. As seen in men's complaints about cell-phone use in intimate settings, ideas about manners fluctuate and evolve, and may be negotiated through private and public discourse. As many scholars point out, critics often view popular culture as something debilitating that masks or manipulates "real" culture.[70] Yet conduct literature is both popular *and* real culture. The images described here are a type of visual argument that not only serves as evaluation and critique but as an understanding of social interaction, which is a fundamental aspect of culture. These new grammars of sociability allow readers to willingly be disciplined and brought to order while at the same time making them feel as if they are doing it for their own betterment and advancement. There is a degree of instant gratification involved. In place of years of good breeding one can acquire knowledge of good conduct, and become a good person, by learning the rules of conduct quickly. The use of images is perhaps the quickest way to process this slippery knowledge.

NOTES

1. The posters had the phrase also written in English as "Please do it at home," but the expression *uchi de yarō* seems slightly less polite. Journalists and others have also been captivated by these posters; see Brett Bull, "Punchy Posters Urge Tokyoites to Mind Manners," *Japan Times*, June 21, 2009. There have even been online parodies of the posters, such as one that has the observing man vomiting and shows the caption "Please do it at the pub."

2. Letting others peer inside of one's purse is a no-no. In her book, Agasa describes "mood breakers" when on a date. The accompanying illustration shows a woman who cannot find her wallet and squats while going through her purse, dumping cosmetics and personal items on the ground as she searches, while her date stands by in embarrassment. Agasa, *Busu kentei: Shinri tesuto de wakaru anata no busu-do* (Ugly chick inspection: Understanding your ugly chickness using psychological tests) (Tokyo: Hōmusha, 2004), 39. Agasa, also known as Agatha, is a TV and radio personality, musician, and prolific author of books on divination and personality classification. She describes herself as a "psychology navigator" and "fortune navigator." See her Web site at http://www.agatha-net.com/index2.html.

3. Amy Chavez, "Get All Animalistic and 'Manner Up,'" *Japan Times*, October 15, 2005. Online at http://search.japantimes.co.jp/cgi-bin/fl20051015cz.html.

4. Ikumi Kaminishi, *Explaining Pictures: Buddhist Propaganda and Etoki Storytelling in Japan* (Honolulu: University of Hawai'i Press, 2006). See also the

DVD produced by David W. Plath, *Preaching From Pictures: A Japanese Mandala* (Media Production Group, Asian Educational Media Service, 2006).

5. Eiko Ikegami, *Bonds of Civility: Aesthetic Networks and the Political Origins of Japanese Culture* (Cambridge: Cambridge University Press, 2005).

6. Ikegami, *Bonds of Civility*, 345.

7. Kaibara Ekiken's name is also romanized as Kaibara Ekken. His work is available in English as *Women and Wisdom of Japan*, trans. K. Hoshino (London: John Murray, 1905).

8. Ishikawa Matsutarō, *Onna daigaku shū* (Collection of greater learning for women) (Tokyo: Heibonsha, 1977).

9. For more on women and bad manners, see Laura Miller, "Bad Girls: Representations of Unsuitable, Unfit, and Unsatisfactory Women in Magazines," *U.S.–Japan Women's Journal English Supplement* 15 (1998): 31–51.

10. A book targeting middle-class women that uses "NG" in numerous illustrations is Shinoda Yasuko, *Josei no utsukushii manā* (Beautiful manners for women) (Tokyo: Seibido Shuppan, 2003).

11. "*Shin manā ressun*" (Lesson in new manners), *Say*, no. 153 (March 1996): 23.

12. Laura Miller, *Beauty Up: Exploring Contemporary Japanese Body Aesthetics* (Berkeley: University of California Press, 2006).

13. Deborah Cameron, *Verbal Hygiene* (New York: Routledge, 1995), 25.

14. "*Barentain dē hisshō manyuaru*" (Manual for certain victory on Valentine's Day), *Seventeen* (February 2003), 96–102.

15. In another guide, Office Ladies are advised on etiquette for giving *giri choko* or obligatory "duty chocolate" to male coworkers. See Mikasa Shobō, *Harōkitii no aisare manā 100* (100 manners that make Hello Kitty lovable) (Tokyo: Mikasa Shobō, 2008), 70–71.

16. For an example, see Urawa Eiko, *Shigoto de "ki ga kiku onna" ni naru hon* (A book to help you become a "savvy woman" in the workplace) (Tokyo: PHP Kenkyūjo, 2006).

17. Although studies of Japanese honorific speech are plentiful, many are based on an assumption that it is an integral aspect of the Japanese language, rather than a social speech register that has class and regional distribution. Claims by writers that failure to use honorific speech is tantamount to showing up at a dinner party in a swimsuit are essentially folk theories of language that exaggerate the expectations for such speech. See Laura Miller, "The Japanese Language and Honorific Speech: Is There a *Nihongo* without *Keigo*?" *Penn Review of Linguistics* 13 (1989): 38–46.

18. Okuaki Yoshinobu, *Keigo no goten* (Dictionary of honorific speech) (Tokyo: Jiyū Kokuminsha, 1994).

19. Chiteki Seikatsu Kenkyūjo, ed. *Gyōgi, sahō no benrichō* (Manual of deportment and manners) (Tokyo: Seishun Shuppansha, 1995).

20. This precise pose for bowing, with exact measurements, is given in countless etiquette manuals. For example, a diagram of proper hand placement and form, with thumbs tucked in and fingers not too far apart, is found in Shufu to Seikatsusha, *Gambaranai! Kurashi no manā tannin ni kikenai kihon to*

kotsu 700 (Don't strain too much! 700 basics and tips on everyday manners you can't ask others about) (Tokyo: Shufu to Seikatsusha, 2007), 76.

21. Tsuda Hideki, *Me kara uroko no kanji no hon* (The revelatory Chinese character book) (Tokyo: Takarajimasha, 2006), 135.

22. Wendy Simonds, *Self-Help Culture: Reading Between the Lines* (New Brunswick, N.J.: Rutgers University Press, 1999).

23. Imai Tomoko, *Nyōbo ni itte ii kotoba, ikenai kotoba* (Words one should say, words one shouldn't say to the wife) (Tokyo: PHP Kenkyūjo, 2004).

24. Examples are found in Isetan Hōhōbu, *OL manā kihon chekku* (A checklist of fundamental Office Lady manners) (Tokyo: Isetan, 1993); and Urawa, *Shigoto de "ki ga kiku onna" ni naru hon.*

25. Zennikkū Eigyōhonbu Kyōikukunrenbu, ed., *OL tabū shū* (Anthology of Office-Lady taboos) (Tokyo: Goma Seibo, 1991).

26. Ibid.

27. Even in their private space, women are subjected to scrutiny. In one article a man comments on his girlfriend's room. Emphasizing its lack of feminine décor, he exclaims that the room looks "exactly like a schoolboy's room." Another complains, "My girlfriend brought home toilet paper from her company restroom." See "*Dansei 100 nin no shōgenshū kawaii onna v. kawiikunai onna*" (One hundred collected male testimonies on women who are cute, women who are not cute), *Say,* no. 229 (July 2002): 115–118.

28. Ryann Connell, "Feminine Faux Pas of Latter-day Ladies Leave Guys Aghast," *Mainichi Daily News*, June 6, 2004.

29. Michael Millett, "Japanese Rail against Women Who Turn Subways into Salons," *World News Asia Pacific,* May 3, 2001.

30. Examples include Shinoda, *Josei no utsukushii manā*, and Ogasawara Keishosai, *Bijin no kyōkasho* (Beauty textbook) (Tokyo: Sōgosha, 2006).

31. Some of the consequences for women who use public space in new ways are explored in Laura Miller and Jan Bardsley, eds., *Bad Girls of Japan* (New York: Palgrave, 2005).

32. Several times I have seen young women in public restrooms do something my mother used to call a "whore's bath," which is to say, they stand at a sink and wash all the odor-producing areas of the body. I once saw a teenager walk into a drug store, pick up a can of spray deodorant, spray both her armpits, replace the can on the shelf, and leave.

33. Ōtawa Fumie, *Choi yaba onna ni tsukeru kusuri* (Medicine for somewhat hideous women). (Tokyo: PHP Kenkyūjo, 2006).

34. Often, women point out that the train molester still operates with relative impunity and is even something of a culture hero. Incredibly, advice given to women dealing with train molestation sometimes say it is best to just stay off crowded trains, to never travel alone, and if one is molested, to very politely say "Please stop."

35. Nōmachi Mineko, *O-kama dakedo OL yattemasu* (I'm queer, but I am an Office Lady) (Tokyo: Take Shobō, 2006). This book is discussed in Vera Mackie, "How to Be a Girl: Mainstream Media Portrayals of Transgendered Lives in Japan," *Asian Studies Review* 32, no. 3 (2008): 411–423.

36. Obuse Makoto, *Joryū otoko to karyū otoko: shinia kaizō kōza, 37 renpatsu* (The classy guy and the low-rent guy: Makeover lessons for seniors, 37 sure-fire tips) (Tokyo: H & I Kenkyūjo, 2005).

37. It is ironic that "super" is frequently used in the very titles and subheadings of advice pieces that deride its use. For example, "*Machigatta keigo tte, chō hazukashii ne*" (It's super embarrassing to use honorifics incorrectly!), *Say*, no. 137 (November 1994):26.

38. Higuchi Yūichi, *Atama ga ii hito, warui hito no kuchiguse* (Favorite sayings of smart people and stupid people) (Tokyo: PHP Kenkyūjo, 2006).

39. Shufu no tomo-sha, *Hitome de wakaru sōgi, hōyō manā jiten* (Dictionary of manners for understanding funeral services and Buddhists memorial rites in one glimpse) (Tokyo: Shufu no tomo-sha, 1994).

40. *Osōshiki* (The funeral), directed by Itami Jūzō (Tokyo: Geneon Entertainment, 1984).

41. Shōgakukan, "*Hajimete no ozashiki asobi*" (Your first time to play at an *ozashiki*), in *Sarai no Kyoto* (Sarai's Kyoto) (Tokyo: Shōgakukan, 2003), 126–127. The name of this magazine is written in *katakana* as *Sarai*, but also transliterated into the Latin alphabet as *Serai*.

42. McVeigh describes JAL manuals being used as texts in a college classroom. Brian J. McVeigh, *Life in a Japanese Women's College: Learning to Be Ladylike* (New York: Routledge, 1996).

43. Kamishichiken Ichimame, *Maiko no osahō* (Etiquette for *maiko*) (Tokyo: Daiwa Shobō, 2007).

44. Ichi Tea House Web site at http://ichi.dreamblog.jp. For more on the *maiko* boom, see Jan Bardsley's "Maiko Boom: The Revival of Kyoto's Novice Geisha," forthcoming in *Japanese Studies Review*.

45. Fusōsha, "*Tachikui pātei NG shū*" (Collection of buffet party gaffes), in *Motto shiritai masutā manā book* (Book for the manners you want to know and master further) (Tokyo: Fusōsha, 1998), 95.

46. "*Otona no manā no dai ippo*" (First steps to adult manners), *Say*, no. 226 (April 2002): 112.

47. Gift-giving entails an enormous level of cultural competence. See Katherine Rupp, *Gift-giving in Japan: Cash, Connections, Cosmologies* (Stanford, Calif.: Stanford University Press, 2003), and Iwashita Noriko and Itō Miki, *Okurikata no manā to kotsu: Kurashi no ehon* (Manners and tips for gift-giving: Daily life picture book) (Tokyo: Gakushū Kenkyūsha, 2004).

48. Mikasa Shobō, *Harōkitii no aisare manā 100*, 70–71.

49. Tanaka Toshiyuki, *Hatachi kara no manā* (Manners for after age twenty) (Tokyo: Shōbunsha, 1993), 131.

50. Richard Lloyd Parry, "Japanese Used to Swear by Code of Good Manners. Now They Just Swear," *The Times*, May 7, 2005. Online at http://www.timesonline.co.uk/tol/news/world/article519499.ece.

51. "*Konna onna no ko tte, dōshitemo suki ni narenai*" (When it comes to women like this, they simply can't be liked), *Say*, no. 147 (September 1995): 48–50.

52. "*Sho dēto: soreyacha dame! dāme! 100 renpatsu*" (The first date: Doing that is wrong! Wrooong! 100 quick hints), *Seventeen*, no. 6 (February 2001): 68–70.

53. "*Chō kinkyori renai mastā manyuaru*" (Master manual for really short-term love), *Seventeen,* nos. 11–12 (May 2005): 123–126.

54. "Shall we *kisu? Yappari shiritai! Kiss no subete*" (Shall we kiss? Of course we want to know! All about kissing), *Seventeen,* no. 6 (February 2003): 47–48.

55. Gakushū Kenkyūsha, *Goshikku and Roriita sutairu bukku* (Gothic and Lolita style book), in *Maizon* (Tokyo: Gakushū Kenkyūsha, 2004), 60.

56. For more on Gal culture, see Laura Miller, "Those Naughty Teenage Girls: Japanese Kogals, Slang, and Media Assessments," *Journal of Linguistic Anthropology* 14, no. 2 (2004): 225–247.

57. "*Māchin Sensei ga kataru NG na gendō, kōdō*" (Professor Martin tells about speech and behaviors that are no good), *egg* 129 (July 2007): 44.

58. The term *ikemen* combines the Japanese *ike* from *ikeike* (lively) with the English loanword *men.*

59. JTB Publishing, *Moe Rurubu Cool Japan Otaku Nippon Guide* (Tokyo: JTB Publishing, 2008), 23. As a marketing device, this publication's title includes the *otaku* (nerd) subculture's slangy term *moe*, a nebulous concept that springs from a fan's fetishization of *manga* and anime characters. Those engaged in *kosupure* (costume play) are also given etiquette rules in this *otaku* guide. The term *rurubu* is a neologism created by the Japan Travel Bureau for its series of guides. It combines the final syllables of the verbs *taberu* (eating), *miru* (looking), and *asobu* (playing), activities associated with traveling.

60. Chris Thangham, "In Japan, Cats and Dogs More Popular Than Babies," *Digital Journal*, May 4, 2008. Online at http://www.digitaljournal.com/article/254232. Manners for pet funerals and pet memorial rites are found in Shufu no tomo-sha, *Hitome de wakaru sōgi.*

61. Shufu to Seikatsusha, *Gambaranai!,* 74.

62. JTB Publishing, "*Kyōto o arukō*" (Let's walk around Kyoto), *Rurubu Kinki,* no. 12 (Tokyo: JTB Publishing, 2007), 30–31.

63. Ian Reader, *Making Pilgrimages: Meaning and Practice in Shikoku* (Honolulu: University of Hawai'i Press, 2006), 58.

64. JTB Publishing, "*O-henro-san dōchū hiki komogomo taikendan*" (Stories about the joys and sorrows of the Henro-san's [pilgrim's] experience), in *Rurubu Shikoku hachijūhakkasho* (Rurubu's Shikoku 88 Pilgrimage) (Tokyo: JTB Publishing, 2008), 11.

65. Yūsei, *Moto karisuma hosuto ga oshieru jikyū hyaku manen kaiwajutsu* (The art of the one hundred million yen conversation taught by a former charismatic host) (Tokyo: Rongu serāzu, 2009).

66. "*Beddo no ue de no ironna manā*" (Various manners for when you're in bed with a guy), *Say,* no. 165 (March 1997): 142–146. Contemporary explicit guides to conduct in bed are an interesting contrast to their absence in writing intended for Edo-period brothel workers in a location that peddled sex as part of its business. As Segawa Seigle notes, books for courtesans in the Yoshiwara district contained advice on beauty and dealings with clients, but rarely sex how-to tips. Segawa Seigle, *Yoshiwara,* 155.

67. "*Dansei 100 nin no shōgenshū.*"

68. "*SEX de NG: Tanoshimu tame no rūru*" (What not to do during sex: Rules for enjoyment), *Say,* no. 253 (July 2004): 85.

69. "*Ettchi no toki otoko ga kizuku Sex igai no aishō*" (Compatibility other than sex that men notice when you do the nasty), *Sign*, no. 110 (June 1997): 53.

70. See Carla Freccero, *Popular Culture, An Introduction* (New York: New York University Press, 1999).

Bibliography

Abe, Hideko. "Lesbian bar talk in Shinjuku, Tokyo." In *Japanese Language, Gender, and Ideology*, edited by S. Okamoto and J. Shibamoto-Smith, 205–221. Oxford: Oxford University Press, 2004.

Abe Hirotada. *Honchō retsujoden* (Biography of women in our country). Edo jidai josei bunko (Edo period women's library), vol. 85. Tokyo: Ōzorasha, 1998.

Abe Shinzō. *Utsukushii kuni e* (To the beautiful country). Tokyo: Bunshun Shinsho, 2006.

Agasa. *Busu kentei: Shinri tesuto de wakaru anata no busu-do* (Ugly chick inspection: Understanding your ugly chickness using psychological tests). Tokyo: Hōmusha, 2004.

Akiyama Ken, ed. *Shin Genji monogatari hikkei* (New *Tale of Genji* handbook). Tokyo: Gakutōsha, 1997.

Aketa Tetsuo. *Nihon hanamachi shi* (History of Japan's *Hanamachi*). Tokyo: Yūzankaku Shuppan, 1990.

Alcock, Rutherford. The Capital of the *Tycoon: A Narrative of a Three Years' Residence in Japan*. New York: Greenwood, 1969. First published in 1863.

Anise for Womyn. Vols. 1–5. Tokyo: Tera Shuppan, 1996–1997.

Aoki Nobuya, dir. and prod. *Dan Dan*. Serialized television drama. Tokyo: Nippon Hōsō Kyōkai, 2008–2009.

Araki, James T. "Sharebon: Books for men of mode." *Monumenta Nipponica* 24, nos. 1, 2 (1969): 31–45.

Araki Kengo and Inoue Tadashi, eds. *Onna daigaku* (Greater learning for women). In *Kaibara Ekiken, Muro Kyūsō*, 201–227. Republished in Nihon shisō taikei (Collection of Japanese thought), vol. 34. Tokyo: Iwanami Shoten, 1970.

Asai Ryōi. *Honchō jokan* (Mirror of women in our country). Edo jidai josei bunko (Edo period women's library), vols. 11–12. Tokyo: Ōzorasha, 1994.

Aso Tarō. *Totetsumonai Nihon* (Incredible Japan). Tokyo: Shinchōsha, 2007.

Aston, W. G. *A History of Japanese Literature*. London: William Heinemann, 1908.

Auslander, Philip. "'Brought to you by Fem-Rage': Stand-up comedy and the politics of gender." In *Acting Out: Feminist Performances*, edited by L. Hart and P. Phelan, 315–36. Ann Arbor: University of Michigan Press, 1993.

Bacon, Alice Mabel. *Japanese Girls and Women*. Boston: Houghton Mifflin, 1896. First published in 1891.

Baelz, Edwin. *Awakening Japan: The Diary of a German Doctor*. Edited by Toku Baelz. Bloomington: Indiana University Press, 1974. First published in 1932.

Bandō Mariko. *Josei no hinkaku* (The dignity of woman). Tokyo: PHP Shinsho, 2006.

Banks, Amanda Carson. *Birthchairs, Midwives, and Medicine*. Jackson: University Press of Mississippi, 1999.

Bardsley, Jan. "Fashioning the people's princess: Women's magazines, Shōda Michiko, and the royal wedding of 1959." *U.S.–Japan Women's Journal English Supplement* 23 (2002): 57–91.

———. "The *maiko* boom: The revival of Kyoto's novice geisha." *Japanese Studies Review* (in press).

Bargen, Doris G. "The problem of incest in *The Tale of Genji*." In *Approaches to Teaching Murasaki Shikibu's The Tale of Genji*, edited by E. Kamens, 115–23. New York: Modern Language Association of America, 1993.

Barr, Pat. *The Deer Cry Pavilion: A Story of Westerners in Japan, 1868–1905*. London: Macmillan, 1968.

Beasley, W. G. *Japanese Imperialism, 1894–1945*. New York: Clarendon, 1987.

Benesse Corporation. *Tamahyo ninshin daihyakka* (Big encyclopedia of pregnancy). Tokyo: Benesse, 2005.

Black, John R. *Young Japan: Yokohama and Yedo 1858–79*. Oxford: Oxford University Press, 1968. First published in 1883.

Bormann, Ernest G. "Fantasy and rhetorical vision: The rhetorical criticism of social reality." *Quarterly Journal of Speech* (1972): 396–407.

Bowring, Richard, trans. *The Diary of Lady Murasaki*. London: Penguin, 1996.

———. *Murasaki Shikibu: Her Diary and Poetic Memoirs*. Princeton, N.J.: Princeton University Press, 1982.

Bramble, Sean P. *Culture Shock! Japan: A Survival Guide to Customs and Etiquette*. Portland, Ore.: Graphic Arts Center Publishing, 2005.

Brown, J. D. *The Sudden Disappearance of Japan: Journeys through a Hidden Land*. Santa Barbara, Calif.: Capra, 1994.

Browne, G. Waldo. *Japan: The Place and the People*. Boston: Dana Estes and Company, 1904.

Bull, Brett. "Punchy posters urge Tokyoites to mind manners." *Japan Times*, June 21, 2009.

Bungei Shunjū. *Genji monogatari no Kyōto annai* (A *Tale of Genji* guide to Kyoto). Tokyo: Bungei Shunjū, 2008.

Burns, Susan L. "The body as text: Confucianism, reproduction and gender in Tokugawa Japan." In *Rethinking Confucianism: Past and Present in China, Japan, Korea and Vietnam*, edited by B. A. Elman, J. B. Duncan, and H. Ooms, 178–219. Los Angeles: UCLA Asian Pacific Monograph Series, 2002.

Butler, Judith. *Gender Trouble: Feminism and the Subversion of Identity*. New York: Routledge, 1990.
Caddeau, Patrick W. *Appraising Genji: Literary Criticism and Cultural Anxiety in the Age of the Last Samurai*. Albany: State University of New York Press, 2006.
Cameron, Deborah. *Verbal Hygiene*. New York: Routledge, 1995.
Carmilla. Vols. 1–10. Tokyo: Potto Shuppan, 2002–2005.
Carter, Steven D. *Regent Redux: A Life of the Statesman-Scholar Ichijō Kaneyoshi*. Ann Arbor: The Center for Japanese Studies, University of Michigan, 1996.
Chakrabarty, Dipesh. "The difference-deferral of a colonial modernity: Public debates on domesticity in British Bengal." In *Tensions of Empire: Colonial Cultures in a Bourgeois World*, edited by F. Cooper and A. L. Stoler, 373–405. Berkeley: University of California Press, 1997.
Chalmers, Sharon. *Emerging Lesbian Voices from Japan*. New York: Routledge-Curzon, 2002.
Chamberlain, Basil Hall, and W. B. Mason. *Handbook for Travellers in Japan*, 7th ed. London: John Murray, 1903.
Charlton, Frank. *The Eastern Traveller's Guide*. London: Wm. Clowes and Sons, 1901.
Chavez, Amy. "Get all animalistic and 'manner up.'" *Japan Times*, October 15, 2005.
Chicago Shimpō, The. "'Herbivorous' men changing Japan's consumer society." *The Chicago Shimpō*, July 10, 2009.
Chiteki Seikatsu Kenkyūjo, ed. *Gyōgi, sahō no benrichō* (Manual of deportment and manners). Tokyo: Seishun Shuppansha, 1995.
Connell, Ryann. "Feminine faux pas of latter-day ladies leave guys aghast." *Mainichi Daily News*, June 6, 2004.
Cooper, Michael. *They Came to Japan: An Anthology of European Reports on Japan, 1543–1640*. Berkeley: University of California Press, 1965.
Cortazzi, Hugh. *Victorians in Japan: In and around the Treaty Ports*. London: Athlone, 1987.
Dalby, Liza. *Geisha*. Berkeley: University of California Press, 1983.
Danly, Robert Lyons. *In the Shade of Spring Leaves: The Life and Writings of Higuchi Ichiyō, A Woman of Letters in Meiji Japan*. New Haven, Conn.: Yale University Press, 1981.
Dasgupta, Romit. "Creating corporate warriors: The 'salaryman' and masculinity in Japan." In *Asian Masculinities: The Meaning and Practice of Manhood in China and Japan*, edited by K. Louie and M. Low, 118–134. London: RoutledgeCurzon, 2003.
Davidson, Cathy N. *36 Views of Mount Fuji: On Finding Myself in Japan*. New York: Dutton, 1993.
De Bary, Wm. Theodore, Wing-tsit Chan, and Burton Watson. *Sources of Chinese Tradition*. New York: Columbia University Press, 1960.
De Gruchy, John Walter. *Orienting Arthur Waley: Japonism, Orientalism, and the Creation of Japanese Literature in English*. Honolulu: University of Hawai'i Press, 2003.
De Mente, Boyé Lafayette. *Etiquette Guide to Japan: Know the Rules that Make the Difference!* Tokyo: Tuttle Publishing, 1990.

Dickins, F. Victor. *Primitive and Mediaeval Japanese Texts.* Oxford: Clarendon, 1906.

Dickson, E. Jane. *Debrett's Manners for Men: What Women Really Want.* Surrey, U.K.: Debrett's Limited, 2007.

Dixon, J. M. "Japanese etiquette." *Transactions of the Asiatic Society of Japan* 13 (1885): 1–21.

Downer, Lesley. *On the Narrow Road: Journey into a Lost Japan.* New York: Summit Books, 1989.

Dulles, Foster Rhea. *Yankees and Samurai: America's Role in the Emergence of Modern Japan, 1791–1900.* New York: Harper and Row, 1965.

Duus, Peter. *The Japanese Discovery of America: A Brief History with Documents.* Boston: Bedford, 1997.

Edelson, Loren. "The female Danjūrō: Revisiting the acting career of Ichikawa Kumehachi." *Journal of Japanese Studies* 34, no. 1 (Winter 2008): 69–98.

egg. "Māchin Sensei ga kataru NG na gendō, kōdō" (Professor Martin tells about speech and behaviors that are no good). Vol. 129 (July 2007): 44.

Eisenberg, Arlene, H. E. Murkoff, and E. Hathaway. *What to Expect When You're Expecting.* New York: Workman, 1996.

Engel, Dean, and Ken Murakami. *Passport Japan: Your Pocket Guide to Japanese Business, Customs and Etiquette,* 2nd ed. Novato, Calif.: World Trade Press, 2003.

Esenbel, Selçuk. "The Meiji elite and Western culture." In *Leaders and Leadership in Japan,* edited by I. Neary, 103–115. Richmond, Surrey, U.K.: Japan Library, 1996.

Field, Norma. *The Splendor of Longing in the Tale of Genji.* Princeton, N.J.: Princeton University Press, 1987.

Fisher, Walter R. *Human Communication as Narration: Toward a Philosophy of Reason, Value, and Action.* Columbia: University of South Carolina Press, 1987.

Fodor, Eugene, and Robert C. Fisher, eds. *Fodor's Japan and Korea.* New York: David McKay, 1977.

Foreman, Kelly M. "Bad girls confined: Okuni, geisha, and the negotiation of female performance space." In *Bad Girls of Japan,* edited by L. Miller and J. Bardsley, 32–47. New York: Palgrave, 2005.

———. *The Gei of Geisha: Music, Identity and Meaning.* London: Ashgate, 2008.

Franck, Harry A. *Glimpses of Japan and Formosa.* New York: The Century Company, 1924.

Freccero, Carla. *Popular Culture: An Introduction.* New York: New York University Press, 1999.

Friend, Tad. "The parachute artist: Have Tony Wheeler's guidebooks travelled too far?" *The New Yorker,* April 8, 2005.

Frühstück, Sabine. *Colonizing Sex: Sexology and Social Control in Modern Japan.* Berkeley: University of California Press, 2003.

Fujita, Fumiko. "Encounters with an alien culture: Americans employed by *kaitakushi.*" In *Foreign Employees in Nineteenth-Century Japan,* edited by E. R. Beauchamp and A. Iriye, 89–119. Boulder, Colo.: Westview, 1990.

Fujiwara Masahiko. *Kokka no hinkaku* (The dignity of the nation). Tokyo: Shinchō Shinsho, 2005.

———. *Kono kuni no kejime* (The distinction of this country). Tokyo: Bunshun Bunko, 2008.

———. *Sokoku towa kokugo* (The motherland is the national language). Tokyo: Shinchō Bunko, 2005.

Fujiwara no Shunzei no musume. "*Mumyōzōshi*" (The nameless tale). Annotated by Kitagawa Tadahiko. Republished in *Kodai chūsei geijutsuron* (Theories of the arts from ancient and medieval periods), annotated by Hayashiya Tatsusaburō, 347–407. Republished in Nihon shisō taikei (Collection of Japanese thought), vol. 23. Tokyo: Iwanami Shoten, 1973.

Fukui Masahyō. *Ninshin yori ikuji made to taikyō* (Pregnancy, childbirth, and fetal education). Tokyo: Kaibunsha, 1930.

Fukuoka Yagoshirō. "*Ayamegusa*" (The words of Ayame). In *Yakusha banashi*, edited by Hachimonji Jishō. Republished in *Kabuki jūhachibanshū* (Eighteen great Kabuki plays), edited by Gunji Masakatsu, 317–326. Nihon koten bungaku taikei (Collection of Japanese classical literature), vol. 98. Tokyo: Iwanami Shoten, 1965.

———. "The words of Ayame." In *The Actors' Analects*, translated and edited by Charles J. Dunn and Bunzō Torigoe, 49–66. New York: Columbia University Press, 1969.

Fukuzawa, Yukichi. *Fukuzawa Yukichi on Japanese Women: Selected Works*. Translated and edited by Eiichi Kiyooka. Tokyo: Tokyo University Press, 1988.

Furuki, Yoshiko. *A Biography of Ume Tsuda: Pioneer in Higher Education of Japanese Women*. New York: Weatherhill, 1991.

Fushimi Noriaki. *Gei to yū keiken* (Experience as gay). Tokyo: Potto Shuppan, 2004.

———. *Kuiā Japan retānzu* (Queer Japan returns). Tokyo: Potto Shuppan, 2007.

———. *Kuiā sutadizu 96* (Queer studies 96). Tokyo: Nanatsumori Shokan, 1996.

Fusōsha. "*Tachikui pātei NG shū*" (Collection of buffet party gaffes). In *Motto shiritai masutā manā book* (Book for the manners you want to know and master further). Tokyo: Fusōsha, 1998.

Gakushū Kenkyūsha. "*Goshikku and Roriita sutairu bukku*" (Gothic and Lolita style book). In *Maizon* 60. Tokyo: Gakushū Kenkyūsha, 2004.

———. *Ninshin seikatsu kōki* (Pregnant living in the later stages). Tokyo: Gakushū Kenkyūsha, 2006.

Garner, Ana, Helen M. Sterk, and Shawn Adams. "Narrative analysis of sexual etiquette in teenage magazines." *International Communication Association* (Autumn 1998): 59–78.

Genji Monogatari Sennenki Kinen Gaidobukku Seisaku Iinkai, eds. *Genji monogatari o aruku tabi* (A walking tour of the *Tale of Genji*). Tokyo: El Shuppan, 2008.

Goff, Janet. *Noh Drama and* The Tale of Genji*: The Art of Allusion in Fifteen Classical Plays*. Princeton, N.J.: Princeton University Press, 1991.

Goffman, Erving. *The Presentation of Self in Everyday Life*. New York: Anchor, 1959.

Grant, Julia Dent. *The Personal Memoirs of Julia Dent Grant*. Edited by J. Y. Simon. Carbondale: Southern Illinois University Press, 1975.

Hachimonji Jishō. *Yakusha zensho* (The complete book on actors). In *Kabuki*, edited by Gondō Yoshikazu, Munemasa Isoo, and Moriya Takeshi, 199–241. Nihon shomin bunka shiryō shūsei (Collected historical documents of Japanese popular culture), vol. 6. Tokyo: San'ichi Shobō, 1973.

Hall, Richard W. "Ann and Abby: The agony column on the air." *TESOL Quarterly* 5, no. 3 (1971): 247–249.

Halttunen, Karen. *Confidence Men and Painted Ladies: A Study of Middle-Class Culture in America, 1830–1870*. New Haven, Conn.: Yale University Press, 1982.

Hane, Mikiso. *Modern Japan: A Historical Survey*. Boulder, Colo.: Westview, 1986.

Harootunian, Harry, and Tomiko Yoda, eds. "Introduction." In *Japan after Japan: Social and Cultural Life from the Recessionary 1990s to the Present*, edited by T. Yoda and H. Harootunian, 1–15. Durham, N.C.: Duke University Press, 2006.

Harris, Townsend. *Some Unpublished Letters of Townsend Harris*. Edited by Shio Sakanishi. New York: Japan Reference Library, 1941.

Hastings, Sally A. "The Empress' new clothes and Japanese women, 1868–1912," *The Historian* 55, no. 4 (Summer 1993): 677–692.

Hatoyama Haruko. *Waga jijoden* (My autobiography). Tokyo: Nihon Tosho Sentā, 1997.

Hawkins, Joseph R. "Invisible People: An Ethnography of Same-Sexuality in Contemporary Japan." PhD dissertation, University of Southern California, 1999.

Hayashi Dōshun. *Tsurezuregusa nozuchi* (*Tsurezuregusa* field hammer). Edited by Muromatsu Iwao. Kokubun chūshaku zensho (Complete collection of commentaries on native texts). Tokyo: Kokugakuin Daigaku Shuppan, 1909.

Hellerstein, Erna Olafson, Leslie Parker Hume, and Karen M. Offen, eds. *Victorian Women: A Documentary Account of Women's Lives in Nineteenth-Century England, France, and the United States*. Stanford, Calif.: Stanford University Press, 1981.

Heusken, Henry. *Japan Journal 1855–1861*. Translated and edited by Jeannette C. Van der Corput and Robert A. Wilson. New Brunswick, N.J.: Rutgers University Press, 1964.

Higashibaba, Ikuo. *Christianity in Early Modern Japan: Kirishitan Belief and Practice* Leiden: Brill, 2001.

Higuchi Yūichi. *Atama ga ii hito, warui hito no kuchiguse* (Favorite sayings of smart people and stupid people). Tokyo: PHP Kenjyūjo, 2006.

Hildreth, Richard. *Japan and the Japanese*. Boston: Bradley, Dayton, 1860.

Hirakawa, Sukehiro. "Japan's turn to the West." In *The Cambridge History of Japan, Volume 5: The Nineteenth Century*, edited by M. B. Jansen, 432–498. Cambridge: Cambridge University Press, 1989.

Hirota, Aki. "*The Tale of Genji*: From Heian classic to Heisei comics." *Journal of Popular Culture* 31, no. 2 (1997): 29–68.

Hirota, Masaki. "Notes on the 'process of creating women' in the Meiji Period." In *Gender and Japanese History, Volume 2: The Self and Expression/ Work and Life*, edited by H. Wakita, A. Bouchy, and C. Ueno, 197–219. Osaka: Osaka University Press, 1999.

Hodgson, C. Pemberton. *A Residence at Nagasaki and Hakodate in 1859–1860 with an Account of Japan Generally*. London: Richard Bentley, 1861.

Hodson, Peregrine. *A Circle around the Sun: A Foreigner in Japan*. London: Mandarin, 1992.
Homei, Aya. "Birth attendants in Meiji Japan: The rise of a medical birth model and the new division of labour." *Social History of Medicine* 19, no. 3 (2006): 407–422.
Horikawa Tonkō, dir. *Sennen no koi: Hikaru Genji monogatari* (Genji: A thousand-year love, 2001). Tokyo: Tōei, 2001.
Howard, Ron, dir. *Gung Ho*. Culver City, Calif.: Paramount Pictures, 1986.
Huffman, James L. *Creating a Public: People and Press in Meiji Japan*. Honolulu: University of Hawai'i Press, 1997.
Hsu, Francis L. K. *Iemoto: The Heart of Japan*. New York: Halsted, 1975.
Ii, Haruki. "Didactic readings of *The Tale of Genji*: Politics and women's education." In *Envisioning The Tale of Genji: Media, Gender, and Cultural Production*, edited by H. Shirane, 157–70. New York: Columbia University Press, 2008.
Iida, Yumiko. *Rethinking Identity in Modern Japan: Nationalism as Aesthetics*. New York: Routledge, 2002.
Ikeda Tomoka. "*Komyunikeeshon to shite no minoue sōdan: Minoue sōdan ni arawareru kachi ishiki no henka*" (Life advice as communication: Changes in the values that appear in advice columns). *Ritsumeikan Sangyō Shakai Ronshū* 35, no. 1 (1999): 103–123.
Ikegami, Eiko. *Bonds of Civility: Aesthetic Networks and the Political Origins of Japanese Culture*. Cambridge: Cambridge University Press, 2005.
IKKO. *Onna no hōsoku* (Woman's rules). Tokyo: Sekai Bunkasha, 2008.
Imai Tomoko. *Nyōbo ni itte ii kotoba, ikenai kotoba* (Words one should say, words one shouldn't say to the wife). Tokyo: PHP Kenkyūjo, 2004.
Inaga Keiji. "Genji *hyōbyaku*" (Invocations for *Genji*). In *Nihon koten bungaku daijiten* (Full dictionary of Japan's classical literature), vol. 2, 405–406. Tokyo: Iwanami Shoten, 1984.
Inoue Fumio. *Dejitaru shakai no nihongo sahō* (Japanese-language etiquette for the digital society). Tokyo: Iwanami Shoten, 2007.
Inoue Hiromi, Koike Kazuo, Tanaka Kyōji and Matsuoka Kenji. *Shakaijin no tessoku 2001: 21-seiki o ikinuku bijinesuman no shin-jōshiki* (Iron-clad rules for the adult 2001: The new common-sense for the businessman's survival in the 21st century). Tokyo: Takarajimasha, 2001.
Isaka, Maki. "The gender of *onnagata* as the imitating imitated: Its historicity, performativity, and involvement in the circulation of femininity." *positions: east asia cultures critique* 10, no. 2 (Fall 2002): 245–284.
———. "Images of *onnagata*: Complicating the binarisms, unraveling the labyrinth." In *PostGender: Gender, Sexuality and Performativity in Japanese Culture*, edited by A. Zohar, 17–33. Newcastle-upon-Tyne, U.K.: Cambridge Scholars Press, 2009.
———. "Osanai Kaoru's dilemma: 'Amateurism by professionals' in modern Japanese theatre." *TDR/The Drama Review* 49, no. 1 (Spring 2005): 119–133.
———. *Secrecy in Japanese Arts: "Secret Transmission" as a Mode of Knowledge*. New York: Palgrave, 2005.

———. "Women *onnagata* in the porous labyrinth of femininity: On Ichikawa Kumehachi I." *U.S.–Japan Women's Journal English Supplement*, vols. 30–31 (2006): 105–131.

Isetan Hōhōbu. *OL manā kihon chekku* (A checklist of fundamental Office Lady manners). Tokyo: Isetan, 1993.

Ishikawa Matsutarō. *Onna daigaku shū* (Collection of greater learning for women). Tokyo: Heibonsha, 1977.

Itami Jūzō, dir. *Osōshiki* (The funeral). Tokyo: Geneon Entertainment, 1984.

———. *Tampopo* (Dandelion). Tokyo: Itami Productions, 1986.

Iwabuchi Junko, ed. *"Danna" to asobi to Nihon bunka* ("Patrons," recreation, and Japanese culture). Tokyo: PHP Kenkyūjo, 1996.

Iwashita Noriko and Itō Miki. *Okurikata no manā to kotsu: Kurashi no ehon* (Manners and tips for gift-giving: Daily life picture book). Tokyo: Gakushū Kenkyūsha, 2004.

JapanCareer, no. 3 (Spring 2009): 18–19.

JTB Publishing. 2007. "Kyōto o arukō" (Let's walk around Kyoto). *Rurubu Kinki* 12. Tokyo: JTB Publishing, 2007.

———. *Moe Rurubu Cool Japan Otaku Nippon Guide*. Tokyo: JTB Publishing, 2008.

———. "O-henro-san dōchū hiki komogomo taikendan" (Stories about the joys and sorrows of the Henro-san's [pilgrim's] experience). In *Rurubu Shikoku hachijūhakkasho* (Rurubu's 88 Shikoku pilgrimage), 10–11. Tokyo: JTB Publishing, 2008.

Kabuki Hyōbanki Kenkyūkai, ed. *Kabuki hyōbanki shūsei* (Collected actor-critique booklets), vol. 3. Tokyo: Iwanami Shoten, 1973.

Kahn, Robbie Pfeufer. *Bearing Meaning: The Language of Birth*. Urbana: University of Illinois Press, 1995.

Kaibara Ekken. *Women and Wisdom of Japan*. Translated by K. Hoshino. London: John Murray, 1905.

Kaminishi, Ikumi. *Explaining Pictures: Buddhist Propaganda and Etoki Storytelling in Japan*. Honolulu: University of Hawai'i Press, 2006.

Kamishichiken Ichimame. *Maiko no osahō* (Etiquette for *maiko*). Tokyo: Daiwa Shobō, 2007.

Kaneko Kichizaemon. "Zoku Nijinshū" (The dust in the ears). In *Yakusha banashi* (The actors' analects), edited by Hachimonji Jishō. Republished in *Kabuki jūhachibanshū* (Eighteen great kabuki plays), edited by Gunji Masakatsu, 327–345. Nihon koten bungaku taikei (Collection of Japanese classical literature), vol 98. Tokyo: Iwanami Shoten, 1965.

Kano, Ayako. *Acting Like a Woman in Modern Japan: Theater, Gender, and Nationalism*. New York: Palgrave, 2001.

Kasson, John. *Rudeness and Civility: Manners in Nineteenth-Century Urban America*. New York: Hill and Wang, 1990.

Kasulis, Thomas P. "Editor's introduction." In *The Body: Toward an Eastern Mind-Body Theory*, Y. Yasuo, translated by Shigenori Nagatomo and Thomas P. Kasulis, edited by T. Kasulis, 1–15. New York: State University of New York Press, 1987.

Kato, Hidetoshi. *Media, Culture, and Education in Japan.* Chiba: National Institute of Multimedia Education, 1992. Also available online at http://homepage3.nifty.com/katodb/doc/text/2606.html.

Katarogu Hausu, ed. *Taishō jidai no minoue sōdan* (Life counseling in the Taisho period). Tokyo: Chikuma Shobō, 2002.

Kaufman, Philip, dir. *Rising Sun.* Los Angeles: 20th Century Fox, 1993.

Kawaki Jun. *Josei ga furimuku menzu fasshon tekunikkushū* (Collection of men's fashion techniques to make women take a second look). Tokyo: Daisan Shokan, 1997.

Kawano, Satsuki. "Japanese bodies and Western ways of seeing in the late nineteenth century." In *Dirt, Undress and Difference: Critical Perspectives on the Body's Surface,* edited by A. M. Masquelier, 149–167. Bloomington: Indiana University Press, 2005.

Kawashima, Yasuhide. "America through foreign eyes: Reactions of the delegates from Tokugawa Japan, 1860." *Journal of Social History* 5 (Summer 1972): 491–511.

Kazama Takeshi and Kawaguchi Kazuya. *Dōseiai to iseiai* (Homosexuality and heterosexuality). Tokyo: Iwanami Shinsho, 2010.

Keene, Donald. *Modern Japanese Diaries: The Japanese at Home and Abroad as Revealed through Their Diaries.* New York: Henry Holt, 1995.

Kelsky, Karen. *Women on the Verge: Japanese Women, Western Dreams.* Durham, N.C.; Duke University Press, 2001.

Kelts, Roland. "Witch women and father hunters: Japan's new generation gap." *Doubletake* (Spring 2002): 75–79.

Keyes, Frances Parkinson. "From the Land of the Rising Sun." *Good Housekeeping* 82 (January 1926): 24–25, 134, 139–141.

Kimura Mokurō. *Gekijō ikkan mushimegane* (Theater under the microscope), edited by Munemasa Isoo. Republished in *Kabuki,* edited by Gondō Yoshikazu, Munemasa Isoo, and Moriya Takeshi, 309–338. Nihon shomin bunka shiryō shūsei (Collected historical documents of Japanese popular culture), vol 6. Tokyo: San'ichi Shobō, 1973.

Kinjinsai Shin'ō. *Kokon yakusha rongo sakigake* (The pioneering analects from past and present actors), edited by Gunji Masakatsu. Republished in *Kinsei geidōron* (Theory on the way of the arts in the premodern period), edited by Nishiyama Matsunosuke, Watanabe Ichirô, and Gunji Masakatsu, 463–492. Nihon shisō taikei (Collection of Japanese thought), vol. 61. Tokyo: Iwanami Shoten, 1972.

Kirby, Vicki. *Telling Flesh: The Substance of the Corporeal.* New York: Routledge, 1997.

Kitamura. "The room of Dr. Kitamura." *Mainichi Shimbun,* October 18, 2007. Online at http://mainichi.jp/life/love/kitamura.

Kitamura Kigin. *Genji monogatari kogetsushō* (*Tale of Genji* moon on the lake commentary). 3 vols. Annotated by Arikawa Takehiko. Kōdansha gakujutsu bunko (Kōdansha academic library). Tokyo: Kōdansha, 1982.

Kitamura, Yuika. "Sexuality, gender, and *The Tale of Genji* in modern Jap
Translations and *manga.*" In *Envisioning* The Tale of Genji: *Medi*

and Cultural Production, edited by H. Shirane, 329–357. New York: Columbia University Press, 2008.
Kornicki, Peter. "Unsuitable books for women? *Genji monogatari* and *Ise monogatari* in late seventeenth-century Japan." *Monumenta Nipponica* 60, no. 2 (Summer 2005): 147–193.
———. "Manuscript, not print: Scribal culture in the Edo period." *Journal of Japanese Studies* 32, no. 1 (2006): 23–52.
Kriska, Laura J. *The Accidental Office Lady*. Rutland, Vt.: Tuttle Publishing, 1997.
Kuno, Akiko. *Unexpected Destinations: The Poignant Story of Japan's First Vassar Graduate*. Translated by Kristen McIvor. Tokyo: Kodansha, 1993.
Lawson, Kate. *Highways and Homes of Japan*. London: T. Fisher Unwin, 1910.
Lebra, Takie S. *Japanese Women: Constraint and Fulfillment*. Honolulu: University of Hawai'i Press, 1984.
Leupp, Gary. *Male Colors: The Construction of Homosexuality in Tokugawa Japan*. Berkeley: University of California Press, 1995.
Lindsey, William. *Fertility and Pleasure: Ritual and Sexual Values in Tokugawa Japan*. Honolulu: University of Hawai'i Press, 2007.
———. "Religion and the good life: Motivation, myth, and metaphor in a Tokugawa female lifestyle guide." *Japanese Journal of Religious Studies* 32, no. 1 (2005): 35–52.
Lunsing, Wim. "What masculinity? Transgender practices among Japanese 'men.'" In *Men and Masculinities in Contemporary Japan: Dislocating the 'Salaryman' Doxa*, edited by J. Roberson and N. Suzuki, 20–36. London: RoutledgeCurzon, 1998.
———. "*Yaoi ronsō*: Discussing depictions of male homosexuality in Japanese girls' comics, gay comics and gay pornography." *Intersections: Gender, History and Culture in the Asian Context* 12 (January 2006), http://wwwsshe.murdoch.edu.au/intersections.
MacFarlane, Charles. *Japan: An Account, Geographical and Historical*. New York: George P. Putnam, 1852.
Mackie, Vera. "How to be a girl: Mainstream media portrayals of transgendered lives in Japan." *Asian Studies Review* 32, no. 3 (2008): 411–423.
Makihara, Kumiko. "Japan's subtle etiquette code." *International Herald Tribune*, July 10, 2007.
Marra, Michele. "Mumyōzōshi: Introduction and translation." *Monumenta Nipponica* 39, no. 2 (Summer 1984): 115–145.
———. "Mumyōzōshi, Part 2." *Monumenta Nipponica* 39, no. 3 (Autumn 1984): 281–305.
———. "Mumyōzōshi, Part 3." *Monumenta Nipponica* 39, no. 4 (Winter 1984): 409–434.
...tin, Sam. *How to Live Like a Gentleman: Lessons in Life, Manners, and ...* Guilford, Conn.: Lyons, 2007.
... Sherrie. *Forever Cool*. New York: Clarkson Potter, 2006.
... *Atomic Sushi: Notes from the Heart of Japan*. Surrey, U.K.: Alma,
... *Maternal Impressions: Pregnancy and Childbirth in Litera-* ...aca, N.Y.: Cornell University Press, 2002.

McCullough, Helen Craig. *Genji & Heike: Selections from* The Tale of Genji *and* The Tale of the Heike. Stanford, Calif.: Stanford University Press, 1994.
McKinstry, John A., and Asako Nakajima McKinstry. *Jinsei an'nai: Glimpses of Japan through a Popular Advice Column.* Armonk, N.Y.: M. E. Sharpe, 1991.
McLelland, Mark. "Live life more selfishly: An on-line gay advice column in Japan." In *Internationalizing Cultural Studies: An Anthology*, edited by A. Abbas and J. Nguyet Erni, 244–360. Malden, Mass.: Blackwell, 2005.
———. *Queer Japan from the Pacific War to the Internet Age.* Lanham, Md.: Rowman and Littlefield, 2005.
McLelland, Mark, Katsuhiko Suganuma, and James Welker, eds. *Queer Voices from Japan: First-Person Narratives from Japan's Sexual Minorities.* Lanham, Md.: Rowman and Littlefield, 2007.
McVeigh, Brian J. *Life in a Japanese Women's College: Learning to Be Ladylike.* New York: Routledge, 1996.
Meech-Pekarik, Julia. *The World of the Meiji Print: Impressions of a New Civilization.* New York: Weatherhill, 1986.
Mikasa Shobō. *Harōkitii no aisare manā 100* (100 manners that make Hello Kitty lovable). Tokyo: Mikasa Shobō, 2008.
Miller, Laura. "Bad girls: Representations of unsuitable, unfit, and unsatisfactory women in magazines." *U.S.–Japan Women's Journal English Supplement* 15 (1998):31–51.
———. *Beauty Up: Exploring Contemporary Japanese Body Aesthetics.* Berkeley: University of California Press, 2006.
———. "The Japanese language and honorific speech: Is there a *nihongo* without *keigo?*" *Penn Review of Linguistics* 13 (1989):38–46.
———. "Mammary mania in Japan." *positions: east asia cultures critique* 11, no. 2 (2003): 271–300.
———. "Those naughty teenage girls: Japanese Kogals, slang, and media assessments." *Journal of Linguistic Anthropology* 14, no. 2 (2004): 225–247.
———. "You are doing *burikko!*" In *Japanese Language, Gender, and Ideology: Cultural Models and Real People*, edited by S. Okamoto and J. Shibamoto-Smith, 148–165. Oxford: Oxford University Press, 2004.
Miller, Laura, and Jan Bardsley, eds. *Bad Girls of Japan.* New York: Palgrave, 2005.
Millett, Michael. "Japanese rail against women who turn subways into salons." *World News Asia Pacific,* May 3, 2001.
Mishima Yukio. "Onnagata." In *Hanazakari no mori, Yūkoku: Jisen tanpenshū* (The forest in full bloom, Patriotism: Short stories selected by the author), by Mishima Yukio, 161–186. Tokyo: Shinchōsha, 1968.
Mitamura Engyō. "Karyū fūzoku" (Culture of the geisha community). In *Engyō Edo bunka* (Engyō Edo collection), vol. 27, edited by Asakura Haruhiko. Tokyo: Chūō Kōronsha, 1998.
Mitani Eiichi. "Kiritsubo." *Genji monogatari yōkai* (Essential explanations of *Tale of Genji*). Bunpō kaimei sōsho (Grammar explication series), vol. 7. Tokyo: Yūseidō, 1954.
Morita Akio and Ishihara Shintarō. *NO to ieru Nippon* (The Japan that can say "no"). Tokyo: Kappa, 1989.

Moriyama Yutaka. *Kekkon to shussan zenshū* (Complete guide to marriage and childbirth). Tokyo: Shufu no Tomo-sha, 1932.

———. *Kekkon to shussan zenshu* (Complete guide to marriage and childbirth). Tokyo: Shufu no Tomo-sha, 1950.

Morsbach, Helmut. *Customs and Etiquette of Japan*, 3rd ed. London: Bravo, 2005.

Moskin, Julia. "Here comes ramen, the slurp heard round the world." *The New York Times*, December 10, 2004.

Mostow, Joshua. "*Genji monogatari* to jokunsho" (*Tale of Genji* and instruction books for women). Translated by Kazuko Kameda. In *Genji monogatari to Edo bunka—kashika sareru gazoku* (*Tale of Genji* and Edo culture—*Ga* and *zoku* visualized), edited by Kojima Naoko, Komine Kazuaki, and Watanabe Kenji, 337–346. Tokyo: Sōwasha, 2008.

Motschenbacher, Heiko. "Can the term "genderlect" be saved? A postmodernist re-definition." *Gender and Language* 1, no. 2 (2007): 255–279.

Muller, Karin. *Japanland: A Year in Search of "Wa."* Emmaus, Penn.: Rodale, 2005.

Mura, David. *Turning Japanese: Memoirs of a Sansei*. New York: Atlantic Monthly Press, 1991.

Murakami Shosuke, dir. *Densha otoko* (Train man). Tokyo: Toho Co. Ltd, Fuji Television Network, SDP Inc., and Hakuhodo DY Media Partners, 2005.

Murasaki Shikibu. 1990. *The Tale of Genji*. Translated and abridged by Edward G. Seidensticker. Vintage Classics edition. New York: Vintage, 1990.

———. *The Tale of Genji*, 2 vols. Translated by Royall Tyler. New York: Viking, 2001.

———. *The Tale of Genji*. Translated and abridged by Royall Tyler. Penguin Classics abridged edition. New York: Penguin, 2006.

Nakajima, Bun. *Japanese Etiquette*. Tokyo: Japan Travel Bureau, 1955.

Nakano Kōichi. *Genji monogatari no kyōju shiryō—Chōsa to hakkutsu* (Materials on the reception of *Tale of Genji*—Survey and discovery). Tokyo: Musashino Shoin, 1997.

Namkibashi (Kojima Junji and Kobayashi Kentarō), dir. *Nihon no kata* (The Japanese tradition). Tokyo: Japan Culture Lab, 2007.

Namura Jōhaku. "Onna chōhōki" (Women's treasury). In *Onna chōhōki nan chōhōki* (Women's treasury and men's treasury), edited by Nagatomo Chiyoji, 9–196. Tokyo: Shakai Shisōsha, 1993.

Nara, Hiroshi. "Translation of *Iki no Kozo*." In *The Structure of Detachment: The Aesthetic Vision of Kuki Shūzō*, edited by H. Nara, J. T. Rimer, and J. M. Mikkelson, 9–92. Honolulu: University of Hawai'i Press, 2005.

Narita Ryuichi. "Women and views of women within the changing hygiene conditions of late nineteenth- and early twentieth-century Japan." *U.S.–Japan Women's Journal English Supplement* 8 (1995): 64–86.

Nihon Bunka Tsū Kenkyūkai. *Nihon bunka tsū shiriizu: "Genji monogatari tsū to yobaretai!"* (Japanese culture expert series: So you want to be a *Genji* expert!) *Micro Magazine*, 2008.

Nishide Hiroko. *Aisare OL no isshūkan oshigoto jutsu* (The art of being a lovable OL from Monday through Friday). Tokyo: Sōgō Hōrei Shuppan, 2006.

Nōmachi Mineko. *O-kama dakedo OL yattemasu* (I'm queer but I am an Office Lady). Tokyo: Take Shobō, 2006.

Norbury, Paul. *Culture Smart! Japan: The Essential Guide to Customs and Culture*, rev. ed. London: Kuperard, 2008.

Obuse Makoto. *Jōryū otoko to karyū otoko: Shinia kaizō kōza, 37 renpatsu!* (The classy guy and the low-rent guy: Makeover lessons for seniors: 37 surefire tips) Tokyo: H & I Kenkyūjo, 2005.

Ogasawara Keishosai. *Bijin no kyōkasho* (Beauty textbook). Tokyo: Sōgosha, 2006.

Ogasawara Yuko. *Office Ladies and Salaried Men: Power, Gender, and Work in Japanese Companies*. Berkeley: University of California Press, 1998.

Ogura Chikako. *Kekkon no jōken* (Conditions for marriage). Tokyo: Asahi Shinbunsha, 2004.

Okamoto, Shigeko, and Janet S. Shibamoto-Smith. "Constructing linguistic femininity in contemporary Japan: Scholarly and popular representations." *Gender and Language* 2, no. 1 (2008): 87–112.

Okuaki Yoshinobu. *Keigo no goten* (Dictionary of honorific speech). Tokyo: Jiyū Kokuminsha, 1994.

Onishi, Norimitsu. "Japanese author guides women to 'dignity,' but others see dullness." *New York Times*, March 29, 2008.

Otsubo, Sumiko. "Feminist maternal eugenics in wartime Japan." *U.S.–Japan Women's Journal English Supplement* 17 (1999): 39–76.

Ōtsuka Takashi. "Baipasu to shite no yōshi engumi" (Adoption as a by-pass). In *Bessatsu Takarajima: Gei no gakuen tengoku* (Takarajima special issue: Campus heaven for gays), 142–143. Tokyo: Takarajimasha, 1994.

Ōtawa Fumie. *Choi yaba onna ni tsukeru kusuri* (Medicine for somewhat hideous women). Tokyo: PHP Kenkyūjo, 2006.

Ōzasa Yoshio. *Nihon gendai engekishi: Meiji Taishō hen* (History of Japanese contemporary theater: The Meiji and Taisho eras). Tokyo: Hakusuisha, 1985.

Parker, Jr., L. Craig. *The Japanese Police System Today: A Comparative Study*. New York: East Gate, 2001.

Parry, Richard Lloyd. "Japanese used to swear by code of good manners. Now they just swear." *The Times*, May 7, 2005.

Pflugfelder, Gregory. *Cartographies of Desire: Male–Male Sexuality in Japanese Discourse, 1600–1950*. Berkeley: University of California Press, 1999.

Plath, David W., prod. *Preaching from Pictures: A Japanese Mandala*. Media Production Group, Asian Educational Media Service, University of Illinois at Urbana-Champaign, 2006.

Post, Peter. *Essential Manners for Men: What to Do, When to Do It, and Why*. New York: HarperResource, 2003.

Pyle, Kenneth B. "Meiji Conservatism." In *The Cambridge History of Japan, Volume 5: The Nineteenth Century*, edited by M. B. Jansen, 674–720. Cambridge: Cambridge University Press, 1989.

Reader, Ian. *Making Pilgrimages: Meaning and Practice in Shikoku*. Honolulu: University of Hawai'i Press, 2006.

Reiber, Beth, and Janie Spencer. *Frommer's Japan*, 9th ed. Hoboken, N.J.: Wiley Publishing, 2008.

Reischauer, Haru Matsukata. *Samurai and Silk: A Japanese and American Heritage*. Cambridge, Mass.: Harvard University Press, 1986.
Rich, Adrienne. "Compulsory heterosexuality and lesbian existence." *Signs* 5 (1980): 631–661.
Roberson, James E., and Nobue Suzuki, eds. "Introduction." In *Men and Masculinities in Contemporary Japan: Dislocating the 'Salaryman' Doxa*, edited by J. Roberson and N. Suzuki, 1–19. New York: RoutledgeCurzon, 2003.
Robertson, Jennifer. "The Shingaku woman: Straight from the heart." In *Recreating Japanese Women, 1600–1945*, edited by G. L. Bernstein, 88–107. Berkeley: University of California Press, 1991.
———. *Takarazuka: Sexual Politics and Popular Culture in Modern Japan*. Berkeley: University of California Press, 1998.
Rose, Barbara. *Tsuda Umeko and Women's Education in Japan*. New Haven, Conn.: Yale University Press, 1992.
Rosenberger, Nancy R. *Gambling with Virtue: Japanese Women and the Search for Self in a Changing Nation*. Honolulu: University of Hawai'i Press, 2001.
Rosenstone, Robert A. *Mirror in the Shrine: American Encounters with Meiji Japan*. Cambridge, Mass.: Harvard University Press, 1988.
Ross, Christopher. *Mishima's Sword: Travels in Search of a Samurai Legend*. London: Fourth Estate, 2006.
Rowley, G. G. *Yosano Akiko and the Tale of Genji*. Ann Arbor: The Center for Japanese Studies, University of Michigan, 2000.
Rupp, Katherine. *Gift-giving in Japan: Cash, Connections, Cosmologies*. Stanford, Calif.: Stanford University Press, 2003.
Rutherford, Scott. *Insight Guide, Japan*. 3rd ed. Singapore: Insight Guides, 2003.
Rüttermann, Marcus. "Urbane Schreib-Anleitungen zu femininer Sanftheit (*yawaraka*): Übersetzung und Interpretation eines Abschnittes aus dem japanisch-neuzeitlichen Frauen-Benimmbuch *Onna chôhôki*" (Urban written instructions for feminine "softness": A translation and explication of an excerpt from the early modern Japanese women's manual *Onna chōhōki*). *Japonica Humboldtiana* 6 (2002):5–56.
Sakai Junko. *Makeinu no tōboe* (The howl of the loser dog). Tokyo: Kōdansha, 2003.
Sakura Momoko. *Sō iu fū ga dekite iru* (That's how I did it). Tokyo: Shinchō Bunko, 1995.
Sand, Jordan. *House and Home in Modern Japan: Architecture, Domestic Space, and Bourgeois Culture, 1880–1930*. Cambridge, Mass.: Harvard University Press, 2003.
Say. "Beddo no ue de no ironna manā" (Various manners for when you're in bed with a guy). *Say*, no. 165 (March 1997): 142–146.
———. "Dansei 100 nin no shōgenshū kawaii onna v. kawiikunai onna" (One hundred collected male testimonies on women who are cute, women who are not cute). *Say*, no. 229 (July 2002): 115–118.
———. "E-mēru, pasokon no manā" (Manners for e-mail and personal computers). *Say*, no. 226 (April 2002): 107.
———. "Konna onna no ko tte, dōshitemo suki ni narenai" (When it comes to women like this, they simply can't be liked). *Say*, no. 147 (September 1995): 48–50.

———. "Machigatta keigo tte, chō hazukashii ne" (It's super embarrassing to use honorifics incorrectly!). *Say*, no. 137 (November 1994): 26.

———. "Shin manā ressun" (Lesson in new manners). *Say*, no. 153 (March 1996): 23.

———. "Otona no manā no dai ippo" (First steps to adult manners). *Say*, no. 226 (April 2002): 112.

———. "SEX de NG: Tanoshimu tame no rūru" (What not to do during sex: Rules for enjoyment). *Say*, no. 253 (July 2004): 85.

Schepisi, Fred, dir. *Mr. Baseball*. Universal City, Calif.: Universal Pictures, 1992.

Seidensticker, Edward, trans. *As I Crossed a Bridge of Dreams: Recollections of a Woman in Eleventh-Century Japan*. London: Penguin, 1975.

———. *Low City, High City. Tokyo from Edo to the Earthquake: How the Shogun's Ancient Capital Became a Great Modern City, 1867–1923*. New York: Knopf, 1983.

Seigle, Cecilia Segawa. *Yoshiwara: The Glittering World of the Japanese Courtesan*. Honolulu: University of Hawai'i Press, 1993.

Seventeen. "Barentain dē hisshō manyuaru" (Manual for certain victory on Valentine's Day). *Seventeen* (February 2003): 96–102.

———. "Chō kinkyori renai mastā manyuaru" (Master manual for really short-term love). *Seventeen*, no. 11–12 (May 2005): 123–126.

———. "Shall we kisu? Yappari shiritai! Kiss no subete" (Shall we kiss? Of course we want to know! All about kissing). *Seventeen*, no. 6 (February 2003): 47–48.

———. "Sho dēto: Soreyacha dame! Dāme! 100 renpatsu" (The first date: Doing that is wrong! Wrooong! 100 quick hints). *Seventeen*, no. 6 (February 2001): 68–70.

Shibamoto-Smith, Janet S. "Changing lovestyles: Fictional representations of contemporary Japanese men in love." *positions: east asia cultures critique* 16, no. 2 (2008): 359–387.

———. "From *hiren* to *happī-endo*: Romantic expression in the Japanese love story." In *Languages of Sentiment: Pragmatic and Conceptual Approaches to Cultural Constructions of Emotional Substrates*, edited by G. Palmer and D. J. Occhi, 147–166. Amsterdam: John Benjamins, 1999.

Shibusawa Ei'ichi. *The Autobiography of Shibusawa Ei'ichi: From Peasant to Entrepreneur*. Translated by Teruko Craig. Tokyo: Tokyo University Press, 1994.

Shibusawa, Naoko. *America's Geisha Ally: Reimagining the Japanese Enemy*. Cambridge, Mass.: Harvard University Press, 2006.

Shimizu Katsumi. *Subete ga wakaru kankonsōsai manā daijiten* (Encyclopedia of important ceremonial occasions [so you] will know everything). Tokyo: Nagaoka Shoten, 2005.

Shinoda Yasuko. *Josei no utsukushii manā* (Beautiful manners for women). Tokyo: Seibido Shuppan, 2003.

Shiotsuki Yaeko. *Suteki na josei no tame no jōkyū manā ressun* (Advanced manner lessons for the attractive woman). Tokyo: Shogakkan, 2005.

Shirane, Haruo. *The Bridge of Dreams: A Poetics of "The Tale of Genji."* Stanford, Calif.: Stanford University Press, 1987.

———. "*The Tale of Genji* and the dynamics of cultural production: Canonization and popularization." In *Envisioning the Tale of Genji: Media, Gender, and Cultural Production*, edited by H. Shirane, 1–46. New York: Columbia University Press, 2008.

Shively, Donald H. "The Japanization of the Middle Meiji." In *Tradition and Modernization in Japanese Culture*, edited by D. H. Shively, 77–119. Princeton, N.J.: Princeton University Press, 1971.

Shōgakukan. "Hajimete no ozashiki asobi" (Your first time to play at an *ozashiki*). In *Sarai no Kyoto*, 126–127. Tokyo: Shōgakukan, 2003.

———. *Nihon kokugo daijiten* (Comprehensive dictionary of Japan's national language). Tokyo: Shōgakukan, 2001. First published in 1974.

Shufu no Tomo-sha. *Ansan to ikujiho* (Methods for safe birth and childrearing). Tokyo: Shufu no Tomo-sha, 1932.

———. *Hitome de wakaru sōgi, hōyō manā jiten* (Dictionary of manners for understanding funeral services and Buddhists memorial rites in one glimpse). Tokyo: Shufu no Tomo-sha, 1994.

Shufu to Seikatsusha. *Gambaranai! Kurashi no manā tannin ni kikenai kihon to kotsu 700* (Don't strain too much! 700 basics and tips on everyday manners you can't ask others about). Tokyo: Shufu to Seikatsusha, 2007.

Shūkan Hikaru Genji Henshūbu, ed. *Shūkan Hikaru Genji* (Weekly shining Genji). Tokyo: Naapuru, 1998.

Shutō Shinchirō. *Moteru otoko no midashinami* (Good grooming for the popular man). Tokyo: C & R Kenkyūjo, 2008.

Sievers, Sharon L. *Flowers in Salt: The Beginnings of Feminist Consciousness in Modern Japan*. Stanford, Calif.: Stanford University Press, 1983.

Sign. "Ettchi no toki otoko ga kizuku Sex igai no aishō" (Compatibility other than sex that men notice when you do the nasty). *Sign*, no. 110 (June 1997): 53.

Simonds, Wendy. *Self-Help Culture: Reading Between the Lines*. New Brunswick, N.J.: Rutgers University Press, 1999.

Spain, Daphne. *Gendered Spaces*. Chapel Hill: University of North Carolina Press, 1992.

Steele, M. William, and Tamiko Ichimata, eds. *Clara's Diary: An American Girl in Meiji Japan*. Tokyo: Kōdansha, 1979.

Stoler, Ann Laura, and Frederick Cooper. "Between metropole and colony: Rethinking a research agenda." In *Tensions of Empire: Colonial Cultures in a Bourgeois World*, edited by F. Cooper and A. L. Stoler, 1–58. Berkeley: University of California Press, 1997.

Sugitatsu Yoshikazu. *Osan no rekishi: Jōmon jidai kara gendai made* (A history of childbirth from the Jōmon era to the present). Tokyo: Shūeisha Shinsho, 2002.

Suyematz, Kenchio. "Introduction by the translator." In *Oriental Literature: The Literature of Japan*, rev. ed. Freeport, N.Y.: Books for Libraries Press, 1971.

Suzuki, Tomi. "Gender and genre: Modern literary histories and women's diary literature." In *Inventing the Classics: Modernity, National Identity, and Japanese Literature*, edited by H. Shirane and T. Suzuki, 71–83. Stanford, Calif.: Stanford University Press, 2000.

———. "*The Tale of Genji*, national literature, language, and modernism." In *Envisioning the Tale of Genji: Media, Gender, and Cultural Production*, edited by H. Shirane, 243–287. New York: Columbia University Press, 2008.

Takashima Keiko. *Ninpu wa hutocha ikenai no?* (Pregnant women shouldn't get fat, right?) Tokyo: Shinchōsha, 2004.

Takayama Tadao. *Hajimete mama ni naru hito no ninshin to shussan* (The first-time mother's guide to the ten months of pregnancy and childbirth). Tokyo: Seibido Shobō, 1999.

Takechi Tetsuji. *Teihon Takechi kabuki: Takechi Tetsuji zenshū* (Takechi kabuki, the standard edition: The complete works of Takechi Tetsuji), vol. 1, edited by Ariki Daisaburō. Tokyo: San'ichi Shobō, 1978.

Tamiya Kōon Shirogorō. "Zoku Nijinshū" (Sequel to "The dust in the ears"). In *Yakusha banashi* (The actors' analects), edited by Hachimonji Jishō. Republished in *Kabuki jūhachibanshū* (Eighteen great kabuki plays), edited by Gunji Masakatsu, 317–326. Nihon koten bungaku taikei (Collection of Japanese classical literature), vol. 98. Tokyo: Iwanami Shoten, 1965.

Tanaka Toshiyuki. *Hatachi kara no manā* (Manners for after age twenty). Tokyo: Shōbunsha, 1993.

Taniguchi, Hiroaki. "The legal situation facing sexual minorities in Japan." *Intersections: Gender, History and Culture in the Asian Context* 12 (January 2006), http://wwwsshe.murdoch.edu.au/intersections.

Terazawa, Yuki. "Gender, knowledge, and power: Reproductive medicine in Japan, 1790–1930." PhD dissertation, University of California–Los Angeles, 2001.

Thangham, Chris. "In Japan, cats and dogs more popular than babies." *Digital Journal* (May 4, 2008), http://www.digitaljournal.com/article/254232.

Thorne, Susan. "'The conversion of Englishmen and the conversion of the world inseparable': Missionary imperialism and the language of class in early industrial Britain." In *Tensions of Empire: Colonial Cultures in a Bourgeois World*, edited by F. Cooper and A. L. Stoler, 238–262. Berkeley: University of California Press, 1997.

Tsuda Hideki. *Me kara uroko no kanji no hon* (The revelatory Chinese character book). Tokyo: Takarajimasha, 2006.

Ueda Kikan, Kishigami Shinji, and Akiyama Ken, eds. *Makura no sōshi, Murasaki Shikibu nikki* (*The Pillow Book* and journal of Murasaki Shikibu). Republished in Nihon koten bungaku taikei (Collection of Japanese classic literature), vol. 19. Tokyo: Iwanami Shoten, 1958.

Urawa Eiko. *Shigoto de"ki ga kiku onna" ni naru hon* (A book to help you become a "savvy woman" in the workplace). Tokyo: PHP Kenkyūjo, 2006.

Vincent, Keith, Takashi Kazama, and Kazuya Kawaguchi. *Gay Studies*. Tokyo: Seidosha, 1997.

———. "A Japanese Electra and her queer progeny." *Mechademia* 2 (2007):64–82.

Wallace, Bruce. "Japan talks dignity, or lack thereof." *Los Angeles Times*, September 22, 2007.

Walthall, Anne. *The Weak Body of a Useless Woman: Matsuo Taseko and the Meiji Restoration*. Chicago: University of Chicago Press, 1998.

Watanuki Toyoaki and Sue Tomoko, comps. *E de miru Meiji, Taishō reigi sahō jiten* (A dictionary for Meiji and Taisho etiquette as seen in pictures). Tokyo: Kashiwa Shobō, 2007.

Welcome Society of Japan. *Guidebook for Tourists in Japan*, 5th ed. Tokyo: Tokyo Chamber of Commerce, 1910.

Whitney, Clara A. N. *Clara's Diary: An American Girl in Meiji Japan*. Edited by M. W. Steele and T. Ichimata. Tokyo: Kōdansha, 1979.

World Fellowship Committee of the Young Women's Christian Association of Tokyo, Japan. *Japanese Etiquette: An Introduction*. Rutland, Vt.: Charles E. Tuttle, 1955.

Yakusha Hyōbanki Kenkyūkai, ed. *Kabuki hyōbanki shūsei dai 2-ki* (Collected kabuki actor-critiques booklets, series 2). Tokyo: Iwanami Shoten, 1988.

Yama Asako. *Onna Genji kyōkun kagami* (Women's mirror of *Genji* lessons). Edo jidai josei bunko (Edo period women's library), vol. 1. Tokyo: Ōzorasha, 1994.

Yamamura Kōzō and John Whitney Hall, eds. *The Cambridge History of Japan, Volume 3, Medieval Japan,* edited by M. B. Jansen, 432–498. Cambridge: Cambridge University Press, 1990.

Yamasaki Takeya. *Otoko no sahō: Senren sareta otona no sutairu* (Men's etiquette: The refined adult's style). Tokyo: PHP Kenkyūjo, 2007.

Yamazaki Kiyoshi. *Ninshin, bunben, sanji no chōsetsu* (The regulation of pregnancy, labor, and childbirth). Tokyo: Bunka Seikatsu Kenkyūkai, 1927.

Yamato, Waki. *The Tale of Genji, Flowers: Part I*. Translated by Stuart Atkin and Yoko Toyozaki. Kodansha Bilingual Comics edition. Tokyo: Kōdansha, 2003.

Yano, Christine. *Tears of Longing: Nostalgia and the Nation in Japanese Popular Song* Cambridge, Mass.: Harvard University Press, 2003.

Yasui Shuhei. *Ninshin kara shussan made* (From pregnancy to childbirth). Tokyo: Handbook-sha, 1928.

Yoda, Tomiko. *Gender and National Literature: Heian Texts in the Constructions of Japanese Modernity*. Durham, N.C.: Duke University Press, 2004.

———. "A roadmap to millennial Japan." In *Japan after Japan: Social and Cultural Life from the Recessionary 1990s to the Present*, edited by T. Yoda and H. Harootunian, 16–53. Durham, N.C.: Duke University Press, 2006.

Yoda, Tomiko, and Harry Harootunian, eds. *Japan after Japan: Social and Cultural Life from the Recessionary 1990s to the Present*. Durham, N.C.: Duke University Press, 2006.

Yomiuri Shinbun Fujinbu, eds. *Nihonjin no jinsei annai* (Japanese people's life guide). Tokyo: Heibonsha, 1998.

Yoshikawa Yoshio. "Kabuki-geki no onnagata" (*Onnagata* in the kabuki theater). In *Engekishi kenkyū, dai-1 shū* (Study of the history of theater, part 1), edited by Engekishi Gakkai, 51–80. Tokyo: Daiichi Shobō, 1932.

———. "Genroku-ki no onnagata" (*Onnagata* in the Genroku era). In *Engekishi kenkyū, dai-2 shū* (Study of the history of theater, part 2), edited by Engekishi Gakkai, 180–228. Tokyo: Daiichi Shobō, 1932.

Yuasa Yasuo. *Shintairon: Tōyōteki shinshinron to gendai* (Theory of the body: An Eastern mind–body theory and the present). Tokyo: Kōdansha, 1990.

Yūsei. *Moto karisuma hosuto ga oshieru jikyū hyaku manen kaiwajutsu* (The art of the one hundred million yen conversation taught by a former charismatic host). Tokyo: Rongu serāzu, 2009.

Zennikkū Eigyōhonbu Kyōikukunrenbu, ed. *OL tabū shū* (Anthology of Office-Lady taboos). Tokyo: Goma Seibo, 1991.

Zwick, Edward, dir. *The Last Samurai*. Burbank, Calif.: Warner Bros., 2003.

Contributors

HIDEKO ABE is an assistant professor of Japanese language and linguistics in the Department of East Asian Studies at Colby College. Her area of specialization is language, gender, and sexuality. Her most recent essay, entitled "Lesbian Bar Talk in Shinjuku, Japan," appeared in *Japanese Language, Gender, and Ideology*, ed. Shigeko Okamoto and Janet S. Shibamoto-Smith (Oxford University Press, 2004) and was reprinted in *The Language and Sexuality Reader*, ed. Deborah Cameron and Don Kulick (Routledge, 2006). Her most recent book, *Queer Japanese: Gender and Sexual Identities through Linguistic Practices*, was published in 2010 (Palgrave).

JAN BARDSLEY is an associate professor of Japanese humanities and chair of the Department of Asian Studies at the University of North Carolina at Chapel Hill. She is the author of *The Bluestockings of Japan: New Women Essays and Fiction from* Seitō, *1911–1916* (Center for Japanese Studies, University of Michigan, 2007), and coeditor, with Laura Miller, of *Bad Girls of Japan* (Palgrave, 2005).

GAVIN JAMES CAMPBELL is a professor of American studies at Doshisha University in Kyoto, Japan. His previous publications have been mainly in the field of U.S. Southern cultural history, including *Music and the Making of a New South* (University of North Carolina Press, 2004). He is currently writing a book centered on the trans-Pacific journeys of Niijima Jo and Lafcadio Hearn as a way to examine the cultural interactions between the United States and Japan during the Meiji period.

LINDA H. CHANCE is an associate professor of Japanese language and literature in the Department of East Asian Languages and Civilizations at the University of Pennsylvania. Her specialization is nonfiction prose of the medieval era.

She is the author of *Formless in Form: Kenkō, Tsurezuregusa, and the Rhetoric of Japanese Fragmentary Prose* (Stanford University Press, 1997).

KELLY M. FOREMAN is an instructor in the Department of Music at Wayne State University. She has published articles on Japanese music and geisha in Japan and authored liner notes for Japanese traditional music recordings. Her book entitled *The Gei of Geisha: Music, Identity, and Meaning* (Ashgate, 2008) details the relationships between geisha and music. She is also an active composer.

SALLY A. HASTINGS is an associate professor of history at Purdue University, where she chairs the Asian Studies Program. She is editor of the *U.S.–Japan Women's Journal* and author of *Neighborhood and Nation in Tokyo, 1905–1937* (University of Pittsburgh Press, 1995). She has published several essays on the history of Japanese women, most recently "Gender and Sexuality in Modern Japan," in *A Companion to Japanese History*, ed. William Tsutsui (Blackwell, 2007), and "Hatoyama Haruko: Ambitious Woman," in *The Human Tradition in Modern Japan*, ed. Anne Walthall (Scholarly Resources, 2002). During her tenure as a Fulbright Fellow in Japan, she is completing work on a book manuscript entitled "Gender and Japanese Politics: Women Legislators, 1946–1974."

HIROKO HIRAKAWA is an associate professor of Japanese and intercultural studies at Guilford College in Greensboro, North Carolina. She has published articles on popular culture and gender in contemporary Japan. Her current book project examines popular commentary on the lives of young career women in Japan at the turn of the new millennium.

MAKI ISAKA is an associate professor of Japanese literature and theater at the University of Minnesota, Twin Cities, teaching Japanese theater and premodern literature. She is currently working on a book manuscript that analyzes the construction of femininity by *onnagata* (actors specializing in women's roles in the kabuki theater). Her future projects include an examination of Osanai Kaoru in terms of modernity and a study of *gei* (acquired artistic technique) in Japanese arts and thought. She is the author of *Secrecy in Japanese Arts: "Secret Transmission" as a Mode of Knowledge* (Palgrave, 2005).

LAURA MILLER is the Ei'ichi Shibusawa-Seigo Arai Professor of Japanese Studies and Professor of Anthropology at the University of Missouri–St. Louis. She has published widely on Japanese popular culture and language, including on such topics as the wizard boom, the Korean Wave, girls' slang, and print club photos. She is the author of *Beauty Up: Exploring Contemporary Japanese Body Aesthetics* (University of California Press, 2006), and is a coeditor, with Jan Bardsley, of *Bad Girls of Japan* (Palgrave, 2005).

AMANDA C. SEAMAN is an associate professor of Japanese Literature at the University of Massachusetts Amherst, and is the author of *Bodies of Evidence: Women, Society, and Detective Fiction in 1990s Japan* (University of Hawai'i Press, 2004). She is currently working on a book on representations of pregnancy in contemporary Japanese society.

JANET S. SHIBAMOTO-SMITH is a professor of anthropology at the University of California–Davis. She is a specialist in Japanese language, society, and culture, with an emphasis on the interaction between ideology and practice. She is the author of *Japanese Women's Language* (Academic Press, 1985) and a co-editor, with Shigeko Okamoto, of *Japanese Language, Gender, and Ideology* (Oxford University Press, 2004). Her latest project addresses contemporary cultural models of femininity/masculinity and romantic love through textual analyses of popular print and televisual materials.

Index

Page numbers in **bold** indicate illustrations.

TEXT
10/13 Sabon

DISPLAY
Sabon

COMPOSITOR
Westchester Book Group

INDEXER
AnDix Indexing

PRINTER AND BINDER
Maple-Vail Book Manufacturing Group